Robert Thornton and his Books

YORK MEDIEVAL PRESS

Robert Thornton and his Books

Essays on the Lincoln and London Thornton Manuscripts

Edited by

Susanna Fein
Michael Johnston

YORK MEDIEVAL PRESS

First published 2014

A York Medieval Press publication
in association with The Boydell Press
an imprint of Boydell & Brewer Ltd
PO Box 9   Woodbridge   Suffolk IP12 3DF   UK
and of Boydell & Brewer Inc.
668 Mt Hope Avenue   Rochester   NY 14620–2731   USA
website: www.boydellandbrewer.com
and with the
Centre for Medieval Studies, University of York

ISBN 978–1–903153–51–2

A CIP catalogue record for this book is available
from the British Library

The publisher has no responsibility for the continued existence or accuracy
of URLs for external or third-party internet websites referred to in this book,
and does not guarantee that any content on such websites is, or will remain,
accurate or appropriate.

This publication is printed on acid-free paper

Contents

Illustrations

Contributors

Julie Nelson Couch	Texas Tech University
Susanna Fein	Kent State University
Rosalind Field	Royal Holloway, University of London
Joel Fredell	Southeastern Louisiana University
Ralph Hanna	University of Oxford
Michael Johnston	Purdue University
George R. Keiser	Independent scholar, formerly Kansas State University
Julie Orlemanski	University of Chicago
Mary Michele Poellinger	University of Leeds
Dav Smith	University of York
Thorlac Turville-Petre	University of Nottingham

Acknowledgements

This book is dedicated to the memory of Robert Thornton, gentleman, reader and scribe.

The editors acknowledge the goodwill and generosity of all the contributors to this volume, who helped to make this book a truly collaborative project. Exceptional moral support has been provided by George Keiser, whose learned scholarship over past decades has immeasurably advanced our understanding of the scribe and the texts he collected. Others who have been most helpful in their support are John J. Thompson and Phillipa Hardman. We also wish to thank the Early Book Society for sponsoring two sessions devoted to Robert Thornton and his books, which allowed several contributors to present early versions of their chapters. We thank the audiences at these sessions, which were held at the Forty-Eighth International Congress on Medieval Studies in Kalamazoo, Michigan, May 2013, and at the Thirteenth Biennial Early Book Society Conference in St Andrews, Scotland, July 2013. We also wish to acknowledge the support of Peter Biller at York Medieval Press and Caroline Palmer, Rohais Haughton, Rob Kinsey and Rosie Pearce at Boydell and Brewer, whose collective professionalism and expertise made the process of making this book a pleasure. The Research Council of Kent State University generously underwrote the costs for illustrations in this volume, and a Creative Incentive Grant from the Department of English, Purdue University, underwrote other production costs. We express our gratitude to them. The editors also wish to thank our spouses, David Raybin and Robyn Malo, for their unflagging willingness to indulge our predilections for studying the contents of miscellanies and the habits of scribes.

Abbreviations

ANTS	Anglo-Norman Text Society
Archiv	*Archiv für das Studien der neueren Sprachen und Literaturen*
BL	British Library
Briquet	C.-M. Briquet, *Les filigranes*, 4 vols. (Leipzig, 1923)
CUL	Cambridge University Library
DIMEV	L. R. Mooney, D. W. Mosser, E. Solopova and D. H. Radcliffe, *The Digital Index of Middle English Verse*, www.dimev.net
DNB	*Dictionary of National Biography*
EETS ES	Early English Text Society, Extra Series
EETS OS	Early English Text Society, Original Series
EETS SS	Early English Text Society, Supplementary Series
IPMEP	R. E. Lewis, N. F. Blake and A. S. G. Edwards, *Index of Printed Middle English Prose* (New York, 1985)
LALME	A. McIntosh, M. L. Samuels and M. Benskin, with M. Laing and K. Williamson, *A Linguistic Atlas of Late Mediaeval English*, 4 vols. (Aberdeen, 1986)
Manual	J. B. Severs, A. E. Hartung and P. G. Beidler, eds., *A Manual of Writings in Middle English, 1050–1500*, 11 vols. (New Haven, 1967–2005)
Manual 1, I	M. J. Donovan, C. W. Dunn, L. H. Hornstein, R. M. Lumiansky, H. Newstead and H. M. Smyser, 'I. Romances', in *Manual*, ed. J. B. Severs, vol. 1 (New Haven, 1967)
Manual 2, V	C. D'Evelyn and F. A. Foster, 'V. Saints' Legends', in *Manual*, ed. J. B. Severs, vol. 2 (New Haven, 1970)
Manual 3, VII	F. L. Utley, 'VII. Dialogues, Debates, and Catechisms', in *Manual*, ed. A. E. Hartung, vol. 3 (New Haven, 1972)
Manual 5, XIII	R. H. Robbins, 'XIII. Poems Dealing with Contemporary Conditions', in *Manual*, ed. A. E. Hartung, vol. 5 (New Haven, 1975)
Manual 6, XIV	R. L. Greene, 'XIV. Carols', in *Manual*, ed. A. E. Hartung, vol. 6 (New Haven, 1980)
Manual 6, XVI	A. Renoir and C. D. Benson, 'XVI. John Lydgate', in *Manual*, ed. A. E. Hartung, vol. 6 (New Haven, 1980)

Manual 7, XX	R. R. Raymo, 'XX. Works of Religious and Philosophical Instruction', in *Manual*, ed. A. E. Hartung, vol. 7 (New Haven, 1986)
Manual 9, XXII	C. Louis, 'XXII. Proverbs, Precepts, and Monitory Pieces', in *Manual*, ed. A. E. Hartung, vol. 9 (New Haven, 1993)
Manual 9, XXIII	V. M. Lagorio and M. G. Sargent, with R. Bradley, 'XXIII. English Mystical Writings', in *Manual*, ed. A. E. Hartung, vol. 9 (New Haven, 1993)
Manual 9, XXIV	T. D. Cook, with P. Whiteford and N. M. Kennedy, 'XXIV. Tales', in *Manual*, ed. A. E. Hartung, vol. 9 (New Haven, 1993)
Manual 10, XXV	G. R. Keiser, 'XXV. Works of Science and Information', in *Manual*, ed. A. E. Hartung, vol. 10 (New Haven, 1998)
MED	H. Jurath, S. H. Kuhn *et al.*, *Middle English Dictionary* (Ann Arbor MI, 1954–2001), http://www.quod.lib.umich.edu/m/med
NIMEV	J. Boffey and A. S. G. Edwards, *A New Index of Middle English Verse* (London, 2005)
NLS	National Library of Scotland
NLW	National Library of Wales
PMLA	*Publications of the Modern Language Association*
STC	A. W. Pollard and G. R. Redgrave, *A Short-Title Catalogue of Books Printed in England, Scotland, and Ireland, and of English Books Printed Abroad, 1475–1640*, 2nd rev. edn, ed. W. A. Jackson, F. S. Ferguson and K. F. Pantzer, 3 vols. (London, 1976–91)
STS	Scottish Text Society
TCD	Trinity College Dublin
Thompson, *London Thornton MS*	J. J. Thompson, *Robert Thornton and the London Thornton Manuscript: British Library MS Additional 31042*, Manuscript Studies 2 (Cambridge, 1987)
The Thornton MS, intro. Brewer and Owen	*The Thornton Manuscript (Lincoln Cathedral MS. 91)*, intro. D. S. Brewer and A. E. B. Owen (London, 1975)

Note on the Presentation of Thornton Texts

When items from the Thornton manuscripts are accompanied by article numbers, the numbering conforms to the List of Contents provided in Chapter One of the present volume (Susanna Fein, 'The Contents of Robert Thornton's Manuscripts'). Titles also agree with the List of Contents. In quoting specific Thornton texts, the authors usually rely on critical editions, as cited. When quotations are drawn directly from the manuscripts, folio numbers are provided, and the manner of transcription accords with that detailed in Fein's chapter, p. 21.

Introduction
The Cheese and the Worms
and Robert Thornton

Michael Johnston

Why an entire essay collection on one manuscript compiler, who has left us but two manuscripts? Or so might the sceptical reader justifiably ask. And yet the value in sustained, focused and collective analysis of Robert Thornton and his manuscripts lies in the amazing wealth of detail we can find – details about the compilation and scribal practices of an identifiable historical figure; about the diversity and contours of vernacular and Latin literary culture in a provincial fifteenth-century English locale; about one specific instantiation of lay piety; about one individual's understanding of literary genres and verse forms; about medieval medicinal beliefs and practices; about conceptions of illumination and decoration in the non-commercial book; about the book production industry in regions beyond London; and about the literary activities of the late medieval gentry. Of course, I could go on, but these occur to me as the primary ways in which Robert Thornton and his books matter, and these are the primary topics taken up in the essays to follow.

I want briefly to propose here that micro-history provides us with a model through which we might better understand Thornton and his two manuscripts – and why they matter. As Giovanni Levi states,

> The unifying principle of all microhistorical research is the belief that microscopic observation will reveal factors previously unobserved ... Phenomena previously considered to be sufficiently described and understood assume completely new meanings by altering the scale of observation. It is then possible to use these results to draw far wider generalizations although the initial observations were made within relatively narrow dimensions and as experiments rather than examples.[1]

---

* I wish to thank my colleague from Purdue's Department of History, William Gray, for a series of stimulating discussions about micro-history and current trends in historiography.

[1] G. Levi, 'On Microhistory', in *New Perspectives on Historical Writing*, ed. P. Burke, 2nd edn (University Park PA, 2001), pp. 93–119 (pp. 101–2). For further reflection on the practice of microhistory, see E. Muir, 'Introduction: Observing Trifles', in *Microhistory and the Lost Peoples*

Or, as Carlo Ginzburg more gnomically puts it, 'A close-up look permits us to grasp what eludes a comprehensive viewing, and vice versa.'[2] Micro-historians exploit understudied archives that reveal information about the marginalized, those whose voices tend to be ignored or, more often, studiously written out of most surviving records. Most often these are freak survivals that happened to record the testimony of peasants or other non-dominant voices. Attending to such archives, these historians demonstrate, gives us access to the *mentalités* and ideologies of both the dominant and the marginalized – and of the tensions therein – and thus yields a richer picture than when we rely on documents constructed by the dominant powers in society, like chronicles, statutes, courtly literature or epistolary correspondence. Micro-history offers a leftist counter-narrative to the leftist, *longue durée* view of the Annales School, known to medievalists primarily through the work of Marc Bloch, Georges Duby and Jacques Le Goff, who attempt to think in large-scale terms about the structures governing social life across broad geopolitical and temporal swathes.

In the essays to follow, by putting Thornton and his two codices under the microscope, so to speak, the contributors take up Levi's and Ginzburg's challenges. Of course, Thornton was not a marginalized figure in his society – far from it. The fact that he had the power of the pen/quill, was an active landowner, had the place of honour in his parish church and served on county commissions all suggest that we should not include him within the normal purview of micro-history. Yet when we turn our attention to late medieval book production as a whole, Thornton does come into focus as a marginalized figure, of sorts. That is, he does not fit any of the larger patterns in which most historians of English book production have been interested of late. Thornton is, in the vein of micro-historiography, the marginalized exception that can help us understand better the rules governing book production and circulation in fifteenth-century England.

For example, scholars have recently delved into the role of Middle English authors in the production and dissemination of their own texts or their role in manuscript production, particularly works by Hoccleve, Bokenham and Capgrave.[3] We have also paid particular attention to the growth of the London

of Europe, ed. E. Muir and G. Ruggiero, trans. E. Branch (Baltimore, 1991), pp. vii–xxviii; and C. Ginzburg, 'Microhistory: Two or Three Things That I Know about It', trans. J. Tedeschi and A. C. Tedeschi, *Critical Inquiry* 20 (1993), 10–35.

2   Ginzburg, 'Microhistory', p. 26.

3   On Hoccleve, see J. J. Thompson, 'Thomas Hoccleve and Manuscript Culture', in *Nation, Court and Culture: New Essays on Fifteenth-Century English Poetry*, ed. H. Cooney (Dublin, 2001), pp. 81–94; D. Watt, '"I this book shal make": Thomas Hoccleve's Self-Publication and Book Production', *Leeds Studies in English* n.s. 34 (2003), 133–60; and L. R. Mooney, 'A Holograph Copy of Thomas Hoccleve's *Regiment of Princes*', *Studies in the Age of Chaucer* 33 (2011), 263–96; on Bokenham, see S. Horobin, 'A Manuscript Found in Abbotsford House and the

book production industry, as it slowly emerged in the late fourteenth century from being just one city amongst many in England, to its position as the dominant production centre for the entire nation. We have recovered much about high-end, commercially produced copies of the works of Gower, Chaucer and Langland from this period.[4] In these years, the commercial industry fitfully centralized its processes: at the beginning of the fifteenth century, the process was largely decentralized. Take, for example, the well-known case of the Trinity Gower manuscript, where five different scribes were at work separately on individual quires. At the same time, Adam Pinkhurst was cobbling together the Hengwrt manuscript of the *Canterbury Tales* from loose quires.[5] By the mid to late fifteenth century, commercially organized copyists were producing multiple copies of the prose *Brut* and *Nova statuta*, almost certainly on a speculative basis, alongside the more decentralized method that continued to operate.[6]

Legendary of Osbern Bokenham', in *Regional Manuscripts 1200–1700*, ed. A. S. G. Edwards, English Manuscript Studies 1100–1700, vol. 14 (London, 2008), pp. 132–64; and on Capgrave, see P. J. Lucas, *From Author to Audience: John Capgrave and Medieval Publication* (Dublin, 1997).

4   On the production of Chaucer manuscripts, see, for example, L. R. Mooney, 'Chaucer's Scribe', *Speculum* 81 (2006), 97–138; and S. Horobin, 'Adam Pinkhurst, Geoffrey Chaucer, and the Hengwrt Manuscript of the *Canterbury Tales*', *Chaucer Review* 44 (2010), 351–67; on Gower, see K. Harris, 'Ownership and Readership: Studies in the Provenance of the Manuscripts of Gower's *Confessio Amantis*' (unpublished D.Phil. thesis, University of York, 1993); and D. Pearsall, 'The Manuscripts and Illustrations of Gower's Works', in *A Companion to Gower*, ed. S. Echard (Cambridge, 2004), pp. 73–97; on Langland, see A. I. Doyle, 'Remarks on the Surviving Manuscripts of *Piers Plowman*', in *Medieval English Religious and Ethical Literature: Essays in Honour of G. H. Russell*, ed. G. Kratzmann and J. Simpson (Cambridge, 1986), pp. 35–48; L. R. Mooney and S. Horobin, 'A *Piers Plowman* Manuscript by the Hengwrt/Ellesmere Scribe and Its Implications for London Standard English', *Studies in the Age of Chaucer* 26 (2004), 65–112; and S. Horobin, 'Adam Pinkhurst and the Copying of British Library, MS Additional 35287 of the B Version of *Piers Plowman*', *Yearbook of Langland Studies* 23 (2009), 61–83.

5   Cambridge, Trinity College, MS R. 3. 2, and Aberystwyth, NLW, MS Peniarth 392D (Hengwrt). See A. I. Doyle and M. B. Parkes, 'The Production of Copies of the *Canterbury Tales* and the *Confessio Amantis* in the Early Fifteenth Century', in *Medieval Scribes, Manuscripts, and Libraries: Essays Presented to N. R. Ker*, ed. M. B. Parkes and A. G. Watson (London, 1978), pp. 163–210; and Horobin, 'Adam Pinkhurst'.

6   On the generally decentralized methods of commercial book production in late fourteenth- and early fifteenth-century London, see Doyle and Parkes, 'The Production'; C. P. Christianson, *Memorials of the Book Trade in Medieval London: The Archives of Old London Bridge* (Cambridge, 1987); C. P. Christianson, 'The Rise of London's Book Trade', in *The Cambridge History of the Book in Britain: Volume 3, 1400–1557*, ed. L. Hellinga and J. B. Trapp (Cambridge, 1999), pp. 128–47; and L. R. Mooney, 'Locating Scribal Activity in Late Medieval London', in *Design and Distribution of Late Medieval Manuscripts in England*, ed. M. Connolly and L. R. Mooney (York, 2008), pp. 183–204. On the development of centralized commercial scriptoria producing books on a speculative basis, see K. L. Scott, 'A Late Fifteenth-Century Group of *Nova Statuta* Manuscripts', in *Manuscripts at Oxford: An Exhibition in Memory of Richard William Hunt (1908–1979), Keeper of Western Manuscripts at the Bodleian Library Oxford, 1945–1975*, on *Themes*

Thus the industry was slowly evolving into the more properly centralized oper-ations of Caxton's press at Westminster.[7] Finally, we have been interested in and learned a great deal about book production and circulation within specific communities with specific textual needs, most notably the Lollards, various noble households, religious institutions and London merchants and clerics who shared 'common-profit' books and libraries.[8]

Thornton, however, fits none of these patterns; his methods are better thought of as both ad hoc and atomized – ad hoc in his compiling and scribal methods, atomized in his individuality and divergence from any of the major trends I have just outlined from this period. R. J. Lyall suggests three basic models for how books were made in late medieval England: they could be made on commission, they could be produced within a religious house for use in that religious house, and they could be made by an individual for his or his family's domestic use.[9] It is this last category that eludes scholarly systemization, largely because it is not, by its very nature, systemizable. Those producing books for their own use were not compelled to follow the best practices of commercial

Selected and Described by Some of His Friends, ed. A. C. de la Mare and B. C. Barker-Benfield (Oxford, 1980), pp. 102–5; and L. R. Mooney and L. M. Matheson, 'The Beryn Scribe and His Texts: Evidence for Multiple-Copy Production of Manuscripts in Fifteenth-Century England', *The Library* 7th ser. 4 (2003), 347–70.

7   N. F. Blake, *Caxton and His World* (London, 1969); and L. Hellinga, *William Caxton and Early Printing in England* (London, 2010).

8   On Lollard book production and circulation see, for example, M. Aston, *Lollards and Reformers: Images and Literacy in Late Medieval Religion* (London, 1984); A. Hudson, 'Lollard Book Production', in *Book Production and Publishing in Britain, 1375–1475*, ed. J. Griffiths and D. Pearsall, Cambridge Studies in Publishing and Printing History (Cambridge, 1989), pp. 125–42; M. Dove, *The First English Bible: The Text and Context of the Wycliffite Versions* (Cambridge, 2007); and R. Copeland, 'Lollard Writings', in *The Cambridge Companion to Medieval English Literature, 1100–1500*, ed. L. Scanlon (Cambridge, 2009), pp. 111–23. On noble houses and book production see, for example, R. Hanna, 'Sir Thomas Berkeley and His Patronage', *Speculum* 64 (1989), 878–916; and R. Hanna and A. S. G. Edwards, 'Rotheley, the De Vere Circle, and the Ellesmere Chaucer', *Huntington Library Quarterly* 58 (1996), 11–35. On religious houses and the production of vernacular literature see, for example, M. Sargent, 'The Transmission by the English Carthusians of Some Late Medieval Spiritual Writings', *Journal of Ecclesiastical History* 27 (1976), 225–40; A. I. Doyle, 'Publication by Members of the Religious Orders', in *Book Production*, ed. Griffiths and Pearsall, pp. 109–23; and V. Gillespie, 'Dial M for Mystic: Mystical Texts in the Library of Syon Abbey and the Spirituality of the Syon Brethren', in *The Medieval Mystical Tradition in England, Ireland and Wales*, ed. M. Glasscoe (Cambridge, 1999), pp. 241–68. On 'common-profit' books and libraries see, for example, J. A. H. Moran, 'A "Common Profit" Library in Fifteenth-Century England and Other Books for Chaplains', *Manuscripta* 28 (1984), 17–25; and W. Scase, 'Reginald Pecock, John Carpenter and John Colop's "Common-Profit" Books: Aspects of Book Ownership and Circulation in Fifteenth-Century London', *Medium Ævum* 61 (1992), 261–74.

9   R. J. Lyall, 'Materials: The Paper Revolution', in *Book Production*, ed. Griffiths and Pearsall, pp. 11–29.

scribal culture, for they had no patron or commissioner to please. They were, then, not creating a commodity so much as an idiosyncratic artefact. Many such 'own-use' Middle English books survive; however, what makes Thornton so valuable is both that he has left us two large artefacts of this nature and that we know a reasonable amount about his life and social world, which we can read in the context of his compilation, shedding light on both the man and his books. Thus, with Thornton, we can fill out much of the personality subtending his idiosyncratic codices.

These idiosyncrasies are precisely what make Thornton so valuable to literary historians and book historians alike. As micro-historians rightly insist, the idiosyncratic matters because it disrupts grand narratives about cultural, social, economic and political history. For example, Emmanuel Le Roy Ladurie's study of the village of Montaillou (about 100 km south of Toulouse) in the early four-teenth century reveals how variant its culture was from the model which medieval historians have offered for the Comté de Foix and for France *in toto*.[10] Ladurie reveals how Catharism survived long after the Albigensian Crusade in this locale, largely on a domus-by-domus basis, where individual homes formed the primary social unit of the society, and where such homes comprised isolated Cathar communities, linked to one another by informal neighbourly relations. There was also, Ladurie reveals, remarkably little feudal class conflict in Montaillou, for there were no resident noblemen; however, what the residents lacked in acrimony towards aristocratic landlords they made up in acrimony towards the Church, which vigorously defended its tithe-collecting prerogatives. From this histor-ical study we also learn much about peasant *mentalités*, in particular their atti-tudes towards aesthetics, gender relations, marital fidelity, animals and dogma, among many others, none of which can be encompassed by larger-scale histories. Although the most ardent Cathars in the village scorned Mass and the sacra-ment of the Eucharist, everyone participated in All Saints' Day masses, which were tied to the beginning of the winter sheep pasturing. Moreover, the entire village seems to have believed passionately in the dogma of Original Sin (and hence baptism) and confession, in spite of the widespread anticlerical attitudes and even the Catharism of their lone parish priest. Ultimately, then, Ladurie's analysis shows a village of such complexity as to elude larger grand narratives about medieval French peasant society and about medieval popular religion.

Likewise, Natalie Zemon Davis's *The Return of Martin Guerre* provides insight into the epistemology of sixteenth-century peasants in Artigat (coin-cidentally, located in the same county as Montaillou).[11] Davis tells the story of Martin Guerre, who fled his home when he was accused of stealing from his

---

[10] E. L. R. Ladurie, *Montaillou: The Promised Land of Error*, trans. B. Bray (New York, 1978).
[11] N. Z. Davis, *The Return of Martin Guerre* (Cambridge MA, 1983).

father, a major transgression in French peasant society. Later, Arnaud du Tilh, a down-on-his-luck soldier, was mistaken for Martin Guerre and, realizing that he must look like this stranger and that this stranger must be absent from his native society, pulled a brilliant confidence trick by going to Guerre's village and passing himself off as the prodigal son returned home. Arnaud even took up with Martin's wife and had children by her. Eventually his ruse was uncovered, and this is where Davis's historical work is most penetrating. She shows how multivalent and complex were the peasants' understandings of juridical truth. At the various trials of Arnaud, witnesses displayed a startling variety of epistemological approaches to truth, some pertinaciously insisting that Arnaud was in fact Guerre, others insisting he was an impostor.

But perhaps the most memorable and well-known example of micro-history is Carlo Ginzburg's *The Cheese and the Worms*, which analyses the strange and brilliant theories of a sixteenth-century Italian miller, Menocchio, who was tried and convicted of heresy by the Inquisition and was executed, at the pope's command, in 1601. Menocchio's trial records reveal a man who espoused a materialist, pantheistic, sceptical and pluralistic theology. His ecclesiology even replicated cutting-edge radical Protestant thought of the most erudite type, yet as Ginzburg shows, Menocchio arrived at his own ideas independently, primarily through a heady mix of oral tradition, selective reading of numerous books (from Jacobus de Voragine to Mandeville to possibly even the Koran) and an active imagination. His cosmogony is the most memorable thing to survive from his trial, whence the title of Ginzburg's book:

> 'I have said that, in my opinion, all was chaos ... and out of that bulk a mass formed – just as cheese is made out of milk – and worms appeared in it, and these were the angels. The most holy majesty decreed that these should be God and the angels, and among that number of angels, there was also God, *he too having been created out of that mass at the same time*.'[12]

As Ginzburg demonstrates, 'An almost exclusively oral culture such as that of the subordinate classes of preindustrial Europe tends not to leave traces, or, at least, the traces left are distorted.'[13] By reconstructing Menocchio's *mentalité*, as well as those of the villagers of Montaillou or Artigat, we are left with a richer, and more accurate, picture of cultural attitudes.

In some ways, then, Thornton can be thought of as a fifteenth-century English Menocchio – minus the idiosyncratic metaphysics and heterodox theology. That is, he was an eager textual collector whose own personal tastes and predilections are borne out by the volume(s) he has left us, and whose

---

[12]   C. Ginzburg, *The Cheese and the Worms: The Cosmos of a Sixteenth-Century Miller*, trans. J. Tedeschi and A. Tedeschi (Baltimore, 1980), p. 53; italics in original.
[13]   Ibid., p. 126.

tastes were sufficiently catholic to leave us traces of a wide range of cultural practices, all of which stands outside the *longue durée* narrative of book production in this period. So although Thornton is not at all counter-cultural, he is like Menocchio in that snippets of both of their personalities come through in the artefacts they have left us. This glimpse is all the more valuable in Thornton's case, since most surviving Middle English books are silent about both their production and their early provenance – and with Thornton, he himself is the key to *both* production and provenance.

What we know about Thornton and his books

Before launching into these essays that reveal new information about Thornton, it is worth pausing to take stock of the picture scholarship has hitherto painted of Thornton. Here, I will briefly suggest that we have approached Thornton from five main angles, each of which provides valuable insight into his working methods and cultural world, and each of which the essays to follow profitably expand upon. The diversity of these approaches also testifies to the cultural diversity contained within the medieval book, and to the complexity of the codex. The first such category involves codicological and palaeographical analyses, which have shed much light on Thornton's working methods.[14] From such

---

[14] On Thornton's compiling methods see, for example, A. McIntosh, 'The Textual Transmission of the Alliterative *Morte Arthure*', in *English and Medieval Studies Presented to J. R. R. Tolkien on the Occasion of His Seventieth Birthday*, ed. N. Davis and C. L. Wrenn (London, 1962), pp. 231–40; G. R. Keiser, 'Lincoln Cathedral Library MS. 91: Life and Milieu of the Scribe', *Studies in Bibliography* 32 (1979), 158–79; J. J. Thompson, 'The Compiler in Action: Robert Thornton and the "Thornton Romances" in Lincoln Cathedral MS 91', in *Manuscripts and Readers in Fifteenth-Century England: The Literary Implications of Manuscript Study: Essays from the 1981 Conference at the University of York*, ed. D. Pearsall (Cambridge, 1983), pp. 113–24; Thompson, *London Thornton Manuscript*; R. Hanna, 'The Growth of Robert Thornton's Books', *Studies in Bibliography* 40 (1987), 51–61; R. Kennedy, 'The Evangelist in Robert Thornton's Devotional Book: Organizing Principles at the Level of the Quire', *Journal of the Early Book Society* 8 (2005), 71–95; and J.-P. Pouzet, '"Space this werke to wirke": Quelques figures de la complémentarité dans les manuscrits de Robert Thornton', in *La Complémentarité: Mélanges offerts à Josseline Bidard et Arlette Sancery à l'occasion de leur depart en retraite*, ed. M.-F. Alamichel (Paris, 2005), pp. 27–42. On Thornton's scribal habits see, for example, P. R. Robinson, 'A Study of Some Aspects of the Transmission of English Verse Texts in Late Mediaeval Manuscripts' (unpublished B.Litt. thesis, University of Oxford, 1972), pp. 66–70; D. Lawton, 'Gaytryge's Sermon, "Dictamen", and Middle English Alliterative Verse', *Modern Philology* 76 (1979), 329–43; M. Hamel, 'Scribal Self-Corrections in the Thornton *Morte Arthure*', *Studies in Bibliography* 36 (1983), 119–37; H. N. Duggan, 'Alliterative Patterning as a Basis for Emendation in Middle English Alliterative Poetry', *Studies in the Age of Chaucer* 8 (1986), 73–105; J. A. Jefferson and A. Putter, 'Alliterative Patterning in the *Morte Arthure*', *Studies in Philology* 102 (2005), 415–33; and J. I. Carlson, 'Scribal Intentions in Medieval

analyses, a general picture of Thornton as scribe and compiler has emerged: we now know of Thornton as someone who worked at his compilations over a long period of time and who sought to compile texts into booklets marked by a rough generic homogeneity. Thanks to codicological analyses of both manuscripts together, we have recovered Thornton as someone who struggled to maintain this rough homogeneity by simultaneously juggling numerous booklets that were constantly evolving, and as someone who frequently 'circled back' to expand quires as he came across new texts. Thus, he often added to quires after he had begun copying by nesting smaller quires inside already-folded ones. We also know that Thornton was a scribe who, in the words of the most recent analyst, 'engaged in predictable [scribal] interventions motivated by a desire to present these tales orally for the moral education of his family'.[15]

Second, we now know of Thornton as someone who had a rough sense of the need for thematic coherence to his codices and who sought to elicit certain responses from readers based on the pairing or series of texts he compiled.[16] For example, he copied out the alliterative *Morte Arthure* very early in his compilation process, following it with several other texts, primarily romances, that do not seem thematically related (viz., Northern *Octavian*, *Sir Isumbras*, *Earl of Toulouse*, *Life of Saint Christopher*, *Sir Degrevant* and *Sir Eglamour of Artois*). Later in the process of compiling the Lincoln manuscript, however, he came across a prose *Life of Alexander*, which he added to the front of the alliterative *Morte*. As a result, based on their codicological proximity, the prose *Life*

Romance: A Case Study of Robert Thornton', *Studies in Bibliography* 58 (2007–8), 49–71. Yet more light on Thornton and his texts may soon emerge, as Fred Porcheddu and Patrick J. Murphy are currently studying Cambridge, CUL, MS Dd. 11. 45, containing a letter which they argue originates with Thornton and refers to his alliterative *Morte Arthure*. I thank Fred for sharing these details with me in private correspondence.

[15] Carlson, 'Scribal Intentions', p. 53.

[16] See, for example, O. J. Daly, 'This World and the Next: Social and Religious Ideologies in the Romances of the Thornton Manuscript' (unpublished Ph.D. dissertation, University of Oregon, 1977); S. Fein, '*Quatrefoil* and *Quatrefolia*: The Devotional Layout of an Alliterative Poem', *Journal of the Early Book Society* 2 (1999), 26–45; P. Hardman, 'The *Sege of Melayne*: A Fifteenth-Century Reading', in *Tradition and Transformation in Medieval Romance*, ed. R. Field (Cambridge, 1999), pp. 71–86; P. Hardman, 'Compiling the Nation: Fifteenth-Century Miscellany Manuscripts', in *Nation, Court and Culture*, ed. Cooney, 50–69; J. Finlayson, 'Reading Romances in Their Manuscript: Lincoln Cathedral Manuscript 91 ("Thornton")', *Anglia* 123 (2005), 632–66; E. Leverett, 'Holy Bloodshed: Violence and Christian Piety in the Romances of the London Thornton Manuscript' (unpublished Ph.D. dissertation, The Ohio State University, 2006); M. Johnston, 'Robert Thornton and *The Siege of Jerusalem*', *Yearbook of Langland Studies* 23 (2009), 125–62; J. Finlayson, 'The Context of the Crusading Romances in the London Thornton Manuscript', *Anglia* 130 (2012), 240–63; and D. Gorny, 'Reading Robert Thornton's Library: Romance and Nationalism in Lincoln, Cathedral Library MS 91 and London, British Library MS Additional 31042' (unpublished Ph.D. dissertation, University of Ottawa, 2013).

of Alexander and the alliterative *Morte* speak to one another hauntingly, both reflecting on the pitfalls of imperial ambition and both offering a vision of the body politic ineluctably waxing and waning in tandem with the physical body of the king. Thornton, moreover, added a decorative scheme to both of these romances, something he did not do elsewhere in the Lincoln manuscript, further underscoring both their material and literary interpenetration.

Third, scholars have uncovered Thornton as someone who saw the decoration of his books as fundamental to the meanings of the texts they contained.[17] Beyond the decorative scheme for the prose *Alexander* and the alliterative *Morte*, he also, in the London manuscript, left space for a large illustration at the beginning of the *Northern Passion*, which was likely intended to contain a depiction of the crucified Christ, the central image of this text. Since the *Northern Passion* was originally the opening text for this manuscript, it seems that Thornton wanted a devotional image to head the devotional series of texts with which this manuscript was to open.

Fourth, scholars have attended to Thornton's identity as a gentry landowner and his socio-economic place within late medieval England.[18] Analysis of Thornton's local networks of cultural exchange has revealed him sharing literature with local clerics and local landowners. He may have been involved with the Percy family, one of the scions of North Riding politics, perhaps even taking part in the Percy-Neville violence in the summer of 1453. And, moreover, recent investigation has focused more broadly on the gentry socio-economics of his romances and how such issues relate to and mediate the social anxieties of one in Thornton's position within aristocratic, landowning society.

Finally, we know a good deal about Thornton and the sorts of piety he practised.[19] His catholic, and always orthodox, devotional impulses attest to the

---

[17] See, for example, J. Fredell, 'Decorated Initials in the Lincoln Thornton Manuscript', *Studies in Bibliography* 47 (1994), 78–88; P. Hardman, 'Reading the Spaces: Pictorial Intentions in the Thornton MSS, Lincoln Cathedral MS 91, and BL MS Add. 31042', *Medium Ævum* 63 (1994), 250–74; and T. H. Crofts, 'The Occasion of the *Morte Arthure*: Textual History and Marginal Decoration in the Thornton MS', *Arthuriana* 20 (2010), 5–27.

[18] See, for example, Keiser, 'Lincoln Cathedral Library MS. 91'; G. R. Keiser, 'More Light on the Life and Milieu of Robert Thornton', *Studies in Bibliography* 36 (1983), 111–19; D. Youngs, 'Cultural Networks', in *Gentry Culture in Late-Medieval England*, ed. R. Radulescu and A. Truelove (Manchester, 2005), pp. 119–33; M. Johnston, 'A New Document Relating to the Life of Robert Thornton', *The Library* 7th ser. 8 (2007), 304–13; and M. Johnston, *Romance and the Gentry in Late Medieval England* (forthcoming, Oxford, 2014), ch. 5.

[19] See, for example, G. R. Keiser, 'Þe Holy Boke Gratia Dei', *Viator* 12 (1981), 289–317; G. R. Keiser, '"To Knawe God Almyghtyn": Robert Thornton's Devotional Book', in *Spätmittelalterliche geistliche Literatur in der Nationalsprache*, vol. 2, Analecta Cartusiana, ed. J. Hogg (Salzburg, 1984), pp. 103–29; S. G. Fein, '"Have Mercy of Me" (Psalm 51), An Unedited Alliterative Poem from the London Thornton Manuscript', *Modern Philology* 86 (1989), 223–41; J. J. Thompson, 'Another Look at the Religious Texts in Lincoln, Cathedral Library, MS 91', in *Late-Medieval Religious*

catholicity of devotional practices available to the late medieval literate laity. He compiled texts of various devotional strands: *inter alia*, affective piety, catechetical instruction, reflections on the so-called 'mixed life', hagiography, religious lyrics, Marian devotion, penitential reflections, mystical visions and biblical translations. He also copied out numerous romances that have a pious or devotional strain to them, and even a series of romances at the beginning of the London manuscript which seem intended as part of a Christian historical schema, with the Jews being vanquished in the *Siege of Jerusalem* followed by the Muslims in the *Sege of Melayne* and *Duke Roland and Sir Otuel of Spain*. And though the majority of Thornton's texts were in Middle English, he does preserve a healthy smattering of Latin religious literature. This diversity, then, attests to the complexity and diversity available to an overridingly orthodox compiler.

Our volume commences with Susanna Fein's comprehensive listing of all the texts in both of Thornton's manuscripts, updating older lists by accounting for scholarship and critical editions of Thornton's texts that have appeared in the intervening years. Fein also attends more carefully to the various scribal colophons and signatures that Thornton composed than do any previous lists. For the first time, Fein's list allows readers to compare the contents of both of Thornton's volumes and to consider which works Thornton brought together within any given booklet. This list thus forms the bedrock and reference point for the essays to follow.

These essays expand upon the five main critical approaches to Thornton, as outlined above. George R. Keiser begins with 'Robert Thornton: Gentleman, Reader and Scribe', which contributes new information on Thornton, including new insight into his family life and cultural milieu. Most importantly, Keiser reveals a wealth of new insights into Thornton's script, with a particular focus on his formation of several graphemes. By such a detailed analysis, Keiser fruit-fully complicates existing theories about the order in which Thornton compiled his texts. But Keiser also extends his analyses beyond the palaeographical, showing how his proposed chronology of Thornton's copying can bear on our understanding of how Thornton understood the relationships among his texts. In short, Keiser's essay shows how manuscript details and literary analysis can be mutually informing. Joel Fredell then similarly asks how knowledge of the makeup of Thornton's manuscripts might allow us to reconstruct the processes Thornton went through to achieve each manuscript's present form. Whereas previous analyses have focused on watermarks, dialect and quiring, Fredell takes

Texts and Their Transmission: Essays in Honour of A. I. Doyle, ed. A. J. Minnis (Cambridge, 1994), pp. 169–87; and E. Duffy, *The Stripping of the Altars: Traditional Religion in England, 1400–1580* (New Haven, 1992), 272–5.

up decoration to show how we might understand the various steps Thornton went through in compiling his codices. By dividing the manuscript up into its component parts based on the role of various decorators, Fredell – like Keiser – complicates previous attempts at understanding Thornton's working methods.

The next two essays take up the alliterative *Morte Arthure*, certainly the most famous of Thornton's texts. Ralph Hanna and Thorlac Turville-Petre argue that, in light of *A Linguistic Atlas of Late Mediaeval English* and recent work on the metre of alliterative verse, we need a new edition of the *Morte*. In particular, they identify the grounds on which one might emend lines in Thornton's text – the only surviving copy of this canonically central poem – that alliterate irregularly, while also giving greater credence to the evidence about the *Morte* poet's alliterative practice surviving from Malory's *Morte D'Arthur* than has any editor to date. Following from this, Mary Michele Poellinger examines the intersections between the language of violence, so central to the *Morte*, and the language of affective piety animating so many of Thornton's texts across both manuscripts. As she concludes, 'In the identification of a shared language of violence between genres, exemplified by the *Morte*, we can begin to understand the sympathies and judgements passed upon the knights who are encountering the affective language'.

In my own contribution to the present volume, I analyse what the linguistic and codicological evidence can tell us about how much of the final shape of the London manuscript reveals Thornton's intentions versus how much was simply transmitted from his exemplars. By examining the dialect strata underlying the opening texts in the London manuscript, I show that Thornton was selecting texts from multiple exemplars, and thus the salvational scheme one meets in that codex, discussed by numerous scholars, was by and large his own invention. Continuing with an interest in the London manuscript's religious literature, Julie Nelson Couch examines the figure of the Christ child in Thornton. By examining the tradition of narratives about Christ's childhood, and by placing Thornton's 'Romance of the childhode of Ihesu Criste þat clerkes callys Ipokrephum' in relation to other texts in the London manuscript, she demonstrates that 'This referential narrative enacts the dialectic at play within and among the manuscript's texts between affective devotion to and righteous indignation for Christ's sacrifice.'

Julie Orlemanski next draws our attention to what are the least literary texts in Thornton's compilations: the *Liber de Diversis Medicinis* and the fragmentary herbal that mark the end of the Lincoln manuscript. By considering how Thornton places his medical texts alongside other literary genres, Orlemanski shows how he is unique in bringing together romance and medical texts; at the same time, Orlemanski suggests that Thornton is very much of his cultural moment: as a collector of vernacular medical lore, Thornton was part of a widespread and rapidly emerging trend among the fifteenth-century English laity.

Finally, Rosalind Field and Dav Smith argue for a re-assessment of Thornton's socio-cultural milieu, demonstrating that the North Riding was quite vibrant – culturally, religiously and politically. The volume concludes with their exciting new discoveries about the fate of Robert Thornton's tomb within his parish church, Holy Trinity, Stonegrave.

This collection takes its cue from four previous edited collections that have similarly focused on a single, late medieval English manuscript, putting it under the microscope of a team of scholars working from different scholarly perspectives.[20] We also envision this as a call for further such endeavours, for numerous manuscripts from late medieval England were similarly produced by ad hoc methods that elude systemization and thus demand their own sustained analyses. In this regard, one thinks of Cambridge, CUL, MS Ff. 1. 6 (the Findern Anthology) and Oxford, Bodleian Library, MS Lat. Misc. c. 66 (the commonplace book of Humphrey Newton), both of which arose from the efforts of individuals about whom we know a good deal.[21] If, in addition to revealing new information about Thornton and inspiring further work on his manuscripts, this collection can also testify to the need for more such work on other codices, then this enterprise will have been well worth the effort.

[20] D. Pearsall, ed., *Studies in the Vernon Manuscript* (Cambridge, 1990); M. Stevens and D. H. Woodward, eds., *The Ellesmere Chaucer: Essays in Interpretation* (San Marino CA, 1995); S. Fein, ed., *Studies in the Harley Manuscript: The Scribes, Contents, and Social Contexts of British Library MS Harley 2253* (Kalamazoo MI, 2000); and K. K. Bell and J. N. Couch, eds., *The Texts and Contexts of Oxford, Bodleian Library, MS Laud Misc. 108: The Shaping of English Vernacular Narrative*, Medieval and Renaissance Authors and Texts 6 (Leiden, 2011). See also S. Fein, ed., *My Wyl and My Wrytyng: Essays on John the Blind Audelay* (Kalamazoo MI, 2009) (on Oxford, Bodleian Library, MS Douce 302); and W. Scase, ed., *The Making of the Vernon Manuscript: The Production and Contexts of Oxford, Bodleian Library MS Eng. poet. a. 1*, Texts and Transitions 6 (Turnhout, 2013).

[21] On the Findern manuscript, see R. H. Robbins, 'The Findern Anthology', *PMLA* 69 (1954), 610–42; K. Harris, 'The Origins and Make-up of Cambridge University Library MS Ff.1.6', *Transactions of the Cambridge Bibliographical Society* 8 (1983), 299–333; R. Hanna, 'The Production of Cambridge University Library MS. Ff.1.6', *Studies in Bibliography* 40 (1987), 62–70; J. J. Thompson, 'Collecting Middle English Romances and Some Related Book-Production Activities in the Later Middle Ages', in *Romance in Medieval England*, ed. M. Mills, J. Fellows and C. Meale (Cambridge, 1991), pp. 17–38 (pp. 30–8); S. C. Marshall, 'Manuscript Agency and the Findern Manuscript', *Neuphilologische Mitteilungen* 108 (2007), 339–49; and L. Olson, 'Courting Romance in the Provinces: The Findern Manuscript', in K. Kerby-Fulton, M. Hilmo and L. Olson, *Opening up Middle English Manuscripts: Literary and Visual Approaches* (Ithaca NY, 2012), pp. 139–51. On Humphrey Newton and his manuscripts, see R. Hanna, 'Humphrey Newton and Bodleian Library, MS Lat. Misc. C.66', *Medium Ævum* 69 (2000), 279–91; D. Marsh, '"I see by sizt of evidence": Information Gathering in Late Medieval Cheshire', in *Courts, Counties and the Capital in the Later Middle Ages*, ed. D. E. S. Dunn (New York, 1996), pp. 71–92; and D. Youngs, *Humphrey Newton (1466–1536): An Early Tudor Gentleman* (Woodbridge, 2008).

The Contents of
Robert Thornton's Manuscripts

Susanna Fein

In keeping with the purpose of this volume, I offer here an overview of Robert Thornton of Yorkshire's surviving corpus and an updated list of contents. The Thornton manuscripts – hereafter called 'Lincoln' and 'London' – have been frequently described in terms of content and makeup. The treatments still considered the definitive starting-points for any new work are by Derek Brewer and A. E. B. Owen, in a 1975 facsimile of Lincoln, and by John J. Thompson, in a 1987 book that examines London.[1] Supplementing these authorities is a plethora of descriptions over the years, dating at least from 1844 (James Orchard Halliwell's edition of what he termed the *Thornton Romances*) to 2012 (Linda Olson's chapter in *Opening Up Middle English Manuscripts*).[2] In between, many have contributed steady, gradual refinements to the growing portrait of Thornton's substantial achievement as a self-fashioned scribe tending prayerfully and paternally to the mental nourishment and spiritual well-being of a familial household, providing them with romances and edifying entertainments, religious meditations and *exempla*, liturgical services, and an encyclopedia of medical remedies.

As scholarship on Thornton has advanced, much of it has centred on codicological details, with investigators using booklet and quire makeups, watermarks, palaeography, dialect of scribe versus exemplar, detectable scribal error, and styles of ornament to produce divergent answers to a host of questions: In what order did Thornton receive and copy texts? What were his methods of book construction? How fully did he follow (as he most apparently did) generic criteria for selections and arrangements? What other hands are present in the manuscript? Did the manuscripts ever leave the Thornton household during

---

[1]   *The Thornton MS*, intro. Brewer and Owen; and Thompson, *London Thornton MS*.

[2]   *The Thornton Romances*, ed. J. O. Halliwell, Camden Society 30 (London, 1844), pp. xxv–xxxvi (treating Lincoln only); and L. Olson, 'Romancing the Book: Manuscripts for "Euerich Inglische"', in K. Kerby-Fulton, M. Hilmo and L. Olson, *Opening Up Middle English Manuscripts: Literary and Visual Approaches* (Ithaca NY, 2012), pp. 95–151 (pp. 116–39), who treats both manuscripts.

the period of their making? And what cultural assumptions, social allegiances, and literary tastes do the chosen texts reveal?

Taken collectively, the wide array of studies of Thornton's books has sketched an ever-deepening portrait of the scribe. With few exceptions, though, individual scholars and editors are wont to examine Thornton through a specific lens of interest, examining, for example, a featured text or, alternatively, one of the dominant strands in his books: romance, religion, medicine. Consequently, individual attention is apt to fall on one manuscript or the other, not both, and frequently on just an isolated portion of that book. My purpose here is to umpire for a moment this ongoing scholarship by compiling an updated descriptive list of the contents of *both* manuscripts, and, insofar as may be possible, to collate our many advances in defining and assessing individual items.[3]

This List of Contents serves as the touchstone for titles and article numbers that appear in the essays of this volume. It presents the incipits, first and final phrases, and explicits for each item according to my own transcription, taken from the facsimile of Lincoln and a British Library microfilm of London. By means of these framing words, one may use this descriptive list to readily survey Thornton's entire codicological labour and acquire a sense of his literate

---

[3] The main descriptions consulted here include (listed chronologically): (1) *Lincoln manuscript*: *Yorkshire Writers: Richard Rolle and His Followers*, ed. C. Horstmann, 2 vols. (London 1895–6; repr. Cambridge, 1999), I, 184–5; *The Life of Richard Rolle Together with an Edition of His English Lyrics*, ed. F. M. M. Comper (London, 1928), pp. 207–9; *The 'Liber de Diversis Medicinis' in the Thornton Manuscript (MS. Lincoln Cathedral A.5.2)*, ed. M. S. Ogden, EETS OS 207 (London, 1938), pp. x–xvii; *The Thornton MS*, intro. Brewer and Owen, pp. vii–xxii; G. Guddat-Figge, *Catalogue of Manuscripts Containing Middle English Romances* (Munich, 1976), pp. 135–42; J. J. Thompson, 'The Compiler in Action: Robert Thornton and the "Thornton Romances" in Lincoln Cathedral MS 91', in *Manuscripts and Readers in Fifteenth-Century England: The Literary Implications of Manuscript Study. Essays from the 1981 Conference at the University of York*, ed. D. Pearsall (Cambridge, 1983), pp. 113–24 (p. 115); G. R. Keiser, '"To Knawe God Almyghtyn": Robert Thornton's Devotional Book', in *Spätmittelalterliche geistliche Literatur in der Nationalsprache*, vol. 2, Analecta Cartusiana, ed. J. Hogg (Salzburg, 1984), pp. 103–29 (pp. 125–9); R. Hanna III, 'The Growth of Robert Thornton's Books', *Studies in Bibliography* 40 (1987), 51–61; R. M. Thomson, *Catalogue of the Manuscripts of Lincoln Cathedral Chapter Library* (Woodbridge, 1989), pp. 65–9; and *Richard Rolle: Uncollected Prose and Verse*, ed. R. Hanna, EETS OS 329 (Oxford, 2007), pp. xxxvi–xxxix. (2) *London manuscript*: 'Hs. Brit. Mus. Additional 31042', ed. K. Brunner, *Archiv* 132 (1914), 316–37 (pp. 316–27); *The Northern Passion*, ed. F. A. Foster, 2 vols., EETS OS 145, 147 (London, 1913–16), II, 12–13; K. Stern, 'The London "Thornton" Miscellany: A New Description of British Museum Additional Manuscript 31042', and 'The London "Thornton" Miscellany (II): A New Description of British Museum Additional Manuscript 31042', *Scriptorium* 30 (1976), 26–40, 201–18; Guddat-Figge, *Catalogue*, pp. 159–63; Thompson, *London Thornton MS*; Hanna, 'The Growth', pp. 51–61; *Wynnere and Wastoure*, ed. S. Trigg, EETS OS 297 (Oxford, 1990), pp. xiv–xv; and *The Siege of Jerusalem*, ed. R. Hanna and D. Lawton, EETS OS 320 (Oxford, 2003), pp. xv–xvi.

presence – as scribe and rubricator, as devout Christian and *paterfamilias*, as engaged reader and collector of texts – as he expresses it by distinctive markers.

The inscribing that flowed from Thornton's hand is voluminous. Nearly five hundred folios survive more or less intact. Numerous others are just fragments, and many of these are meagre scraps salvaged from pages once affixed to the end of Lincoln. Both manuscripts begin and end imperfectly, and both have suffered internal losses. Measurable gaps within the books as we have them come to more than thirty folios.[4] Nonetheless, a majority of items survive fully intact as Thornton copied them.[5] In these many leaves we witness a fifteenth-century English gentleman's long-term, worshipful endeavour to compile a sizeable library for his own personal use and the edification of his family. How Christian faith drove Thornton's inner life is evident by the presence of many meditations and prayers, as well as by the scribe's instinctive insertions of invocations and blessings. Thornton's manorial home supported a private chapel,[6] which helps to explain the inclusion of texts for liturgical or meditative practice. There are, moreover, numerous romances collected by Thornton with deliberation and discernment, which would have held particular appeal for a gentry family.[7] And comprising a discrete booklet in Lincoln are medical texts and a herbal (now fragmentary), which gave the Thorntons a storehouse of information on the properties of natural substances, scientific lore and practical remedies. While one cannot determine how many or what texts are now lost from the Thornton oeuvre, the extensive corpus that survives tells us that Thornton's self-made library was ambitious in scope and substantial in its actual execution.[8]

---

4   According to the accepted collations. See D. Brewer and A. E. B. Owen, 'Collation of the Manuscript', in *The Thornton MS*, intro. Brewer and Owen, p. xii; and Thompson, *London Thornton MS*, p. 19. These collations have been subsequently refined by examination of watermarks, quires, and stubs. See, in particular, Stern, 'The London "Thornton" Miscellany' and 'The London "Thornton" Miscellany (II); S. M. Horrall, 'The London Thornton Manuscript: A New Collation', *Manuscripta* 23 (1979), 99–103; S. M. Horrall, 'The Watermarks of the Thornton Manuscripts', *Notes and Queries* n.s. 27 (1980), 385–6; R. Hanna III, 'The London Thornton Manuscript: A Corrected Collation', *Studies in Bibliography* 37 (1984), 122–30; Hanna, 'The Growth'; and the chapters by Fredell and Keiser in the present volume.

5   Some articles suffering severe damage, for example, include a miracle of the Virgin, Thornton's herbal, and the romances the *Sege of Melayne* and *Richard Coer de Lyon* (Lincoln arts. 17, 100; London arts. 8, 32).

6   Keiser, '"To Knawe God Almyghtyn"', pp. 121–2; see also Keiser's chapter in the present volume.

7   M. Johnston, 'A New Document Relating to the Life of Robert Thornton', *The Library* 7th ser. 8 (2007), 304–13.

8   Keiser suggests large losses from the front of London in his chapter in the present volume. In addition, he provides an astute assessment of the herbal lost at the end of Lincoln (see Lincoln art. 100).

The primary language of Lincoln and London is English. Yet Thornton shows himself ready, as both scribe and reader, to pivot casually to Latin, which he often does, mainly in religious contexts and incipits. In carrying out his vast scrivenal undertaking, though, Thornton chooses English most of the time, and in this language he copies more verse than prose, the ratio being roughly two to one when measured by number of folios filled. Aside from the abridged, yet long, *Psalter of Saint Jerome* (Lincoln art. 84), which occupies about twenty-five pages, the presence of Latin seems incidental to Thornton's main compiling purpose. Outside the *Psalter*, Latin totals only about a dozen pages, appearing mainly as prayers, charms, proverbs and pious tags.[9] Despite its secondary status, Latin contributes to Thornton's books a cultivated manner of dignity and reverence. Thornton regularly interchanges Latin with English in his own incipits and explicits, and he often turns to Latin to inscribe brief prayers.

In the following paragraphs, I summarize the nature and contents of each book and some ways in which Thornton signified his presence as their maker.

The Lincoln manuscript

As it stands today, Lincoln holds 312 folios before ending with a set of severely damaged fragments that represent all that remains of Thornton's lost herbal. Lincoln's basic structure of four booklets is evident on empirical grounds and provokes no dispute.[10] **Booklet 1** (fols. 3–52; arts. 1–6) holds the prose *Life of Alexander*, which was added to preface booklet 2 after the latter was completed, Thornton deciding to set the life of an ancient Worthy before that of a medieval one: King Arthur of Britain in the alliterative *Morte Arthure*. In Arthur's second dream in the alliterative poem, he has a spectacular vision of Fortune's

---

9   Thornton ascribes a Latin prayer and two meditations to Richard Rolle (Lincoln arts. 49, 55, 56), nestling these items among much by Rolle in English prose or verse (Lincoln arts. 46, 47, 51–4, 57–60). Clusters of very short Latin texts fill space near the opening or close of booklets (London arts. 17–19; Lincoln arts. 88–96), or mix with similar texts in English (Lincoln arts. 26–36). Two articles of English devotional prose frequently include Latin (Lincoln arts. 61, 62).

10   For some significant broad efforts to define discrete codicological units (commonly called 'booklets') within manuscripts, see P. R. Robinson, 'The "Booklet": A Self-Contained Unit in Composite Manuscripts', *Codicologica* 3 (1980), 46–69, and 'Booklets in Medieval Manuscripts: Further Considerations', *Studies in Bibliography* 39 (1986), 100–11; R. Hanna III, *Pursuing History: Middle English Manuscripts and Their Texts* (Stanford CA, 1996), pp. 21–34; J. Boffey and J. J. Thompson, 'Anthologies and Miscellanies: Production and Choice of Texts', in *Book Production and Publishing in Britain, 1375–1475*, ed. J. Griffiths and D. Pearsall (Cambridge, 1989), pp. 279–315; J. Fredell, '"Go Litel Quaer": Lydgate's Pamphlet Poetry', *Journal of the Early Book Society* 9 (2006), 51–74; and E. Kwakkel, 'Late Medieval Text Collections: A Codicological Typology Based on Single-Author Manuscripts', in *Author, Reader, Book: Medieval Authority in Theory and Practice*, ed. S. Partridge and E. Kwakkel (Toronto, 2012), pp. 56–79.

Wheel, sees eight riders being tossed off in succession and then becomes the ninth, signifying how he is the last of the great imperial leaders of history. The first of the Worthies is Alexander, who declares in Arthur's dream that 'I was lorde ... of londes inewe, / And all ledis me lowttede that lenegede in erthe' (lines 3285–86).[11] Thornton has framed his manuscript as a World History, secular in its thrust for these first booklets. Blank space at the end of booklet 1 holds family records, signatures and scribbles by Thornton's descendants, a prognostication on thunder according the days of the week and chivalric drawings. There is also the lyric *Sinner's Lament* that ruminates on the fates of men, situated strategically between the falls of Alexander and Arthur.[12] The blank space thus formed a spot for filler material, some related to the core romances on either side, some demonstrating the book's intergenerational status as a Thornton household treasure.

As a full unit in its own right, **booklet 2** (fols. 53–178; arts. 7–36) stands as one of the premier medieval collections of Middle English verse romance. When one joins to it *Alexander* and the four crusades-oriented romances of the London manuscript, we find in Thornton's body of work a set of romances that rivals the Auchinleck manuscript (Edinburgh, NLS, MS Advocates' 19. 2. 1) in quantity and significance. The booklet leads off with the alliterative *Morte Arthure* and then serves up *Octavian*, *Sir Isumbras*, the *Earl of Toulouse*, *Sir Degrevant*, *Sir Eglamour of Artois*, *Awntyrs off Arthure* and *Sir Perceval of Gales*. Tucked into this sequence are other kinds of narrative that the scribe may have regarded as romance-like: the *Life of Saint Christopher*, a miracle of the Virgin called *The Wicked Knight and the Friar*, *Lyarde* (a comic satire on friars and husbands)[13] and *Thomas of Erceldoune's Prophecy*. A good number of these items are preserved solely in Lincoln, adding to its value as a witness to romances circulating in Thornton's region.

The next section of Lincoln, **booklet 3** (fols. 179–279; arts. 37–98), holds Thornton's collection of religious devotions and treatises, often in prose (mainly English), with a hefty number of attributions to specific authors: Richard Rolle, Saint Jerome, Saint Ambrose, William of Nassington and Edmund Rich of Abingdon. Three treatises by Walter Hilton (one an extract from the *Scale of Perfection*) appear without any attribution. Alliterative English prose or verse makes an appearance in Gaytryge's *Sermon*, the alliterative *John Evangelist Hymn*

---

[11] Fol. 88r. See *Morte Arthure: A Critical Edition*, ed. M. Hamel, Garland Medieval Texts 9 (New York, 1984), p. 221.

[12] On the regular use of this song to comment on great men who have fallen low, see *The Sinner's Lament*, in *Moral Love Songs and Laments*, ed. S. G. Fein (Kalamazoo MI, 1998), pp. 361–94 (pp. 367–9).

[13] *Lyarde*, the most secular and comic work in Thornton's oeuvre (Lincoln art. 18). It seems to draw on monastic goliardic traditions.

and a treatise *On Prayer*. Other anonymous religious items include the *Privity of the Passion*, the *Holy Boke Gratia Dei*, an extract from the *Prick of Conscience* and several lyrics, prayers and hymns. The English lyrics include versions of *When Adam Delved* and *Earth upon Earth*. The unique *Revelation Shown to a Holy Woman* offers a glimpse of the pains of purgatory; Thornton annotates this text and copies after it the psalm and hymn most useful to escape that fate. Lincoln's final section, **booklet 4** (fols. 280–321; arts. 99–100), preserves the medical collection *Liber de Diversis Medicinis*, which survives on thirty-five leaves, and the herbal now mostly lost.

The London manuscript

The smaller London (179 folios) is more homogeneous and less obviously segmented than Lincoln. Its collation and watermarks nonetheless suggest that it too was constructed progressively in parts. Begun as an account of Sacred History, it initially opened with the *Northern Passion*. But again, as with Lincoln, Thornton's plans evolved as time passed, and he eventually augmented London's opening with a new beginning – a long extract and a short allegorical dialogue taken from the *Cursor Mundi* – thereby setting up an expansive preface to the *Northern Passion*. This new opening forms **booklet 1** (fols. 3–32; arts. 1–3).[14] The succeeding **booklet 2** (fols. 33–97; arts. 4–20) has the *Northern Passion* joined to three romances that continue a narrative of Christian history, from the *Siege of Jerusalem* (situated AD 70) to the crusading Middle Ages: the *Sege of Melayne* and *Duke Roland and Sir Otuel of Spain*. Interspersed here are lyrics by John Lydgate. Thornton's corpus of Lydgatiana is comprised of the *Complaint That Christ Makes of His Passion*, *Verses on the Kings of England*, the *Dietary*, a refrain poem *O Florum Flos*, and (in the next booklet) *Virtues of the Mass*, which has a scribal ascription to Lydgate (fol. 103r). Aside from Lydgate's *Virtues*, **booklet 3** (fols. 98–124; arts. 21–31) features a selection of anonymous religious verse: the alliterative *Four Leaves of the Truelove* in thirteen-line stanzas; *Have Mercy of Me* (an alliterating paraphrase of Vulgate Psalm 50); a filler poem hailing one's guardian spirit; more English lyrics on mercy, mutability and wisdom; the *Rose of Ryse* (a carol with allusions to Henry V); and the narrative *Three Kings of Cologne* in rhyme royal stanzas. *Three Kings* is the last lengthy item in booklet 3, and its dignified rhyme royal seems matched to Lydgate's rhyme royal *Verses on the Kings of England* at the end of booklet 2. These are the only items in this metre in Thornton's entire corpus.

When Thornton added **booklet 4** (fols. 125–168; arts. 32–3), he was able

---

[14] According to the analysis of Hanna, 'The London Thornton Manuscript', and Hanna, 'The Growth'.

to introduce another romance of sacred history – *Richard Coer de Lyon* – furthering his accumulated themes of royalty, crusade and national mission. And finally, after *Richard*, he rounds London's interests back to the scriptural *Cursor Mundi* and *Northern Passion* material of his two beginnings: Thornton now includes the apocryphal *Childhood of Christ*, which he names a 'romance' in the incipit. One final section remains: **booklet 5** (fols. 169–181; arts. 34–5) supplies a moralizing commemoration of the Nine Worthies and an allegory of the world in decline: the *Parlement of the Thre Ages* and *Wynnere and Wastoure*. Both drawn apparently from one of Thornton's favourite exemplars,[15] this pair of alliterative debate poems gives London a provocative if incomplete ending.

Thornton's signatures

As Robert Thornton acquired a personal household library by selecting and copying the texts he wished to own, it is clear that in scrivening he was ever-cognizant that his deeds were under God's watchful eye. His own embellishments reveal how profoundly he considered scribal work to be pious work. Thornton's personal voice emerges in the consistently prayerful idiom employed to frame texts according to a fairly methodical system of incipits and explicits.[16] His name appears eleven times in Lincoln, twice in London. Four times it surfaces as 'R Thornton', four times 'Thornton', once 'Robert Thornton', once (on an illustrator's scroll) 'Robart Thornton', once (in a Latin context) 'Robertus Thornton', once (oddly) 'Robert of Thornton',[17] and once (in a Latin prayer) 'Robertum'. In addition, in the prose *Life of Alexander* there appears a rebus drawing that puns on the Thornton name (Lincoln, fol. 23v).

But it is not merely in the signatures that Thornton's devout presence may be heard and felt in his books. He habitually embellishes the endings of texts with multiple strung-out 'Amens', often with 'per charite' added for good measure. This final benediction is so common that when one finds it as the last line of a romance – that is, set *inside* the last stanza, not outside it – one may suspect that Thornton has doctored the ending to conform to his own religio-aesthetic sensibilities. This event happens twice: in the romances *Octavian* ('Amen Amen per charyte') and *Sir Perceval of Gales* ('Amen for charyte') (Lincoln arts. 10, 21). Appended to some texts there are also couplets (or near-couplets) that bear

---

[15] On the basis of dialect, their shared exemplar is also thought to have contained the *Sege of Melayne* (London art. 8) and *Octavian, Sir Isumbras, Earl of Toulouse, Sir Perceval of Gales*, and the *Abbey of the Holy Ghost* (Lincoln arts. 10, 11, 13, 21, 85).

[16] And in the occasional annotation: see Lincoln arts. 81 and 84, and also London art. 24 (an ascription to Lydgate).

[17] This one is not in Thornton's hand. It and the ascription on a scroll accompany the alliterative *Morte Arthure* (Lincoln art. 8).

a distinct Thorntonian air because they tend to recur as devout ways to sign off the copying task. The most familiar is the Latin rhyme wherein Thornton names himself ('R Thornton dictus qui scripsit sit benedictus amen'), which appears twice in Lincoln (arts. 9, 68), once in London (art. 7), and twice in abbreviated form *sans* signature ('Qui scripsit [carmen] sit benedictus Amen'; Lincoln arts. 50, 60). This ending implores a blessing for the scribe after his pious labour. At one point Thornton embeds his name deep inside a prayer (Lincoln art. 28), showing how personalized the copying has become. He also names himself in a plea to God for mercy ('Thornton misereatur mei dei'; Lincoln art. 93), invoking Vulgate Psalm 50, which he elsewhere records in Lincoln in Latin (art. 82) and in London in an English verse paraphrase (art. 23). At other points, he inserts an English couplet as a colophon-prayer, and one of these is certainly his own invention: 'Amen Amen per charite / And louynge to god þerfore gyfe we / R Thornton' (London art. 5).[18] Twice in Lincoln, Thornton's enthusiasm for naming Christ and Mary erupts as a rhyming Latin prayer that must reflect a personal pious reflex: 'Ihesus Marie filius sit michi clemens & propecius' (Lincoln arts. 59, 95). Thornton's most intrusive moment comes when he describes his compilatory reordering of texts as scribal fantasy, 'fantasiam scriptoris' (London art. 3; fol. 32vb). There are other instances where Thornton mixes piety with deep family pride, as in the birth record of his grandson (Lincoln art. 2) and the apparent family motto inscribed at the base of the opening folio of the alliterative *Morte Arthure* (Lincoln art. 7): 'Espoyez / Thornton / ygl En esperance may …' (Lincoln art. 7).[19]

List of Contents

The List of Contents given below itemizes individual articles found in Robert Thornton's Lincoln and London manuscripts. Each article's opening and closing phrases are given. Boldface indicates Thornton's own verbal insertions, that is, those words he adds as incipits, explicits, signatures, prayers, pious invocations or final 'amens'. When these insertions show Thornton to be using verse (usually a single couplet in Latin or English), the item is listed separately.

The article numbering represents a new count of the contents of Lincoln and London. The count is different because of a finer discrimination within and between separate articles (in accord with recent scholarship) as well as because Thornton's signatures, insertions and meaningful blank sections are enumer-

---

[18] This couplet is not recorded in the *NIMEV*. For a second example, see Lincoln art 48: 'Ihesu þe sone of þe gloriouse virgyne / Now lorde haue mercy one all thyne / Amen Amen pur charite Amen' (*NIMEV* 1779.3).

[19] See details in the List of Contents, Lincoln arts. 2, 7.

ated separately. As reference points, the numbers in the Brewer and Owen facsimile of Lincoln ('F') and the Thompson 1987 analysis of London ('T') are also provided. Not counted are marginal writing exercises (which generally involve later hands) and nonscribal signatures.[20]

For convenient reference, titles are assigned to most articles itemized here. For familiar works, the given titles are the ones currently in use; for less well-known works, titles are generally drawn from an item's opening phrase in its own language, either English or Latin. Textual witnesses from other manuscripts are listed except where their number is relatively high, that is, more than twelve. The List of Contents also provides in the footnotes the printed editions of each article with most post-1850 editions included.

In transcribing Thornton's handwriting, I have expanded abbreviations silently and not reproduced his punctuation or flourishes.[21] A slash-mark (/) indicates a scribal change in line. Thornton's frequent marks over final *n* are not expanded, although editors often print them as *-n* , *-e*, or *-ne*. Thornton's abbreviations for forms of *Christ* are expanded to forms without the letter *h* (*Crist, Cristi*, etc.). I have striven to reproduce Thornton's capitalizations, but it must be noted that many instances are ambiguous. Initial *ff* is transcribed as capital F. Estimates of missing leaves are based on collations found in the Brewer and Owen facsimile (for Lincoln) and Thompson's 1987 book (for London).

Lincoln Cathedral Library, MS 91 (321 folios)

Lincoln booklet 1 (Quires A–C; fols. 1–52): Prose *Life of Alexander*
1.   fols. 1r–49r English prose [F1].[22] *Begins imperfectly*: ... down into þe dyke and thare he felle. *Ends*: þe twelfed / es called Egipt **Explicit Vita Alexandry magni co[n]questoris / Here ende3 þe lyf of gret Allexander conquerour of all þe worlde**

Prose *Life of Alexander*.[23] Prose romance, with spaces left open for a programme of illustration, not filled in except for an ornate initial

---

[20] For discussion of these marks, see Olson, 'Romancing the Book', pp. 126–7, 132–5.

[21] For a list of Thornton's most common abbreviations, see *The Prose Alexander of Robert Thornton: The Middle English Text with a Modern English Translation*, ed. J. Chappell (New York, 1992), pp. 31–2.

[22] Numbers prefixed 'F' refer to the list of Lincoln contents as itemized in the facsimile: *The Thornton MS*, intro. Brewer and Owen, pp. xvii–xx. A detail from fol. 9v is reproduced as Figure 1 in Fredell's chapter in the present volume. Fols. 6r, 7r, 23v, 27r are reproduced in colour in Olson, 'Romancing the Book', pp. 121, 123, 137 (figs. 24, 23, 27, 25, respectively).

[23] Editions: *The Prose Life of Alexander from the Thornton MS*, ed. J. S. Westlake, EETS OS 143 (London, 1913); *The Prose Alexander: A Critical Edition*, ed. M. Neeson (Los Angeles, 1971); and *The Prose Alexander of Robert Thornton*, ed. Chappell.

Q on fol. 6r (compare London art. 1). Most of the romance is intact, but substantial losses occur at the beginning, where four leaves are missing, and between fols. 18 and 19, and 19 and 20, where two leaves are missing. A rebus on Thornton's name appears in a large red initial *A* on fol. 23v (a 'thorn' sprouting from a 'tun' [barrel]). *IPMEP* 158. *Manual* 1, I [67].

No other manuscript.

2.   fol. 49v Latin prose.[24] **Isto die natus Fuit sancta maria ante domini nostri Ihesu Cristi Robertus Thornton in Ridayll anno domini Mᵒ cccc liij**

    Birth record for Thornton's grandson, also named Robert, perhaps in Thornton's hand (top of folio). This leaf, originally blank, was used over time for pen and writing trials, scribbles and the ownership inscription of Thornton's son or great-grandson William (bottom): 'Wylliam thorntson armiger this Boke'.[25]

3.   fol. 50r–v English prose [F2]. *Begins*: Notandum þat by tokyns off þe Element. *Ends*: of þat / rewme þer yt falles In

    Thunder Prognostications.[26] Predictions regarding thunder by the days of the week, probably in Thornton's hand. *IPMEP* 475. *Manual* 10, XXV [122b].

    Twelve other manuscripts: Aberdeen University Library, MS 272; Cambridge, Trinity College, MS R. 14. 52; London, BL, MSS Cotton Vespasian D. xiv, Sloane 213, Sloane 989, Sloane 2270, Sloane 2584; New York, Pierpont Morgan Library, MS 776; Oxford, Bodleian Library, MSS Ashmole 189, Ashmole 342; San Marino, Huntington Library, MSS HM 64, HM 1336.

4.   fol. 51r Blank except for a few late pen trials.

5.   fols. 51va–52ra English verse [F3]. *Begins*: **Lamentacio Peccatoris**. All crystyn men þat wawkes me bye. *Ends*: All crystyn men be war by me / **Explicit Lamentacio**

    Sinner's Lament.[27] Penitential lyric, probably in Thornton's hand;[28] ten

---

[24] Fol. 49v is reproduced in colour in Olson, 'Romancing the Book', p. 134 (fig. 28). 'Family pride' is discussed on pp. 132–3. Olson attributes this hand to either Thornton or his son (p. 126).

[25] See *Richard Rolle*, ed. Hanna, pp. xxxviii–xxxix; and Thomson, *Catalogue*, p. 65. Both read the abbreviation as *ar*, 'armiger', while Olson reads it as *aro*, 'armigero' ('Romancing the Book', p. 126).

[26] Edition: *Religious Pieces in Prose and Verse*, ed. G. G. Perry, EETS OS 26 (New York, 1905), p. 114. On the hand, see note 28 below.

[27] Editions: *Religious Pieces*, ed. Perry, pp. 115–18; *Altenglische Legenden: Neue Folge*, ed. C. Horstmann (Heilbronn, 1881), pp. 529–30. See also *The Sinner's Lament*, ed. Fein, pp. 361–94 (critical edition based on Corpus Christi 237).

[28] On the hand, see *The Sinner's Lament*, ed. Fein, pp. 367–68; and compare Olson,

8-line stanzas; much variety among versions.[29] Dragon drawings on fols. 51v and 52r match one on fol. 161r. *DIMEV* 317, *NIMEV* 172. *Manual* 9, XXII [338].

Five other manuscripts: Edinburgh, NLS, Advocates' MS 19. 3. 1; London, Lambeth Palace Library, MS 560; Oxford, Bodleian Library, MSS Ashmole 61, Rawlinson C. 813; Oxford, Corpus Christi College, MS 237.

6. fol. 52v Sketches of knights and a horse.[30]

Lincoln booklet 2 (Quires D–K; fols. 53–178): Romances

7. fol. 53r English or French prose.[31] **Espoyez / Thornton / ygl En espyrance may ...**

    Scribal signature at base of booklet 2's opening page. The inscription may be a Thornton family motto or a variant of the Percy motto 'Esperaunce ma comforte'.[32]

8. fols. 53r–98v English verse [F4].[33] *Begins:* **H[er]e begynnes Morte Arthure** / Now grett glorious godd thurgh grace of hym selven. *Ends:* Into Bretayne the brode as þe bruytte tellys &c explicit / **Hic iacet**

'Romancing the Book', p. 116 n. 121. See also J. Finlayson, 'Reading Romances in the Manuscript: Lincoln Cathedral Manuscript 91 ("Thornton")', *Anglia* 123 (2006), 632–66 (pp. 639–40), who notes that there is no 'extensive published analysis' of Thornton's own varying script – his apparent 'spreading hand' – though analogies have been offered to M. B. Parkes's demonstration of wide variation by a scribe copying *Brut: English Cursive Book Hands 1250–1500* (Oxford, 1969), Plate 21. On verifiably different hands contemporary with Thornton's own, see Keiser's chapter in the present volume (and notes to Lincoln arts. 8, 38, 39, 40).

[29] A chart of the stanzaic variation among versions is available in *The Sinner's Lament*, ed. Fein, p. 381.

[30] Fol. 52v is reproduced in colour and discussed in Olson, 'Romancing the Book', pp. 124, 125 n. 140 (fig. 19); see also Thomson, *Catalogue*, p. 65; and T. H. Crofts, 'The Occasion of the *Morte Arthure*: Textual History and Marginal Decoration in the Thornton MS', *Arthuriana* 20 (2010), 5–27 (pp. 6, 13).

[31] Fol. 53r is reproduced in colour in Olson, 'Romancing the Book', p. 121 (fig. 15); and in Thompson, *London Thornton MS*, plate 1.

[32] The transcription follows *The Thornton MS*, intro. Brewer and Owen, p. vii. The phrase and its meaning are puzzling; if it is meant to represent pseudo-heraldic French, one should note that French elsewhere in Thornton's books is virtually nonexistent. Olson, 'Romancing the Book', p. 126, reads 'ygl' as an abbreviation for 'ynglish'. On the Percy motto, see Johnston, 'A New Document', p. 309 n. 28; and Olson, pp. 122–3. Compare also Lincoln art. 13 (note 38).

[33] For fol. 53r, see Figure 1. For a detail from fol. 56v, see Fredell's chapter, Figure 10, in the present volume. For fol. 98v, see Keiser's chapter, Figure 1, in the present volume. Fols. 53r, 80r, 84r, 93v and 98v are reproduced in colour in Olson, 'Romancing the Book', pp. 121, 123, 137 (figs. 15, 31a, 31b, 18, 17, respectively). See also the marginal decorations reproduced in Crofts, 'The Occasion', pp. 15, 16, 19, 20 (fols. 75v, 66r, 78v, 73r, 95r, respectively).

Arthurus rex quondam rexque futurus / [*in a different hand*] Here endes Morte Arthure Writen By Robert of / Thornton[34]

Alliterative *Morte Arthure*.[35] Romance; 4346 unrhymed alliterative long lines (see Figure 1). Two ascriptions to Thornton as scribe: an illustrator's scroll on fol. 93v ('Robart Thornton') and the English 'Here endes' explicit on fol. 98r. The latter was not written by Thornton himself; the former might not have been.[36] This item and Lincoln art. 38 (*Privity of the Passion*) probably derive from a single exemplar in a southwest Lincolnshire dialect. The visual presentation of the *Morte* is singular among Thornton's texts for its fuller degree of ornamentation: elaborated initials, marginal flourishes, and animate faces and figures.[37] *NIMEV* 2322. *Manual* 1, I [16].

No other manuscript.

9. fol. 98v Latin verse. **R Thornton dictus qui scripsit sit benedictus amen** Scribal signature-couplet. Compare Lincoln arts. 55, 60, 68 and London art. 7.

10. fols. 98va–109rb English verse [F5].[38] *Begins:* **Here Bygynnes The Romance off Octovyane** / Mekyll and littill Olde & 3ynge. *Ends:* Thou gyffe vs alle thi dere blyssynge / **Amen Amen per charyte Amen** *Octavian* (Northern version).[39] Romance; 1731 lines; 12-line tail-rhyme stanzas; last line of poem appears to be Thornton's altered ending. A loss of text occurs between fols. 102 and 103, where one leaf is missing. *DIMEV* 3132, *NIMEV* 1918 (for Southern version, see *DIMEV* 2930,

---

[34] This line is written by a trained scribe, not Thornton. The same hand appears on fol. 189r (Lincoln arts. 38–40); see Keiser's chapter and his Figures 1 and 2 in the present volume; and also Olson, 'Romancing the Book', pp. 116 nn. 121, 126.

[35] Editions: *Morte Arthure, or The Death of Arthur*, ed. E. Brock, EETS OS 8 (London, 1871); *Morte Arthure: An Alliterative Poem of the 14th Century, from the Lincoln MS*, ed. M. M. Banks (London, 1900); *Morte Arthure*, ed. E. Björkman (Heidelberg, 1915); *The Alliterative* Morte Arthure: *A Critical Edition*, ed. V. Krishna (New York, 1976); and *Morte Arthure*, ed. Hamel. For an edition with regularized spelling, see *King Arthur's Death: The Middle English Stanzaic* Morte Arthur *and Alliterative* Morte Arthure, ed. L. D. Benson, rev. E. E. Foster (Kalamazoo MI, 1994), pp. 131–284. A new facing-page translation has recently been published: *The Death of King Arthur*, trans. S. Armitage (New York, 2012).

[36] Olson, 'Romancing the Book', pp. 116 n. 121, 123, 126.

[37] Crofts, 'The Occasion', pp. 11–24; Olson, 'Romancing the Book', pp. 136–7; and J. Fredell, 'Decorated Initials in the Lincoln Thornton Manuscript', *Studies in Bibliography* 47 (1994), 78–88.

[38] Fol. 98v is reproduced in colour in Olson, 'Romancing the Book', p. 123 (fig. 17).

[39] Editions: *Octavian*, ed. G. Sarrazin (Heilbronn, 1885) (in parallel with CUL Ff. 2. 38); *Octavian*, ed. F. McSparran, EETS OS 289 (London, 1986) (in parallel with CUL Ff. 2. 38 and de Worde); *Four Middle English Romances: Sir Isumbras, Octavian, Sir Eglamour of Artois, Sir Tryamour*, ed. H. Hudson (Kalamazoo MI, 1996), pp. 45–114. See also *Six Middle English Romances*, ed. M. Mills (London, 1973), pp. 75–124 (CUL Ff. 2. 38).

Figure 1. Lincoln Cathedral Library, MS 91, fol. 53r (opening of the alliterative *Morte Arthure*)

NIMEV 1774). This item likely shared a single exemplar with Lincoln arts. 11, 13, 21, 85 and London arts. 8, 34, 35.[40] *Manual* 1, I [81].

> *One other manuscript: Cambridge, CUL, MS Ff. 2. 38. One early print: de Worde (STC 18779). Southern version: London, BL, MS Cotton Caligula A. ii.*

11.   fols. 109rb–114va English verse [F6].[41] *Begins:* **Here begynnes the Romance / Off Sir ysambrace** / Ihesu Crist lorde of heven kynge. *Ends:* Nowe and euer mare **Amen Amen / Explicit Sir ysambrace**

Sir Isumbras.[42] Romance; 12-line tail-rhyme stanzas. This item likely

---

[40] On the matter of shared exemplars for Thornton's texts, see A. McIntosh, 'The Textual Transmission of the Alliterative *Morte Arthure*', in *English and Medieval Studies Presented to J. R. R. Tolkien on the Occasion of His Seventieth Birthday*, ed. N. Davis and C. L. Wrenn (London, 1962), pp. 231–40 (pp. 231–2); and R. Hanna, 'The Growth of Robert Thornton's Books', *Studies in Bibliography* 40 (1987), 51–61 (esp. p. 55). Thornton scholars have by and large accepted these conclusions. All further references to shared exemplars in the present chapter rely on these sources.

[41] A detail from fol. 109v is reproduced in Fredell's chapter, Figure 5, in the present volume.

[42] Edition: *Thornton Romances*, ed. Halliwell, pp. 88–120. See also *Six Middle English Romances*, ed. Mills, pp. 125–47 (based on Cotton); *Four Middle English Romances*, ed. Hudson, pp. 7–44 (based on Gonville and Caius).

shared a single exemplar with Lincoln arts. 10, 13, 21, 85 and London arts. 8, 34, 35. *DIMEV* 1934, *NIMEV* 1184 (lines 1–3 are different in Lincoln). *Manual* 1, I [78].

Nine other manuscripts: Cambridge, Gonville and Caius College, MS 175/96; Edinburgh, NLS, Advocates' MS 19. 3. 1; London, BL, MS Cotton Caligula A. ii; London, Gray's Inn, MS 20; Naples, Biblioteca Nazionale, MS XIII. B. 29; Oxford, Bodleian Library, MSS Ashmole 61, Douce 261 (transcript of early print), Malone 941; Oxford, University College, MS 142 (extract). *Four early prints:* STC 14280.5, 14280.7, 14281, 14282.

12. fol. 114va Latin verse. Vt dicunt multi cito transit lancea stulti
Aphorism written in lower margin; couplet.
Other manuscripts unknown.

13. fols. 114vb–122ra English verse [F7]. *Begins:* **Here bygynnes þe Romance off Dyoclicyane / þe Emperour & þe Erle Berade of Tholous And / of þe Emprice Beaulilione**[43] / Ihesu Criste god and lorde in trynyte. *Ends imperfectly:* Bothe þaire flesche & þaire bones ...
Earl of Toulouse.[44] Romance; 12-line tail-rhyme stanzas. This item likely shared a single exemplar with Lincoln arts. 10, 11, 21, 85 and London arts. 8, 34, 35. *DIMEV* 2813, *NIMEV* 1681. *Manual* 1, I [94].
Three other manuscripts: Cambridge, CUL, MS Ff. 2. 38; Oxford, Bodleian Library, MSS Ashmole 45, Ashmole 61.

14. fols. 122vb–129vb English verse [F8]. *Begins:* **Vita Sancti Cristofori / [...] e bygynnes þe lyffe of þe Story of / [...]aynte Cristofre to þe heryng or þe / [...]yng of þe whilke storye langes / [...]ete mede & it be don with deuocion** / Lordynges if it be 3owre will. *Ends:* God bryng vs thedir when his will es **Amen / Explicit Vita sancti Cristofori / Thornton**
Life of Saint Christopher.[45] Saint's life; 1013 lines in couplets. Scribal signa-

---

[43] In the right margin, beside this word, one finds a obscure inscription: 'Ky gray [*or* graþ] Espoyere' with the numeral 'xix' written above 'Espoyere'. Compare the presence of the word 'Espoyez' in Lincoln art. 7 (possibly a motto), and see note 30.

[44] The Lincoln Thornton text is not printed. For editions based on CUL Ff. 2. 38, see *The Erl of Tolous and the Emperes of Almayne*, ed. G. Lüdtke, Sammlung englischer Denkmäler 3 (Berlin, 1881); *Middle English Romances*, ed. W. H. French and C. B. Hale, 2 vols. (New York, 1930), I, pp. 383–419; *Breton Lays in Middle English*, ed. T. C. Rumble (Detroit, 1965), pp. 135–77; *Of Love and Chivalry: An Anthology of Middle English Romance*, ed. J. Fellows (London, 1992), pp. 231–65; *The Middle English Breton Lays*, ed. A. Laskaya and E. Salisbury (Kalamazoo MI, 1995), pp. 309–65. See also *Codex Ashmole 61: A Compilation of Popular Middle English Verse*, ed. G. Shuffelton (Kalamazoo MI, 2008), pp. 83–111 (Ashmole 61).

[45] Edition: *Altenglische Legenden*, ed. Horstmann, pp. 454–66.

ture by Thornton. A loss of text occurs between fols. 122 and 123, where one leaf is missing. *DIMEV* 3246, *NIMEV* 1990.

No other manuscript.

15. fols. 130ra–139va English verse [F9].[46] *Begins*: **Sir degreuante** / Ihesu lorde in trynite / Graunte þam heuen for to see. *Ends*: Thy worthy face for to see / And gyff vs wele to spede **Amen / Amen Explicit Sir degreuant / Explicit ser Degreuant**

    Sir Degrevant.[47] Romance; 107 16-line tail-rhyme stanzas. *DIMEV* 3197, *NIMEV* 1953. *Manual* 1, I [97].

    One other manuscript: Cambridge, CUL, MS Ff. 1. 6 (Findern).

16. fols. 139va–147rb English verse [F10]. *Begins*: **InCipit Sir Eglamour of Artasse**[48] / Ihesu þat es heuens kyng. *Ends*: þat lastis withowttyn ende **Amen / Amen Amen per charyte Amen**

    Sir Eglamour of Artois.[49] Romance; 1341 lines, generally in 12-line tail-rhyme stanzas. *DIMEV* 2867, *NIMEV* 1725. *Manual* 1, I [79].

    Five other manuscripts: Cambridge, CUL, MS Ff. 2. 38; London, BL, MSS Additional 27879 (Percy Folio), Cotton Caligula A. ii, Egerton 2862; Oxford, Bodleian Library, MS Douce 261 (transcript of an early print). *One fragment:* Ann Arbor, University of Michigan, MS 225. *Two early prints:* STC 7541, 7542.

17. fols. 147ra–148rb English verse [F11]. *Begins*: **De miraculo beate Marie** / Ihesu lorde in trynyte / þat was & es and aye schall be. *Ends*: And duelle Angells Amange / þus Endis here our talkyng / Ihesu till his blysse vs brynge / þat es euer lastande **Amen per charite**

    The Wicked Knight and the Friar.[50] Miracle of the Virgin; 12-line tail-rhyme stanzas plus 3-line coda. A loss of text occurs between fols. 147 and 148, where one leaf is missing. The poem was originally about 300

---

[46] Fol. 130v is reproduced in colour in Olson, 'Romancing the Book', p. 118 (fig. 12).

[47] Editions: *Thornton Romances*, ed. Halliwell, pp. 177–256; *Sir Degrevant*, ed. K. Luick, Wiener Beiträge zur englischen Philologie 47 (Vienna, 1917), pp. 1–123 (in parallel with Findern); *The Romance of Sir Degrevant*, ed. L. F. Casson, EETS OS 221 (London, 1949), pp. 2–115 (in parallel with Findern). See also *Sentimental and Humorous Romances*, ed. E. Kooper (Kalamazoo MI, 2006), pp. 53–126 (Findern).

[48] Before this line is written 'Incipit Sir Eglamour off in artas' in lighter ink. The line is possibly a writing exercise performed by a later hand.

[49] Editions: *Thornton Romances*, ed. Halliwell, pp. 121–76; *Sir Eglamour. Eine englische Romanze des 14. Jahrhunderts*, ed. G. Schleich, Palaestra 53 (Berlin, 1906); *Sir Eglamour: A Middle English Romance*, ed. A. S. Cook (New York, 1911); *Sir Eglamour of Artois*, ed. F. E. Richardson, EETS 256 (London, 1965) (in parallel with Cotton and Egerton). See also *Four Middle English Romances*, ed. Hudson, pp. 115–71 (Cotton); *Bishop Percy's Folio Manuscript: Ballads and Romances*, ed. J. W. Hales and F. J. Furnivall, 3 vols. (London, 1867–8), II, 338–89 (Percy Folio).

[50] Edition: *Altenglische Legenden*, ed. Horstmann, pp. 503–4.

lines long, but only the first 97 and last 43 lines survive. *DIMEV* 2864, *NIMEV* 1722. *Manual* 9, XXIV [186].

No other manuscript.

18. fols. 148rb–149r English verse [F12]. *Begins:* **Lyarde** / Lyarde es ane olde horse & may noght wele drawe. *Ends:* yf a man thynke mekill kepe somewhate in horde / **Here Endys Lyarde**

    Lyarde.[51] Satire on friars and husbands; 130 lines (imperfect); couplets. *DIMEV* 3304, *NIMEV* 2026.

    No other manuscript.

19. fols. 149va–153vb English verse [F13]. *Begins:* **Tomas Off Ersseldoune** / Lystyns lordyngs bothe grete & smale. *Ends:* [...]nge vs to his heuen so hyee **Amen Amen** / **Explicit Thomas** / **Of Erseledownn**

    Thomas of Erceldoune's Prophecy.[52] Prophecy with romance prologue, in three fits; 134 quatrains; imperfect because of losses on fols. 152–53. The Lincoln prologue is not found elsewhere but appears in a seventeenth-century printing. Numerous medieval prophecies are attached to the name Thomas of Erceldoune, a shadowy thirteenth-century Scots poet. *DIMEV* 620, *NIMEV* 365. *Manual* 5, XIII [290].

    Five other manuscripts: Cambridge, CUL, MS Ff. 5. 48; London, BL, MSS Cotton Vitellius E. x, Lansdowne 762, Sloane 2578; Oxford, Bodleian Library, MS Hatton 56. *Four fragments:* London, BL, MSS Harley 559, Additional 6702; Oxford, Bodleian Library, MSS Ashmole 337, Ashmole 1386.

20. fols. 154r–161r English verse [F14].[53] *Begins:* **Here Bygynnes The Awntyrs off Arthure at the Terne Wathelyn** / In Kyng Arthure tym ane awntir bytyde. *Ends:* In yggillwede Foreste at þe Tern Wathelayne / **Explicit Libere Explicit** [*dragon drawing*] **Libere**

    Awntyrs off Arthure.[54] Romance; 715 lines in 13-line alliterative stanzas.

---

[51] Editions: *Reliquiæ Antiquæ*, ed. T. Wright and J. O. Halliwell, 2 vols. (London, 1841–3), II, 280–2; J. Reakes, 'Lyarde and Goliard', *Neuphilologische Mitteilungen* 83 (1982), 34–41; and 'A Minor Comic Poem in a Major Romance Manuscript: "Lyarde"', ed. M. Furrow, *Forum for Modern Language Studies* 32 (1996), 289–302..

[52] Editions: *The Romances and Prophecies of Thomas of Erceldoune*, ed. J. A. H. Murray, EETS OS 61 (London, 1875), pp. 1–46 (in parallel with other versions); *Thomas of Erceldoune, Parts 1–2*, ed. I. Nixon (Copenhagen, 1980, 1983), pp. 27–85 (in parallel with CUL Ff. 5. 48, Cotton and Lansdowne). For the Lincoln prologue in a 1652 printing, see *Thomas of Erceldoune*, ed. Nixon, pp. 90–103.

[53] A detail from fol. 154r is reproduced in Fredell's chapter, Figure 9, in the present volume.

[54] Editions: *Scottish Alliterative Poems in Riming Stanzas*, ed. F. J. Amours, STS 27, 38 (1892; repr. London, 1966), pp. 115–71 (in parallel with Douce); and *Syr Gawayne: A Collation of Ancient Romance-Poems by Scottish and English Authors Relating to the Celebrated Knight of the Round Table*, ed. F. Madden (London, 1839), pp. 95–128. For editions based on Douce, see *The Awntyrs*

The dragon drawing matches others found on fols. 51v and 52r. *DIMEV* 2628, *NIMEV* 1566. *Manual* 1, I [30].

Three other manuscripts: London, Lambeth Palace Library, MS 491; Oxford, Bodleian Library, MS Douce 324; Princeton University Library, MS Taylor Medieval 9 (Ireland Blackburn).

21.   fols. 161ra–176ra English verse [F15].[55] *Begins:* **Here Bygynnes The Romance Off Sir Perecyuell of Gales** / Lef lythes to me / Two wordes or thre. *Ends:* Grante vs all his blyssyng / Amen for charyte / **quod Robert Thornton / Explicit Sir Percevell De Gales Here / endys þe Romance of Sir Percevell of Gales Cosyn to kyng Arthoure**

Sir Perceval of Gales.[56] Romance; 2288 lines generally in 16-line tail-rhyme stanzas. Scribal signature by Thornton. This item likely shared a single exemplar with Lincoln arts. 10, 11, 13, 85 and London arts. 8, 34, 35. *DIMEV* 3074, *NIMEV* 1853. *Manual* 1, I [39].

No other manuscript.

22.   fol. 176rb English verse [F16].[57] *Begins:* **A charme for þe tethe werke / Say þe charme thris to it be sayd ix ty … / and ay thris at a / charemynge** / I conjure the laythely beste with þat ilke spere. *Ends:* To þe erde & þe stane

Thornton Toothache Charm.[58] Medical charm in seven imperfect couplets. Invokes spear of Longinus, the crown of thorns, the words of the Mass, Jesus and other holy beings. Material appropriate for booklets 3 and 4 begins here to spill over onto the originally blank fols. 176v–178v of booklet 2. *DIMEV* 2153, *NIMEV* 1292. *Manual* 10, XXV [331].

No other manuscript.

23.   fol. 176rb English verse [F16]. *Begins:* Thre gude breþer are 3e. *Ends:* To þe erthe & þe stane

---

off Arthure at the Terne Wathelyn, ed. R. Hanna (Manchester, 1974); *The Awntyrs off Arthure at the Terne Wathelyne*, ed. R. J. Gates (Philadelphia, 1969); *Middle English Romances*, ed. S. H. A. Shepherd (New York, 1995), pp. 219–42; and *Eleven Gawain Romances and Tales*, ed. T. Hahn (Kalamazoo MI, 1995), pp. 178–226. For editions based on Ireland Blackburn, see *Six Middle English Romances*, ed. Mills, pp. 161–82; and *Three Early English Metrical Romances*, ed. J. Robson, Camden Society 19 (London, 1842), pp. 1–26. For a modern-spelling edition, see *The Awnytrs off Arthure*, ed. H. Phillips (Lancaster, 1988).

[55] Fol. 163va is reproduced in colour in Olson, 'Romancing the Book', p. 133 (fig. 26).

[56] Editions: *Thornton Romances*, ed. Halliwell, pp. 1–87; *Sir Perceval of Gales*, ed. J. Campion and F. Holthausen (Heidelberg, 1913); *Middle English Romances*, ed. French and Hale, II, 529–604; *Six Middle English Romances*, ed. Mills, pp. 103–60; *Syr Perecyvelle of Gales*, ed. F. S. Ellis (Hammersmith, 1985); *Sir Perceval of Galles and Yvain and Gawain*, ed. M. F. Braswell (Kalamazoo MI, 1995), pp. 1–83.

[57] Fol. 176r is reproduced in colour in Olson, 'Romancing the Book', p. 119 (fig. 13).

[58] Editions: *Religious Pieces*, ed. Perry, p. 119; *Yorkshire Writers*, ed. Horstmann, I, 375.

Three Good Brothers Charm (Version B).[59] Medical charm for toothache; 28 lines, mostly couplets. Widespread in medieval Europe, extant in two very different forms in Middle English. *DIMEV* 5900, *NIMEV* 3709. Manual 10, XXV [343b]

No other manuscripts. Version A (for wounds) in five manuscripts: Durham, Cathedral Library, MS Cosin V.v.8; London, BL, MSS Harley 2378, Sloane 706, Sloane 3160, Sloane 3217.

24. fol. 176v Latin prose [F16]. *Begins*: **A Charm for the T[...]** / In dei nomine amen +. *Ends*: patris + et Filii + et spiritus sancti + Amen ... [P]ater noster & iij Aue Maria + Amen +

Latin Toothache Charm.[60] Medical charm.

Other manuscripts unknown.

25. fol. 176v Latin prose [F17]. *Begins*: **Epistola Sancti Saluatoris** / Hec est Epistola Sancti Saluatoris quam Leo Papa transmisit Karolo Regi. *Ends*: creatura eius nocere poterit illo die.

Epistola Sancti Salvatoris.[61] Preface to the Heavenly Letter, said to have been miraculously received by Pope Leo III (795–816) and delivered to Charlemagne.[62] This item apparently introduces Lincoln art. 26.

Other manuscripts unknown.

26. fol. 176v Latin prose. *Begins*: ... Crux Cristi que es Arma invincibilis +. *Ends*: In nomine Patris et Filii et Spiritus Sancti Amen

O crux Cristi.[63] Charm invoking the cross for protection. Lincoln art. 25 presents this text as the Heavenly Letter.

Other manuscripts unknown.

27. fols. 176v–177r English prose. *Begins*: He þat devotely sayse þis Orysene dayly sall hafe remyssyone of alle his synnys. *Ends*: For alle þe vertu þereof may man telle.

Occasions for the Latin Prayer for Deliverance.[64] Preface to Lincoln art. 28, explaining how to use and wear the prayer as a protective amulet. Ascribed to Saint Paul, the prayer is said to be an indulgence granted by Pope Innocent. *IPMEP* 283.

---

[59] Editions: *Religious Pieces*, ed. Perry, pp. 119–20; *Yorkshire Writers*, ed. Horstmann, I, 375.

[60] Edition: *Yorkshire Writers*, ed. Horstmann, I, 375–6.

[61] Edition: *Yorkshire Writers*, ed. Horstmann, I, 376.

[62] See D. C. Skemer, *Binding Words: Textual Amulets in the Middle Ages* (University Park PA, 2006), pp. 98–105.

[63] Edition: *Yorkshire Writers*, ed. Horstmann, I, 376. On textual amulets based on the cross, see Skemer, *Binding Words*, pp. 221–7.

[64] Edition: *Yorkshire Writers*, ed. Horstmann, I, 376.

One other manuscript: London, BL, MS Harley 2253 (an older version in French prose).[65]

28. fols. 177r Latin prose. *Begins* **Oracio sequitur** / Domine deus omnipotens Pater et Filius et Spiritus Sanctus. *Ends:* rignas deus per omnia secula seculorum **Amen**

Prayer for Deliverance.[66] Talismanic prayer, which the user may wear into battle, among other uses and occasions as provided in English (Lincoln art. 27). The scribe's name 'Robertum' is inserted. Vulgate Psalms 66, 129 and 141 are incorporated into the prayer, which also invokes biblical examples of God's intervening protection.

Numerous manuscripts: A standard item in Books of Hours. See London, BL, MS Harley 2253 (a shorter version).[67]

29. fol. 177v English verse [F18]. **A Preyere Off The Fyve Ioyes of owre Lady [in] Inglys and Of The Fyve Sorowes** / Lady For thy Ioyes Fyve Wysse me the waye of Rightwys lyffe **Amen**.

Lady for Thy Joys Five.[68] Invocation to the Virgin; couplet written as prose; heads Lincoln art. 30. *DIMEV* 3414, *NIMEV* 2099.

One other manuscript: London, BL, MS Royal 8 F.vi (Mary for thine yoys five / teche me þe vey to ryth lyve). *One wall painting:* Life of Virgin on chancel wall of Broughton church, Oxon.

30. fols. 177v–178r English prose. *Begins:* Now mekest and ioyfulleste lady Saynt Marye For þe Ioye þou hadde when þou conceyuede thy dere / sone. *Ends:* and of alle those þat haly kyrke preyes fore qwyke and dede **Amen Pater noster Aue Maria Amen**

Prayer on Mary's Five Joys.[69] Prayer to the Virgin. Each joy ends with a Paternoster and an Ave. Spaces are left for eight large initials. *IPMEP* 479.

No other manuscript.

31. fol. 178r Latin and English prose. *Begins:* **Psalmus Voce mea ad Dominum clamaui** / Say þis Psalme Voce me Ad dominum clamaui with this **Colett folowande þat es full Merytorye** / Domine Ihesu Criste. *Ends:* visibilium et invisibilium **Amen**

A Meritorious Collect.[70] English instructions to recite Vulgate Psalm 76,

---

[65] *The Complete Harley 2253 Manuscript in Three Volumes*, ed. and trans. S. Fein, with D. Raybin and J. Ziolkowski (Kalamazoo MI, forthcoming 2014), III, 266–7, 345–6.

[66] Edition: *Yorkshire Writers*, ed. Horstmann, I, 376–7.

[67] *The Complete Harley 2253 Manuscript.* ed. Fein, III, 266–9, 345–6.

[68] Edition: *Yorkshire Writers*, ed. Horstmann, I, 377.

[69] Edition: *Yorkshire Writers*, ed. Horstmann, I, 377–9.

[70] Edition: *Yorkshire Writers*, ed. Horstmann, I, 379.

which heads a Latin collect for mercy and protection from tribulation. Space is left for a large initial *D*. Not in *IPMEP*.

Other manuscripts unknown.

32. fol. 178r–v Latin prose [F19]. *Begins*: **Here Bygynnys Fyve prayers to the wirchipe of the Fyve Wondys of oure lorde Ihesu Cryste** / Adoro te Crucem in Honore Crucis. *Ends*: per omnia secula seculorum **Amen**

    Adoro te crucem.[71] Five prayers on the five wounds with an English incipit; a quasi-liturgical service with a prayer on each wound and a final collect. Spaces are left for six large initials.

    Other manuscripts unknown.

33. fol. 178v English prose.[72] *Begins*: **Oracio in Inglys** / Now Ihesu goddis sone giffere of alle vertus. *Ends*: And graunte me of thy Blyssedhede vertuose lyffynge

    Prayer on the Seven Gifts of the Holy Ghost.[73] Prayer invoking the seven gifts, but only the gift of understanding is named. *IPMEP 477.*

    No other manuscript.

34. fol. 178v Latin prose. *Begins*: **A Colett to owre lady Saynt Marye** / Sancta Maria Regina celorum Mater Cristi. *Ends*: Exaudi Exaudi / Exaudi me dulcissime Ihesu vt terrorem Sathane per te queam Euadere **Amen**

    Sancta Maria mater Cristi.[74] A quasi-liturgical service dedicated to Mary with suffrage and two collects. Space left for large initials *D* and *O*.

    Other manuscripts unknown.

35. fol. 178v Latin prose. *Begins*: **Oracio in Modo Collecte pro amico** / Omnipotens sempiterne deus miserere Famulo tuo N. *Ends*: per dominum nostrum Ihesum Cristum filium tuum qui tecum

    Omnipotens sempiterne Deus.[75] Prayer for mercy through Mary's intercession.

    Other manuscripts unknown.

36. fol. 178v Latin prose. *Begins*: **Antiphon Sancti Leonardi cum Collecte** / O virtutum domine per secula benedicimus te. *Ends*: rignat deus per omnia secula seculorum **Amen**

    O virtutum Domine.[76] A quasi-liturgical service dedicated to Saint Leonard with suffrage and two collects. This text appears to be complete, though

---

[71] Edition: *Yorkshire Writers*, ed. Horstmann, I, 379–80.

[72] Thomson, *Catalogue*, and the editors of the facsimile (*The Thornton MS*, intro. Brewer and Owen) do not differentiate Lincoln arts. 33–6 from Lincoln art. 32.

[73] Edition: *Yorkshire Writers*, ed. Horstmann, I, 380.

[74] Edition: *Yorkshire Writers*, ed. Horstmann, I, 380.

[75] Edition: *Yorkshire Writers*, ed. Horstmann, I, 380.

[76] Edition: *Yorkshire Writers*, ed. Horstmann, I, 381.

it should be noted that damage has occurred after fol. 178: the last leaf of booklet 2 is missing.

Other manuscripts unknown.

Lincoln booklet 3 (Quires L–P; fols. 179–279): Religious and devotional texts

37.   fol. 179r Latin prose.[77] **In Nomine Patris et Filii et Speritus Sancti Amen** Invocation of the Trinity, written at the head of booklet 3.

38.   fols. 179r–189r English prose [F20]. *Begins:* **Here Begynnes the Previte off the Passione of owre lorde Ihesu** / Who so desyres to Fynd comforthe and gostely gladnes in þe Pa/ssione. *Ends:* with his / precious blode boghte vs Ihesus Cristus **Amen Amen Amen pur charite** / [*in a different hand*] Explicit Bonauenture de misteriis Passionis Ihesu Cristi[78]

   Privity of the Passion.[79] English translation of Pseudo-Bonaventure, *Meditationes vitae Christi.* This item and Lincoln art. 8 (alliterative *Morte Arthure*) probably derive from a single exemplar in a southwest Lincolnshire dialect. The explicit is written in the formal script used for the explicit to the alliterative *Morte Arthure* (fol. 98v). *IPMEP* 837. *Manual* 9, XXIII [62].

   Three other manuscripts: Cambridge, Trinity College, MS B. 10. 12; Durham, Cathedral Library, MS Cosin V.iii.8; New Haven, Yale University Beinecke Library, MS 600.

39.   fol. 189r English verse. Of all thynge it is the best / Ihesu in herte fast to fest / And lufe hym ower all thynge

   Of All Things It Is the Best.[80] Lyric (part of the explicit for Lincoln art. 38); three lines written in a formal hand not Thornton's.[81] *DIMEV* 4144, *NIMEV* 2616.

---

[77]   For fol. 179r, see Keiser's chapter, Figure 3, in the present volume. Fol. 179r is reproduced in colour in Olson, 'Romancing the Book', p. 122 (fig. 16).

[78]   This line is written by a trained scribe, not Thornton; the hand also appears on the remainder of this page and on fol. 98v (explicit to the alliterative *Morte Arthure*). For fol. 189r, see Keiser's chapter, Figure 2, in the present volume.

[79]   Edition: *Yorkshire Writers*, ed. Horstmann, I, 198–218. Translation: *Some Minor Works of Richard Rolle with The Privity of the Passion by S. Bonaventure*, trans. G. E. Hodgson (London, 1923), pp. 178–225. See also 'A Critical Edition of *The Privity of the Passion* and *The Lyrical Meditations*', ed. S. M. Day (unpublished Ph.D. thesis, University of York, 1991), pp. 123–347 (based on Cambridge, Trinity College).

[80]   Edition: *Writings Ascribed to Richard Role Hermit of Hampole and Materials for His Biography*, ed. H. E. Allen (New York, 1927), p. 403. Translation: *Some Minor Works*, trans. Hodgson, p. 225.

[81]   The hand also appears in the explicits to Lincoln arts. 8 and 38, and the opening of Lincoln art. 40.

No other manuscript.

40. fols. 189r–191v English verse [F21]. *Begins:* **Incipit tractatus Willelmi Nassyngton quondam aduocati Iuris / Eboraci[82] de Trinitate & Vnitate cum declaracione operum dei & de pas/sione domini nostri ihesu Cristi &c /** A lord god of myghtes maste. *Ends:* Be led to þe blyse þat sall last ay **Amen**

    William of Nassington, *Tractatus de Trinitate et Unitate.*[83] Devotional treatise; 216 couplets. *DIMEV* 100, *NIMEV* 11. *Manual* 9, XXIII [44]. The incipit and the opening on fol. 189r is in a formal hand not Thornton's (see also Lincoln arts. 8, 38 and 39).

    Two other manuscripts: London, BL, MS Additional 33995; New Haven, Yale University Beinecke Library, Osborn MSS File Folder 19558 (wrapper).

41. fol. 191v English verse [F22]. *Begins:* Lorde gode Ihesu cryste godd almyghty. *Ends:* þat I may wonne with þe in blisse Endlesse **Amen**

    Lord God Jesus Christ, God Almighty.[84] Lyric prayer of thanksgiving; 23 couplets. *DIMEV* 3198, *NIMEV* 1954.

    One other manuscript: Wellesley College, MS 8.

42. fol. 191v English verse [F22]. *Begins:* Almyghty god in trinite. *Ends:* Be til þi name withowttyn endyng **Amen**

    Almighty God in Trinity.[85] Lyric prayer; 4 couplets. This poem is joined to Lincoln art. 43 in both other copies. It is not separate in Lincoln except for the final *Amen*, which is likely a scribal addition. *DIMEV* 424, *NIMEV* 246.

    Two other manuscripts: London, BL, MS Egerton 3245 (*olim* Gurney); Princeton University Library, MS Kane 21 (*olim* Huth).

43. fol. 191v English verse [F22]. *Begins:* Lorde god alweldande I beteche todaye into þi hande. *Ends:* alls thow for vs died one a tree **Graunte vs lorde þat swa bee Amen Amen pur charite**

    Lord God All-Wielding.[86] Lyric morning prayer; 10 couplets. The Egerton version lacks the final couplet (perhaps added by Thornton). This lyric

---

[82] Perry transcribes the abbreviated words as 'Iuris Eboraci' (*Religious Pieces*, p. 63), while Horstmann reads 'curie Eboraci' (*Yorkshire Writers*, II, 334) and Thomson reads 'ciuitatis Eboracensis' (*Catalogue*, p. 66).

[83] Editions: *Religious Pieces*, ed. Perry, pp. 63–75; *Yorkshire Writers*, ed. Horstmann, II, 334–9.

[84] Editions: *Religious Pieces*, ed. Perry, pp. 75–6; *Yorkshire Writers*, ed. Horstmann, I, 363.

[85] Editions: *Religious Pieces*, ed. Perry, p. 77; *Yorkshire Writers*, ed. Horstmann, I, 363; *The Life*, ed. Comper, pp. 293–94. See also 'The Gurney Series of Religious Lyrics', ed. R. H. Robbins, *PMLA* 54 (1939), 369–90 (p. 376) (Egerton); 'A Middle English Versified Prayer to the Trinity', ed. C. F. Bühler, *Modern Language Notes* 66 (1951), 312–14 (p. 314) (Princeton).

[86] Editions: *Religious Pieces*, ed. Perry, p. 77; *Yorkshire Writers*, ed. Horstmann, I, 364; *The*

and Lincoln art. 42 probably form a single item. *DIMEV* 3193, *NIMEV* 1950.5.

Two other manuscripts: London, BL, MS Egerton 3245 (*olim* Gurney); Princeton University Library, MS Kane 21 (*olim* Huth).

44. fols. 191v–192r English verse [F22]. *Begins:* Ihesu that diede one the rude for þe lufe of me. *Ends:* Be it me lefe be it me lathe do it awaye fra me
Jesus That Died on the Rood for the Love of Me.[87] Lyric prayer ; monorhyming quatrain. *DIMEV* 2909, *NIMEV* 1757.

One other manuscript: Oxford, Bodleian Library, MS Eng. poet. a. 1 (Vernon).

45. fol. 192r English verse [F22]. *Begins:* Ihesu of whayme all trewe luffe sprynges. *Ends:* That for my lufe walde be slayne / **Amen Amen Amen Amen pur charite**
Jesus of Whom All True Love Springs.[88] Lyric prayer; one 8-line stanza. *DIMEV* 2892, *NIMEV* 1741.

No other manuscript.

46. fols. 192r–193v English prose [F23].[89] *Begins:* **Of the vertuȝ of the haly name of Ihesu / Ricardus herimita super Versiculo / Oleum effusum nomen tuum in canticis &c** / That es on Inglysce Oyle owtȝettede es thi name. *Ends:* For thare may na wykked spyritte / noye þare Ihesu es mekyll in mynde or es neuennyd in mouthe &c **Explicit**
Richard Rolle, *Oleum effusum in English* (Version A).[90] Devotional treatise. *IPMEP* 506. *Manual* 9, XXIII [16].

Two other manuscripts: London, BL, MSS Harley 1022, Stowe 38. *Version B:* Dublin, TCD, MS 155. A third version is embedded in the *Pore Caitif* (see *Manual*).

47. fol. 193v English prose [F24].[91] *Begins:* **Narracio / A tale þat Richerde hermet** / When I hade taken my syngulere purpos & lefte þe seculere /

Life, ed. Comper, p. 294. See also 'The Gurney Series', ed. Robbins, p. 376 (Egerton); 'A ME Versified Prayer', ed. Bühler, p. 314 (Princeton).

[87] Editions: *Religious Pieces*, ed. Perry, p. 78; *Yorkshire Writers*, ed. Horstmann, I, 364; *The Life*, ed. Comper, pp. 280–1. For Vernon, see *The Minor Poems of the Vernon MS., Part I*, ed. C. Horstmann, EETS OS 98 (London, 1892), p. 22; *The Middle English Penitential Lyric*, ed. F. A. Patterson (New York, 1966), p. 137.

[88] Editions: *Religious Pieces*, ed. Perry, p. 78; *Yorkshire Writers*, ed. Horstmann, I, 364; *The Life*, ed. Comper, pp. 281–2.

[89] Fols. 192v, 193r are reproduced in colour in Olson, 'Romancing the Book', p. 135 (figs. 30a, 30b).

[90] Editions: *Yorkshire Writers*, ed. Horstmann, I, 186–91 (in parallel with Harley); *The English Prose Treatises of Richard Rolle de Hampole*, ed. G. G. Perry, EETS OS 20, 2nd edn (London, 1921), pp. 1–5; *Richard Rolle*, ed. Hanna, pp. 3–11 (in parallel with Dublin).

[91] Fol. 193v is reproduced in colour in Olson, 'Romancing the Book', p. 135 (fig. 29a).

habyte. *Ends*: Tharefore blysside be þe nam of Ihesu in the worlde of worldes **Amen Amen Amen &c**

Richard Rolle, *A Tale of Hampole's Temptation*.[92] Meditative *exemplum*. This item forms a separate article in Lincoln, but it is attached as a conclusion to Lincoln art. 46 in the Latin source and Harley 1022.[93] *IPMEP* 821.

One other manuscript: London, BL, MS Harley 1022.

48. fol. 193v English verse. **Ihesu þe sone of þe gloriouse virgyne / Now lorde haue mercy one all thyne / Amen Amen pur charite Amen**
Jesus the Son of the Glorious Virgin.[94] Lyric prayer-couplet; inserted by Thornton to conclude Lincoln art. 47. *NIMEV* 1779.33.
No other manuscript.

49. fol. 193v. Latin prose [F25]. *Begins*: **A prayere þat þe same**[95] **Richerd hermet made þat es beried at hampulle.** Deus noster refugium O creator noster. *Ends*: perueniamus ab omnibus peccatis mundati & absoluti **Amen**
Deus noster refugium.[96] Prayer ascribed to Richard Rolle.
Other manuscripts unknown.

50. fols. 193v–194r Latin verse [F26].[97] *Begins*: **Ympnus quem composuit Sanctus Ambrosyus & est valde bonus** / Ihesu nostra redempcio amor & desiderium deus creator omnium homo / in fine temporum. *Ends*: **Amen Amen Amen per charyte Amen. Qui scripsit carmen sit benedictus Amen Amen In nomine domini Ihesu Amen**
Ihesu nostra redempcio amor.[98] Hymn ascribed to Saint Ambrose. Closing phrase echoes words used elsewhere for Thornton signatures; compare Lincoln arts. 9, 60, 68.
Other manuscripts unknown.

51. fol. 194r English prose [F27]. *Begins*: **De inperfecta contricione / Rycharde hermyte reherces a dredfull tale of vnperfitte contrecyone.** *Ends*: Wharefore Sentence of / dampnacyone Felle one me & wente agaynes mee

---

[92] Editions: *Yorkshire Writers*, ed. Horstmann, I, 192; *English Prose Treatises*, ed. Perry, pp. 5–6.

[93] *Richard Rolle*, ed. Hanna, p. xxxvi.

[94] Edition: *Yorkshire Writers*, ed. Horstmann, I, 192.

[95] The words *þe same* are written in the left margin with an indication of insertion.

[96] Edition: *Yorkshire Writers*, ed. Horstmann, I, 192.

[97] Fols. 193v, 194r are reproduced in colour in Olson, 'Romancing the Book', p. 135 (figs. 29a, 29b, respectively).

[98] See *Yorkshire Writers*, ed. Horstmann, I, 192. Compare *Thesaurus hymnologicus sive hymnorum canticorum sequentiarum circa annum MD usitatarum collectio amplissima*, ed. H. A. Daniel, 5 vols. (Leipzig, 1855) I, 63–4.

Richard Rolle, *Imperfect Contrition.*[99] Meditative *exemplum. IPMEP* 564. *Manual* 9, XXIII [17].

No other manuscript.

52. fol. 194r English prose. *Begins:* Allswa he reherces anothyre tale of verraye contrecyone. *Ends:* and he with gret Ioye thanked god

Richard Rolle, *True Contrition.*[100] Meditative *exemplum. IPMEP* 58. *Manual* 9, XXIII [17].

One other manuscript: Oxford, Bodleian Library, MS Ashmole 751.

53. fol. 194r–v English prose [F28]. *Begins:* **Moralia Richardi heremite de natura apis vnde quasi apis argumentosa** / [*in right margin*] **Apis** / The bee has thre kyndis. *Ends:* þay are so chargede Wyth othyre / affeccyons and othire vanytes **Explicit**

Richard Rolle, *The Bee and the Stork.*[101] Meditative *exemplum. IPMEP* 657. *Manual* 9, XXIII [4].

One other manuscript: Durham, Cathedral Library, MS Cosin V.i.12. *Latin version:* London, BL, MS Harley 268.

54. fols. 194v–195r English prose [F29]. *Begins:* **De vita cuiusdam puelle incluse propter Amorem Cristi** / Alswa Heraclides þe clerke telles þat A mayden forsuke / hir Cete. *Ends:* Richard herymyte reherces þis / tale in Ensampill.

Richard Rolle, *A Woman Enclosed for Love of Christ.*[102] Meditative *exemplum. IPMEP* 59.

No other manuscript.

55. fol. 195r Latin prose [F30]. *Begins:* **Richardus herymyta** / Meliora sunt vbera tua vino. *Ends:* quando ab hac luce deus dignetur me vocare &c

Meliora sunt.[103] Latin meditation ascribed to Richard Rolle.

Other manuscripts unknown.

56. fol. 195r Latin prose [F31]. *Begins:* **Item inferius idem Richardus** / O quam delectabile gaudium et delicatum solacium Amare dei filium.

---

[99] Editions: *Yorkshire Writers*, ed. Horstmann, I, 192–3; *English Prose Treatises*, ed. Perry, pp. 6–7; *Richard Rolle*, ed. Hanna, p. 12. Translation: *Some Minor Works*, trans. Hodgson, p. 62.

[100] Editions: *Yorkshire Writers*, ed. Horstmann, I, 193; *English Prose Treatises*, ed. Perry, p. 7; *Richard Rolle*, ed. Hanna, pp. 12–13. Translation: *The Form of Perfect Living and Other Prose Treatises, by Richard Rolle of Hampole, A.D. 1300–1349*, trans. G. E. Hodgson (London, 1910), pp. 190–1.

[101] Editions: *Yorkshire Writers*, ed. Horstmann, I, 193–4; *English Prose Treatises*, ed. Perry, pp. 8–9; *English Writings of Richard Rolle Hermit of Hampole*, ed. H. E. Allen (Oxford, 1931), pp. 54–5; *Richard Rolle*, ed. Hanna, pp. 13–14. Translation: *Richard Rolle: The English Writings*, trans. R. S. Allen (Mahwah NJ, 1988), pp. 127–9.

[102] Editions: *Yorkshire Writers*, ed. Horstmann, I, 194; *English Prose Treatises*, ed. Perry, p. 9; *Richard Rolle*, ed. Hanna, p. 14. Translation: *Some Minor Works*, trans. Hodgson, p. 78.

[103] Edition: *Yorkshire Writers*, ed. Horstmann, I, 194.

Ends: Quia nichil in presenti desidero quod me in eternum habere non confido &c

O quam delectabile.[104] Latin meditation ascribed to Richard Rolle. *Other manuscripts unknown.*

57. fols. 195v–196r English prose [F32]. *Begins*: **A notabill Tretys off the ten Comandementys Drawen by / Richerde the hermyte off hampull / The fyrste comandement es.** *Ends*: And þat / he lufe his neghtbour saule mare þane his body or Any gude3 of þe worlde &c **Explicit**

Richard Rolle, *Commentary on the Decalogue* (Shorter Version).[105] Devotional treatise. *IPMEP* 667. *Manual* 9, XXIII [8].

No other manuscript. The Longer Version appears in Oxford, Bodleian Library, MS Hatton 12.

58. fol. 196r–v English prose [F33]. *Begins*: **Item Idem de septem donis spiritus sancti / Also of the gyftes of the haly gaste /** Þe seuen gyftes of þe haly gaste þat ere gyfen to men and / wymmen. *Ends*: þat we kan / knawe and flese it als venym **Explicit**

Richard Rolle, *Seven Gifts of the Holy Spirit.*[106] Devotional meditation. The item is embedded in Rolle's *Form of Living* in Cambridge, CUL, MS Dd. 5. 64 (3). *IPMEP* 700. *Manual* 9, XXIII [7].

Two other manuscripts: Cambridge, CUL, MS Dd. 5. 64 (3); London, BL, MS Arundel 507.

59. fol. 196v Latin verse. **Ihesus Marie filius sit michi / clemens & propecius Amen**

Scribal prayer-couplet written to the right of the incipit for Lincoln art. 60. Compare Lincoln art. 95.

60. fol. 196v English prose [F34]. *Begins*: **Item Idem de dilectacione in deo / Also of þe same delyte and ȝernyng of gode /** Gernyng and delite of Ihesu Criste þat has na thyng of worldes thoghtes / es wondyrfull pure haly and faste. *Ends*: withowttene gruchynge or heuynese of thoghte3 &c **Explicit / Explicit carmen Qui scripsit sit benedictus Amen**

Richard Rolle, *Desire and Delight.*[107] Devotional meditation. The final words of the explicit correspond to Thornton signatures found else-

---

104 Edition: *Yorkshire Writers*, ed. Horstmann, I, 194–5.

105 Editions: *Yorkshire Writers*, ed. Horstmann, I, 195–6; *English Prose Treatises*, ed. Perry, pp. 10–12; *Richard Rolle*, ed. Hanna, pp. 16–18.

106 Editions: *Yorkshire Writers*, ed. Horstmann, I, 196–7; *English Prose Treatises*, ed. Perry, p. 13; *Richard Rolle*, ed. Hanna, p. 19. Translation: *Some Minor Works*, trans. Hodgson, pp. 92–3.

107 Editions: *Yorkshire Writers*, ed. Horstmann, I, 197; *English Prose Treatises*, ed. Perry, pp. 14–15; *English Writings*, ed. H. E. Allen, pp. 57–8. For Longleat, see also *Writings*, ed. H. E. Allen, pp. 271–2; *Richard Rolle: Prose and Verse*, ed. S. J. Ogilvie-Thomson, EETS OS 293 (Oxford, 1988), p. 40. Translation: *Richard Rolle*, trans. R. S. Allen, pp. 130–1.

where; compare Lincoln arts. 9, 68 (and also 50) and London art. 7. *IPMEP* 863. *Manual* 9, XXIII [5].

One other manuscript: Longleat House, Marquess of Bath, MS 29.

61. fols. 197r–209v English and Latin prose [F35]. *Begins:* **Incipit Speculum Sancti Edmundi Cantuariensis Archipiscopi in Anglicis / Here begynnys The Myrrour of Seynt Edmonde þe Ersebechope of Canterberye.** / Uidete Vocacionem Vestram. This wordes sayse saynte / paule in his pistyll and thay are thus mekill to saye one ynglysche. Seese ȝowre callynge. This worde falles till vs folke of / religioun. *Ends:* Ihesu with his swete / blude and his preciouse passion **Amen Expliculum speculum sancti Edmundi Cantuariensis Archiepiscopi / Dulce nomen Domini nostri Ihesu Cristi sit benedictum in secula seculorum Amen**

Mirror of Saint Edmund.[108] Devotional treatise; a translation of Edmund Rich of Abingdon, *Speculum ecclesie*. *IPMEP* 800. *Manual* 9, XXIII [72].

Two other manuscripts: Aberystwyth, NLW, MS Peniarth 395D; Oxford, Bodleian Library, MS Eng. poet. a. 1 (Vernon). See *Manual* for a list of the many other versions.

62. fols. 209v–211r English and Latin prose [F36]. *Begins: [in left margin]* **Tractatus de dominica / oracione secundum** [*name omitted*] **&c /** Pater noster qui es in celis In all the wordes þat er stabilled. *Ends:* Que nobis prestare dingneris qui viuis & rignas &c **Explicit / Benedicta sit sancta trinitas Amen**

Tract on the Lord's Prayer.[109] Devotional meditation. *IPMEP* 533. *Manual* 7, XX [36] (Version I).

No other manuscript (but see other versions listed in *Manual*).

63. fol. 211ra–va English verse [F37]. *Begins:* Ihesu criste saynte Marye sone. *Ends:* And wonn ay with the stylle **Amen / Explicit Tractatus Explicit Amen Thornton Amen**

Jesus Christ Saint Mary's Son.[110] Lyric prayer; twenty quatrains. Scribal signature by Thornton. *DIMEV* 2826, *NIMEV* 1692.

No other manuscript.

64. fols. 211vb–212rb English verse [F38]. *Begins:* Fadir and son and haly gaste. *Ends:* Fadir and sonn and þe haly gaste **Amen / Explicit &c**

---

[108] Editions: *Religious Pieces*, ed. Perry, pp. 16–50; *Yorkshire Writers*, ed. Horstmann, I, 219–40. Translation: *Some Minor Works*, trans. Hodgson, pp. 94–147. See also *Yorkshire Writers*, ed. Horstmann, I, 240–61 (Vernon).

[109] Edition: *Yorkshire Writers*, ed. Horstmann, I, 261–4.

[110] Editions: *Religious Pieces*, ed. Perry, pp. 79–82; *Yorkshire Writers*, ed. Horstmann, I, 364–5; *The Life*, ed. Comper, pp. 235–9.

Father and Son and Holy Ghost.[111] Hymn to the Trinity, Mary and Jesus; thirteen 8-line stanzas. *DIMEV*, 1280, *NIMEV* 775. In Lambeth the poem is incorporated in *DIMEV* 3918, *NIMEV* 2451, beginning at line 9.

Three other manuscripts: London, BL, MS Additional 37787; London, Lambeth Palace Library, MS 559; Oxford, Bodleian Library, MS Eng. poet. a. 1 (Vernon).

65. fol. 212rb English prose [F39]. *Begins:* Ihesu criste goddes sun of heuen. *Ends:* for þe lufe þat þou / schewede to mankynde **Amen / Explicit Prayer to Christ.**[112] Prayer. *IPMEP* 415.
No other manuscript.

66. fol. 212rb–vb Latin verse and prose [F40]. *Begins: [in right margin]* **Incipit A Meditacione / of þe Fyve woundes / of oure lorde Ihesu Criste / with a prayere in þe same** / Adoro te piissime Ihesu qui / redimisti me. *Ends:* Per eundem Cristum dominum nostrum **Amen**
Adoro te piissime Ihesu.[113] Verse meditation on the five wounds with prose prayer and collect; six 5-line stanzas.
Other manuscripts unknown.

67. fols. 212vb–213r Latin verse and prose [F41]. *Begins:* **A medytacion of the Crosse of / Criste with a prayere** / O crux frutex saluificus vino fonte rigatus. *Ends:* Per omnia secula seculorum **Amen**
O crux frutex.[114] Verse meditation on the cross with prose antiphon and collect; a common extract from Saint Bonaventure's *Arbor vitae Christi.*
Other manuscripts unknown.

68. fol. 213r Latin verse and prose. **Ihesus pie flos Marie peccatorum miserere Amen / Ihesus Maria Iohannes / Nomina digna coli Ihesus coque Maria Iohannes / R Thornton dictus qui scripsit sit benedictus amen**
Thornton invokes Jesus (with Mary and John the Evangelist) for mercy, concluding with a scribal signature-couplet found elsewhere. Compare Lincoln arts. 9, 60 and London art. 7.

69. fol. 213r–v English verse [F42]. *Begins:* When Adam dalfe and Eue spane.

---

[111] Editions: *Religious Pieces*, ed. Perry, pp. 83–6; *Yorkshire Writers*, ed. Horstmann, I, 365–6. See also *The Minor Poems of the Vernon MS. I*, ed. Horstmann, pp. 16–19 (Vernon); *Religious Lyrics of the XIVth Century*, ed. C. Brown (Oxford 1924), pp. 121–4 (Additional 37787); 'Unpublished Verses in Lambeth Palace MS. 559', ed. S. J. Ogilvie-Thomson, *Review of English Studies* n.s. 25 (1974), 387–9 (Lambeth).

[112] Editions: *Religious Pieces*, ed. Perry, p. 87; *Yorkshire Writers*, ed. Horstmann, I, 367.

[113] Edition: *Yorkshire Writers*, ed. Horstmann, I, 381–2.

[114] Edition: *Yorkshire Writers*, ed. Horstmann, I, 382–3.

Ends: A nyghte vndir þi schete / **Sit nomen Domini benedictum ex hoc nunc et usque in seculum Amen**

When Adam Delved.[115] Religious lyric; eight 6-line stanzas. *DIMEV* 6265, *NIMEV* 3921 (compare *DIMEV* 6266, *NIMEV* 3922).

One other manuscript: Cambridge, CUL, MS Dd. 5. 64 (3).

70.　fol. 213v English verse. *Begins:* Ihesu criste haue mercy one me. *Ends:* Till heuen to wonn ay with þe styll **Amen**

Jesus Christ, Have Mercy on Me.[116] Lyric prayer; three couplets; copied as the colophon to Lincoln art. 69. *DIMEV* 2806, *NIMEV* 1674.

No other manuscript.

71.　fols. 213v–218v English prose [F43]. *Begins:* **Here begynnes A sermon þat Dan Iohn Gaytryge made þe / whilke teches how scrifte es to be made & whareof and in scrifte / how many thynge3 solde be consederide / Et est petrus / sentenciarum discrecione prima /** Als a grete doctour schewes in his buke Of all the creatoures. *Ends:* To þe whilke / blysse He brynge vs oure lorde gode Almyghty **Amen Amen Amen / Per dominum nostrum Ihesum Cristum qui cum deo patri & Spiritu Sancto viuit & rignat / omnipotens deus in secula seculorum Amen Amen Amen**

John Gaytryge, *Sermon* (or *Lay Folks' Catechism*).[117] Religious treatise (or 'sermon') composed in semi-alliterative prose written as verse in some manuscripts. It is a translation made in 1357 by Gaytryge, a monk at St Mary's, York, of Archbishop Thoresby's Latin catechism. The English version is much longer than the Latin original. *NIMEV* 406 (Version A). *IPMEP* 71. *Manual* 7, XX [19].

Eighteen other manuscripts.

72.　fol. 219ra–v English verse [F44]. *Begins:* Ihesu thi swetnes wha moghte it se. *Ends:* With þe to wonn withowtten ende **Amen / Explicit**

Jesus Thy Sweetness.[118] Lyric prayer; fifteen 8-line stanzas. *NIMEV* 1781.

Eighteen other manuscripts.

73.　fols. 219v–221v English prose [F45]. *Begins:* Dere Frende wit þou wele þat

---

[115]　Edition: *Religious Pieces*, ed. Perry, pp. 88–91; *Yorkshire Writers*, ed. Horstmann, I, 367–8. See also *Religious Lyrics of the XIVth Century*, ed. Brown, pp. 96–7 (CUL Dd. 5. 64 (3)).

[116]　Editions: *Religious Pieces*, ed. Perry, p. 91; *Yorkshire Writers*, ed. Horstmann, I, 368; *The Life*, ed. Comper, pp. 294–5.

[117]　Editions: *Religious Pieces*, ed. Perry, pp. 1–15; *Middle English Religious Prose*, ed. N. F. Blake (London, 1972), pp. 73–87. See also *The Lay Folks' Cathechism, or the English and Latin Versions of Archbishop Thoresby's Instruction for the People*, ed. T. F. Simmons and H. E. Nolloth, EETS OS 118 (London, 1901), pp. 1–98 (York, Archbishop Thoresby's Register).

[118]　Editions: *Religious Pieces*, ed. Perry, pp. 92–6; *Yorkshire Writers*, ed. Horstmann, I, 368–70.

þe ende and þe soueraynte of per / feccione. *Ends*: It sufficith to me for to lyffe in / trouthe princypally and noghte in felynge / **Explicit &c**

Walter Hilton, *Of Angels' Song*.[119] Devotional treatise. *IPMEP* 146. *Manual* 9, XXIII [31].

Five other manuscripts: Cambridge, CUL, MSS Dd. 5. 55, Ff. 5. 40; London, BL, MS Additional 27592; Oxford, Bodleian Library, MS Bodley 576; Tokyo, MS Takamiya 3. *One early print*: STC 20972.

74. fol. 222r–v English verse [F46]. *Begins*: Þi Joy be ilke a dele to serue thi godd to paye. *Ends*: in swete lufe ay brennande

Richard Rolle, *Thy Joy Be in the Love of Jesus*.[120] Religious lyric; twelve 8-line stanzas; joined to Lincoln art. 75 as in Longleat. *DIMEV* 5940, *NIMEV* 3730. *Manual* 9, XXIII [12].

Two other manuscripts: Cambridge, CUL, MS Dd. 5. 64 (3). Longleat House, Marquess of Bath, MS 29.

75. fol. 222v English verse [F46]. *Begins*: All vanytese forsake If þou his lufe will fele. *Ends imperfectly*: And come to criste thi frende …

Richard Rolle, *All Vanities Forsake*.[121] Religious lyric; ten 8-line stanzas; joined to Lincoln art. 74 as in Longleat. A loss of text occurs at the end because one leaf is missing between fols. 222 and 223. *DIMEV* 401, *NIMEV* 229. *Manual* 9, XXIII [12].

Two other manuscripts: Cambridge, CUL, MS Dd. 5. 64 (3); Longleat House, Marquess of Bath, MS 29.

76. fols. 223r–229r English prose [F47]. *Begins imperfectly*: … men þat ware in prelacye and oþer also þat ware haly temporalle men. *Ends*: gret clennes / and meknes sall be ouerlayde and oppresside of hym selfe &c **Explicit**

Walter Hilton, *Epistle on the Mixed Life (Shorter Version)*.[122] Devotional

---

[119] Editions: *Yorkshire Writers*, ed. Horstmann, I, 175–82 (in parallel with CUL Dd. 5. 55); *English Prose Treatises*, ed. Perry, pp. 15–20. See also *English Mystics of the Middle Ages*, ed. B. Windeatt (Cambridge, 1994), pp. 131–6 (Additional 27592).

[120] Editions: *Religious Pieces*, ed. Perry, pp. 107–10; *Yorkshire Writers*, ed. Horstmann, I, 370–2; *The Life*, ed. Comper, pp. 260–4. For CUL Dd. 5. 64 (3), see *Richard Rolle*, ed. Hanna, pp. 29–30; *Religious Lyrics of the XIVth Century*, ed. Brown, pp. 107–9; *English Writings*, ed. H. E. Allen, pp. 52–3. For Longleat, where Lincoln arts. 74 and 75 are joined, see *Richard Rolle*, ed. Ogilvie-Thomson, pp. 46–8.

[121] Editions: *Religious Pieces*, ed. Perry, pp. 110–13; *Yorkshire Writers*, ed. Horstmann, I, 79–81, 371–2; *The Life*, ed. Comper, pp. 264–8. For CUL Dd. 5. 64 (3), see *Richard Rolle*, ed. Hanna, pp. 31–2; *English Writings*, ed. H. E. Allen, pp. 49–51. For Longleat, see *Richard Rolle*, ed. Ogilvie-Thomson, pp. 48–9.

[122] Editions: *English Prose Treatises*, ed. Perry, pp. 27–43; *Yorkshire Writers*, ed. Horstmann, I, 270–92 (in parallel with Vernon). See also *English Mystics of the Middle Ages*, ed. Windeatt, pp. 108–30 (Longer Version in Lambeth 472).

treatise. A loss of text occurs at the beginning where one leaf is missing between fols. 222 and 223. *IPMEP* 147. *Manual* 9, XXIII [30].

Nine other manuscripts (Shorter Version): London, BL, MSS Additional 22283 (Simeon), Harley 2254; Longleat House, Marquess of Bath, MS 29; Manchester, Chetham's Library, MS 6690; New York, Columbia University Library, MS Plimpton 271; Tokyo, MS Takamiya 15; Oxford, Bodleian Library, MSS Laud Misc. 685, Eng. poet. a. 1 (Vernon), Rawlinson A. 355 (*plus six manuscripts of the Longer Version, many fragments and five early prints*).

77. fols. 229v–230v English prose [F48]. *Begins:* Wit thou wele dere Frende. *Ends:* With his precyouse / Passion Ihesu criste goddis sone of heuen Amen

    Walter Hilton, *Epistle of Salvation*.[123] Devotional treatise, extracted from *The Scale of Perfection*, Book I, chap. 44. *IPMEP* 848 (compare 255). *Manual* 9, XXIII [29].

    Numerous other manuscripts: In addition to London's unique extract from Book I, there are twenty-three manuscripts of the complete text, twenty manuscripts of Book I alone, and six early prints.

78. fols. 231r–233v English verse [F49]. *Begins:* **Of Sayne Iohn þe euangelist.** Of all mankynde þat he made þat maste es of myghte. *Ends:* þat euermore sall laste **Amen / Explicit**

    Alliterative *John Evangelist Hymn*.[124] Salutation to Saint John the Evangelist; nineteen alliterative 14-line stanzas. *DIMEV* 4132, *NIMEV* 2608. *No other manuscript.*

79. fols. 233v–236v English prose [F50]. *Begins:* Prayng es a gracyous gyfte of owre lorde godd tyll / ylk manne diuysed as he vouches safe. *Ends imperfectly*: All if þay hafe will and grace for to serue godd ȝitt may þay make / bot lyttill owtwarde myrthe …

    On Prayer.[125] Devotional treatise in rhythmic prose with frequent alliteration.[126] Even though the guide initial is a *P*, the decorated initial is,

---

[123] Edition: *English Prose Treatises*, ed. Perry, pp. 44–7. Translation: *Some Minor Works*, trans. Hodgson, pp. 56–61. Compare W. Hilton, *The Scale of Perfection*, ed. T. H. Bestul (Kalamazoo MI, 2000), pp. 79–82 (based on Lambeth 472).

[124] Editions: *Altenglische Legenden*, ed. Horstmann, pp. 467–71; *Religious Pieces*, ed. Perry, pp. 97–105; *Three Alliterative Saints' Hymns*, ed. R. Kennedy, EETS OS 321 (Oxford, 2003), pp. 10–18.

[125] Edition: *Yorkshire Writers*, ed. Horstmann, I, 295–300. Translation: *Some Minor Works*, trans. Hodgson, pp. 148–60.

[126] Hodgson ascribes this work to Richard Rolle (*Some Minor Works*, trans. Hodgson, p. 148).

erroneously, an S. A loss of text occurs at the end because four leaves are missing between fols. 236 and 237. *IPMEP* 548.

Three other manuscripts: Liverpool University Library, MS F.4; London, BL, MS Royal 18 A.x; Oxford, Bodleian Library, MS e Mus. 35.

80.   fols. 237r–250v English prose [F51, F52, F53]. *Begins imperfectly:* ... mercy habydes & sythen for all þat myster hase qwykk & dede. *Ends:* & he sall noghte fayle for to come / to grace of gode & ay lastand hele to þe wylke hele &c

Holy Boke Gratia Dei.[127] Devotional treatise having three parts in Lincoln: 'On Prayer', 'On Grace' and 'Our Daily Work'.[128] Its fourth part, 'Meditation on the Passion and of Three Arrows of Doomsday', is absent. A loss of text occurs at the beginning because four leaves are missing between fols. 236 and 237. *IPMEP* 502. *Manual* 9, XXIII [85].

Two other manuscripts: London, BL, MS Arundel 507; San Marino, Huntington Library, MS HM 148. *One fragment:* Edinburgh, NLS, MS 6126.

81.   fols. 250v–258r English prose [F54]. *Begins:* **Hic incipit quedam reuelacio A Reuelacyon Schewed to ane / holy woman now one late tyme /** Alle manere of thyng þat es bygun þat may turne to the profyte of / mannes saule. *Ends:* No / more fadir at þis tyme bot god bryng vs to his kyngdome **Amen / Explicit tractatus de visione**

Revelation Shown to a Holy Woman.[129] Vision of purgatory; marked by Thornton's annotations, which 'point to the efficacy of prayers and masses'.[130] *IPMEP* 50. *Manual* 2, V [325]. A loss of text occurs between fols. 253 and 254, where one leaf is missing. Lincoln arts. 82–83 are sequenced after this item.

Two other manuscripts: Longleat House, Marquess of Bath, MS 29; Oxford, Bodleian Library, MS Eng. th. c. 58.

82.   fol. 258r–v Latin prose [F55]. *Begins:* Miserere mei deus secundum

---

[127]   Editions: *Yorkshire Writers*, ed. Horstmann, I, 300–21; *Richard Rolle and þe Holy Boke Gratia Dei: An Edition with Commentary*, ed. M. L. Arntz, S.N.D. (Salzburg, 1981), pp. 1–131 (with variants from Arundel and Huntington). See also *Yorkshire Writers*, ed. Horstmann, I, 112–31 (Arundel).

[128]   Thornton treats this work as separate treatises; see the analysis of parts given in *Richard Rolle*, ed. Arntz, pp. vi–ix; G. R. Keiser, 'Þe Holy Boke Gratia Dei', *Viator* 12 (1981), 289–317; and Thomson, *Catalogue*, p. 68.

[129]   Edition: *Yorkshire Writers*, ed. Horstmann, I, 383–92. Translation: Anonymous, 'A Revelation of Purgatory', trans. E. Spearing, in *Medieval Writings on Female Spirituality*, ed. E. Spearing (New York, 2002), pp. xlvii, 205–25. See also *A Revelation of Purgatory by an Unknown Fifteenth-Century Woman Visionary: Introduction, Critical Text, and Translation*, ed. M. P. Harley (Lewiston NY, 1985), pp. 59–86 (Longleat).

[130]   Olson, 'Romancing the Book', p. 136.

magnam misericordiam tuam. *Ends*: Tunc acceptabis sacrificium Iusticie oblaciones et holocausta tunc / Imponent super altare tuum vetulos **Gloria Patri & filio & spiritui sancto / sicut erat in principio & nunc & semper & in secula seculorum Amen**

Vulgate Psalm 50, concluded with a benediction.[131] Lincoln arts. 82–83 are sequenced after Lincoln art. 81, wherein they are named efficacious when uttered on behalf of souls in purgatory. Compare Lincoln art. 93 and the English verse paraphrase of Psalm 50 copied elsewhere by Thornton (London art. 23).

83. fol. 258v Latin prose [F55]. *Begins*: **ympnus** / Ueni creator spiritus. *Ends*: Sit laus Patri cum filio sancto / simul Paraclito nobisque mittat filius karisma sancti spiritus **Amen**

Hymn *Veni creator spiritus* with a variant ending.[132] Lincoln arts. 82–83 are sequenced after Lincoln art. 81, wherein they are named efficacious when uttered on behalf of souls in purgatory.

84. fols. 258v–270v Latin prose [F56, F57]. *Begins*: **Here Bygynnys Sayne Ierome Spaltyre** / Beatus vero Ieronimus in hoc modo disposuit hoc spalterium. *Ends*: Qui uiuis & rignas deus per omnia secula seculorum **Amen Amen Amen**

Abridged *Psalter of Saint Jerome* with Office.[133] Lengthy liturgical text.
Unique abridgement of text with numerous manuscripts.

85. fols. 271r–276r English prose [F58]. *Begins*: **Religio Sancti Spiritus** / **Religio Munda** / Off the abbaye of saynte spirite that es in a place that es / callede conscyence. *Ends*: blyssede mot he be withowtten ende **Amen / Explicit Relegio Sancti Spiritus Amen**

Abbey of the Holy Ghost (Northern Version).[134] Devotional treatise. Thornton's frequent annotations focus on basic concepts of Christian faith. This item likely shared a single exemplar with Lincoln arts. 10, 11, 13, 21 and London arts. 8, 34, 35. *IPMEP* 39. Manual 7, XX [184].
Twenty-three manuscripts and three early prints.

86. fols. 276va–277ra English verse [F59]. *Begins*: The begynnyng es of thre. *Ends*: Full of caytefte and of care

First Age of Man's Life.[135] Extract of 111 lines from the *Prick of Conscience* (lines 438–551). *DIMEV* 5398, *NIMEV* 3428. Manual 7, XX [18].

---

[131] The Lincoln Thornton text is not printed.

[132] The Lincoln Thornton text is not printed.

[133] Edition: *Yorkshire Writers*, ed. Horstmann, I, 392–408. Thomson, *Catalogue*, p. 68, itemises the Psalter's devotional components (psalms, litany, prayers).

[134] Editions: *Religious Pieces*, ed. Perry, pp. 51–62; *Yorkshire Writers*, ed. Horstmann, I, 321–37. See also *Middle English Religious Prose*, ed. Blake, pp. 88–102 (Laud 210).

[135] Edition: *Yorkshire Writers*, ed. Horstmann, I, 372–3. See also *The Prick of Conscience*

Ninety-seven other manuscripts and many variants (see DIMEV).[136]

87. fol. 277rb Originally blank column with a trial alphabet added later.

88. fol. 277va–b Latin verse and prose [F60]. *Begins:* **Ista oracio que sequitur est de vij gaudia beate marie virginis per Sanctum Thomam / et martirem Cantuariensem Archiepiscopum Edita** / Gaude Flore virgenali. *Ends:* qui viuis & rignas deus per omnia secula seculorum **Amen**

Gaude flore virgenali.[137] Salutation to Mary for her Seven Joys; ascribed to Saint Thomas of Canterbury; seven 6-line stanzas, concluding with versicle and prose collect.

Other manuscripts unknown.

89. fols. 277vb–278r Latin verse and prose [F61]. *Begins:* **Anoþer salutacioun till our lady / of hir fyve Ioyes** / Gaude virgo Mater Cristi. *Ends:* per eundem Cristum dominum nostrum

Gaude virgo mater Cristi.[138] Salutation to Mary for her Five Joys; three 6-line stanzas, concluding with versicle and prose collect. Spaces left for large initials.

Other manuscripts unknown.

90. fol. 278r Latin prose [F62]. *Begins:* **Ane Antyme to þe Fadir of heuen with a Colett** / Benedictio et Claritas et Sapiencia et graciarum accio. *Ends:* per Cristum dominum nostrum

Benedictio et claritas.[139] Hymn, concluding with versicle and collect. Spaces left for large initials *B* and *D*.

Other manuscripts unknown.

91. fol. 278r Latin prose [F62]. *Begins:* **Anoþer Antym of þe passyoun of criste Ihesu** / Tuam crucem adoramus domine. *Ends:* qui viuis & rignas deus per omnia secula seculorum **Amen**

Tuam crucem adoramus Domine.[140] Hymn on the Passion, concluding with versicle and collect. Spaces left for large initials *T* and *P*.

Other manuscripts unknown.

(*Stimulus Conscientiae*), ed. R. Morris (Berlin, 1863), pp. 13–16 (London, BL, MS Cotton Galba E. ix), which has been reprinted as *Richard Morris's Prick of Conscience: A Corrected and Amplified Reading Text*, ed. R. Hanna and S. Wood, EETS OS 342 (Oxford, 2013); and *Prik of Conscience*, ed. J. H. Morey (Kalamazoo MI, 2012), pp. 21–4 (New Haven, Yale University Beinecke Library, MS Osborn a. 13).

[136] See R. E. Lewis and A. McIntosh, *A Descriptive Guide to the Manuscripts of the* Pricke of Conscience, Medium Ævum Monographs n.s. 12 (Oxford, 1982), especially pp. 152–3.

[137] Edition: *Yorkshire Writers*, ed. Horstmann, I, 408–9. Compare *Thesaurus hymnologicus*, ed. Daniel, I, 346–7.

[138] Edition: *Yorkshire Writers*, ed. Horstmann, I, 409.

[139] Edition: *Yorkshire Writers*, ed. Horstmann, I, 409.

[140] Edition: *Yorkshire Writers*, ed. Horstmann, I, 409–10.

92.   fol. 278r Latin prose [F62]. *Begins:* **A Colecte of grete perdon vnto crist Ihesu** / *Domine Ihesu Criste Fili dei viui qui pendens in cruce. Ends: Salue sancta facies nostri redemptoris cum tota oracione & versu & colecta &c*

    Domine Ihesu Criste Fili Dei.[141] Prayer for pardon. Space left for large initial *D*.

    Other manuscripts unknown.

93.   fol. 278v Latin prose. **Thornton misereatur mei dei / miserere mei deus**

    Scribal signature in upper right margin, invoking Vulgate Psalm 50. Compare Lincoln art. 82 and London art. 23.

94.   fol. 278v Latin verse and prose [F62]. *Begins:* Crucem coronam spiniam. *Ends: per Cristum dominum nostrum*

    Crucem coronam spiniam.[142] Hymn on the *arma Christi*, with concluding prose prayer and collect; four 6-line stanzas.

    Other manuscripts unknown.

95.   fol. 278v Latin verse. **Ihesus Marie filius sit michi clemens / & propicius**

    Latin prayer-couplet written beside the incipit for Lincoln art. 96. Compare Lincoln art. 59.

96.   fols. 278v–279r Latin verse and prose [F62]. *Begins:* **A Preyere to þe wounde in Crystis syde** / *Salue plaga lateris nostri redemptoris. Ends: per Cristum dominum nostrum* **Amen**

    Salva plaga lateris.[143] Hymn on Christ's side wound with concluding anthem and prose collect; four 4-line stanzas.

    Other manuscripts unknown.

97.   fol. 279r–v English verse. [F63][144] *Begins:* **Memento Homo Quod Cinis Es / Et in cenerem Reuerteris** / [*in right margin*] **Perce michi domine nichil enim [sunt] / dies mei quid est homo [quia]** / [*in left margin*] **Limus** / Erthe owte of erthe es wondirly wroghte. *Ends:* Thane schalle erthe of erthe hafe a foulle stynke / **Mors Soluit Omnia**

    Earth upon Earth (Version B).[145] Moral lyric; five monorhyming quatrains. *DIMEV* 1170, *NIMEV* 704. *Manual* 9, XXII [264].

    Sixteen other manuscripts.

---

[141]   Edition: *Yorkshire Writers*, ed. Horstmann, I, 410.

[142]   Edition: *Yorkshire Writers*, ed. Horstmann, I, 410, who notes that 'The 2 following hymns may possibly be by R. Rolle. In 1276, Innocent V had ordered festival days in memory of the spear, nails, crown of thorns.'

[143]   Edition: *Yorkshire Writers*, ed. Horstmann, I, 410–11.

[144]   Fol. 279r is reproduced in colour in Olson, 'Romancing the Book', p. 120 (fig. 14).

[145]   Editions: *Religious Pieces*, ed. Perry, p. 106; *Yorkshire Writers*, ed. Horstmann, I, 373–4; *The Middle English Poem, Erthe upon Erthe, Printed from Twenty-Four Manuscripts*, ed. H. M. R. Murray, EETS OS 141 (London, 1911), p. 6 (printed with other versions).

98. fol. 279v English prose. **For the scyatite** / Tak a gowpyn full of sawge &
    Als mekyll of rewe / and choppe þam smale
    For the Sciatica. Medical recipe. Not in *IPMEP*.
    Other manuscripts unknown.

Lincoln booklet 4 (Quires Q–R; fols. 280–321): Practical medicine

99. fols. 280r–314v English prose [F64].[146] *Begins:* **Hic incipit Liber De
    diuersis medicinis & Primo pro Capite / For werke and vanytee in
    þe hede** / Take veruayne or vetoyn. *Ends imperfectly:* menge þerwith
    alde swyn grese & lay it to / þe kankir
    Liber de Diversis Medicinis.[147] Book of medical recipes. A loss of text
    occurs at the end because the last leaf of the quire is missing after fol.
    314. *IPMEP* 647 (compare 446, 447). *Manual* 10, XXV [272]; see also
    [336], [339], [347], [348], [349].
    No other manuscript. See *Manual* 10, pp. 3596–8.[148]

100. fols. 315r–321v English verse and prose. *Begins imperfectly:* … an oþer …
     Ends imperfectly: … n …
     Thornton Herbal.[149] Herbal that survives in fragments only; drawn from
     A Tretys of Diverse Herbis.

London, BL, MS Additional 31042 (179 folios)

London booklet 1 (Quires a–b; fols. 3–32): Sacred History (*Cursor Mundi* extracts)[150]

1. fols. 3ra–32rb English verse [T1].[151] *Begins imperfectly:* Sche was & that
   was sone appon hir sene. *Ends:* he brynge me vnto gode endyng **Amen**
   Life of Christ.[152] Narrative of sacred history (childhood of Mary, early life

---

[146]   For fol. 280r, see Orlemanski's chapter, Figure 1, in the present volume.

[147]   Edition: *The 'Liber de Diversis Medicinis'*, ed. Ogden.

[148]   On the provenance of an exemplar, see Olson, 'Romancing the Book', p. 138.

[149]   See G. R. Keiser, 'Reconstructing Robert Thornton's Herbal', *Medium Ævum* 65 (1996), 35–53.

[150]   On the booklet structure of London, see Hanna, 'The London Thornton MS' and 'The Growth'; and also the chapters by Fredell and Keiser in the present volume. Numbers prefixed 'T' refer to the list of London contents as itemized by Thompson, *London Thornton MS*.

[151]   Fols. 2v (flyleaf), 3r, 8v, 9r, 31v, 32r are reproduced in Thompson, *London Thornton MS*, plates 2a, 2b, 3a, 3b, 4a, 4b, respectively. See also the colour reproduction of fol. 8vb in Olson, 'Romancing the Book', p. 130 (fig. 22).

[152]   Editions (diplomatic transcriptions): *The Southern Version of Cursor Mundi: Volume II*, ed. R. R. Fowler (Ottawa, 1990), pp. 151–92 (lines 10630–12710); and *The Southern Version of*

and ministry of Christ); couplets corresponding to *Cursor Mundi*, lines 10630–14915, with variation. There are section headings and spaces left open for a programme of illustration, which is not filled in (compare Lincoln art. 1).[153] This *Cursor Mundi* extract begins mid Fifth Age and ends mid Sixth Age. *NIMEV* 2153. *Manual* 7, XX [31].

Nine other manuscripts: Cambridge, Trinity College, MS R. 3. 8; Edinburgh, NLS, Deposit 313/3633; Edinburgh, Royal College of Physicians, Edinburgh MS *Cursor Mundi, Northern Homily Cycle*; Göttingen University Library, MS Theol. 107; London, BL, MSS Cotton Vespasian A. iii, Additional 36983; London, College of Arms, MS Arundel 57; Oxford, Bodleian Library, MSS Fairfax 14, Laud Misc. 416. *One fragment:* Montreal, McGill University Library, MS 142.

2. fol. 32rb English verse.[154] *Begins:* **For now I thynke of this make ende.** *Ends:* **He brynge me vnto gode endyng Amen**

A unique bridge (seven couplets) between two *Cursor Mundi* extracts, possibly composed by Thornton. The lines are copied continuously with London art. 1.[155]

No other manuscripts.

3. fol. 32rb–vb English verse [T2].[156] *Begins:* Ihesu was of Mary borne. *Ends:* Come to thi Ioye withowtten ende **Amen / Amen Amen Per charite Amen Amen / Et Sic Procedendum ad Passionem / domini nostri Ihesu Cristi que incipit in folio / proximo sequente secundum Fantasiam scriptoris &c**

Discourse between Christ and Man.[157] Post-Passion allegorical dialogue; thirty-nine couplets, corresponding to *Cursor Mundi*, Sixth Age, lines

---

Cursor Mundi: Volume III, ed. H. J. Stauffenberg (Ottawa, 1985), pp. 165–208 (lines 12713–14915). See also *Cursor Mundi, Parts II–III*, ed. R. Morris, EETS OS 59, 62 (London, 1875–6), pp. 610–978 (four other versions in parallel).

153   Olson, 'Romancing the Book', p. 130.

154   Fol. 32r is reproduced in Johnston's chapter, Figure 1, in the present volume, and in Thompson, *London Thornton MS*, plate 4b.

155   *The Southern Version III*, ed. Stauffenberg, pp. 208–9. Johnston proposes Thornton's authorship; see his chapter in the present volume. See also S. Fein, 'The Literary Scribe: The Ludlow Scribe of Harley 2253 and Robert Thornton as Case Studies', in *Insular Books: Vernacular Miscellanies in Late Medieval Britain*, ed. M. Connolly and R. Radulescu, Proceedings of the British Academy (London, forthcoming 2015).

156   For fols. 32r, 32v, see Johnston's chapter, Figures 1–2, in the present volume, and Thompson, *London Thornton MS*, plates 4b, 1 (colour), respectively.

157   Edition: *The Southern Version III*, ed. Stauffenberg, pp. 209–10. Ten couplets are printed in 'Hs. Brit. Mus. Additional 31042', ed. Brunner, *Archiv* 132 (1914), 316–37 (pp. 316–17). See also *Cursor Mundi, Part III*, ed. Morris, pp. 978–82 (Cotton and Göttingen in parallel).

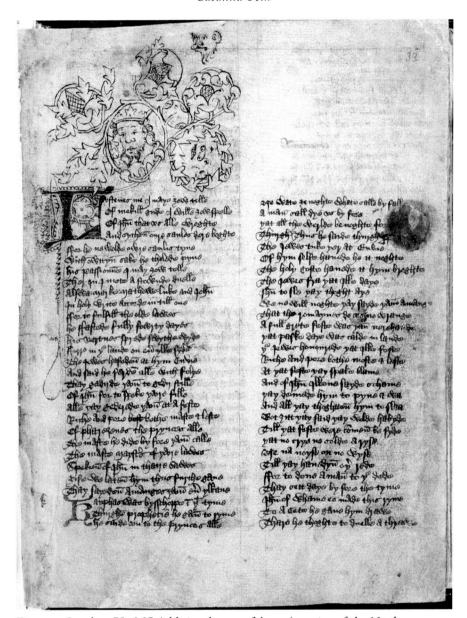

Figure 2. London, BL, MS Additional 31042, fol. 33r (opening of the *Northern Passion*

17111–86, with variations. *DIMEV* 2945, *NIMEV* 1786. *Manual* 3, VII [2b], 7, XX [31].

Four other manuscripts: Göttingen University Library, MS Theol. 107; London, BL, MS Cotton Vespasian A. iii; Tokyo, Keio University Library, Hopton Hall MS; Tokyo, MS Takamiya 15.

London booklet 2 (Quires c–e; fols. 33–96): *Northern Passion* **and Romances**

4. fols. 33ra–50rb English verse [T3].[158] *Begins:* Lystenes me I maye ʒow telle / Of mekill gude I wille ʒow spelle. *Ends:* And alle þat hafe herde this passioun / Sall haue a thowsande ʒeris to perdone (see Figure 2). *Northern Passion.*[159] Narrative of sacred history; couplets. Scribal signature by Thornton (see London art. 5). *DIMEV* 3124, *NIMEV* 1907. *Manual* 2, V [303c].

   Twelve other manuscripts: Cambridge, CUL, MSS Dd. 1. 1, Ff. 5. 48, Gg. 1. 1, Gg. 1. 12, Gg. 5. 31, Ii. 4. 9; Cambridge MA, Harvard University Houghton Library, MS Eng. 1031; London, BL, MSS Cotton Vespasian D. ix, Harley 215; Oxford, Bodleian Library, MSS Ashmole 61, Rawlinson C. 86, Rawlinson C. 655.

5. fol. 50rb English verse.[160] **Amen Amen per charite / And louynge to god þerfore gyfe we / R Thornton / Explicit Passio Domini nostri Ihesu Cristi**

   Scribal colophon concluding London art. 4; couplet. Not in *DIMEV, NIMEV*.

6. fols. 50r–66r English verse [T4].[161] *Begins:* **Hic Incepit Distruccio Ierarusalem Quomodo Titus & Vaspasianus / Obsederunt & distruxerunt Ierusalem et Vi[n]dicarunt mortem domini Ihesu Cristi / The Segge of Ierusalem / Off Tytus And Vaspasyane / In tyberyus tym that trewe Emperoure.** *Ends:* And rydis to Rome thare rede vs oure lorde **Amen Amen Amen / Explicit la Sege de Jerusalem**

---

[158] Fol. 33r is Figure 2 in this chapter. For fols. 40v, 50r, see Johnston's chapter, Figures 4, 3, respectively, in the present volume. Fols. 33r, 40v, 41r, 41v, 42r, 49r, 50r are reproduced in Thompson, *London Thornton MS*, plates 7, 5a, 5b, 6a, 6b, 8, 9, respectively. See also the colour reproduction of fol. 33r in Olson, 'Romancing the Book', p. 128 (fig. 20), and in Thompson, *London Thornton MS*, plate 1.

[159] Edition: *The Northern Passion*, ed. Foster (in parallel with CUL Dd. 1. 1, CUL Gg. 5. 31 and Harley 215).

[160] Fol. 50r is reproduced in Thompson, *London Thornton MS*, plate 9; and in colour in Olson, p. 129 (fig. 21).

[161] Fols. 50r, 66r are reproduced in Thompson, *London Thornton MS*, plates 9, 10, respectively; and fol. 50r is reproduced in colour in Olson, 'Romancing the Book', p. 129 (fig. 21).

Siege of Jerusalem.[162] Romance; 1334 unrhymed alliterative long lines. A loss of text occurs between fols. 53 and 54, where one leaf is missing. Scribal signature by Thornton (see London art. 7). *DIMEV* 2651, *NIMEV* 1583 (compare *DIMEV* 3107, *NIMEV* 1881). *Manual* 1, I [107].

> *Eight other manuscripts:* Cambridge, CUL, MS Mm. 5. 14; Exeter, Devon Record Office, MS 2507; London, BL, MSS Cotton Caligula A. ii, Cotton Vespasian E. xvi; London, Lambeth Palace Library, MS 491; Oxford, Bodleian Library, MS Laud Misc. 656; Princeton University Library, MS Taylor Medieval 11; San Marino, Huntington Library, MS HM 128.

7. fol. 66r Latin verse.[163] **R Thornton dictus qui scripsit sit benedictus Amen**

> Scribal signature; couplet. Compare Lincoln arts. 9, 59, 68.

8. fols. 66v–79v English verse [T5].[164] *Begins:* **Here Bygynnys the Sege off Melayne** / All worthy men that luffes to here. *Ends imperfectly:* And Bendis vp þaire engyne …

> *Sege of Melayne.*[165] Romance; 134 12-line stanzas plus six lines. This item is a companion to London art. 10.[166] This item likely shared a single exemplar with London arts. 34, 35 and Lincoln arts. 10, 11, 13, 21, 85. Losses occur between fols. 77 and 78, where one leaf is missing, and at the end, where another leaf is missing. *DIMEV* 408, *NIMEV* 234. *Manual* 1, I [56].
>
> *No other manuscript.*

9. fols. 80r–81v English verse [T6].[167] *Begins imperfectly:* … With humble hert I praye iche creature. *Ends:* O Florum flos O Flos pulcherime **Amen / Explicit Cantus Amen**

---

[162] The London Thornton text is not printed, but a diplomatic transcription will soon be available: *The Seige of Jerusalem Electronic Archive,* ed. T. J. Stinson, www.siegeofjerusalem.org. For editions based on Laud, see *The Siege of Jerusalem,* ed. E. Kölbing and M. Day, EETS OS 188 (London, 1932), pp. 1–78; *The Siege of Jerusalem,* ed. R. Hanna and D. Lawton, EETS OS 320 (Oxford, 2003), pp. 1–90; *Siege of Jerusalem,* ed. M. Livingston (Kalamazoo MI, 2004), pp. 41–83.

[163] Fol. 66r is reproduced in Thompson, *London Thornton MS,* plate 10.

[164] Fols. 66v, 73v, 79v are reproduced in Thompson, *London Thornton MS,* plates 11, 12, 13a, respectively.

[165] Editions: *The English Charlemagne Romances, Part II. 'The Sege off Melayne' and 'The Romance of Duke Rowland and Sir Otuell of Spayne',* ed. S. J. Herrtage, EETS ES 35 (London, 1880), pp. 1–52; *Six Middle English Romances,* ed. Mills, pp. 1–45; *Three Middle English Charlemagne Romances,* ed. A. Lupack (Kalamazoo MI, 1990), pp. 105–60; *Middle English Romances,* ed. Shepherd, pp. 268–312.

[166] Stern, 'The London "Thornton" Miscellany (II)', p. 216.

[167] Fols. 80r, 80v, 81v are reproduced in Thompson, *London Thornton MS,* plates 13b, 14, 15, respectively.

John Lydgate, *O Florum Flos*.[168] English refrain lyric in praise of the Virgin; twenty-three 8-line stanzas. This item begins imperfectly because there is a leaf lost between fols. 79 and 80. *DIMEV* 3495, *NIMEV* 2168.

One other manuscript: London, BL, MS Harley 3869.

10. fols. 82r–94r English verse [T7].[169] *Begins*: **Þe Romance Of Duke Rowlande and of Sir Ottuell of Spayne / Off Cherlls of Fraunce** / Lordynges þat bene hende and Free. *Ends*: Brynge vs to thi Blisses sere / Amen, per charite / **Charlles /Here Endes þe Romance / of Duk Rowland & sir Otuell of Spayne / Explicit sir Ottuell**

Duke Roland and Sir Otuel of Spain.[170] Romance; 133 12-line stanzas. The text is incomplete because leaves are lost between fols. 85 and 86 and between fols. 86 and 87. *DIMEV* 3254, *NIMEV* 1996. *Manual* 1, I [57].

No other manuscript.

11. fol. 94r English verse [T8].[171] *Begins*: **Passionis Cristi Cantus / Hic incipit quedam Tractatus Passionis Domini nostri Iesu Cristi in Anglicis** / Man to reforme thyne exile and thi losse. *Ends imperfectly*: Thynke and remembir the appon my blody face …

John Lydgate, *Complaint That Christ Makes of His Passion*, lines 1–9.[172] Religious lyric (fragment); one 8-line stanza plus one line. This item is Thornton's first start, aborted apparently because he found fault with the exemplar; he left a gap of half a page and then copied the poem again (London art. 14). *DIMEV* 3388 (and cf. *DIMEV* 3974), *NIMEV* 2081. *Manual* 6, XVI [24].

Six other manuscripts: Cambridge, CUL, MS Kk. 1. 6; Cambridge, Trinity College, MS R. 3. 21 (601); London, BL, MSS Harley 372, Harley 7333; Oxford, Bodleian Library, MS Laud Misc. 683.

12. fol. 94v English verse [T9].[173] Exultit celum laudibus / In bathelem in that fare sete Ihesus was borne of mare fre / for he ys prens / Exultet celum lawdibus

Nativity carol (fragment);[174] copied by a later hand in space left blank by the scribe. *DIMEV* 2481, *NIMEV* 1471. *Manual* 6, XIV [20].

Five other manuscripts: Cambridge, CUL, MS Ee. 1. 12; Cambridge, Trinity

---

[168] Edition: 'Lydgatiana: 14. O Flos Pulcherrime!', ed. H. N. MacCracken, *Archiv* 131 (1913), 60–3.

[169] Fol. 94r is reproduced in Thompson, *London Thornton MS*, plate 16.

[170] Edition: *The English Charlemagne Romances*, ed. Herrtage, pp. 55–104.

[171] Fol. 94r is reproduced in Thompson, *London Thornton MS*, plate 16.

[172] The London text is not printed. See J. Lydgate, *The Minor Poems of John Lydgate I–II*, ed. H. N. MacCracken, 2 vols., EETS OS 107, 192 (London, 1911–34), I, 216–21 (Laud).

[173] Fol. 94v is reproduced in Thompson, *London Thornton MS*, plate 17.

[174] Editions: 'Two Unpublished Middle English Carol-Fragments', ed. K. Hodder, *Archiv*

College, MS O. 3. 58 (1230); Oxford, Balliol College, MS 354; Oxford, Bodleian Library, MS Eng. poet. e. 1; Oxford, Lincoln College, MS Lat. 141.

13. fol. 94v English verse [T10].[175] Mare moder cum and se þin awne dere chyld ys nalyd on tre / both fowt & hand he may not go þat blyssyd chyld ys lappyd in wo / þat blyssyd chy

 Passion carol (fragment);[176] copied by a later hand in space left blank by the scribe. *DIMEV* 3424, *NIMEV* 2111. *Manual* 6, XIV [159].

 One other manuscript: London, BL, MS Sloane 2593. *One early print:* STC 5204.3. *Variants in:* Edinburgh, NLS, Advocates' MS 18. 7. 21; Oxford, Bodleian Library, Eng. poet. e. 1; STC 15045.

14. fols. 94v–96r English verse [T11].[177] *Begins:* Mman to refourme thyn exile and thi losse. *Ends:* Than ofte to thynke one Cristes passioun / **Explicit Passio Cristi**

 John Lydgate, *Complaint That Christ Makes of His Passion.*[178] Religious lyric; fifteen 8-line stanzas. Compare London art. 11. *DIMEV* 3388 (and cf. *DIMEV* 3974), *NIMEV* 2081. *Manual* 6, XVI [24].

 Six other manuscripts: Cambridge, CUL, MS Kk. 1. 6; Cambridge, Trinity College, MS R. 3. 21 (601); London, BL, MSS Harley 372, Harley 7333; Oxford, Bodleian Library, MS Laud Misc. 683.

15. fol. 96r–v English verse [T12].[179] *Begins:* **Willelmus conquestor Dux Normannorum** / This myghty Willyam Duke of Normandy. *Ends imperfectly:* And alle wales in despite of alle þaire myghte ...

 John Lydgate, *Verses on the Kings of England* (to Henry VI).[180] Political lyric; eight rhyme royal stanzas plus four lines. The poem generally has fifteen stanzas; some versions are longer. *DIMEV* 5731 (cf. *DIMEV* 3158), *NIMEV* 3632. *Manual* 6, XVI [100].

 Thirty-six other manuscripts plus other versions.

---

205 (1969), 378–83; *The Early English Carols*, ed. R. L. Greene, 2nd edn (Oxford, 1977), pp. 10–12 (no. 21E).

[175] Fol. 94v is reproduced in Thompson, *London Thornton MS*, plate 17.

[176] Editions: 'Two Unpublished Middle English Carol-Fragments', ed. Hodder, pp. 378–83; *The Early English Carols*, ed. Greene, pp. 105–7 (no. 157E).

[177] Fol. 94v is reproduced in Thompson, *London Thornton MS*, plate 17.

[178] The London Thornton text is not printed. See Lydgate, *Minor Poems*, ed. MacCracken, I, 216–21 (Laud).

[179] Fol. 96v is reproduced in Thompson, *London Thornton MS*, plate 18a.

[180] The London Thornton text is not printed. See Lydgate, *Minor Poems*, ed. MacCracken, II, 710–16 (Harley 372; thirty stanzas); *Historical Poems of the XIVth and XVth Centuries*, ed. R. H. Robbins (New York, 1959), pp. 3–6 (Rawlinson C. 48; fifteen stanzas).

16. fol. 97r–v English verse [T13].[181] *Begins imperfectly:* … Be noghte hasty nore sodanly vengeable. *Ends:* To alle in deferent recheste dyetarye
John Lydgate, *Dietary*.[182] Moral lyric; seven lines plus eight 8-line stanzas. *NIMEV* 824. *Manual* 6, XVI [34].
Fifty-five other manuscripts and one early print.

17. fol. 97v Latin verse [T14].[183] Post visum risum post risum transit in usum / Post vsum tactum post tactum transit in actum / Nisu geste tactus vix enacubitur actus / Tactus eretur vita ne moriaris ita
Latin aphorism.[184]

18. fol. 97v Latin verse [T15]. Lex est defuncta quia iudicis est manus vncta / Proptter vnguentum ius est incarcere tentum
Latin aphorism.[185]

19. fol. 97v Latin verse [T16]. Alterius lingue dic quis moderatur habenas / Vix est conni proprie possit habere modum
Latin aphorism.[186]

20. fol. 97v English verse [T17].[187] **A gud scherte songe of this dete / This werlde es tournede vp so downne** / To thynke it es a wondir thynge / Of this werldis mutabilytee / I ame matede in my mosynge / Of the variaunce the whilke þat I now see.
To Think It Is a Wonder Thing.[188] Lyric on mutability; four lines, abab. *DIMEV* 6025, *NIMEV* 3778. *Manual* 5, XIII [94].
No other manuscript.

London booklet 3 (Quire f, fols. 98–124): Religious Verse

21. fols. 98r–101v English verse [T18].[189] *Begins:* In a moruenynge of Maye when Medowes sall spryng. *Ends:* In a mornynge of may / When medowes sall sprynge

---

[181]   Fols. 97r, 97v are reproduced in Thompson, *London Thornton MS*, plates 18b, 19a, respectively.

[182]   The London Thornton text is not printed. See Lydgate, *Minor Poems*, ed. MacCracken, II, 702–7 (Lansdowne 699; ten stanzas).

[183]   Fol. 97v is reproduced in Thompson, *London Thornton MS*, plate 19a.

[184]   *Carmina medii aevi posterioris latina*, II/1–3: *Lateinische Sprichwörter und Sentenzen des Mittelalters in alphabetischer Anordnung A-E, F-M, N-P*, ed. H. Walther (Göttingen, 1963–65), II/3, p. 904 (no. 72, a variant).

[185]   *Carmina*, ed. Walther, II/2, p. 721 (no. 95).

[186]   *Carmina*, II/1, ed. Walther, p. 101 (no. 64).

[187]   Fol. 97v is reproduced in Thompson, *London Thornton MS*, plate 19a.

[188]   Edition: 'Hs. Brit. Mus. Additional 31042', ed. Brunner, p. 318.

[189]   Fols. 98r, 101v are reproduced in Thompson, *London Thornton MS*, plates 19b, 20a, respectively.

Four Leaves of the Truelove.[190] Moral poem; forty 13-line alliterative stanzas. This Northern devotional poem is crafted to be presented on a bifolium of four leaves, a layout Thornton comes very close to replicating.[191] *DIMEV* 2452, *NIMEV* 1453. *Manual* 7, XX [176].
One other manuscript: Oxford, Bodleian Library, MS Additional A. 106. *One early print:* de Worde (*STC* 15345).

22. fol. 101v English verse [T19].[192] *Begins:* Haile holy spyritt & Ioy be vnto the. *Ends:* þat regnys god in trynyte in worlde withowten ende Amen
Hail Holy Spirit.[193] Lyric prayer to guardian angel, added as filler; couplets. *DIMEV* 1720, *NIMEV* 1051.
One other manuscript: Cambridge, Magdalene College, MS 13.

23. fol. 102r–v English verse [T20].[194] *Begins:* Miserere mei deus secundum magnam miserecordiam tuam / God þou haue mercy of me After thi mercy mekill of mayne. *Ends imperfectly:* Flitt me noghte lorde fra thi face All if I falle in fandynges fell ...
Have Mercy of Me.[195] Paraphrase of Vulgate Psalm 50; eleven alliterating 12-line stanzas plus three lines. Compare Lincoln arts. 82, 93. This item ends imperfectly because five leaves are missing after fol. 102. Compare Lincoln art. 93 and the copy of Vulgate Psalm 50 copied elsewhere by Thornton (Lincoln art. 82). *DIMEV* 1618, *NIMEV* 990. *Manual* 2, IV [22].
No other manuscript.

24. fols. 103r–110v English verse [T21].[196] *Begins imperfectly:* ... Iudica me deus with hole hert and entere / Their conscyence purge fro þe synnes

---

[190] Edition: *The Quatrefoil of Love*, ed. I. Gollancz and M. M. Weale, EETS OS 195 (London, 1935), pp. 1–18. See also *The Four Leaves of the Truelove*, in *Moral Love Songs*, ed. Fein, pp. 180–96 (based on Additional A. 106).

[191] S. Fein, 'Quatrefoil and Quatrefolia: The Devotional Layout of an Alliterative Poem', *Journal of the Early Book Society* 2 (1999), 26–45; and S. Fein, 'The Epistemology of Titles in Editing Whole-Manuscripts: The Lyric Sequence, in Particular', *Poetica* 71 (2009), 49–74 (pp. 52–53).

[192] Fol. 101v is reproduced in Thompson, *London Thornton MS*, plate 20a.

[193] Editions: 'Hs. Brit. Mus. Additional 31042', ed. Brunner, p. 318; *Religious Lyrics of the XVth Century*, ed. R. H. Robbins (Oxford, 1939), pp. 204–5.

[194] Fols. 102r, 102v are reproduced in Thompson, *London Thornton MS*, plates 20b, 21a, respectively.

[195] Editions: 'Have Mercy of Me (Psalm 51): An Unedited Alliterative Poem from the London Thornton Manuscript', ed. S. G. Fein, *Modern Philology* 86 (1989), 223–41; 'Literary Associations of an Anonymous Middle English Paraphrase of Vulgate Psalm L', ed. J. J. Thompson, *Medium Ævum* 55 (1988), 38–55 (pp. 53–5).

[196] Fols. 103r, 103v, 104r, 110v are reproduced in Thompson, *London Thornton MS*, plates 21b, 22a, 22b, 23a, respectively.

seuen. *Ends*: Withe goostely supporte to doo correccyone / The reforme
where as þay see nede **Amen**

John Lydgate, *Virtues of the Mass*.[197] Poem of religious instruction;
seventy-six 8-line stanzas (stanzas 1–7 missing). In the right margin of
fol. 103r, next to Lydgate's name (v. 88), Thornton has written: '**Hunc
librum qui dictauit / Lydgate Cristus nominauit**'. This item begins
imperfectly because five leaves are missing after fol. 102. *DIMEV* 6820,
NIMEV 4246. *Manual* 6, XVI [87].

Nine other manuscripts: Cambridge, Gonville and Caius College, MS
174/95; Cambridge, Trinity College, MS R. 3. 21 (601); London, BL,
MSS Arundel 396, Harley 2251; London, Lambeth Palace Library, MS
344; Oxford, Balliol College, MS 354; Oxford, Bodleian Library, MSS
Laud Misc. 683, Hatton 73; Oxford, St John's College, MS 56. *One early
print*: de Worde (*STC* 17037.5).

25.   fol. 110v Latin verse. Nunc diues dupis cum poblico crimine purus / hoc
opus expleuit quod mentis robore cleuit

Nunc dives dupis. This appears to be a Latin aphorism in two couplets. It
has not been previously identified as separate from London art. 24.

Other manuscripts unknown.

26.   fol. 110v English verse [T22].[198] *Begins*: [*in left margin*] **A Carolle For
/ Crystynmesse** / The Rose es the fayreste Floure of alle / [*in right
margin*] **The Rose of Ryse**. *Ends imperfectly*: In plesance of the Rose
so trewe ...

Rose of Ryse.[199] A carol for Christmas alluding to Henry V and the
Agincourt campaign; three 6-line stanzas and 4-line burden. *DIMEV*
5456, *NIMEV* 3457. *Manual* 6, XIV [436].

No other manuscript.

27.   fols. 111r–119vb English verse [T23].[200] *Begins imperfectly*: ... For wynde
or Rayne For wate or colde or hete. *Ends*: To his honour whom þay in
Bedlem soghte / **Amen** / **Explicit Tractatus Amen** / **Trium Magum**

Three Kings of Cologne.[201] Religious verse narrative; five lines plus 122
rhyme royal stanzas. *DIMEV* 1419, *NIMEV* 854.3 (*IMEV* *31; *IMEV
Suppl.* *854.3). *Manual* 6, XVI [98].

---

197   The London Thornton text is not printed. See Lydgate, *Minor Poems*, ed. MacCracken,
I, 87–115 (Cambridge, Trinity College with variants listed).

198   Fol. 110v is reproduced in Thompson, *London Thornton MS*, plate 23a.

199   Edition: *The Early English Carols*, ed. Greene, p. 258 (no. 427).

200   Fols. 111r, 117r, 119v are reproduced in Thompson, *London Thornton MS*, plates 23b, 26,
24a, respectively.

201   Edition: 'Lydgatiana: III. The Three Kings of Cologne', ed. H. N. MacCracken, *Archiv*
192 (1912), 50–68.

No other manuscript. One early print: STC 5572.

28.   fols. 120r–122rb English verse [T24].[202] *Begins:* **Hic Incipit Cantus Cu[i]usdam Sapientis / Here Bygynnys a louely song of Wysdome** / Waste makes a kyngdome in nede. *Ends:* That we may wynn of blysse þe crowne **Amen / Amen**

   A Lovely Song of Wisdom.[203] Moral lyric, elsewhere entitled *The Proverbs of Solomon*; thirty-eight 8-line stanzas. *DIMEV* 6159, *NIMEV* 3861.

   Two other manuscripts: Cambridge, CUL, MS Ff. 2. 38; Cambridge, Magdalene College, MS Pepys 1584.

29.   fols. 122va–123ra English verse [T25]. *Begins:* **A Song How þat Mercy Passeth Rightwisnes** / By one foreste als I gan walke. *Ends:* And thus mercy passes Rightwysnes **Amen / Explicit Cantus Amen**

   Mercy Passes Rightwisnes.[204] Lyric dialogue between Mercy and Justice; fourteen 8-line stanzas with refrain. *DIMEV* 923, *NIMEV* 560. *Manual* 3, VII [27].

   Three other manuscripts: Aberystwyth, NLW, MS Brogyntyn II. 1 (*olim* MS Porkington 10); Chichester, West Sussex Record Office, Cowfold Churchwarden's Accounts; London, Lambeth Palace Library, MS 853.

30.   fol. 123ra–vb English verse [T26]. *Begins:* **A songe how Mercy comes bifore þe Iugement / Doo mercy Bifore thi Iugement** / There es no creatoure bot one. *Ends:* Bitwix vs and thi Iugement **Amen / Explicit Cantus Amen**

   Do Mercy before Thy Judgment.[205] Lyric on mercy; seven 12-line stanzas with refrain. *DIMEV* 5577, *NIMEV* 3533.

   Three other manuscripts: London, BL, MSS Harley 1704, Additional 39574; London, Lambeth Palace Library, MS 853.

31.   fols. 123vb–124vb English verse [T27].[206] *Begins:* **A Songe how þat Mercy passeth alle thynge** / Be weste vndir a wilde wodde syde. *Ends:* That mercy passes alle thynge **Amen Explicit Cantus Amen / Explicit Cantus Amen**

---

[202]   Fols. 120r, 120v, 121r are reproduced in Thompson, *London Thornton MS*, plates 24b, 25a, 25b, respectively.

[203]   Edition: 'Spätme. Lehrgedichte', ed. K. Brunner, *Archiv* 164 (1933), 178–99 (pp. 193–9); see also pp. 178–91 for the longer version in CUL Ff. 2. 38.

[204]   Editions: 'Hs. Brit. Mus. Additional 31042', ed. Brunner, pp. 319–21; '"Mercy and Justice": The Additional MS 31042 Version', ed. J. Brazire, *Leeds Studies in English* n.s. 16 (1985), 259–71.

[205]   Edition: 'Hs. Brit. Mus. Additional 31042', ed. Brunner, pp. 321–2. See also *Hymns to the Virgin & Christ, The Parliament of Devils, and Other Religious Poems*, ed. F. J. Furnivall, EETS OS 24 (London, 1868), pp. 18–21 (Lambeth 853).

[206]   Fol. 124v is reproduced in Thompson, *London Thornton MS*, plate 27.

Mercy Passes All Things.[207] Lyric on mercy; sixteen 12-line stanzas with refrain. The last stanza is written in the bottom margin of fol. 124v. *DIMEV* 950, *NIMEV* 583.

Two other manuscripts: London, BL, MS Additional 22283 (Simeon); Oxford, Bodleian Library, MS Eng. poet. a. 1 (Vernon).

London booklet 4 (Quires g–h; fols. 125–168): *Richard Coer de Lyon* and *Childhood of Christ*

32. fols. 125ra–163va English verse [T28].[208] *Begins imperfectly*: Lorde Ihesu Criste kyng of glory. *Ends*: And god grante vs alle gude endynge **Amen / Explicit The Romance / Of Kyng Richerd þe Conqueroure**

Richard Coer de Lyon.[209] Romance; couplets. Losses of text occur at the beginning because two leaves are missing after fol. 124 and three are missing between fols. 143 and 144. *DIMEV* 3231, *NIMEV* 1979. *Manual* 1, I [106].

Nine other manuscripts: Badminton, Duke of Beaufort, MS 704.1.16; Cambridge, Gonville and Caius College, MS 175/96; Edinburgh University Library, MS 218; Edinburgh, NLS, Advocates' MS 19. 2. 1 (Auchinleck); London, BL, MSS Egerton 2862, Harley 4690; London, College of Arms, MS Arundel 58; Oxford, Bodleian Library, MS Douce 228; St Andrews University Library, MS PR 2065.R4. *Two early prints:* STC 21007, 21008.

33. fols. 163va–168vb English verse [T29].[210] *Begins*: [*in left margin*] **Ihesus Cristus / Here Bigynnys the Romance / of the childhode of Ihesu Criste þat / clerkes callys Ipokrephum / Allemyghty god in Trynytee.** *Ends*: Thare Ioyes are euer & myrthe & playe **Amen / Moralitus dicit in verbis prophecie**

---

[207] Edition: 'Hs. Brit. Mus. Additional 31042', ed. Brunner, pp. 323–27. See also *Religious Lyrics of the XIVth Century*, ed. Brown, pp. 125–31 (Vernon).

[208] For fol. 163v, see Couch's chapter, Figure 1, in the present volume. Fols. 139v, 142r, 159v, 160r are reproduced in Thompson, *London Thornton MS*, plates 28, 29, 30a, 30b, respectively.

[209] The London Thornton text is not printed. For editions based on Auchinleck, see 'Kleine Publicationen aus der Auchinleck-hs. III.', ed. E. Kölbing, *Englische Studien* 8 (1885), 115–19; 'Two Newly-Discovered Fragments from the Auchinleck MS', ed. G. V. Smithers, *Medium Ævum* 18 (1949), 1–11; *Auchinleck Manuscript*, ed. D. Burnley and A. Wiggins (Edinburgh, 2003), http://auchinleck.nls.uk/editorial/project.html. For an edition based on Gonville and Caius, see *Der mittelenglische Versroman über Richard Löwenherz*, ed. K. Brunner, Wiener Beiträge zur englischen Philologie 42 (Vienna, 1913).

[210] Fols. 163v, 168v are reproduced in Thompson, *London Thornton MS*, plates 34, 31a, respectively.

Childhood of Christ.[211] Religious narrative poem, called a 'romance'; 925 lines in 12- and 8-line stanzas. *DIMEV* 429, *NIMEV* 250. *Manual* 2, V [311].

Two other manuscripts: London, BL, MSS Harley 2399, Harley 3954.

London booklet 5 (Quire i; fols. 169–181): Two Alliterative Debates

34. fols. 169r–176v English verse [T30].[212] *Begins:* **The Parlement of the thre Ages** / In the monethes of maye When mirthes bene fele. *Ends:* And Marie þat es mylde qwene amende vs of synn Amen Amen / **Thus Endes The Three Ages**

Parlement of the Thre Ages.[213] Allegorical debate; 665 unrhymed alliterative long lines. This item likely shared a single exemplar with London arts. 8, 35 and Lincoln arts. 10, 11, 13, 21, 85. *DIMEV* 2611, *NIMEV* 1556. *Manual* 5, XIII [244].

One other manuscript: London, BL, MS Additional 33994.

35. fols. 176v–181vb English verse [T31].[214] *Begins:* **Here Begynnes a Tretys and god Schorte refreyte** / **Bytwixe Wynnere and Wastoure** / Sythen that Bretayne was biggede and Bruyttus it aughte. *Ends imperfectly:* To þe kirke of Colayne þer þe kynges ligges …

Wynnere and Wastoure.[215] Allegorical debate; 503 unrhymed alliterative long lines; incomplete at end. This item likely shared a single exemplar with London arts. 8, 34 and Lincoln arts. 10, 11, 13, 21, 85. *DIMEV* 4918, *NIMEV* 3137. *Manual* 5, XIII [243].

No other manuscript.

---

[211] Edition: 'Nachträge zu den Legenden: 1. Kindheit Jesu aus Ms. Addit. 31,042', ed. C. Horstmann, *Archiv* 74 (1885), 327–39. See also *Sammlung altenglischer Legenden*, ed. C. Horstmann (Heilbronn, 1878), pp. 101–23 (Harley 2399, Harley 3954).

[212] Fol. 169r is reproduced in Thompson, *London Thornton MS*, plate 31b.

[213] Editions: *The Parlement of the Three Ages: An Alliterative Poem on the Nine Worthies and the Heroes of Romances*, ed. I. Gollancz, Select Early English Poems 2 (London, 1915); *The Parlement of the Thre Ages*, ed. M. Y. Offord, EETS OS 246 (London, 1959), pp. 1–30 (in parallel with Additional 33994); *The Parlement of the Thre Ages*, in *Alliterative Poetry of the Middle Ages: An Anthology*, ed. T. Turville-Petre (Washington DC, 1989), pp. 67–100; *Middle English Debate Poetry: A Critical Anthology*, ed. J. W. Conlee (East Lansing MI, 1991), pp. 99–138; *Wynnere and Wastoure and The Parlement of the Thre Ages*, ed. W. Ginsberg (Kalamazoo MI, 1992), pp. 43–79.

[214] For fol. 181r, see Keiser's chapter, Figure 4, in the present volume. Fols. 180v, 181r, 181v are reproduced in Thompson, *London Thornton MS*, plates 32a, 32b, 33a, respectively.

[215] Editions: *A Good Short Debate between Winner and Waster*, ed. I. Gollancz, Select Early English Poems 3 (London, 1920); *Wynnere and Wastoure*, in *Alliterative Poetry*, ed. Turville-Petre, pp. 38–66; *Wynnere and Wastoure*, ed. Trigg; *Middle English Debate Poetry*, ed. Conlee, pp. 63–98; *Wynnere and Wastoure*, ed. Ginsberg, pp. 1–42.

Appendix
Index of manuscripts sharing items with the Thornton manuscripts[216]

---

[216] This appendix collates the manuscripts cited in the List of Contents of this chapter. Thornton articles with more than twelve additional witnesses – Gaytryge's *Sermon*, *Jesus Thy Sweetness*, Hilton's *Epistle of Salvation*, *Psalter of Saint Jerome*, *Abbey of the Holy Ghost*, *Prick of Conscience*, *Earth upon Earth*, Lydgate's *Verses on the Kings of England*, and Lydgate's *Dietary* (Lincoln arts. 71, 72, 77, 84, 85, 86, 97; London arts., 15, 16) – are not included because of the high number of manuscripts. For the manuscripts holding these works, see *DIMEV*, *NIMEV*, and *Manual*.

Magdalene College, MS Pepys 1584	London art. 28
Trinity College, MS B. 10. 12	Lincoln art. 38
Trinity College, MS O. 3. 58 (1230)	London art. 12
Trinity College, MS R. 3. 8	London art. 1
Trinity College, MS R. 3. 21 (601)	London arts. 11, 14, 24
Trinity College, MS R. 14. 52	Lincoln art. 3
Cambridge MA	
Harvard University Houghton Library, MS Eng. 1031	London art. 4
Chichester	
West Sussex Record Office, Cowfold Churchwarden's Accounts	London art. 29
Dublin	
TCD, MS 155	Lincoln art. 46
Durham	
Cathedral Library, MS Cosin V.i.12	Lincoln art. 53
Cathedral Library, MS Cosin V.iii.8	Lincoln art. 38
Cathedral Library, MS Cosin V.v.8	Lincoln art. 23
Edinburgh	
NLS, Advocates' MS 19. 2. 1 (Auchinleck)	Lincoln arts. 5, 11, London art. 32
NLS, Advocates' MS 19. 3. 1	Lincoln arts. 5, 11
NLS, Deposit 313/3633	London art. 1
NLS, MS 6126	Lincoln art. 80
Royal College of Physicians, Edinburgh MS	London art. 1
University Library, MS 218	London art. 32
Exeter	
Devon Record Office, MS 2507	London art. 6
Göttingen	
University Library, MS Theol. 107	London art. 1
Liverpool	
University Library, MS F.4	Lincoln art. 79
London	
BL, MS Additional 6702	Lincoln art. 19
BL, Additional 22283 (Simeon)	Lincoln art. 76, London art. 31
BL, MS Additional 27592	Lincoln art. 73
BL, MS Additional 27879 (Percy Folio)	Lincoln art. 16
BL, MS Additional 33994	London art. 34
BL, MS Additional 33995	Lincoln art. 40
BL, MS Additional 36983	London art. 1
BL, MS Additional 37787	Lincoln art. 64

College of Arms, MS Arundel 58	London art. 32
Gray's Inn, MS 20	Lincoln art. 11
Lambeth Palace Library, MS 344	London art. 24
Lambeth Palace Library, MS 491	Lincoln art. 20, London art. 6
Lambeth Palace Library, MS 559	Lincoln art. 64
Lambeth Palace Library, MS 560	Lincoln art. 5
Lambeth Palace Library, MS 853	London arts. 29, 30
Longleat House, Wiltshire	
Marquess of Bath, MS 29	Lincoln arts. 60, 74, 75, 76, 81
Manchester	
Chetham's Library, MS 6690	Lincoln art. 76
Montreal	
McGill University Library, MS 142	London art. 1
Naples	
Biblioteca Nazionale, MS XIII. B. 29	Lincoln art. 11
New Haven	
Yale University Beinecke Library, MS 600	Lincoln art. 38
Yale University Beinecke Library, Osborn MSS File, Folder 19558	Lincoln art. 40
New York	
Columbia University Library, MS Plimpton 271	Lincoln art. 76
Pierpont Morgan Library, MS 776	Lincoln art. 3
Oxford	
Balliol College, MS 354	London arts. 12, 24
Bodleian Library, Additional A. 106	London art. 21
Bodleian Library, MS Ashmole 45	Lincoln art. 13
Bodleian Library, MS Ashmole 61	Lincoln arts. 5, 11, 13, London art. 4
Bodleian Library, MS Ashmole 189	Lincoln art. 3
Bodleian Library, MS Ashmole 337	Lincoln art. 19
Bodleian Library, MS Ashmole 342	Lincoln art. 3
Bodleian Library, MS Ashmole 751	Lincoln art. 52
Bodleian Library, MS Ashmole 1386	Lincoln art. 19
Bodleian Library, MS Bodley 576	Lincoln art. 73
Bodleian Library, MS Douce 228	London art. 32
Bodleian Library, MS Douce 261	Lincoln arts. 11, 16
Bodleian Library, MS Douce 324	Lincoln art. 20
Bodleian Library, MS Eng. poet. a. 1 (Vernon)	Lincoln arts. 44, 61, 64, 76, London art. 31
Bodleian Library, MS Eng. poet. e. 1	London art. 12

2

Robert Thornton: Gentleman, Reader and Scribe*

George R. Keiser

> The volume appears to have been a family book, and to have belonged to several persons of the name of Thornton.... This compilation must have formed a cyclopedia of amusement and instruction, when books were few and scarce.
>
> Edward James Willson[1]

The establishment of a private chapel in 1397 by the Thornton family of the manor of East Newton in Ryedale, Yorkshire, initiated a series of events that likely culminated in the copying of the two important and well-known Middle English miscellanies, Lincoln Cathedral Library, MS 91, and London, BL, MS Additional 31042. Piety and prosperity are the obvious explanations for the desire to establish this chapel. Apparently, the Thornton family had attained a sufficient level of prosperity to afford the costs of establishing and furnishing a chapel, where they could engage in celebration of formal liturgical exercises and also participate in exercises of individual piety. Such private chapels were common at the time, partly in response to a burgeoning desire among the laity to participate in private devotional exercises that were adapted from monastic spirituality.[2]

---

*   I would like to express my gratitude to Vincent Gillespie and the late Jeremy Griffiths for an invitation in 1995 to present the earliest version of this paper at their series, University of Oxford Seminars on Authors, Scribes and Owners of Middle English Texts, and for their support and encouragement to develop the paper. I am also indebted to Ralph Hanna for reading a very late version of the paper and making astute and useful recommendations for improvement.

[1] Letter to Thomas Frognall Dibdin, 22 May 1837 (San Marino, Huntington Library, MS DI 626).

[2] N. Orme, 'Education and Recreation', and C. Carpenter, 'Religion', in *Gentry Culture in Late-Medieval England*, ed. R. Radulescu and A. Truelove (Manchester, 2005), pp. 63–83 (p. 68), and pp. 134–50 (p. 138), respectively; C. Richmond, 'Religion and the Fifteenth-Century Gentleman', in *The Church, Politics and Patronage in the Fifteenth Century*, ed. B. Dobson (Gloucester, 1984), pp. 193–208 (p. 199); and G. Harriss, *Shaping the Nation: England 1360–1461* (Oxford, 2005), pp. 162–3.

With only the formulaic licence for the East Newton chapel and the testamentary evidence of Alice Thornton that it 'was long since demolished' in the seventeenth century, we have almost no basis for speculation about its original cost.[3] It would surely not have been on the scale of the chapels built by the Multons of Frampton and their associates, but perhaps it was comparable to the modest chapel built by Humphrey Newton in the early sixteenth century.[4] Such a chapel would certainly require furniture and, likely, vestments and sacred vessels, and probably wood or stone statues of the Virgin and the Christ and favourite saints. It is not impossible that the Thornton chapel had a wall painting, for the very beautiful wall paintings preserved at nearby Pickering church suggest that these were popular and may have been frequent in the churches of Ryedale.[5] Imitating that style of decoration in a private chapel would seem a real possibility.

The chapel at East Newton was not only a sign of the family's prosperity and piety, but a means to preserve them, for the chapel would have brought into the household, at least for temporary periods, a clergyman, perhaps a chantry priest from a nearby monastic institution, with some responsibility for the education of the young Robert Thornton. About twenty years prior to the establishment of the chapel, another Robert Thornton, likely the scribe's grandfather, was a plaintiff in a case involving possession of the nearby manor of Great Edston. Though the lawsuit was not successful, later documents show that the Thornton family maintained an active interest in that manor, for the scribe was in the witness list of several documents concerning Great Edston and the neighbouring manor of Northolm.[6] As well as literacy, some knowledge of land law would have been almost essential for the heir to the family manor and the landholding interests of the family elsewhere in Yorkshire. The advice

[3] University of York Borthwick Institute for Archives, Archbishop's Register 5a, fol. 235v; *The Autobiography of Mrs. Alice Thornton of East Newton, Co. York*, ed. C. Jackson, Surtees Society Publications 62 (Durham, 1875), p. 884. See also *The Autobiographies and Letters of Thomas Comber*, ed. C. E. Whiting, Surtees Society Publications 156 (Durham, 1946), xxii: 'The old chapel, which Mrs. Thornton wished to restore, has disappeared, unless a small building standing in an adjacent field, still known as the Chapel Garth, may represent some portion of it.'

[4] P. Coss, *The Foundations of Gentry Life: The Multons of Frampton and Their World* (Oxford, 2010), pp. 32, 35; and D. Youngs, *Humphrey Newton (1466–1536): An Early Tudor Gentleman* (Woodbridge, 2008), pp. 128–33.

[5] See 'Pickering Church', at Britain Express, http://www.britainexpress.com/attractions.htm?attraction=4600, and 'Pickering Parish Church', http://www.pickeringchurch.com/wall paintings.html. Of interest is a wall painting of Saint Christopher that recalls the *vita* in the Lincoln manuscript.

[6] For details about this and the public record of Thornton's activities, see G. R. Keiser, 'Lincoln Cathedral Library MS. 91: The Life and Milieu of the Scribe', *Studies in Bibliography* 32 (1979), 158–79 (pp. 161–2), and 'More Light on the Life and Milieu of Robert Thornton', *Studies in Bibliography* 36 (1983), 111–19 (pp. 112–13).

of Agnes Paston and Peter Idley to their sons is only the most obvious evidence of the desire for legal knowledge among the English gentry.[7] A monastic priest with access to formularies and knowledge of land interests would have been an ideal tutor for the young heir.

The two manuscripts Robert Thornton compiled offer abundant evidence that his education had been shaped, directly or indirectly, by a monastic sensibility. Almost every work in the devotional collection in the Lincoln manuscript has its roots in monastic spirituality, most obviously Walter Hilton's *Mixed Life* (art. 76), the *Holy Boke Gratia Dei* (art. 80) and the *Abbey of the Holy Ghost* (art. 85). A little noticed fragment, *Lyarde* (art. 18), amid the romance collection in the first part of the Lincoln manuscript, is an antifraternal satire obviously of monastic origin. The opening text in the London manuscript is *Cursor Mundi* (art. 1), which Sarah M. Horrall identified as a work of monastic origin. The most recent editors of the *Siege of Jerusalem* (London, art. 6) identify it as also of monastic origin, probably Bolton Abbey in Craven, West Yorkshire.[8]

Owing to literary history and literary tastes, the Thornton manuscripts were long looked upon primarily as a source for Middle English romances, and they have been plundered for editions over a very long time. When the great nineteenth-century antiquarians – Frederic Madden, Thomas Frognall Dibdin and James Orchard Halliwell – introduced the Lincoln manuscript to students of later medieval England, they held it in esteem for the fact that it preserved numerous small treasures of Middle English literature.[9] In a limited way, they recognized its value as a document of later medieval culture, a repository of many fascinating puzzles, whose solutions might lead toward a more thorough understanding of its age. Understandably, though, given contemporary tastes and interests, they lavished far more attention on its romances than on the collection of devotional works or the medical book at the end of the volume.

---

[7] *Paston Letters and Papers of the Fifteenth Century*, ed. N. Davis, R. Beadle and C. Richmond, 3 vols., EETS SS 20, 21, 22 (Oxford, 2004–5), I, 27; *Peter Idley's Instructions to His Son*, ed. C. D'Evelyn (Boston, 1935), p. 83. See also N. Orme, *From Childhood to Chivalry* (London, 1984), pp. 77–9; Coss, *The Foundations of Gentry Life*, pp. 209–29; and Youngs, *Humphrey Newton*, pp. 41–68, for informed discussions of the gentry's need for legal knowledge.

[8] S. M. Horrall, '"For the cummun at understand": *Cursor Mundi* and Its Background', and G. R. Keiser, '"Noght how lang man lifs; but how wele": The Laity and the Ladder of Perfection', in *De Cella in Saeculum: Religious and Secular Life and Devotion in Late Medieval England*, ed. M. G. Sargent (Cambridge, 1989), pp. 97–107, 145–59; J. Reakes, 'Lyarde and Goliard', *Neuphilologische Mitteilungen* 83 (1982), 34–41; N. R. Rice, 'Spiritual Ambition and the Translation of the Cloister: The *Abbey* and *Charter of the Holy Ghost*', *Viator* 33 (2002), 222–60; N. R. Rice, *Lay Piety and Religious Discipline in Middle English Literature* (Cambridge, 2008); and *The Siege of Jerusalem*, ed. R. Hanna and D. Lawton, EETS OS 320 (Oxford, 2003), pp. liv–lv.

[9] G. R. Keiser, 'The Nineteenth-Century Discovery of the Thornton Manuscript', *Papers of the Bibliographical Society of America* 77 (1983), 167–90.

So it continued until well into the twentieth century, with one exception. The devotional book received significant attention from students of Richard Rolle, who recognized its importance as a witness to the circulation of his works in his native county.[10] Meanwhile, in the late nineteenth century the British Museum acquired the second Thornton manuscript, which was also mined for editions of its romances, though until recently these did not receive the critical attention accorded to the romances preserved in the Lincoln volume, with its wealth of Arthuriana. Indeed, some have viewed the London miscellany as a volume of much less consequence than the Lincoln volume.

In 1983 I expressed a hope that the facsimile of Lincoln would enable students to 'respond to the challenge of a manuscript which, taken as a whole, incorporates a vision of human experience that has yet to be fully explored'.[11] A substantial body of admirable work by various scholars has moved that hope closer to achievement, not only in regard to the Lincoln manuscript, but to the London manuscript as well. In the present chapter I hope to move toward a greater fulfilment of my hope. To do so, I will focus first on what we know about Robert Thornton in his historical context. I want, further, to consider his scribal activities in detail, with special attention to his experiments with graphic forms in the course of his copying and to what they tell us about him as a compiler. From that information we can, I believe, reach a better understanding of his intentions and how these evolved as he undertook the selection, copying and arrangement of texts for his two manuscripts.

Robert Thornton first came to public attention with a notice in *Bibliotheca Britannico-Hibernica* (London, 1748). The learned antiquarian Thomas Tanner, who had apparently visited the Lincoln Cathedral Library and examined the manuscript, attributed the alliterative *Morte Arthure* (art. 8) and a verse life of Saint Christopher (art. 14) to Thornton. In the years after 1748, information about Robert Thornton accumulated slowly and not always deliberately. In the 1830s Edward James Willson, a Lincolnshire architect and antiquary, was the first to recognize that the miscellany was a book compiled for a specific medieval household and worthy of serious attention in that respect. Willson, putting aside common assumptions about a clerical compiler, proposed that Thornton was a member of the Yorkshire gentry, and soon afterward Madden confirmed and improved slightly upon that identification.[12] And so the matter rested for about a century, except for a few incidental notices in collections of Yorkshire wills published by the Surtees Society. It was an era in which histo-

---

[10] *English Prose Treatises of Richard Rolle de Hampole*, ed. G. G. Perry, EETS OS 20 (London, 1886, rev. 1921); *Yorkshire Writers: Richard Rolle and His Followers*, ed. C. Horstmann, 2 vols. (London, 1895–6; repr. Cambridge, 1999), I, 184–337, 363–411.

[11] Keiser, 'The Nineteenth-Century Discovery', p. 190.

[12] Ibid., pp. 168–9, 180–1.

rians assumed that great men make history, and they were unlikely to look closely at a man of such relatively low social standing as Robert Thornton, especially one from rural Yorkshire.

In 1938 the Early English Text Society published an edition of the medical treatise found at the end of the Lincoln volume, the *Liber de Diversis Medicinis* (art. 99). Its editor, Margaret Sinclair Ogden, included previously unknown information about Robert Thornton in her introduction, providing the first real glimpse into the life of the scribe and his worldly activities.[13] This information had been collected from published calendars of Public Record Office documents by Virginia Everett Leland for a 1935 term paper presented to Edith Rickert at the University of Chicago during the days of the Chaucer factory there, where scribes and their identities and social networks were receiving serious attention, perhaps more than at any time in the past. My own work, in essays published in 1978 and 1983, built upon the work of Leland. Inspired by the new movements in historical studies, particularly the Annales School, I searched national and local archives for documentary evidence concerning Robert Thornton and other bookowners in fifteenth-century Yorkshire. In the time since that work appeared, more extensive research permits us a fuller view of book-owning among Yorkshire residents.[14]

Though still scant, the documentary evidence reveals that Robert Thornton was a prosperous member of the minor gentry, who had connections with others among whom he must have been known as a man of probity and strength of character, as well as a man of bookish piety. His continuing involvement with other Ryedale gentry of greater social standing than he, for example, Richard Pickering and William Holthorp, seems telling. Pickering was descended from a knightly family that had its origins in the thirteenth century. He held several important Yorkshire offices, and he was clearly Thornton's superior. Yet the families had close relations, for Pickering made bequests to Robert Thornton and his siblings and entrusted him to serve as an executor of his will in 1441. Holthorp was a distant cousin and the grandson of Joan de Holme, against whom Thornton's grandfather brought suit concerning possession of Great Edston in 1376. His sister Katherine married John Stillington of Nether Acaster and was the mother of Robert Stillington, the powerful archbishop of Bath and

---

[13]   'The *Liber de Diversis Medicinis*', ed. M. S. Ogden, EETS OS 207 (London 1938, rev. 1969), pp. x–xv.

[14]   Keiser, 'Lincoln Cathedral Library MS. 91', and 'More Light'. For further information on Yorkshire books and education, see especially J. A. H. Moran, *The Growth of English Schooling, 1340–1548: Learning, Literacy, and Laicization in Pre-Reformation York Diocese* (Princeton, 1985); P. J. P. Goldberg, 'Lay Book Ownership in Late Medieval York: The Evidence of Wills', *The Library* 6th ser. 16 (1994), 181–9; and J. B. Friedman, *Northern English Books, Owners, and Makers in the Late Middle Ages* (Syracuse, 1995).

Wells.[15] While we know little about daily life in fifteenth-century Yorkshire, we can assume that these men were well known to each other and had regular contact. Movement within Yorkshire and, more specifically, Ryedale may have been less difficult than we would imagine, for commerce and trade were of such dimensions as to require adequate roadways to move commodities.[16] Through such contacts, Thornton must have acquired the repute that led to his appointment as collector of taxes in 1453. While this appointment is less important than the numerous commissions on which Richard Pickering served, it does indicate that Thornton was a man of serious standing among his fellow gentry.

That Robert Thornton maintained and perhaps even improved the prosperity of his forebears we can infer from his involvement with land transactions throughout the Ryedale wapentake and perhaps beyond. If, as has long been supposed, one of the effigies in Trinity church at Stonegrave is that of his father, it signals the prosperity and the piety of the family.[17] Nigel Saul points out that burial 'monuments were an essential weapon in the battle for salvation of the soul', encouraging prayerful assistance from observers. In addition, as Deborah Youngs has noted, such monuments also 'functioned to proclaim a family's past, present and future importance to the local area'.[18] Lamentably, we do not have the last testament of Robert Thornton, yet the 1487 will of his son 'William Thorneton of Yorke, gentilman', with its generous bequests to churches, suggests that with wealth he received from his father he maintained a prosperous life in the city of York. Though he designated that he be buried before the altar of Saint Katherine in St Cuthbert in York and bequeathed 'iij s iiij d' to the church, he also bequeathed 'vj s viiij d' for 'Reparacioun of the yle in Steyngrave kyrk'. That and a bequest of 'my newe messe buke to the maner of Newton in Rydale to serve in Seynt Peter chapell to the world end' tell us that among the scribe's legacies to his son were piety and pride in the family. The latter bequest also indicates that the chapel at East Newton was still in service and Mass was still being read there on occasion. The 'newe messe buke' may have joined the two manuscripts we know and still others in the chapel, which

---

[15] Keiser, 'More Light', pp. 112–15.

[16] J. McDonnell, ed., *A History of Helmsley, Rievaulx, and District* (York, 1963), pp. 69–80; J. H. Rushton, 'Life in Ryedale in the 14th Century', 2 parts, *Ryedale Historian* 8 (1976), 19–29, and 9 (1978), 29–51.

[17] On this question, see the afterword by R. Field and D. Smith in the present volume.

[18] N. Saul, *English Church Monuments in the Middle Ages: History and Representation* (Oxford, 2009), p. 120; Youngs, *Humphrey Newton*, p. 140. Concerning the costs of a private tomb, see Richmond, 'Religion', pp. 195–6; and M. G. A. Vale, *Piety, Charity and Literacy Among the Yorkshire Gentry, 1370–1480*, Borthwick Papers 50 (York, 1976), pp. 9–10.

remained a place of importance for the family, particularly, one imagines, when the family was recusant in the sixteenth century.[19]

Clearly, Robert Thornton was a man of confirmed belief and confidence, whose influence on his family continued well after his death. The Lincoln manuscript was an important possession of the family and extended that influence, as we can see from the autographs of later descendants in margins of that book. Arthur Owen, in his introduction to the facsimile of the manuscript, called attention to early repairs made to it and the implications of them:

> some leaves were formerly repaired with needle and thread, a common medieval practice with vellum leaves but surprising to find in a paper manuscript. The old sewing holes remain to show where tears were carefully mended, e.g., ff. 23, 42, 154–9.… Probably the sewing was done when the manuscript was still in the Thornton family and regularly read and, by implication, cherished enough for such tears to be made good.[20]

The extensive use of the manuscript and the concern for its preservation may be due in part, as Phillipa Hardman has suggested, to its use for the instruction of generations of Thornton children.[21]

To understand more about how Robert Thornton successfully extended his influence through both his books, we need to consider what we can discover about his copying and compiling of texts, for that work manifests a sense of confidence and purpose. To demonstrate, I want to begin with his handling of the texts and what that tells us about his attention to the needs of readers of the books. This subject has led his editors to draw different and sometimes

---

[19] Keiser, 'More Light', p. 112, n. 3. For a full transcript of the will, see *The Autobiography of Mrs. Alice Thornton*, ed. Jackson, pp. 324–25. William entered a birth notice for his son, Robert, in the Lincoln manuscript, fol. 49v. Knowledge of the history of the Thornton family has long been dependent on a pedigree pasted into this edition, though its accuracy is uncertain. Another pedigree, in two early modern hands, appears in London, BL, MS Harley 6070, fol. 35r; this is a volume of patrilineal pedigrees for Yorkshire families with heraldic insignia. Recently, a pedigree of the family has appeared on the internet: M. E. Lohman, 'Thornton', freepages.genealogy. rootsweb.ancestry.com/~celticlady/thornton/England_Thorntons.pdf. It is heavily documented with references to www.ancestry.com. Its dependability is also uncertain. The earlier pedigree includes information about Robert Thornton's second wife, Isabel, who turns up in a newly discovered document: M. Johnston, 'A New Document Relating to the Life of Robert Thornton', *The Library*, 7th ser. 8 (2007), 304–13. The internet document contains no reference to Isabel. Regarding the recusant Thorntons, see H. Aveling, *Northern Catholics: The Catholic Recusants of the North Riding of Yorkshire, 1558–1790* (London, 1966), pp. 104, 189, 285.

[20] A. E. B. Owen, 'Collation and Handwriting', in *The Thornton MS*, intro. Brewer and Owen (London, 1975), pp. xiii–xvi (p. xv).

[21] P. Hardman, 'Domestic Learning and Teaching: Investigating Evidence for the Role of "Household Miscellanies" in Late-Medieval England', in *Women and Writing c. 1340–1650*, ed. A. Lawrence-Mathers and P. Hardman (York, 2010), pp. 15–33 (pp. 21–8).

conflicting judgements. Inevitably, an editor must judge whether or not a copy is a scrupulous attempt to produce a text as close as possible to the exemplar(s) used by the scribe and, beyond that, to an ideal text that issued from the author. In reaching that judgement, an editor must attend to a scribe's habits of copying and presentation of a text. In this regard, Robert Thornton provides interesting challenges.

Mary Hamel was the first editor to attempt a definitive statement about Thornton's scribal practices, in the wake of having confronted them while preparing her 1984 edition of the alliterative *Morte Arthure* from the unique text in the Lincoln manuscript. Her analysis of scribal self-correction in that text led her to present a picture of a generally conscientious scribe who memorized an alliterative long line and transcribed it 'with immediate corrections, occasionally checking the exemplar in the process, and then briefly rechecking it before going on to the next line'. Acknowledging that 'there are too many errors remaining in the text, and [that] Thornton undoubtedly committed his share of these', Hamel conceded that 'the scribe's attention to correctness in transcription was not always at a high pitch'. Still, she concludes: 'dialect aside', Thornton 'exhibited a remarkable fidelity to his texts'.[22] In sharp contrast, when Frances McSparran prepared her 1986 edition of Thornton's *Octavian*, she saw 'two different tendencies: on the one hand, casual carelessness and garrulity, on the other a zeal to clarify things by identifying speakers'. Nevertheless, McSparran observed that Thornton frequently preserves original readings where the Cambridge, CUL, MS Ff. 2. 38 copy and the Wynkyn de Worde print, or their common exemplar, do not. The result is a text 'stylistically idiosyncratic and sometimes clumsy, but in its preservation (and augmentation) of source detail it offers a text which is livelier and more colourful'.[23] Other editors of Thornton texts have called attention to scribal interventions in *Sir Degrevant* (Lincoln art. 15), *Sir Eglamour of Artois* (Lincoln art. 16) and *Awntyrs off Arthure* (Lincoln art. 20), though like McSparran, they find much to praise in Thornton's copies.[24]

J. I. Carlson has compared passages of one hundred lines from near the beginnings and endings of *Octavian* (Lincoln art. 10), *Awntyrs off Arthure*, *Sir Degrevant*, *Siege of Jerusalem* (London art. 6), *Richard Coer de Lyon* (London art.

---

[22] M. Hamel, 'Scribal Self-Corrections in the Thornton *Morte Arthure*', *Studies in Bibliography* 36 (1983), 119–37 (pp. 122, 133). See also *Morte Arthure: A Critical Edition*, ed. M. Hamel, Garland Medieval Texts 9 (New York, 1984), pp. 76–8. See also the chapter by Hanna and Turville-Petre in the present volume.

[23] *Octavian*, ed. F. McSparran, EETS OS 289 (London, 1986), pp. 16–17.

[24] *Sir Eglamour of Artois*, ed. F. E. Richardson, EETS OS 256 (London, 1965), pp. xiv–xvii; *The Romance of Sir Degrevant*, ed. L. F. Casson, EETS OS 221 (London, 1949), pp. xvi–xxxi; and *The Awntyrs off Arthure at the Terne Wathelyne*, ed. R. J. Gates (Philadelphia, 1969), pp. 42–73.

32) and the *Parlement of the Thre Ages* (London art. 34) in Thornton's text and those preserved in other manuscripts. From that, he concluded that five forms of scribal intervention are characteristic of Thornton's copying: dialogue attributions, unnecessary conjunctions and conjunctive adverbs to connect syntactic elements, doubling of negative modifiers, a profusion of adverbial intensifiers and 'regular tinkering with both word order and the degree of explicitness in his identification of sentence elements'.[25] While Carlson's demonstration is very persuasive, one must recognize that such interventions are not exclusive to Thornton, as Robert Gates showed in his 1969 edition of *Awntyrs*. Comparing the four texts of that work, Gates found that scribal intervention was common and purposeful: 'The most consistent tendency of scribal substitution,' he observed, 'is the attempt to make the text more explicit'.[26]

Carlson used passages from *Awntyrs* and *Parlement* to illustrate Thornton's propensity for inserting 'and' at the beginning of lines of verse. In the version of *Degrevant* preserved in Cambridge, CUL, MS Ff. 1. 6, we find similar use of an unnecessary 'and' in numerous places where it does not appear in the parallel passages in Thornton's text (lines 85–6, 114–23, 149–59, 182–91, 226–30, 356–63, 911–27, 1073–81, 1203–05, 1314–32, 1346–7, 1746–7). Still, after conducting my own search for parallels to Thornton's scribal interventions in related texts, I am convinced that relative to other scribes, Thornton uses these interventions with greater freedom. Additionally, we find Thornton using them in at least one of the prose devotional works he copied for the Lincoln volume. Unfortunately, because these works have received far less attention than they deserve, only an edition of the *Holy Boke Gratia Dei* (art. 80) by Sr Mary Luke Arntz permits us to search for these interventions. In the first twenty pages of the edition, we find thirteen apparent insertions of 'and' that do not occur in the parallel passages in other manuscripts (1.11, 2.18, 4.21, 5.1, 6.10, 7.6, 8.3, 10.11, 11.8, 12.7, 16.14, 18.22, 19.14) and four examples of the doubling of negatives (5.5, 7.19, 9.1,12.5). Most surprising, given the nature of the work, we find seven instances of unnecessary dialogue attributions inserted into the text (3.6, 3.13, 9.12, 15.1, 17.13, 20.1, 20.6).[27]

To explain Thornton's interventions, Carlson proceeds beyond Gates's suggestion that scribes in general 'attempt to make the text more explicit' and considers the specific purpose that Thornton had in mind when copying his texts:

[25] J. I. Carlson, 'Scribal Intentions in Medieval Romance: A Case Study of Robert Thornton', *Studies in Bibliography* 58 (2007–8), 49–71 (at p. 61).

[26] *The Awntyrs off Arthure*, ed. Gates, p. 56.

[27] *Richard Rolle and þe Holy Boke Gratia Dei: An Edition with Commentary*, ed. M. L. Arntz, S.N.D. (Salzburg, 1981).

> If one remains open to the possibility that Thornton ... intended either to read his texts aloud for friends and family or have them read by another, his copying style begins to make better sense. ... [E]mphasis on syntactic structure and semantic meaning stems from the scribe's belief that his audience would misunderstand more subtle grammatical constructions better suited to the eye than the ear when listening to the tales presented aloud.[28]

Given that oral delivery was altogether common in an age when silent reading was still relatively uncommon, Thornton certainly would have wished to ensure that the texts he copied, when read aloud for the entertainment, education and edification of his family, would more easily provide necessary guidance and instruction for their actions in this world and their preparation for the world beyond.

The same confidence and sense of purpose implied in Robert Thornton's interventions in the texts he copied are apparent when we consider the palaeographical and codicological features of his manuscripts and what they reveal about how Thornton compiled them. Specifically, I will show how in the course of his scribal activities Thornton experimented with letter-forms and adopted some into his permanent repertoire. From this information, sometimes in conjunction with watermark evidence, we can learn more about the order in which Thornton copied works and discover why he placed them in relation to each other. We can also see that as he worked, Thornton developed a sense of a larger design for his books. In neither the Lincoln nor the London manuscripts can we suppose that the design was a rigid one that did not allow for flexibility in choosing the particular texts he copied. Because it is unlikely that Thornton had a full set of exemplars before him as he copied texts for his books or that he always knew far in advance what might be available, his design must have been evolving as he carried out his compilation.

In 1962 Angus McIntosh published an influential study of dialects in the Lincoln manuscript, showing that the alliterative *Morte Arthure* and the *Privity of the Passion* (Lincoln art. 38) were taken from exemplars copied by the same scribe.[29] The *Morte* is the initial piece in a series of verse works, mostly romances, while the *Privity* is the initial piece in a collection of prose and verse devotional works. From this evidence I inferred, in a 1979 study, that Thornton copied these two texts consecutively and prior to copying any other works. Proceeding from that inference, I moved on to two larger speculations: first, that these were the works with which Thornton began his scribal activities and, second, that his decision not to begin the *Privity* at the foot of the page

---

[28] Carlson, 'Scribal Intentions', p. 65.

[29] A. McIntosh, 'The Textual Transmission of the Alliterative *Morte Arthure*', in *English and Medieval Studies Presented to J. R. R. Tolkien on the Occasion of His Seventieth Birthday*, ed. N. Davis and C. L. Wrenn (London, 1962), pp. 231–40.

containing the last lines of the *Morte* indicates that from the earliest point in his process of compilation he intended to create two separate and autonomous books, or booklets, such as we now have in the first and second parts of the Lincoln volume, a book of romances and a devotional book.[30] Over the years these speculations have almost hardened into fact, particularly with the aid of watermark evidence presented in separate publications by Horrall, John J. Thompson and Ralph Hanna.[31]

The alliterative *Morte* fills almost all of three quires, consisting in turn of sixteen, eighteen and sixteen leaves. The first quire and the outer ten leaves of the second are made up of paper containing a single watermark. The inner four leaves of the second quire and all of the third consist of paper containing a different watermark, which also appears in the paper that makes up the first two quires, of twenty-two and twenty-four leaves, of the devotional book, beginning with the leaves onto which Thornton copied the *Privity*. The *Morte* ends about a third of the way down fol. 98v, and the *Privity* ends about halfway down fol. 189r. At the ends of both these works appears a hand other than Thornton's. On fol. 98v this hand writes 'Here endes Morte Arthure writen by Robert of Thornton' (see Figure 1). On fol. 189r, at the end of the *Privity*, this hand writes everything else on the page – an explicit for the *Privity*, a scrap of verse, a rubric for the following work, William of Nassington's *Tractatus de Trinitate*, and its opening lines (see Figure 2). It is notable that this hand, which occurs nowhere else in either Thornton manuscript, appears at the close of the first two works he copied, on partially filled leaves, for which Thornton seems to have had no clear plans.[32] In each case, Thornton had drawn the margins for the rest

[30]   Keiser, 'Lincoln Cathedral Library MS. 91', pp. 177–9.

[31]   S. M. Horrall, 'The Watermarks of the Thornton Manuscripts', *Notes and Queries* n.s. 27 (1980), 385–86; Thompson, *London Thornton MS*; and R. Hanna, 'The Growth of Robert Thornton's Books', *Studies in Bibliography* 40 (1986), 51–61. While these are fine studies by very reputable scholars, the time may be at hand for a reconsideration of their findings, especially with the on-line availability of the *Digital Publication of the 'Piccard' Collection of Watermarks*, German Research Foundation,http:// www.landesarchiv-bw.de/web/44577.

[32]   L. Olson, 'Romancing the Book: Manuscripts for "Euerich Inglische"', in K. Kerby-Fulton, M. Hilmo and L. Olson, *Opening Up Middle English Manuscripts: Literary and Visual Approaches* (Ithaca NY, 2012), pp. 95–151, speculated that these may be 'the work of a different hand' (p. 123). Any suggestion that these represent an attempt on Thornton's part to write in another script seems untenable. Thornton undertakes experiments with writing forms, as we see in the remainder of this paper, slowly, haltingly, and sometimes uncertainly, with regular reversions to original forms. The hand on fols. 98v and 189r is practised and experienced. The appearance of still another hand in corrections on fols. 58r and 62v of the alliterative *Morte*, noted by Hamel, 'Scribal Self-Corrections', p. 126, and described by her as a hand 'more carefully formed with letters more uniform in size, and with book rather than cursive *e*', may be yet another indication that Thornton was copying the work in a communal setting. This would fit with an observation by K. L. Scott that the illustrations of the alliterative *Morte* were the work of a 'pen flourisher

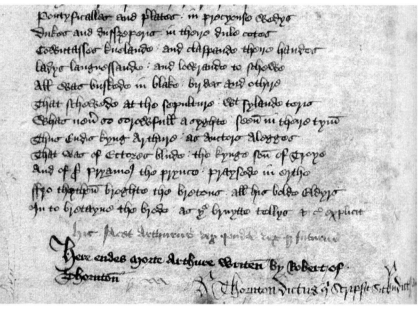

Figure 1. Lincoln Cathedral Library, MS 91, fol. 98v (end of the alliterative *Morte Arthure*, 2nd hand)

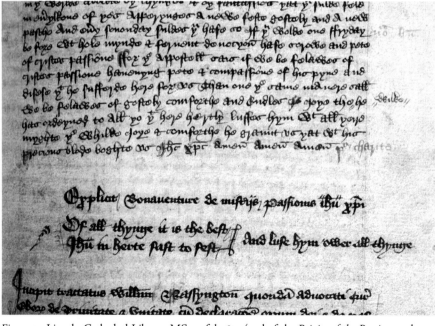

Figure 2. Lincoln Cathedral Library, MS 91, fol. 189r (end of the *Privity of the Passion*, 2nd hand)

of the quire, creating a writing area that was appropriate to the works he had completed, but inadequate for the works that he would eventually copy into the remaining leaves of each quire. The second scribe recognized the problem at the end of the *Privity* and dealt with it by copying the opening of *Tractatus de Trinitate* (art. 40) with two lines of verse across the writing area in the lower portion of fol. 189r, rather than copying each verse on a new line. Thornton continues this method through the next leaves as he copied the remainder of the Nassington work – a method he never uses again in his books. The second scribe was more experienced than Thornton and was also, I believe, the source of Nassington's verses. Perhaps he also supplied a substantial portion of the writings that follow it in the devotional collection, for Thornton had many of those writings on hand after copying Nassington's work, as we will see when we look at his experiment with one particular letter-form.

But first we must look at the ending of the alliterative *Morte* on fol. 98v and notice the opening of *Octavian* on the lower half of that leaf. In contrast to the alliterative long line of the *Morte*, *Octavian* was composed in tail-rhyme stanzas, aabccbddbeeb, with two four-foot lines followed by a three-foot line as the tail. *Octavian* is thriftily presented in double columns, for these shorter lines do not require the full space needed for the alliterative long line. Because of the complexity of the stanza, Thornton cannot use the method adopted for *Tractatus de Trinitate*, of writing lines across the page. Looking more closely, we see that the second column is crowded into the writing area designated by the margins. The problem is magnified by the fact that in the lower half of fol. 98v, Thornton drew inner margins to separate the columns, which further reduced the space in the writing area and exacerbated the crowding. He continues to struggle with this problem for the remainder of the quire, up to fol. 101v, but he remedies it in the next quire by expanding the writing area from about 125 mm to 158–160 mm. With that, the crowding ends.

Looking still more closely at the beginning of *Octavian*, we find that Thornton is using a new graph, the first and one of the most dramatic changes in his writing – a 2-shaped lower-case 'r' in the position immediately following 'o', which is written rapidly in a single stroke. Throughout the *Morte* Thornton had commonly been using a long 'r' in the position following 'o' almost without exception, as he does in 'auctors' in the fifth line from the ending on fol. 98v. In the line immediately following, we see the origin of the new form in 'Ectores' – a formal version of the 2-shaped 'r' with an angular top and a decorative hook at the bottom. In fact, that form first appears on fol. 53v in the heading for the alliterative *Morte* and then in the opening lines of the work, in 'glorious' in line 1 and

[who] had certainly seen and absorbed 14th-century modes of grotesque decoration' (private correspondence, 3 June 1983).

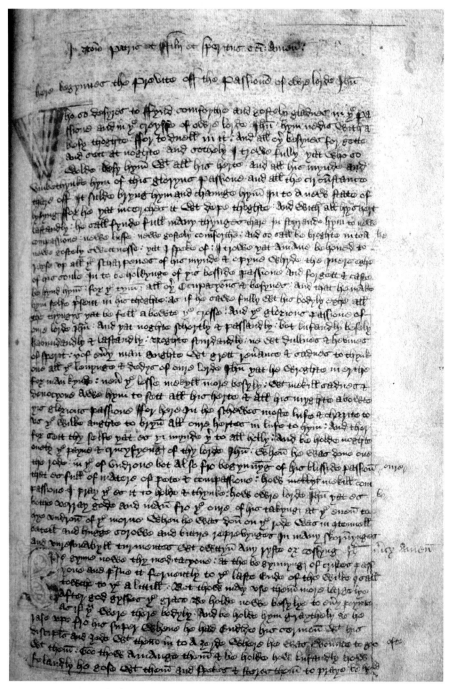

Figure 3. Lincoln Cathedral Library, MS 91, fol. 179r (opening of the *Privity of the Passion*, 2-shaped 'r')

'modyr' in line 2, then again in 'for' in line 12. Throughout the *Morte* Thornton uses the form occasionally with no apparent plan. On fol. 53v it appears in 'Norway' near the top and 'borde' near the bottom, whereas he uses the long 'r' in 'Glamorgan', 'lordys' and 'sorte' in midpage. On fol. 54r it appears four times in 'for' and once in 'or'; elsewhere he uses the long 'r' in 'before', 'wordys', 'for', 'force' and 'more'. While that might lead us to expect greater frequency of this form as he continues to copy, any expectation is thwarted on fol. 54v where he uses it in 'for' near the top of the page and the long 'r' following 'o' in six other words. That he is experimenting seems clear when we find the new form used in 'aftyr' in the first line of fol. 55v, which recalls its use in 'modyr' on fol. 53v. In the last leaves of the *Morte*, we find no reason to suppose that he has a plan to make the new form his standard. It appears three times on fol. 95r ('ffor', 'or', 'cors'), then not again until fol. 97r where it appears in four words ('cadors', '3ondyr', 'walyngfordhe' and 'ffor' – but not in a second use of 'walyngfordhe'), then not again until fol. 98v.

By contrast, when Thornton begins to copy the *Privity*, he seems determined to replace the long 'r' in the position following 'o'. On the first leaf of this text, fol. 179r, we find seven instances of the 2-shaped 'r' and twelve of the long form (see Figure 3); on fol. 179v we find thirteen instances of the 2-shaped 'r' and ten of the long form; on fol. 180r we find twenty-one instances of the 2-shaped 'r' and eight of the long form. It should be noted that the 2-shaped form is used as the final letter in 'fadir' once on fol. 179v, three times in 'fadir' and once in 'aftir' on fol.180r. At this point Thornton is still experimenting. As we come to the end of the *Privity* we see that the new form is displacing the long 'r'. There are nineteen instances of the 2-shaped form and five of the long form on fol. 188v, and eleven instances of the new form and two of the long form in the half-page of writing on fol. 189r, all in the position following 'o'. With the new form taking precedence over the long form, Thornton begins experimenting with ways to write the 2-shaped 'r', for, in the final two uses on fol. 189r, he does not include a hook at the foot of this very angular letter.

Ten leaves later Thornton is still experimenting with the new form. On fol. 208r, in the position following 'o', we find three instances of the long 'r' and eleven of the 2-shaped 'r'. But the shapes of the latter vary. Seven of the eleven have angular tops, but only four of those have a hook at the bottom. The remaining four have rounded tops such as we find in the opening lines of *Octavian*. On fol. 229v we find no long 'r' in the position following 'o' and sixteen instances of the new form, only nine of which have angular tops, with only two of those having hooks at the bottom. On fol. 239r, in all twelve instances, a 2-shaped 'r' follows 'o', and all have rounded tops, just as we find in *Octavian*. So, too, in seventeen instances on fol. 249r. The transition is complete, and the 2-shaped 'r' is standard in positions following 'o'. Among the occurrences of the new form on these two leaves, we find no hooks at the bottom of the graph.

Turning back to *Octavian* and the romances that follow, we find a few anomalies. On fol. 99r, the second page of *Octavian*, there are three appearances of the long 'r', all in 'sorowe'. So, too, on fols. 100r, 101r, 103r and 114r (in *Sir Isumbras*). Also, Thornton consistently uses a long 'r' in the name 'Florent' throughout *Octavian*. In a few instances, he uses the hook at the foot of the 2-shaped 'r' – once on fol. 101r and twice on fol. 120v, in *Earl of Toulouse* (art. 13). Otherwise, through *Octavian* and the successive works in the collection of romances, we find that the 2-shaped 'r' with a rounded top and without a hook is the preferred form. What becomes evident from this is that Thornton returned to the romance book and began copying these texts only after he had copied a good portion of the writings in the devotional book and had established the 2-shaped 'r' as his preferred form.

Whether the romances reached Thornton as a group or as individual works and how this influenced the shape of his romance book are questions to which Thompson and Hanna have offered complementary and fascinating speculative answers based on watermark evidence. Here I wish to offer an alternative explanation based on other evidence. *Octavian* and the four tail-rhyme romances that follow it – *Isumbras*, *Earl of Toulouse*, *Degrevant* and *Eglamour* – may have come to Thornton singly or in the lump. Their associations in other manuscripts indicate that they frequently travelled together and that they appealed to the same set of tastes. When we look at their presentation, we may assume that Thornton acquired *Octavian*, *Isumbras* and *Earl of Toulouse* from the same exemplar, in which all the verses were written one after the other, with no distinction between the tetrameter and trimeter lines, and that he followed that presentation. Thornton then copied a life of Saint Christopher in couplets, and next he copied *Degrevant*, from a different source than that of the three preceding romances. In that exemplar, the tetrameter lines were written one after the other, but with each group of three bracketed, and the tail-rhyme lines written to the right of the brackets. Possibly *Eglamour* came from the same exemplar as the group beginning with *Octavian* or still another with no distinction between the tetrameter and trimeter lines. In any case, the five romances extend from fol. 98v, the twelfth of sixteen leaves in the quire, to fol. 147r, the third leaf of twenty-two in its quire.

Sometime after copying these works, Thornton acquired a text of *Awntyrs off Arthure* and at the same time, or soon afterwards, a text of *Sir Perceval of Gales* (art. 21). *Awntyrs* is written in a complex thirteen-line stanza comprised of nine long alliterative lines, rhyming abababab, and a wheel consisting of four shorter alliterative lines, with two or three stresses, and rhyming dddc. If Thornton had previously copied the alliterative *John Evangelist Hymn* (art. 78; fols. 231r-233v), with its complex fourteen-line stanza, into the devotional book, he failed to see the similarities. In any case, Thornton did not understand the *Awntyrs* stanza at first, but he did recognize that the long alliterative lines could not be accommodated in the remaining seven folios of the first half of the quire, where *Eglamour* ended (fol. 148r), for he had already drawn margins for a double-column writing area on those leaves. Consequently, he moved ahead to fol. 154r, the midpoint of the quire, and drew margins for a narrower, one-column writing area, similar to that which he had used for the *Morte*. (Into the blank leaves, fols. 148r–153v, he would eventually copy *The Wicked Knight and the Friar, Lyarde* and *Thomas of Erceldoune's Prophecy*, arts. 17–19, and confront a serious problem because of line-length in *Lyarde*.)

From fol. 154r to fol. 155v, probably following the design of his exemplar, Thornton copied *Awntyrs* with the four half-lines at the end of the stanza as two whole lines with a bracket setting them apart from the preceding nine lines. At some point, he came to understand the complex stanza and saw that the structure of the last four lines was not unlike that of tail-rhyme romances. Thus on fol. 156r he began to write the first three as separate lines, bracketing them exactly as he had done the lines of *Degrevant*, with the final line to the right of the bracket. Significantly, before he began to write the final twenty-five lines of *Awntyrs* on fol. 161r, he expanded the writing area to accommodate a two-column layout for *Perceval* in the remaining space below those lines. This uncharacteristic foresight suggests that he recalled his difficulties with *Octavian* or, more likely, the problem he had just faced with *Awntyrs*.[33]

In the course of copying the contents of his devotional book, Thornton experimented with still another letter-form. He began using the traditional Caroline 'e' as an alternative to the cursive 'e' that he had used consistently in the *Morte* and the *Privity* and the next works in the devotional collection. It first appears, so far as I can see, near the end of Walter Hilton's *Epistle on the Mixed Life*, on fol. 228v, where it occurs in twelve words, not a large number on a page of prose; it appears only once on fol. 229r. Then he uses it more frequently in the following leaves, fols. 229r–233v, which contain Chapter 44 of Hilton's *Scale of Perfection* (forty-three instances on fol. 230v, for example; art. 77) and the stanzaic hymn to Saint John the Evangelist. Turning back to the romance book, we find that this form of 'e' occurs twelve times in the opening twenty-four lines of *Octavian*. After that, it appears in clusters – for example, eight times on fol. 104r. In the opening two lines of *Awntyrs* on fol. 154r, it appears three times; then nine times in a set of six lines on fol. 156r (with two other occurrences elsewhere on the leaf); then twenty-four times on fol. 156v. From this evidence

---

[33] For an alternative view of the shaping of these materials, see J. J. Thompson, 'The Compiler in Action: Robert Thornton and the "Thornton Romances" in Lincoln Cathedral MS 91', in *Manuscripts and Readers in Fifteenth-Century England: The Literary Implications of Manuscript Study. Essays from the 1981 Conference at the University of York*, ed. D. Pearsall (Cambridge, 1983), pp. 113–24. For an insightful study of scribal presentation of tail-rhyme romances, see R. Purdie, *Anglicising Romance: Tail-Rhyme and Genre in Medieval English Literature* (Cambridge, 2008), pp. 66–90.

it is difficult to detect a larger pattern, except to say that, in works copied after the last pages of Hilton's *Mixed Life*, the Caroline 'e' is available as an alternative form to the cursive 'e', but it certainly never displaces that form.

This form of 'e' does appear with some regularity in the texts of the *Northern Passion* (art. 4) and *Siege of Jerusalem* in the London manuscript, fols. 33r–66r. In these works, the new form of 'r' has displaced the long 'r' in the position following 'o'. As with *Octavian* and several of the romances that follow it, we find the long 'r' in 'sorowe' (e.g., fols. 41r, 61r) and 'thorow' (fol. 61) and a scattering of other words: 'swore' (fol. 50r), 'florence' (fol. 66r), 'torment' (fol. 66r). This evidence, along with other evidence to be presented below, suggests that these works were copied very close in time to the tail-rhyme romances and the portion of the devotional book containing the Hilton texts and the John the Evangelist hymn.

The likelihood that the *Northern Passion* and the *Siege of Jerusalem* were copied and then set aside as Thornton continued to copy works for the Lincoln volume raises a number of intriguing questions, which deserve attention before we proceed to further evidence of graphic changes. First, as to why Thornton did not incorporate them into one of the two parts of the Lincoln collection, the most obvious answer is that they did not fit with his vision of these parts. There is certainly no place for them in the romance collection. As for the devotional collection, the answer is a bit more complicated. First, Thornton already had copied the *Privity*, and a second affective account of the Passion would be superfluous. Second, other works in this collection focus on how the laity should live and behave in this world and are often catechetical, teaching what a good Christian must know about the tenets of the Church. They treat prayer and meditation, describing how these are to be a part of the daily lives of the laity. Also, they teach the importance of grace, constantly reminding the reader that without the help of God's grace, he or she cannot achieve success and happiness in this life and in the afterlife. In contrast, the *Northern Passion* and *Siege* are affective narratives that set out to create a powerful emotional response to the events of the death of Christ, the salvation it brings, and the vengeance for that death upon those who caused it.

One more important point is that at the beginning of the *Northern Passion*, Thornton left a large space empty at the top of the first leaf for an illumination, suggesting that he probably envisioned still another collection of writings in a different vein from those in either the Lincoln romance book or its devotional book, with these as the initial works.[34] From this we may infer that by the

---

[34] P. Hardman, 'Windows into the Text: Unfilled Spaces in Some Fifteenth-Century Manuscripts', *Texts and Their Contexts: Papers from the Early Book Society*, ed. J. Scattergood and J. Boffey (Dublin 1997), pp. 44–70 (p. 59), has commented on the horizontal nature of the space as unusual and suggested that Thornton may have had in mind an image such as that in London,

time he copied these works, Thornton had developed a considerable degree of sophistication about the nature and uses of texts. At least as important, he knew that complementary texts existed and was confident that he could gain access to them. How he was aware of the availability of resources leads to still further speculation. Almost without fail, all discussions of Thornton's activities as a compiler assume that his scribal activities took place at East Newton, where he was surrounded by numerous manuscripts on loan. A more likely possibility that has not been considered is that Thornton visited nearby monastic institutions and other manors, where he became familiar with a large number of resources and where he remained for brief periods to copy texts that were appropriate to his interests, works that addressed matters of urgency and value for the spiritual life of his family. In the course of working with a number of manuscripts, he would have become attentive to graphic forms and methods of presentation.[35]

With that, we may now turn to another major change of letter-form in Thornton's manuscripts, specifically, the thorn.[36] It is difficult to see exactly where Thornton began to move from the graph that is so easy to mistake for a 'y' to the runic form 'þ'. With so much experience in copying and with habits established, Thornton frequently reverts to the older form, which makes tracing his movement rather challenging, to say the least. The change seems to be almost firmly established in Lincoln's fragmentary prose *Alexander* (art. 1) and London's fragmentary *Cursor Mundi* (arts. 1 and 3), the latter attesting to Thornton's desire to create a Spiritual History in the London manuscript. His wavering between the two forms appears in works further along in the London manuscript. In *Sege of Melayne*, fols. 66v–79v (art. 8), the new form is preferred, but with a problem arising regularly in 'other' and 'another', where Thornton reverts to the old form – a problem that persists through this (fols. 67r, 69r, 69v, 70r, 70v, 77r) and several other works.

At about the same time that Thornton begins to use this new thorn, he also introduces a new form of upper-case 'O', a form having a broken left side, with an angle penetrating the inner space of the letter. In the *Sege* it appears for the first time near the bottom of fol. 69r; up to that point he had been using a fully rounded 'O', which was his standard form, with the exception of still another

BL, MS Additional 37049, fol. 45r. He might also have had in mind a horizontal image such as that found in a wall painting at Pickering church: see note 3, above.

[35] Unfortunately, Rievaulx Abbey is not one of the monastic institutions he might have visited. See McDonnell, *History*, p. 118: 'There is no reason to suppose that they offered hospitality on any scale to strangers.'

[36] I first called attention to this change in G. Keiser, 'Review of *Robert Thornton and the London Thornton Manuscript*, by J. J. Thompson', *Envoi* 2 (1990), 155–60. In the intervening years, several scholars have made use of the observation.

form with an outward angle on the left side that he had used very much earlier in his copying. (See, for example, fols. 53r, 55v, 56v, 57r, etc., in Lincoln.) From fol. 69r onwards in London, the broken form prevails, though there are reversions to the rounded form. On 77v, in 'Of ane Olefe', the first is broken, the second rounded; similarly, on 79v, in 'Oure Oste', the first 'O' is a broken form, the second a rounded form. Following a lost leaf that contained the end of the *Sege* is the lyric *O Florum Flos* (art. 9), imperfect at the beginning because of that lost leaf. Throughout this work the use of the new forms of thorn and 'O' are consistent. In *Duke Roland and Sir Otuel of Spain* (art. 10), which follows, Thornton uses the new thorn consistently, even in forms of 'other' (fols. 89v, 90v). The broken 'O' is the preferred form in this text, used in the title on fol. 82r, but on a few occasions he reverts to the rounded form (fols. 84v, 86r).

The short works that follow show considerable variation, with those on fols. 94r–97v using both new forms consistently. In the *Four Leaves of the Truelove* (fols. 98r–101v; art. 21), Thornton uses both forms of the thorn and the 'O' without much consistency. A short prayer at the foot of fol. 101v (art. 22) and the fragmentary paraphrase of Vulgate Psalm 50 (fol. 102r–v; art. 23) use the new thorn consistently along with the broken 'O'. However, in the short works on fols. 103r-110v (arts. 24–26), Thornton uses the old thorn consistently along with the broken 'O', except in the *Rose of Ryse* on fol. 110v where we find both thorns. The first thirteen lines of the imperfect opening of *Three Kings of Cologne* (fols. 111r–119v; art. 27) use the old thorn consistently, but from that point to the end Thornton uses the new form almost consistently, except in forms of 'other'. At the end, in the final stanza, he reverts to the old form of thorn. He uses the broken 'O' with consistency, apparently from the lost beginning, to judge by its appearance on one of small pieces of torn leaf containing that beginning. In the short poems on fols. 120r–122v (arts. 28–29), we find the new thorn and broken 'O' used consistently.

Particularly puzzling is what we find in *Richard Coer de Lyon* (fols. 125r–163v; art. 32) and the *Childhood of Christ* (fols. 163v–168v; art. 33). In the opening of *Richard*, Thornton begins with the new form of thorn and uses it with some consistency. In a few instances, he uses the old thorn in forms of 'other' (fols. 125r, 126r, 128r), though he also uses the new thorn in other instances of 'other' (fols. 128r, 130r–v). Then on fol. 144r, column 1, Thornton begins to waver, shifting from one form of thorn to another, and from fol. 144v onward, he uses the old form consistently, with only an odd occurrence of the new thorn (fol. 147r). Throughout the rest of *Richard*, Thornton uses the broken form of 'O' and a broken form of 'Q' as well (fols. 147r, 150v). And so he continues through the *Childhood*. In the debate poems that follow – the *Parlement of the Thre Ages* and *Wynnere and Wastoure* (arts. 34–35) – Thornton uses the runic thorn almost consistently and the broken 'O' consistently.

Coming to terms with these twists and turns is a challenge. It might be tempting to conclude that *Richard* and the *Childhood* are among the first works Thornton copied after he adopted the new form of thorn. However, the presence of the broken 'O' makes that unlikely. Moreover, given that the two paper stocks used for these works and the two debates do not appear elsewhere in either manuscript, it seems likely that these were the last works Thornton copied, unless more leaves from the end of the London volume have been lost. On this point, the conditions in the manuscript are perplexing, for when Thornton begins to copy the debates on fol. 169r, he writes single lines across the page in order to accommodate the long alliterative line. Then, for no apparent reason, at fol. 181r, he shifts to an awkward and crowded two-column format (see Figure 4). One obvious explanation, as Thompson has observed, is that Thornton was running out of paper and needed to complete as much as possible before doing so. Unfortunately, this likelihood makes the collations for this part of the manuscript proposed by Thompson and Hanna problematic.[37]

One must consider that the stints of copying each work or block of works in the London manuscript were separated by intervals of time, perhaps long intervals of time. And if, as I suggested above, Thornton was copying texts while a guest at a monastic institution or a neighbouring manor, he may have been under pressure from several different directions to accelerate his copying. In such a case, it is rather easy to imagine that after copying a portion of *Richard*, pressed by time or feeling the tedium of this vast undertaking, he simply reverted to the older, more established form of thorn to move the project along. Unfortunately, counting the numbers of each form and establishing frequency in these texts does not seem to be as significant as it was when examining his earlier change of lower-case 'r', where we could easily see that he made a decision to adopt the new form while copying the *Privity of the Passion* and then modified the form in subsequent works. In the case of the thorn, there is no modification of its form. And the wavering within works and among works does not follow any apparent pattern.

Still, we can reach a few useful conclusions. First, as has been argued several times, Thornton added the prose *Alexander* to the Lincoln manuscript (fols. 1r–49r) at a late date, very likely after he had almost completed the collection of romances. In addition to the watermark evidence, mentioned above, we have the fact that when he copied it, Thornton was using the new thorn almost consistently, with a few exceptions, as in 'other' (as on fol. 9r, where the old form appears in three instances). In *Alexander* we find no use of the new 'O'. At about the same time Thornton must have added *Perceval* at the end of the Lincoln romance collection, for he uses the new thorn consistently and the broken 'O' in the second half of the work (fols. 169r–174r) almost consistently.

37 Thompson, *London Thornton MS*, pp. 33–34; and Hanna, 'The Growth', p. 55.

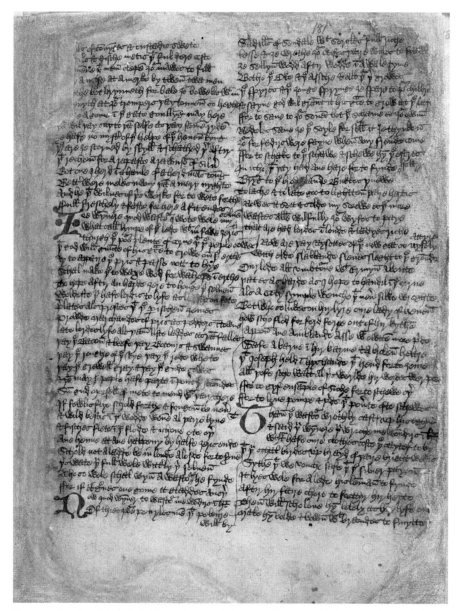

Figure 4. London, BL, MS Additional 31042, fol. 181r (*Wynnere and Wastoure*, abrupt shift in format)

Again watermark evidence is useful, for the greater part of *Perceval* is written on paper with the same watermark as that found in the paper he used for the *Alexander*. It seems important that in *Perceval* Thornton uses the rounded 'O' consistently through fol. 161r until fol. 169v, where he introduces the broken 'O' and then uses it consistently, except for one instance on fol. 175v. It may be that he copied *Perceval* after copying the *Alexander*, but before copying *Cursor Mundi*.

Placing *Alexander* – 'þe lyf of gret Allexander conquerour of all þe worlde' (fol. 49v) – before the alliterative *Morte Arthure* and thus giving the romance collection a new beginning transformed it in many respects. First, this is a work of prose, and English prose romances were an innovation in the middle years of the fifteenth century. Thus, the *Alexander* is a departure from the collection of fourteenth-century verse romances – alliterative and tail-rhyme works – with which he had filled the rest of the book. Second, it is the story of an imperial figure who came from the classical world, not another story of a customary medieval hero. In short, the prose *Alexander* vastly expanded the vision of the collection. Further, as Michael Johnston has observed, placing *Alexander* immediately before the *Morte* 'evinces a literary intelligence, as this pairing allows the haunting statements about fate and death that animate the ... *Alexander* to resonate with King Arthur's similar struggles'.[38]

Concluding the collection with *Perceval* also expands its scope, for the figure of the Fair Unknown is different from the more conventional chivalric heroes of *Octavian*, *Degrevant*, *Isumbras* and *Earl of Toulouse*. While *Perceval* is a serious work, it offers humour and wordplay that are not so often found in those works, thus extending the emotional range of the collection.[39] Finally, it expands the Arthurian collection, adding to the alliterative *Morte Arthure* and *Awntyrs off Arthure* and thus tipping the balance of the book somewhat toward Arthurian works. With a new beginning and ending, the Lincoln romance collection becomes richer and more comprehensive than it had been.

Though enhancing the collection, the addition of these works does not change its central integrity, which is to tell stories, as the author of *Eglamour* puts it, 'Of eldyrs þat by-fore vs were / þat lyved in grete honoure' (fol. 138v; lines 5–6), of exemplary heroes dedicated to achieving honour and upholding justice. Their heroic adventures are filled with a multitude of marvels, their actions are inspired by divine grace, their enemies are usually also the enemies of God, their desire for salvation guides their actions, and they live and act in

---

[38] M. Johnston, 'Robert Thornton and *The Siege of Jerusalem*', *Yearbook of Langland Studies* 23 (2009), 125–62 (p. 137).

[39] This is not to suggest that comedy is lacking in other romances. In her edition of *Octavian*, for example, McSparran calls attention to the author's treatment of the Florent story 'to produce a robust and colourful narrative enlivened by some broad comic strokes' (p. 64).

a world for which there is a divine plan. We read about the adventures of these heroes to satisfy an interest in human character, in the individual's struggle to achieve honour in the face of personal danger and temptation, in the belief in the value of human glory and the joy it brings, and in the reconciliation of that belief with the knowledge that in a world ruled by Fortune all glory fades.[40] The best example of the attempt to counsel both acceptance and rejection of the world is *Awntyrs*. Its author was well read in vernacular literature and attuned to contemporary interests. Thus, he drew upon conventions from purgatorial visions, such as the *Revelation Shown to a Holy Woman* (Lincoln art. 81) that Thornton had copied into his devotional book, to flesh out his reworking of the story of the Trental of Saint Gregory, and he added ominous matter borrowed from the alliterative *Morte*. The author who joined that story with the tournament of Gawain and Galeron achieved a brilliant thematic union that dramatizes the almost irreconcilable desires of his age and of Robert Thornton's. Following hard upon the penitential mode of the first part, with its prophecy of the imminent fall of the Arthurian court, the second part tells an abundantly joyous tale of Gawain's skill in the tournament, thereby restoring the glory of the Round Table that had been tarnished in the first part of *Awntyrs*.

The attempt to teach the reader how to be a part of the world, to partake fully of its activities, and yet to be detached, recognizing its instability and yearning always for the true good and stability of God, preoccupies the writers of the moral and devotional treatises copied by Thornton, and the theme is never far from the attention of the authors of the romances preserved in the Lincoln volume. At the beginnings of most of those romances is an assertion of their moral purpose, such as that in *Eglamour*. In view of the attacks on romances and similar writings by such well-known moralists as Robert Mannyng of Brunne and the author of *Speculum Vitae*, it is not surprising that an assertion of this kind became a convention of the later Middle English romance. The conventionality does not imply insincerity on the part of the authors. Indeed, though we do not know who these authors are, the smell of a cleric's candle often seems detectable, and for such authors the assertion of moral purpose would have been no mere pretext. In the lost opening of Thornton's fragmentary text of the prose *Alexander*, there may have been such a claim, for the work regularly

---

[40] For a similar view, see R. Field, 'Popular Romance: The Material and the Problems', in *A Companion to Medieval Popular Romance*, ed. R L. Radulescu and C. J. Rushton (Cambridge, 2009), pp. 9–30: 'These texts deal with the bases of human existence in society: getting born, surviving childhood, negotiating the family, finding a mate, facing threats, achieving justice and accepting mortality. And they demonstrate the enduring need to find meaning and even comedy in the narratives of human life' (p. 29). Among the earliest observations on the didactic quality of Middle English romances are those of H. Schelp, *Exemplarische Romanzen im Mittelenglischen*, Palaestra 246 (Göttingen, 1967); and D. Mehl, *The Middle English Romances of the Thirteenth and Fourteenth Centuries* (London, 1968).

draws moral conclusions about the action, often delivered by the characters themselves. Thus, we hear from the fallen Darius:

> For if godd hadd ordeyned all thynge₃ esy to man and alwaye withowtten chaungynge sent hym prosperitee, man schulde be lyfted vp so hie in pryde & in vayne glorye, þat he solde no₃te arett all his welefare & his welthe vnto godd, bot till his awenn desert & his awene vertu. And so schulde men gaa fra þaire makare. (fol. 21r)

Alexander recognizes the wisdom of this message, as we see when he tells the Persians, 'I pray ₃ow þat ₃e wirchipe me no₃te as a godd, for sothely I am as ₃e are, a corupteble & a dedly man, and in me þer es na parcell of the godhede' (fol. 23r). After Alexander's great victories, Aristotle reminds him what he owes to God: 'Wharefor thankynge & louynge i₃elde to þe maker of all þis wyde werlde þat swylke victoryes hase grantede vn-to þe' (fol. 46r).

When Degravant puts the old earl to flight, 'He knelid down in þat place / And thanked God of His grace' (lines 365–6). In the alliterative *Morte*, after defeating the Giant of Seynt Mighell Mount, Arthur 'Thankes Gode … of þis grace, and no gome ells; / For it was neuer manns dede, bot myghte of Hym selfen' (lines 1209–10). The failure of Isumbras to remember that all comes from God –

> Bot in his hert a pride was broghte
> Of Goddis werkes gafe he noghte
> His mercys for to nevene (lines 31–3)

brings on sufferings that lead to a discovery of humility in the end: 'Thankede be the heghe kynge of heven / My bale thane has he bett!' (lines 763–4). Unfailingly, the narrator or the hero of *Eglamour* acknowledges the need for God's grace. At the beginning, Eglamour prays that he will win the lady – 'Lorde, ₃e grant me my bone, / On þe rode als þou me boghte' (lines 101–2). At the end, the narrator announces the arrival of the wedding party in Artois, 'Thorow þe myght of God þis fayre naue / Alle in lykynge passed the see' (lines 1336–7), and he comments on the fatal fall of the old earl, 'With God may na man stryue' (line 1347). At the end of *Sir Perceval*, the knight, his mother and his lady

> sett þam down one thaire kne,
> Thanked Godde, alle three,
> That he wolde so appon tham see. (lines 2265–7)[41]

---

[41] *The Romance of Sir Degrevant*, ed. Casson; *Morte Arthure*, ed. Hamel; *Sir Isumbras*, in *The Thornton Romances: The Early English Metrical Romances of Perceval, Isumbras, Eglamour and Degrevant*, ed. J. O. Halliwell, Camden Society 30 (London, 1884), pp. 88–120; *Sir Eglamour of Artois*, ed. Richardson; and *Sir Perceval of Gales*, ed. J. Campion and F. Holthausen (Heidelberg, 1913).

Similar and related messages that 'na gude may I do if ne goddes grace me helpe' (p. 12; fol. 242v) and 'mannes lyfe es lykkynde to the wynde, þat of all thynges es maste vnstabill' (p. 17; fol. 244r) appear throughout the writings that Thornton copied into the Lincoln devotional book, as in these quotations from the *Holy Boke Gratia Dei*.[42] At a pivotal moment in the alliterative *John Evangelist Hymn*, as its recent editor observes, the narrator comments on John's escaping death: 'Grete grace was the gyffen and graunted also / Thurghe His gudnes þat gyfes vs all gyftes of mayne' (lines 141–2).[43]

That the volume ends with the *Liber de Diversis Medicinis* (fols. 280r–314v), whether Thornton intended that or not, fits with the concerns of human weakness and mortality and the hope for at least temporary respite from them, which is evident in the romances and devotional writings. Exactly when Thornton copied *Liber* is not at all clear, though the watermark evidence has led Hanna to suggest that it was copied prior to all the rest of the contents.[44] The evidence of Thornton's use of letter-forms, while far from consistent, would suggest that it was copied at a much later point. The first recipe offers an excellent example of that inconsistency: 'Take vervayne or vetoyn or filles or wormod and make lee þerof and wasche þi heued þerwith thrys in a weke' (fol. 280r). In all three occurrences, the 'r' following 'o' is the final version of the 2-shaped 'r'. The thorn in 'þerof' is Thornton's original form, those in 'þi' and 'þerwith' are the runic form. The final 'e' in 'weke' is the cursive form; all others are the traditional Caroline form. The broken 'O' first appears in this text at a very late point, on fol. 299v. It appears consistently on several pages; then Thornton shifts back and forth between it and the round 'O' in the remaining leaves. This evidence would point to the likelihood that Thornton copied *Liber de Diversis Medicinis* at about the same time as he was copying works that appear in the latter part of the London manuscript.

The same sense of conviction and the imagination that led Thornton to transform the Lincoln romance book by adding the *Alexander* and *Perceval* also led him to place *Cursor Mundi* at the beginning of the London volume, thereby giving shape and focus to what might have been just a collection of assorted texts. All the evidence suggests that he did so at the same time as he concluded shaping the Lincoln romance collection. The watermark found in the leaves containing *Cursor* is the same as that found in the other two works,

---

[42] *Richard Rolle and þe Holy Boke Gratia Dei*, ed. Arntz. For another study of the relation of Middle English romances and devotional writings, see R. Dalrymple, *Language and Piety in Middle English Romance* (Cambridge, 2000).

[43] *Three Alliterative Saints' Hymns*, ed. R. Kennedy, EETS OS 321 (Oxford, 2003); and R. Kennedy, 'The Evangelist in Robert Thornton's Devotional Book: Organizing Principles at the Level of the Quire', *Journal of the Early Book Society* 8 (2005), 71–95.

[44] Hanna, 'The Growth', p. 59.

Perceval and *Alexander*. Further, his letter-forms clearly connect it with them, possibly making it the last work copied among this group. The new thorn is well established, as is the broken 'O'. Thornton's deliberate positioning of *Cursor* to precede the two works copied sometime before, the *Northern Passion* and the *Siege of Jerusalem*, was meant to create what Frances Foster in 1916 described as 'a series of poems on Sacred History'.[45]

The dimensions of that Sacred History are, however, greater than Foster had suggested, for the two Charlemagne romances that follow – the *Sege of Melayne* and *Roland and Otuel* – continue that history. In addition, it seems likely that Thornton copied all of the *Cursor Mundi* preceding the fragment that is now extant. Though the extensive handling of the London volume in recent decades has done much to obscure these marks, a magnifying glass allows one to see, with little doubt, that in the lower right corners of fols. 17r, 18r, 19r and 20r are looped ascenders of the letter 'd' – not in Thornton's hand, but in that of the person responsible for adding catchwords in this portion of the manuscript. (These loops are clearly visible in a microfilm I purchased from the British Library in 1973.) On fols. 8v and 32v are catchwords in *Cursor*, which, in conjunction with watermark evidence, tell us that fols. 9–32 originally constituted a twenty-four-leaf quire. The tops of the ascenders, therefore, appear on what would have been leaves 9–12 of the quire, that is, the last four leaves in the first half-quire as it was originally constituted and the leaves on which we might expect to find signatures. If the folios now numbered 9–32 were Quire d, the leaves now numbered fols. 3–8 would have been the last six leaves of Quire c. The question that arises is whether the missing leaves from Quires a, b and c would have been sufficient to hold the missing first portion of the *Cursor Mundi*, the lines preceding line 10,630 in the modern edition, and the answer would seem to be 'very likely'.

While it is risky to assume any consistency on the part of a scribe who tends to be idiosyncratic, it is worth observing that the two opening quires of Lincoln's prose *Alexander* and the surviving quire of *Cursor* are made up of twenty-four leaves. Therefore, we may suppose that Thornton used twenty-four leaves in Quires a, b and c, and that the London manuscript now lacks sixty-six leaves at its opening. Given that Thornton copied, on average, 147 lines per side of each leaf in fols. 3–32, he would have needed seventy-three leaves to copy the preceding 10,629 lines of *Cursor*, seven more than the sixty-six I suggest

---

[45] *The Northern Passion*, ed. F. A. Foster, 2 vols., EETS OS 145, 147 (London, 1913–16), II, 12–13. The idea that Thornton was compiling a Sacred History has been explored at some length in P. Hardman, 'Reading the Spaces: Pictorial Intentions in the Thornton MSS, Lincoln Cathedral MS 91, and BL MS 31042', *Medium Ævum* 63 (1994), 250–74 (pp. 263–9), and in an abbreviated version of the former, 'Windows into the Text', pp. 59–62; and Johnston, 'Robert Thornton', pp. 143–62.

are missing. The discrepancy is not a serious matter. Without plunging into what Thompson calls the 'complex and protean textual history' of *Cursor*, we can say that Thornton's exemplar may not have had a full set of those 10,629 lines, for the extant manuscripts have serious differences owing, according to Thompson, to an ongoing process of revision by the original author.[46] Further, given what we see of his copying elsewhere, Thornton would not have been reluctant to abbreviate what he found in his exemplar as he copied from it. If, before suffering the depredations of time and fortune, the London manuscript contained a much fuller text of the *Cursor*, the volume would have contained more than 190 leaves, making it almost as large as the Lincoln manuscript.

It is important to know that two other manuscripts offer parallels to Thornton's joining of the *Cursor* with another Passion narrative. In London, BL, MS Cotton Vespasian A. iii, an interpolator scraped one full leaf clean and inserted four new leaves to accommodate the replacement of *Cursor*'s Passion narrative with portions of the Middle English *Southern Passion*. In London, BL, MS Additional 36983, which has several times been invoked for its interesting parallels with the Thornton manuscripts, one of the three (or four) scribes has removed portions of the *Cursor* text and replaced them with a versified translation of the Passion narrative translated from *Meditationes vitae Christi* (the source of Lincoln's *Privity*) and the account of Doomsday from the *Prick of Conscience*.[47] That Thornton was sufficiently audacious to undertake a revision similar to that of experienced and perhaps professional scribes attests to the strong sense of confidence that we have seen elsewhere in his activities as compiler. The rather complicated and even sophisticated process of seamwork with which Thornton joined the two works has been described in careful detail by Thompson.[48] It was further explored by Johnston, who points out that Thornton's moving the *Discourse between Christ and Man* (art. 3) forward from a later position in *Cursor* to make it part of the seamwork 'was an apt choice, as it anticipates the torture that will be inflicted on Christ in greater detail in the *Northern Passion*'.[49]

Whether Thornton or the scribe of his exemplar joined the *Northern Passion* and the *Siege of Jerusalem* is not clear, but the reason for doing so is, for the latter work is meant to show the vengeance wrought for the death of Jesus.[50] The *Northern Passion* is unrelenting in its treatment of the Jews, particularly

---

[46] J. J. Thompson, *The* Cursor Mundi: *Poem, Texts and Contexts*, Medium Ævum Monographs n.s. 19 (Oxford, 1998), p. 22.

[47] Ibid., pp. 75–9; 88–99.

[48] Thompson, *London Thornton MS*, pp. 49–55.

[49] Johnston, 'Robert Thornton', p. 145.

[50] For an argument that this pairing was likely found in Thornton's exemplar, see Johnston's chapter in the present volume.

the version in London. Johnston has shown that Thornton's text contains material not present in other versions, specifically the full story of the Wandering Jew and legend of the Vernicle, as well as other textual variants that shift any blame for the death of Jesus from the Romans to the Jews: 'the Messiah has been violently executed by a people who have wilfully rejected the very Word made flesh'.[51]

A resurgence of interest in the *Siege of Jerusalem* has led to reconsideration of traditional readings of the anti-Jewish expression in the work, which may call into question the success of Thornton's joining of the two works. Much of this revisionism arises from a sympathetic reading of the sufferings of the Jews. One of the best and most influential of these studies is that of Elisa Narin van Court, who points to its likely origin at an Augustinian house, Bolton Abbey in Yorkshire, and argues that that the treatment of Jews in the work reflects a 'dualistic Christological perspective' which 'was developed by Augustine and others into what is called the doctrine of relative toleration'. Specifically, she finds that in his descriptions of the besieged Jews the poet 'complicates his narrative's anti-Judaism' and at times even 'articulates his sympathy for the Jews'. The ultimate effect, Narin van Court concludes, is 'a poem compounded of unequal measures of assertive bigotry and melancholy apologetic'.[52] This attempt to redeem the *Siege* from 'modern reactions of repugnance, brought on by the explicit violence of its anti-Judaism',[53] has influenced two very astute critical responses to the work by Johnston (mentioned above) and Jeremy Citrome.

As the *Northern Passion* and *Siege* are at the heart of the London manuscript, probably were the genesis of it, and as they set the tone for the book, the revisionist readings of *Siege* deserve more than passing comment here. In his detailed examination of these two works and the two Charlemagne romances that follow them, Johnston argues forcefully that in the context of the London manuscript, the grouping of these works creates 'a starkly binaristic worldview, with a stable Christian identity on one side, and a stable, debased, Judaeo-Muslim, non-Christian identity on the other.' If the author of *Siege* intended a nuanced and subtle view of the Jews, Robert Thornton did not recognize that

---

[51] Johnston, 'Robert Thornton', p. 151.

[52] E. Narin van Court, 'The *Siege of Jerusalem* and Augustinian Historians: Writing About Jews in Fourteenth-Century England', *Chaucer Review* 29 (1995), 227–48 (pp. 232–9). The author revisited the subject in E. Narin van Court, 'The *Siege of Jerusalem* and Recuperative Readings', in *Pulp Fictions of Medieval England: Essays in Popular Romance*, ed. N. McDonald (Manchester, 2004), pp. 151–70. For a complementary analysis, which examines the poem in a heady intellectual, historical and theological context, but not in a manuscript context, see S. M. Yeager, *Jerusalem in Medieval Narrative* (Cambridge, 2008), pp. 78–107.

[53] M. Birenbaum, 'Affective Vengeance in *Titus and Vespasian*', *Chaucer Review* 43 (2009), 330–44 (p. 331).

intention. As Johnston concludes, 'In the decentred manuscript culture of late medieval England, authorship was just the beginning'.[54]

In a different kind of study, part of a monograph examining four Middle English works, Citrome argues, 'To the profoundly penitential culture of late medieval England, sin and sickness were inextricably linked, and surgery ... became even more important as a metaphor for the pursuit of spiritual health'.[55] This linkage, as Citrome shows, is pervasive in the *Siege of Jerusalem*. Following the assumptions of Narin van Court that the work is of Augustinian origin and, therefore, is infused with Augustine's emphasis on grace, Citrome argues that 'the poet retains an emphasis upon surgery throughout as the medium through which God's grace works to render Vespasian and his fellow Romans as indestructable'.[56] In contrast, the poet presents the Jews as wounded and suffering spiritual sickness that arises from their refusal to accept the salvation offered by *Christus medicus*. However, in keeping with Narin van Court's argument, Citrome concludes that the focus of the poem is not the violence against Jews, but the 'exhortation to Christian faith, to sustained observance and adherence to Christ the Physician'.[57]

That refusal to accept Christian grace is, I believe, of greater importance than these scholars acknowledge. When the Romans accept that grace and come to Jerusalem to offer the Jews an opportunity to the 'Iewyse for Ihesu by iuggement to take' (line 353), the Jews respond with defiance, mistreating envoys sent by Vespasian and telling them to deliver the message, 'Sayþ vnbuxum we beþ his biddyng to ȝete' (line 369).[58] As the siege takes its toll on the Jews in the city, it is painful, too, for modern readers. Indeed, the narrative voice (not the poet) comments on the pain of describing it: 'Nowe of the tene of the towne tyme ware to saye' (fol. 62v).[59] Titus learns of their plight and responds with compassion: 'Efter proferde thaym peese for pete þat he hade / When þat he wiste thaire wo þat ware with-in closede' (fol. 63v).[60] In response, the leader of

---

[54] Johnston, 'Robert Thornton', pp. 153, 162. Notwithstanding a few favourable comments about Jews in the Nine Worthies sequences of *Parlement of the Thre Ages* and the alliterative *Morte Arthure*, the presentation of Jews in the Thornton manuscripts is very negative. In *Revelation Shown to a Holy Woman*, for example, we learn that there is no place in Purgatory for them: 'Iewes and Saraȝenes dyes and oþer hethyne pople and þay sall neuer come þere bot þay sall streghte to þe paynes of helle, for þay sall neuer be sauede' (Lincoln manuscript, fol. 255v).

[55] J. J. Citrome, *The Surgeon in Medieval English Literature* (New York, 2006), p. 1.

[56] Ibid., p. 71.

[57] Ibid., p. 59.

[58] As the leaves containing these lines are wanting in the London manuscript, citation here is from *The Siege of Jerusalem*, ed. Hanna and Lawton.

[59] Ibid., line 1069, reads '[Now] of þe tene in þe toun were [tore] forto telle'.

[60] Ibid., lines 1135–6 read, 'After profreþ pes for pyte þat he hadde / Whan he wist of here wo þat were withyn stoken'.

the Jews spurns the offer: 'Iosaphus the gentill […] for-suken þan þat profire' (fol. 63v).[61] When Titus sees bodies dead of hunger thrown from the walls of the city, he renews his offer – 'When Titus telled was the tale of trewe god he witnes / that he profirde thaym pese and grete pete hade' (fol. 64r) – and he entreats Iosaphus to proclaim to the citizens that they should save their lives by yielding to the Romans.[62] The context of these offers and the refusals, in both instances, by Ion and Symond show the art of the poet and his skill in demonstrating the justice of the treatment of the Jews.

That public starvation is desperate among the populace is vividly presented in the story of 'a Milde wyfe', who roasts 'hir awen barne' and says, as she eats the child, 'ȝelde þat þou ȝafe and aȝayne torne / Enter þare þou owte come' (fol. 63r).[63] This gruesome parody of the Virgin and child, with echoes of the *planctus Mariae* and at least a suggestion of the Jewish blood libel, may well evoke a response of pathos, but also repugnance in a reader who recognizes the parody. Her neighbours, who break down her door because of the aroma of cooked food, refuse to join her unholy communion and woefully declare their preference to die in battle than to continue suffering. Apparently in preparation for that, they decide 'To voyden all the vyle that vetaylles distroyede' (fol. 63r).[64] Or, as the editors gloss the passage, 'Those who cannot profit from food and thus are wasting it, … should get none'. Their reading and the information that those to be killed are 'women and wayke folke and those þat weryn of Elde' (fol. 63r) is somewhat different from Narin van Court's reading of these lines, that the Jews, 'prompted by moral imperative', decide 'to kill everyone who is dying from hunger' in an act of 'spiritualized martyrology'.[65]

Their continued desperation is illustrated in still another gruesome act, this time a parody of communion, 'Or thaire faa men schulde þam fange thaire florence þay ete' (fol. 64r).[66] When a group comes out of the city to partake of the meal Titus provides, they are unable 'Any fude to defy' (fol. 64r) because their guts are full of gold coins.[67] Their inability to take physical nutrition is symbolic of their inability to take spiritual nutrition. The grotesque humour

---

[61]   Ibid., lines 1137–8 read, 'Ion þe ienfulle … / … forsoke[n] þe profre'.

[62]   Ibid., lines 1155–6 read, 'to trewe God he vouched / þat he propfred hem and grete pite hadde'.

[63]   Ibid., lines 1081–2, 1087–8. Cf. Lamentations 4. 10.

[64]   Ibid., line 1102 reads, 'To voiden alle by vile deþ þat vitelys destruyed'.

[65]   Ibid., line 1103 reads, 'Wymmen and weyke folke þat weren of [e]lde'; Narin van Court, '*The Siege of Jerusalem* and Augustinian Historians', p. 236.

[66]   *The Siege of Jerusalem*, ed. Hanna and Lawton, line 1168 reads, "Lest fomen fongen hem schold, here floreyns þey eten'.

[67]   Ibid., line 1166 reads, 'Any fode to defye'.

here and in the mother's cannibalism presents the Jews in a standard stereotype of the age. As in the *planctus Mariae*, where the Virgin laments the sufferings of her Son, they are hardhearted and lacking in spiritual and emotional strength.[68] Further, they are wilfully blind and greedy and acquisitive, with love of gold surpassing any humane or spiritual concern. In terms that *Siege* establishes, it is altogether understandable that when the Jews refuse to respond to his *pite* and reject another opportunity to receive grace, Titus takes counsel and decides on a final assault of the city, 'Nowthir pete ne pese to profire thaym more' (fol. 64r).[69]

After avenging the death of his beloved friend, Sir Sabyn of Surrye, Titus fiercely rejects an appeal: 'The Iewes prayed þat prynce of pesse this was at the paske tyme' (fol. 64v).[70] The poet signals divine approval of his choice: 'A bryghte birnande swerde over þe burghe hange / With-owttyn helpe or holde save of heuene one' (fol. 64v).[71] Even as the city falls about them, the Jews persist in their blindness and refuse to see the true nature of their sinfulness and to seek the grace of God:

> And þan þe [vilayns] deuysed hem and vengaunce hit helde
> And wyten her wo þe wronge þat þey wroȝte
> Whan þey brutned in þe burwe þe byschup seint Iame;
> Noȝt wolde acounte hit for Crist þe care þat þey hadde.
>
> (lines 1237–40)[72]

Through the remaining lines of the poem, the emphasis is on the justice of their destruction in response to their sinfulness in slaying Jesus (lines 1262, 1299, 1303, 1305–8, 1324) and on the fulfilment of prophecy, 'Thare was no stone standande in the stede lefte' (fol. 65v), echoing Luke 19. 41–4 and signalling the end of biblical history.[73]

The Jews, unlike the Saracens of the fierce *Richard Coer de Lyon*, are not subject to mass execution. Rather, they are spared and dispersed in what the poet found an ironically appropriate way, repeating their treatment of Jesus: 'For thirtty penys in a purse his pastille hym solde / So was he bargande and

---

[68] G. R. Keiser, 'The Middle English *Planctus Mariae* and the Rhetoric of Pathos', in *The Popular Literature of Medieval England*, ed. T. J. Heffernan (Knoxville, 1985), pp. 167–93.

[69] *The Siege of Jerusalem*, ed. Hanna and Lawton, line 1179 reads, 'Neuer pyte ne pees profre hem more'.

[70] Ibid., line 1215 reads, 'þe Iewe preien þe pees – þis was þe Paske euene'.

[71] Ibid., lines 1223–4 read, 'A bryȝt bren[n]yng swerd ouer þe burwe henged / Without ho[l]d oþer helpe saue [of] heuen one'.

[72] As the leaves containing these lines are wanting in the London manuscript, citation here is from *The Siege of Jerusalem*, ed. Hanna and Lawton.

[73] Ibid., line 1289 reads, 'Nas no ston in þe stede stondande alofte'.

boughte and als a beste quellede' (fol. 65v).[74] Titus establishes a market for the sale of the Jews:

> For a peny of pryce who so paye wolde
> Thritty Iewes in a throwe ...
> So ware þay bargande and bought with bale owt of lande (fol. 66r)[75]

They join, in a sense, the Wandering Jew, whose story is told briefly and exclusively in Thornton's version of the *Northern Passion*.

For those wishing to see the influence of Augustine on the *Siege of Jerusalem*, the dispersal of the Jews does comply with his admonition that they be spared. In the *City of God* (XVIII 46), he cites Psalm 58. 12 in support of this admonition: 'Thow shalt not slay them, lest they should at least forget Thy law: disperse them in thy might'. Through their own scriptures the Jews 'bear witness for us that we have not invented the prophecies concerning Christ' – even though the Jews are blind to their fulfilment in the scriptures of the Christians:

> those prophecies which are produced from the books of our adversaries themselves are enough; for we recognize that it is for the sake of such testimony, with which, even against their will, they furnish us by having and preserving those books that they themselves are scattered through all the nations, wherever the Christian Church spreads.[76]

Interestingly, though, at the close of *Siege* there is no mention of books. As the Jews ready for war, we hear of 'psalmes tolde' from 'sawtirs' and the Exodus story read from 'a rolle' (fol. 55r; lines 478, 481), yet at the end when the Romans loot the temple, there are gold and gems and other valuables, not books. The 'clerkes' of Cayphas were burned with their master (fol. 58v; line 725), and Iosaphus was summoned to Rome to write about the destruction and other matters (line 1325). But the carrying away of scripture in fulfilment of Psalm 58. 12 is not mentioned.

A little later in the London manuscript, Thornton copies the unique verse text of the *Three Kings of Cologne*, which complements the *Siege of Jerusalem*.[77] A prose version of this narrative and *Siege* appear together in London, BL, MS Cotton Vespasian E. xvi and London, Lambeth Palace Library, MS 491.

---

[74] Ibid., lines 1307–8 read, 'For þritty penyes in a poke his postel hym solde: / So was he bargayned and bouȝt and as a beste quelled'.

[75] Ibid., lines 1319–21 read, 'Ay for a peny of pris, whoso pay wolde, / Þrytty Iewes in a þrom ... / So were þey bargayned and bouȝt and broȝt out of londe'.

[76] Augustine, *The City of God against the Pagans*, ed. and trans. R. W. Dyson (Cambridge, 1998), p. 892. For an important (and generous) treatment of this topic, see P. Frederiksen, *Augustine and the Jews: A Christian Defense of Jews and Judaism* (New York, 2008).

[77] H. N. MacCracken, 'Lydgatiana: III. The Three Kings of Cologne', *Archiv* 129 (1912), 50–68.

Similarly, a prose version of *Three Kings* is associated with the couplet account of the destruction of Jerusalem known as *Titus and Vespasian* in London, BL, MS Additional 36983, the Bedfordshire miscellany that has notable similarities with the Thornton manuscripts. The prose versions are fuller and more complete than Thornton's verse version, but the general outlines of the two versions are the same.

The obvious connection between the stories is Paul's statement in Romans 11. 11: 'But by their [i.e., the Jews'] offense salvation has come to the Gentiles, that they may be jealous of them.' The prose *Three Kings* begins with the rejection of Jesus by the Jews. The Thornton text is imperfect at the beginning, and it now begins at the point where 'The sterne that Balaam prophecyede be-forne / To þam apperide' (lines 15–16), causing the 'gentile kynges' (line 41) to set out to discover and worship 'the kynge of Iewes' who 'þis ilke nyghte es ybore' (line 28). Very likely, the missing material contained some of the anti-Jewish matter found at the beginning of the prose version, specifically the Jewish rejection of Balaam as a prophet (Numbers 25. 17) that appears in one of the prose versions: 'balaam was þe first prophete þat was no Iewe, and prophecied to hem þat were no Iewes: therfore þe Iewes in her bokys clepe hym a enchantoure and no prophete'.[78] The verse text does emphasize the importance of the notice given to 'gentile kynges': 'O worthy Lorde, thi werke es mervellouse, / ... / One dyuerse wyse thi grace es plentevous' (lines 34, 36).

After the kings have met with Herod and he has tried to trick them into returning and revealing the place where they find the child, the poet delivers three apostrophes condemning Herod and the Jews, one foretelling the destruction of Jerusalem:

> O cursede kynge, and cursede peple bothe,
> Wiche, will ȝee, nyll ȝee, sall neuer hafe gouernaunce,
> The tyme es come, whether thou be lefe or lothe,
> That all the worlde schall knawe of ȝoure myschaunce
> Sall neuer kyng with coron ȝow avaunce,
> ȝoure cruelle will, ȝoure false collusioune
> To ȝow and ȝoures sall be confusione. (lines 265–71)

Of course, these lines echo *Siege of Jerusalem*: 'schal neuer kyng of ȝour kynde with croune be ynoyntid / Ne Iewe for Ihesus sake [i]ouke in ȝou more' (lines 303–4).[79]

The kings visit the infant, and they proclaim their gratitude: 'We thanke the,

[78] *The Three Kings of Cologne: An Early English Translation of the* Historia Trium Regum, ed. C. Horstmann, EETS OS 85 (London, 1886), p. 4.

[79] As the leaves containing these lines are wanting in the London manuscript, citation here is from *The Siege of Jerusalem*, ed. Hanna and Lawton.

Lorde, this specialtee of grace' (line 295). The poem gives in spare detail the events of the rest of their lives, in particular, how the sight of the infant inspires their missionary work to convert their fellow gentiles and the establishment of the patriarchy of Saint Thomas and the high priesthood of Prester John. Helen, mother of Constantine, brings together their bodies long after their deaths and installs them in the church of St Sophia with relics of the life and death of Jesus. A contrast is then drawn between this acceptance of the grace of Christ and the Jews' treatment of the stall where Jesus was born:

> The Iewes for Ire and Envy haden skorne
> Vnto that place, and closede it with stone,
> …
> called it curste, vnhappy and prophane. (lines 762–3, 768)

The story concludes with the translations of the bodies of the kings, first to Milan, then to Cologne. The translations are, of course, symbolic, for the final repose of the kings in Cologne attests to the centrality of the Holy Roman Empire and, implicitly, to the Eurocentrism of Christianity.

This same theme appears in one of the two Charlemagne romances in the London manuscript, *Roland and Otuel*, when the Saracen warrior Otuel meets Roland in a duel and performs with such fierce valour that Charlemagne falls to his knees to beseech aid for Roland.[80] Suddenly, a dove descends upon the helmet of Otuel, and the Saracen renounces his religion to 'be-come a Cristyn knyghte' (line 585). After leading the French to victory over the Saracens and capturing the Sultan, Otuel weds Charlemagne's daughter and is made 'lorde of lumbardye': 'A gud Christyn man is hee' (lines 1588, 1593). Indeed, he is not merely a good Christian man, but also a good western European man. He has been transformed and is no longer a figure of the Other.

Without having the ending of the *Sege of Melayne*, we cannot reach certain conclusions,[81] but it is certainly a fit companion to the story of Otuel and his conversion. In the cause of 'Iesus Criste þat boghte vs dere' (*Otuel*, line 1594), Otuel retrieves Lumbardy and Milan from the Saracens, who captured it in the *Sege*, and he also saves all of Europe from the conquest that the Saracens plan. As Charlemagne several times reminds Otuel, his conversion is a fulfilment

---

[80] *The English Charlemagne Romances, Part II. 'The Sege off Melayne' and 'The Romance of Duke Rowland and Sir Otuell of Spayne'*, ed. S. J. Herrtage, EETS ES 35 (London, 1880).

[81] The anomalies and fragmentary state of *Sege of Melayne* have inspired a wide range of responses, including two of particular interest because they concentrate on the manuscript context: P. Hardman, 'The *Sege of Melayne*: A Fifteenth-Century Reading', in *Tradition and Transformation in Medieval Romance*, ed. R. Field (Cambridge, 1999), pp. 71–86; and S. C. Akbari, 'Incorporation in the *Siege of Melayne*', in *Pulp Fictions of Medieval England*, ed. McDonald, pp. 22–44.

of the Passion of Christ: 'to godde þat diede on rode / þat all schall deme & dighte' (lines 1268–9).

That redeeming Passion is a central theme of the *Sege*, where one of the most dramatic moments is the burning of an image of the crucified Christ by the Sultan, which becomes almost a re-enactment of the Passion. As the image explodes and blinds the Saracens, the Christian knights escape, and Roland points out that

> 'This meracle es schewed thorowe goddis grace
> For all þe saraȝenes in this place
> May noþer see nore here'. (lines 478–80)

The blinding of the Saracens allows Charlemagne's knights to escape their Saracen captors, and it also shows that the Saracens share with the Jews a blindness to the grace offered to them by Christ. Further, in responding to the wounding of the heroic bishop Turpin, Charles expresses a desire to find a surgeon to attend to those wounds; Turpin rejects the idea: 'Criste for me suffered mare; / He askede no salue to his sare' (*Sege*, lines 1348–9).

Despite the fact that the Anglo-French wars hobbled any serious crusading movement in fourteenth- and fifteenth-century England, the ideal itself was esteemed. Christopher Tyerman has amassed significant evidence in support of this contention and concludes, 'Devotion to the Holy Land remained part of the mentality of the period' in England, as well as continental Europe.[82] It is not surprising then that Thornton would copy the Charlemagne romances, about wars against the Saracens, as well as *Richard Coer de Lyon*. In the Lincoln manuscript he had already shown his interest in crusading themes. His life of Saint Christopher is a tale of a series of encounters with Saracens. Three romance heroes in that manuscript – Octavian, Perceval and Isumbras – win their greatest victories against Saracens. A recent study of *Sir Isumbras* has made a strong case for reading it as a work that participates in an active crusade discourse of the fourteenth century and for understanding that 'the crusading romance encompassed more than tales of massed armies'.[83]

With the inclusion of *Richard*, a full-blown crusading romance about the great English king and hero, Thornton achieved his ultimate expression of national and religious pride.[84] It may not be one of the most memorable

---

[82] C. Tyerman, *England and the Crusades, 1095–1588* (Chicago, 1988), p. 260.

[83] L. Manion, 'The Loss of the Holy Land and *Sir Isumbras*: Literary Contributions to Fourteenth-Century Crusade Discourse', *Speculum* 85 (2010), 65–90.

[84] P. Hardman, 'Compiling the Nation: Fifteenth-Century Miscellany Manuscripts', in *Nation, Court and Culture: New Essays on Fifteenth-Century English Poetry*, ed. H. Cooney (Dublin, 2001), pp. 50–69, looks at Thornton's sense of Englishness in the works that he included in his manuscripts.

of Middle English works, but it often surpasses the dramatic, sometimes galloping, action and the energetic vernacular dialogue that we find in other vernacular romances. Richard is, as Malcolm Hebron has described him, 'an indefatigable and zealous agent of God's will, … indiscriminately destroying a common enemy'.[85] Often the action is outrageous and verges on the darkly comical, yet the narrator unfailingly makes clear that in his actions Richard serves the divine will and is always deferential to that will. When his enemies set a hungry lion upon him, Richard cries out, 'Now helpe, lorde Ihesu'. He then tears out the lion's heart, while suffering 'noþer wem ne wounde'. Recognizing that he has been under the protection of his god, Richard falls upon his knees, 'And thanked Ihesu þat of his grace / Hym hade so kende fro schame & harme' (fol. 131v). The compelling dynamic of the work leaves the reader assured that, no matter how outrageous, all is as God intends.

In Walter Hilton's *Epistle on the Mixed Life*, preserved in the Lincoln manuscript (art. 76), Thornton found directions for meditation, particularly on the Passion. As I have shown elsewhere, those directions influenced the choices that he made in compiling the devotional book for that manuscript.[86] Hilton's advice continued to influence Thornton when he copied and set aside the *Northern Passion* and probably the *Siege of Jerusalem* for the beginning of the London manuscript, which was taking shape in his mind as he finished work on Lincoln. As he assembled this miscellany, Thornton continued to heed that advice, particularly when he copied a number of the shorter works, for example, the *Childhood of Christ*, mostly a collection of episodes from the apocryphal infancy gospels in which a very tedious child Jesus has confrontations with other children and their parents, each episode developing an adversarial relation with 'the Jewes' and thus anticipating the Passion.[87] In several, he raises one or more children from death in response to a request from Mary, who fears the Jews, but he warns her of his future pains:

> 'Modir, for 3our sake he sall lyfe als-so skete.
> And 3ete þe childire þat are here
> Salle stande by-fore me one thair fete,
> Agaynes me fals witness for to bere,

---

[85] M. Hebron, *The Medieval Siege: Theme and Image in Middle English Romance* (Oxford, 1997), p. 46.

[86] G. R. Keiser, '"To Knawe God Almyghtyn": Robert Thornton's Devotional Book', in *Spätmittelalterliche geistliche Literatur in der Nationalsprache*, vol. 2, Analecta Cartusiana, ed. J. Hogg (Salzburg, 1984), pp. 103–29. For later explorations of the nature of Thornton's devotional book, see J. J. Thompson, 'Another Look at the Religious Texts in Lincoln, Cathedral Library, MS 91', in *Late Medieval Religious Texts and Their Transmission: Essays in Honour of A. I. Doyle*, ed. A. J. Minnis (Cambridge, 1994), pp. 169–87; and Kennedy, 'The Evangelist', pp. 71–95.

[87] For a discussion of this text, see Couch's chapter in the present volume.

By-fore the Jewes thare thay salle sitte,
And gyffe me boffettes, þat salle me dere,
And nakyne me and one me spitte,
And some with thornnes salle croune my hede
And help at hange me one the Rode.' (lines 558–66)[88]

Other works treat the Passion with somewhat more tact. Lydgate's *Complaint That Christ Makes of His Passion* (London, arts. 11, 14) is a lament spoken by Jesus while on the Cross, and though it is a powerful work, it does not directly address the participation of the Jews in the Crucifixion. Such laments had a strong appeal for Thornton, and most do place guilt upon the Jews. When he created the bridge between *Cursor Mundi* and the *Northern Passion*, Thornton included *Cursor's Discourse between Christ and Man*, a lament spoken from the Cross: 'With thy sin þou pynes me / Als did þe Iewes appon þis tree' (lines 17157–8).[89]

The positive message of the Passion is that the death of Jesus reveals divine mercy and that mercy and grace are easily accessible to those who seek it. The *Four Leaves of the Truelove* recounts the events of the life of Jesus, with particular emphasis on the Passion: 'þat grace graunted grete gode þat dyede on gud fryday' (line 514). It is interesting that the *Truelove* (lines 430–40), *Mercy Passes Rightwisnes* (London art. 29; lines 85–108) and Lydgate's *Virtues of the Mass* (London art. 24; lines 409–16) all tell readers that to partake of divine grace and mercy, they too must show mercy.[90] To remind how that may be done, the poems rehearse the Seven Works of Mercy, with the first two of them putting summaries of Matthew 25. 34–40 into the mouth of Jesus.

Unquestionably, Thornton's London manuscript is a Spiritual History. While the items that follow the Charlemagne romances do not observe chronological order, this is a matter of small concern. The Passion is the central matter of

---

[88] 'Nachträge zu den Legenden: 1. Kindheit Jesu aus Ms. Addit. 31,042', ed. C. Horstmann, *Archiv* 74 (1885), 327–39. M. Dzon, 'Cecily Neville and the Apocryphal *Infantia Salvatoris* in the Middle Ages', *Mediaeval Studies* 71 (2009), 235–300, presents a remarkably comprehensive survey of late medieval accounts of the childhood of Jesus, with particular emphasis on versions circulating in England.

[89] For a complete transcript of Thornton's text of *Cursor Mundi*, see *The Southern Version of Cursor Mundi: Volume II*, ed. R. R. Fowler (Ottawa, 1990), pp. 151–92; and *The Southern Version of Cursor Mundi: Volume III*, ed. H. J. Stauffenberg (Ottawa, 1985), pp. 165–210.

[90] '*Haue Mercy of Me* (Psalm 51): An Unedited Alliterative Poem from the London Thornton Manuscript', ed. S. G. Fein, *Modern Philology* 86 (1989), 223–41, discusses the theme of mercy in the shorter works of the London manuscript. See also 'Literary Associations of an Anonymous Middle English Paraphrase of Vulgate Psalm L', ed. J. J. Thompson, *Medium Ævum* 57 (1988), 38–55.

most of these works, and it is what drew Thornton to them.[91] *Cursor Mundi* was modified to lead to the *Northern Passion*, and almost all the works in the remainder of the manuscript detail events that follow from the birth and, especially, the death of Jesus. Of course, an overwhelming theme throughout the collection is vengeance on those assumed responsible for that death and those unwilling to accept the grace available to them through that death.

The final works in London, the *Parlement of the Thre Ages* and *Wynnere and Wastoure*,[92] form a unit apart from this Spiritual History, and they might have been appended to either the Lincoln or the London volume. They probably went into the latter because it still seemed open-ended when their exemplar(s) came into Thornton's hands. Thornton had the ending of *Wynnere*, which we do not, owing to a lost leaf or leaves, and it is hard to know what led him to copy it. It is, nevertheless, ironic that the line where the work now breaks off contains a reference to the story of the *Three Kings of Cologne*. The work addresses social and national issues that apparently were of interest to Thornton, even though England's economic problems under the rule of Edward III, to which it supposedly alludes, could have been only a dim memory. Surely, Thornton was also drawn to it because it contains so many elements common to other works he copied: romance, vision, satire, alliteration.[93] The *Parlement* and *Wynnere* are, to an extent, works of reflection, and that probably had a particular appeal to the scribe at the time that he copied them. In the *Parlement* Elde has the last word, and Thornton may have been himself 'elde' when he copied it. And of course, its account of the Nine Worthies must have called to mind the first work he copied, the alliterative *Morte Arthure*, where Arthur has a prophetic dream about the Worthies. The rehearsal of past glories in the *Parlement* includes not only the heroes of the Arthurian romances in the Lincoln manuscript and those of the Charlemagne romances in the London manuscript, but also the hero of one of the other romances in the Lincoln book:

> Sir Eglamour of Artas, full euerous in armes,
> And Cristabelle the clere maye es crept in hir graue. (lines 622–3)

At least as important: each debate addresses matters that, as we have seen elsewhere, were of great interest to Robert Thornton. Specifically, they show the beguiling attraction of worldly goods and glory and the troubling moral conflicts they generate. In *Wynnere and Wastoure*, where each of the protago-

---

[91] Hardman, 'Reading the Spaces', discusses the importance of the Passion in the London manuscript. Her discussion covers only a portion of the works in the book.

[92] *The Parlement of the Thre Ages*, ed. M. Y. Offord, EETS OS 246 (London, 1959); *Wynnere and Wastoure*, ed. S. Trigg, EETS OS 297 (London, 1990).

[93] T. H. Bestul, *Satire and Allegory in Wynnere and Wastoure* (Lincoln NE, 1974), skillfully explores the multitude of literary forms which the author incorporated into this very rich poem.

nists attacks the practical and moral shortcomings of the other, while blind to his own, we see that worldly goods and glory distract one from the pursuit of moral virtue. The three protagonists of *Parlement* offer eloquent praise of worldly goods and glory, while blinded to the moral conflicts these raise. Elde concludes with the wisdom of Ecclesiastes and penitential advice, 'schryue ʒow full schirle' (line 646). Yet he does so only after a nostalgic and compelling *ubi sunt* account of the Worthies, as well as history's wisest men and greatest lovers. Once again, as in *Awntyrs off Arthure*, we find the conjunction of the irreconcilable desires of his age and of Robert Thornton.[94]

Despite his limited formal education, Thornton was a man of confidence, piety and purpose, and he responded with intelligence, insight and selectivity to the texts that he read as he assembled them into the two manuscripts. The Lincoln manuscript provided directions and examples to strive for worldly glory, goodness and joy in a world subject to Fortune, while at the same time yearning always for the true good and stability of God. By contrast, the works preserved in the London manuscript give assurance of the inexorable force of divine will, which manifests itself through marvels and ferocity. *Cursor Mundi* assures that, by divine plan, the Old Testament finds true meaning only in the fulfilment of the New Testament. The accounts of the life and, particularly, the death of Jesus are the culmination of all human history that has preceded them and the determinant of all human history that follows them. That later history is often repugnant to modern sensibilities, as we witness the ferocious vengeance visited upon those who refuse to accept the salvation made available through the Passion, who defy the will of God and who deny the meaning of those events.

If my explanation of the assembling of these two volumes and my readings of their contents are well founded, then indeed the London manuscript does demonstrate a very considerable development of the interests and concerns of Robert Thornton, though not a radical one. The presence of *Thomas of Erceldoune's Prophecy*, *Awntyrs off Arthure* and *Revelation Shown to a Holy Woman* in the Lincoln volume attests to a strong interest in visionary and prognosticative writings, which imply a view of history and might well encourage a thoughtful reader to contemplate its meaning. The emphasis on the control of Fortune in three works that incorporate visionary and prognosticative themes – *Alexander*, *Awntyrs* and *Morte* – would surely have encouraged such thoughts. Moving from an understanding that the fulfilment of prophecies implies a world in which a whimsical Fortune is merely the appearance and a providential order

[94] Of the extensive body of critical writings on these two works, I am particularly indebted to T. Turville-Petre, 'The Ages of Man in *The Parlement of the Thre Ages*', *Medium Ævum* 46 (1977), 66–76; and L. Kiser, 'Elde and His Teaching in *The Parlement of the Thre Ages*', *Philological Quarterly* 66 (1987), 303–14.

the reality, to thoughts about the fierce power of the divine grace that underlies that order, is a natural progression.

Still, admirable as it may be on its own terms, the London manuscript does not have the appeal of the Lincoln manuscript. From what we can piece together of the history of these books, later generations of the Thornton family did not look upon them with equal enthusiasm. In an earlier study, I argued that Lincoln remained with the family until the late seventeenth century.[95] Thompson has adduced evidence strong enough to support a persuasive conjecture that the Thorntons parted with the book *c.* 1600, 'perhaps [with] the promise of some limited financial gain' from John Nettleton, whose ownership inscription appears on fol. 49r. Thompson also offers an explanation for the family choosing to keep the Lincoln manuscript in their possession: 'a great number of recusant families in sixteenth-century Yorkshire were probably still using and sharing much older devotional material for their own private reading'.[96] Two *c.* 1600 manuscript copies of John Lydgate's *Life of Our Lady* indicate that this was also happening elsewhere in England.[97] Hardman has made a strong case that the Lincoln manuscript served as a household miscellany of value for its spiritual exercises, but also for the material necessary to teach generations of Thornton children the tenets of the old religion. In that case, this volume would have had sentimental and practical value for the family.[98]

The Lincoln manuscript served still other tastes and needs. Interest in medieval romance persisted well after the Reformation, much to the dismay of religious reformers and humanists.[99] Moreover, we must not underestimate the possible importance of the *Liber de Diversis Medicinis*. Still extant and in use were a great number of medical manuscripts from the fifteenth century and earlier, as well as sixteenth-century manuscript and printed copies of treatises from the earlier period, and interest in their contents persisted after the books

---

[95] G. R. Keiser, 'A Note on the Descent of the Thornton Manuscript', *Transactions of the Cambridge Bibliographical Society* 6 (1976), 347–49. For another theory, see R. M. Thomson, *Catalogue of the Manuscripts of Lincoln Cathedral Chapter Library* (Cambridge, 1989), p. 69.

[96] Thompson, *London Thornton MS*, pp. 6–7.

[97] Liverpool, Liverpool University Library, MS Radcliffe 16, fols. 1r–104v, and Oxford, Bodleian Library, MS Ashmole 59, fols. 136r–181v.

[98] Hardman, 'Domestic Learning and Teaching'.

[99] Middle English romances were still being copied and read in manuscripts well into the sixteenth century: Oxford, Bodleian Library, MS Douce 261, copied in 1564, contains copies of *Sir Isumbras*, fols. 1r–7v (copied from a printed text), and *Sir Eglamour*, fol. 26r (a fragment copied from a printed text). Oxford, Bodleian Library, MS Greaves 60, fols. 1v–20r, preserves a *c.* 1600 fragmentary text of the alliterative *Alisaunder*. J. Boro offers an extensive examination of these and other early modern romance manuscripts in their context; see 'Miscellaneity and History: Reading Sixteenth-Century Romance Manuscripts', in *Tudor Manuscripts 1485–1603*, ed. A. S. G. Edwards, English Manuscript Studies 1100–1700, vol. 15 (London, 2010), pp. 123–51.

were no longer available.[100] The large body of household books prepared in the sixteenth and seventeenth centuries, by women and men, preserve medical recipes that would have been familiar to Robert Thornton and his contemporaries. In the end, the diversity of the Lincoln book, as compared with the more limited focus of the London book, probably determined that it remained a cherished possession of the Thornton family until the end of the family in the late seventeenth century. Though not 'to the worlde end', the book fullfilled the purposes of its scribe and compiler for a surprisingly long period of time.

[100] In his modern edition of the immensely popular and oft-printed household book (1615–1637) – G. Markham, *The English Housewife: containing the inward and outward virtues which ought to be in a complete woman ...*, ed. M. R. Best (Montreal, 1986) – Best demonstrates the use of sources from both manuscript and early printed books. Markham had great affection for manuscripts and made frequent use of them in his very successful books on practical matters, including both human and veterinary medicine. See, for example, G. R. Keiser, 'Medicines for Horses: The Continuity from Script to Print', *Yale University Library Gazette* 69 (1995), 111–28; rev. repr., with addendum, *Veterinary History* n.s. 12 (2004), 125–48 (134–9). On the *Liber de Diversis Medicinis* in Lincoln and its place in Middle English literary culture, see Orlemanski's chapter in the present volume.

3

The Thornton Manuscripts and Book Production in York

Joel Fredell

The two manuscript anthologies inscribed by Robert Thornton of East Newton, in the North Riding of Yorkshire, remain crucial witnesses to literature in late medieval England. Lincoln Cathedral Library, MS 91 and London, BL, MS Additional 31042 provide much of what we know from this period about romances, about devotional literature, and about the relations between the two, given these manuscripts' wide-ranging contents and their suggestive arrangements of texts. These gleanings about literary presentation and distribution have been applied to the North of England or the nation generally. However, our conclusions from the Thornton manuscripts about romance and devotional literature can be applied more accurately to York, a centre of book production that by the end of the fourteenth century rivalled London. Furthermore, these conclusions can be enriched by comparisons with another manuscript of the highest literary importance, London, BL, MS Cotton Nero A. x, the sole witness to the four poems ascribed to the *Pearl* poet or *Gawain* poet. Cotton Nero and the Lincoln Thornton manuscript share decorations that are closely identified with York in the first half of the fifteenth century, and that connection allows us to think about these two great collections as bookends to a vital place and period for the reproduction of literary texts in England from around 1400 (the likely time for production and decoration of Cotton Nero) to around 1450 (the likely time for production and decoration of the Thornton manuscripts).

Furthermore, we can use the decoration in combination with other forms of evidence to separate out likely clusters of texts that probably came to Thornton in pamphlet form, focusing our attention on works that circulated together in small anthologies in Yorkshire, if not York itself. The question of Thornton's interests as evidenced by his manuscripts is undeniably rich and important. Equally important, though, is the evidence of mini-collections that came to Thornton as exemplars, that is, as cultural formations embedded within Thornton's booklets and then enshrined by the larger collections and the decoration that defines them. One point that leaps out from this approach is a complex relationship between romance and devotional literature that develops, apparently deliberately, by the arrangements of their scribes. Two important witnesses to such arrangements are the three devotional poems in Cotton Nero brought together with *Sir Gawain and the Green Knight*, and the various lesser-known poems (the *Life of Saint Christopher* [Lincoln art. 14], the *Siege of Jerusalem* [London art. 5]) embedded within romance collections that form independent units in both of the Thornton manuscripts. These collections testify that romance literature associated with York has its own set of devotional themes and concerns closely allied with upper classes of the laity, connected to but not dominated by the 'vernacular theology' represented by writings associated with Richard Rolle, Walter Hilton and other figures influential in York and the North of England.

Before we can broach these topics, though, the decoration in the Thornton manuscripts demands review.[1] The Thornton manuscripts are not lavishly decorated, a circumstance that led scholars for many decades to speculate that Thornton did all the decoration as well as the writing.[2] It is likely that Thornton did the rubrication, and possibly the unadorned coloured Lombard capitals in both Lincoln and London.[3] The decorated initials in Lincoln, however, and the two sets of drolleries in London represent at least three decorating hands – none of them likely to be Thornton's. Instead, the main decorator for Lincoln uses features exclusive to contemporary manuscripts produced in York. These features include specific penwork elements, wash for sprays and other decoration I have identified during a larger examination of York manuscripts.

Dozens of surviving manuscripts produced in the city of York from around 1390 to the 1450s share several common elements, particularly in border illuminations for deluxe manuscripts.[4] The convenience of these elements is that

---

[1]   For earlier discussions of the decoration in the Lincoln manuscript, see J. Fredell, 'Decorated Initials in the Lincoln Thornton Manuscript', *Studies in Bibliography* 47 (1994), 78–89; and P. Hardman, 'Reading the Spaces: Pictorial Intentions in the Thornton MSS, Lincoln Cathedral MS 91, and BL MS Add. 31042', *Medium Ævum* 63 (1994), 250–74. Standard accounts for each manuscript can be found respectively in *The Thornton MS*, intro. Brewer and Owen, pp. viii–ix (booklets), pp. xii–xvi (collation), pp. xvii–xx (contents); and Thompson, *London Thornton MS*.

[2]   The discussion began to shift with the more cautious assessment by Thompson, *London Thornton MS*, p. 58; for a fuller history of this speculation, see Fredell, 'Decorated Initials', p. 89 note 5.

[3]   Responsibility for the drolleries inhabiting some initials (not the leaf and crosshatching) remains an open question, given the relative lack of skill in some cases, and the likelihood that Thornton produced the Lombard initials in the first place.

[4]   K. L. Scott, *Later Gothic Manuscripts: 1390–1490*, 2 vols. (London, 1996), identifies five major illuminated manuscripts *c*. 1400 with a definite York provenance and shared decorative features: Boulogne-sur-Mer, Bibliothèque Municipale, MS 93, fols. 1r–41v, II, 37–9 (#7); Brussels, Bibliothèque Royale, MS 4862–4869a, II, 97–8 (#24); Cambridge, Trinity College, MS O. 3. 10, II, 117–19 (#32); Dublin, TCD, MS 83, II, 38–9 (no catalogue entry for this manuscript); and York Minster Library, MS Additional 2 (Bolton Hours), II, 119–21 (#33). J. B. Friedman,

Figure 1. York Minster
Library, MS Additional 2
(Bolton Hours), fol. 10v
(detail)

Figure 2. London, BL,
MS Cotton Nero A. x,
fol. 95r (detail)

Figure 3. Lincoln
Cathedral Library,
MS 91, fol. 9v (detail)

they can be found in manuscripts with secure provenance and dating for York
in this period, such as the well-known Bolton Hours (York, Minster Library,
MS Additional 2). Two features are relevant here, given the modesty of the
work in the Lincoln manuscript. First, a pervasive feature of penwork initials in
York manuscripts during this period is the presence of small circles or 'bubbles'
settled into quadrants, anchored on or floating alongside pen flourishes, and
sometimes studded along the outside of the boxing on the initial itself. This
feature, which after an extensive search I have not found in any manuscripts
produced outside of Yorkshire, not only appears regularly in deluxe manuscripts such as the Bolton Hours and San Marino, Huntington Library, MS
HM 1067, but also in more modest manuscripts, including Cotton Nero, which
I also believe was produced in Yorkshire, and in what I have called 'style 1' decoration in the Lincoln manuscript (see Figures 1, 2, 3).[5] These kinds of penwork
initials run throughout Cotton Nero and the style 1 sections of the Lincoln
manuscript, whose red Lombard initials are decorated with violet penwork.
This feature certainly could be imitated by decorators outside the city of York
itself. Nonetheless, its presence in Cotton Nero and Lincoln confirms that the
decoration is closely associated with York.

Northern English Books, Owners, and Makers in the Late Middle Ages (Syracuse NY, 1995), pp.
108–47, examines a larger but overlapping group of manuscripts using a much broader regional
perspective; I have identified many more such manuscripts, some of which are identified in my
'The Pearl-Poet Manuscript in York', forthcoming in *Studies in the Age of Chaucer* 36 (2014).

   [5]   See further Fredell, 'Decorated Initials', pp. 80–84.

Figure 4. San Marino, Huntington Library, MS HM 1067, fol. 130v (detail)

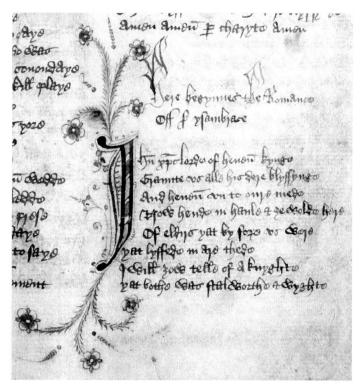

Figure 5. Lincoln Cathedral Library, MS 91, fol. 109r (detail)

Figure 6. York Minster Library, MS XVI.K.6 (Pavement Hours), fol. 25r (detail)

A second feature which I have found to be exclusive to York decoration is an unusual use of green wash appearing at the base of sprays, and sometimes all along the spray lines themselves (see Figure 4).[6] This green appears in the two illuminated initials occurring among the style 1 decorations, along with quatrefoil flowers closely resembling those found in the Pavement Hours, a manuscript very likely produced in the city of York around 1420 (see Figures 5, 6).[7] The illuminated *I* on fol. 154r also follows a standard York pattern by infilling the shaft with bubbles, as can be seen in various York manuscripts including an initial *A* in Cotton Nero, fol. 57r (see Figures 7, 8, 9).

Altogether these features strongly argue for a professional hand from York, or trained there, decorating important sections of the Lincoln manuscript. The sheer bulk and diversity of texts in the Thornton anthologies alone argue for a connection with a major book centre, and York has always been the best candidate in the region.[8] Given that the two illuminated initials (Lincoln fols. 109rb, 154r) are also done in a distinct York style, that same hand, or a close associate, probably inserted these initials as well; consequently I will refer to all decora-

---

[6] Scott uses the effect of green wash on pen squiggles (presumably those squiggles that occur at spray ends and/or off of the little balls that cap penwork lines of spray commonly in the early fifteenth century in English manuscripts) to date borders in English manuscripts and England generally. In *Later Gothic Manuscripts*, she argues that the borders in Cambridge, Trinity College, MS O. 3. 10, due to the 'application of green to all pen squiggles in the borders indicate a later date than Boulogne-Sur-Mer', that is 'c. 1410 or slightly later' (II, 118). Similarly, K. L. Scott, *Dated and Dateable English Manuscript Borders c. 1395–1499* (London, 2002), p. 42, argues that this use of green wash is 'new' in a manuscript she dates 1410–1413. She does not discuss green wash along spray lines. Friedman, *Northern English Books*, p. 74, briefly notes the use of green in northern illuminating generally, but does not note its use in lesser decoration.

[7] Two of the illuminated initials in the Lincoln manuscript, fols. 19r and 19v, include folded acanthus-leaf decoration (sometimes simplified to a form called 'mitten leaves' typical in York illuminated borders in the period, as in Figure 4). However, while the persistence of the latter into the middle of the fifteenth century is also a marker for York decoration, acanthus-leaf decoration itself was used across England. The initial on fol. 19r uses a 'bar band'-style initial (similar to the illuminated initials on fols. 109rb and 154r) with acanthus leaves in a spray. On fol. 19v, similar acanthus 'mittens' are incorporated into penwork spray with bubbles, as is the illuminated initial on fol. 27r. On the Pavement Hours, see most recently A. Grounds, 'Evolution of a Manuscript: The Pavement Hours', in *Design and Distribution of Late Medieval Manuscripts in England*, ed. L. R. Mooney and M. Connolly (York, 2008), pp. 118–38.

[8] Thompson, *London Thornton MS*, p. 6, notes the inscription by 'Willa Frostt' at the top of fol. 73v in red ink in the London manuscript. Thompson suggests a role in decoration for Frost, but the name is much more likely connected to a prominent Yorkshire family with a long series of Williams; see C. D. Liddy, 'William Frost, the City of York and Scrope's Rebellion of 1405', in *Richard Scrope: Archbishop, Rebel, Martyr*, ed. P. J. P. Goldberg (Donington, 2007), pp. 77–82. Also, however, see A. I. Doyle, 'Review of *Robert Thornton and the London Thornton Manuscript*, by J. J. Thompson', *Review of English Studies* n.s. 41 (1990), 242, where Doyle argues that the final graph is an abbreviation rather than a 't', yielding something like 'Frooster'.

Figure 7. University of York
Borthwick Institute for
Archives, Henry Brynsall of
York, 21 August 1395 Prob.
Reg. 1, fol. 85r (detail)

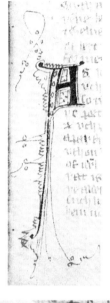

Figure 8. London, BL,
MS Cotton Nero A. x,
fol. 57r (detail)

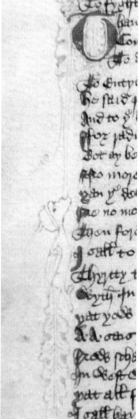

Figure 9. Lincoln
Cathedral Library, MS
91, fol. 154r (detail)

Figure 10. Lincoln
Cathedral Library,
MS 91, fol. 56v
(detail)

tion within these sections as 'style 1'. One variant of this style appears in Lincoln quires M and N, using short sprays in brown ink rather than the violet penwork appearing otherwise. Since this variant is likely to be a late addition, I will look at it below in the context of Thornton's compiling activities, and possibly as Thornton's own work.

The distinct decorating hand of the alliterative *Morte Arthure* (Lincoln art. 8), which I will call 'style 2', is less easily located (see Figure 10).[9] These decorations feature long penwork sprays in light brown that come out of foliate bases – complicated foliage, usually what seem to be modified oak leaves (that is, the round-lobed leaves of the English oak, *Quercus robur*), sometimes edging towards acanthus-like pointed lobes and in many cases with leaf veins drawn in. Both leaf types are enhanced with various forms of dentate edging and cross-hatched infill for shading effects. Scholars have been more interested in the varied drolleries also emerging out of the penwork sprays and inhabiting some initials, but the leaf-forms are the chief distinguishing feature for this style.[10] These leaf-forms do not constitute a stable identifier for the decorator's provenance, though the penwork overall is certainly professional, certainly nothing like the work of the style 1 decorator, and highly unlikely to be the work of Thornton himself.[11] This subsection of the Lincoln manuscript was decorated by a professional who knew Thornton well enough to use his client's name in one drollery (a bird clutching a scroll with the legend 'Robert Thornton', fol. 93v); he was not a decorator with obvious local habits otherwise.

The isolation of style 2 here raises a series of questions if we look at it in combination with other evidence for Thornton's compiling activities.[12] It is no surprise that this style is restricted to the *Morte*, if we follow the common

[9] In an earlier discussion I named the illuminated initials 'style 2', and the decoration for the alliterative *Morte Arthure* 'style 3'; see Fredell, 'Decorated Initials', pp. 80–3.

[10] On these drolleries and the isolation of style 2 generally see also T. H. Crofts, 'The Occasion of the *Morte Arthure*: Textual History and Marginal Decoration in the Thornton MS', *Arthuriana* 20 (2010), 11–22.

[11] The decorator of Cotton Nero uses similar foliate forms for infilling initials; see, for instance, fol. 61r.

[12] On Thornton's compiling activities, see also K. Stern, 'The London "Thornton" Miscellany: A New Description of British Museum Additional Manuscript 31042', *Scriptorium* 30 (1976), 26–40 (pp. 26–37); S. M. Horrall, 'The London Thornton Manuscript: A New Collation', *Manuscripta* 23 (1979), 99–103; C. A. Owen, Jr., 'The Collation and Descent of the Thornton Manuscript', *Transactions of the Cambridge Bibliographical Society* 6 (1975), 218–25; J. J. Thompson, 'The Compiler in Action: Robert Thornton and the "Thornton Romances" in Lincoln Cathedral MS 91', in *Manuscripts and Readers in Fifteenth–Century England: The Literary Implications of Manuscript Study. Essays from the 1981 Conference at the University of York*, ed. D. Pearsall (Cambridge, 1983), pp. 113–24; R. Hanna III, 'The Growth of Robert Thornton's Books', *Studies in Bibliography* 40 (1987), 51–61; and M. Johnston, 'Robert Thornton and *The Siege of Jerusalem*', *Yearbook of Langland Studies* 23 (2009), 125–62 (pp. 135–43).

opinion that Thornton copied this poem early in his compiling, and make the assumption that its isolation indicates a first attempt at literary bookmaking, possibly aligned with an interest in the Nine Worthies.[13] More surprising is the fact that another work scholars regularly assume Thornton copied alongside the *Morte*, the *Privity of the Passion* (Lincoln art. 38), is not decorated in this style despite the latter text's apparent descent from the same 'Lincolnshire exemplar' and Thornton's use of the same paper stock to copy both.[14] Thornton must have included the *Privity* in a plan of compilation separate from the *Morte* both in terms of genre grouping and a time frame for completion: the other text in the Lincoln manuscript celebrating one of the Nine Worthies, the prose *Life of Alexander* (art. 1), precedes the *Morte*, but is decorated (like the *Privity*) in style 1.[15] Also surprising is another peculiarity of decoration: Thornton (who regularly starts off new long texts in the available final folia of a preexisting quire) added the beginning of *Octavian* (art. 10) to the last four folia of this original unit containing the *Morte* (quires D–F). These opening pages of the added romance are decorated in style 2 as well, but the main bulk of *Octavian* in the next quire is decorated in style 1. In other words, the decoration of the *Morte* was not isolated chronologically from the compiling process for the romance booklet as a whole. Consequently, we need to search for other explanations for that isolated decoration (cabbage-leaf decorations and the multitude of drollery animals, humans, dragons and hybrids), and consider its implications for our narratives of Thornton's compiling stages.

Adding to this complication is that the continuation of *Octavian* begins another cluster familiar to students of this section of the Lincoln manuscript: four romances apparently taken from what Ralph Hanna has called the 'Doncaster exemplar'.[16] The first three of these romances – the end of *Octa-*

---

[13] The origin of the Nine Worthies identification here, now regularly cited, is G. R. Keiser, 'Lincoln Cathedral Library MS. 91: Life and Milieu of the Scribe', *Studies in Bibliography* 32 (1979), 159–80 (pp. 177–8). For the argument based on watermark evidence that Lincoln quire N is the earliest of Thornton's proto-booklets, see R. Kennedy, 'The Evangelist in Robert Thornton's Devotional Book: Organizing Principles at the Level of the Quire', *Journal of the Early Book Society* 8 (2005), 71–95 (p. 73).

[14] For discussions of the *Morte* and the *Privity* based on this assumption, see Keiser, 'Lincoln Cathedral Library MS. 91', pp. 178–9; Hanna, 'The Growth'; and Crofts, 'The Occasion', pp. 8–12.

[15] The classic study on dialect evidence for the origins of several texts in the Lincoln manuscript is A. McIntosh, 'The Textual Transmission of the Alliterative *Morte Arthure*', in *English and Medieval Studies Presented to J. R. R. Tolkien on the Occasion of His Seventieth Birthday*, ed. N. Davis and C. L. Wrenn (London, 1962), pp. 231–40. See also the chapter by Johnston in the present volume.

[16] Hanna, 'The Growth', p. 55, follows McIntosh's brief mention (pp. 231–2) of this group 'from the area near the junction of Yorkshire, Lincolnshire and Nottinghamshire', and names it Doncaster.

vian, *Sir Isumbras* (art. 11) and *Earl of Toulouse* (art. 12) – are contained in a single quire (G, fols. 103–122) and decorated (along with the remaining texts in this fascinating subsection) with style 1 initials, including two illuminated initials distinguishing *Isumbras* (fol. 109rb) and *Awntyrs off Arthure* (art. 20; fol. 154r). Yet the fourth romance presumably from the 'Doncaster exemplar', *Sir Perceval of Gales* (art. 21), appears at the end of this section. As in the case of *Octavian, Perceval* begins in the last few folia of quire I, and this opening fragment is decorated in style 1 along with the earlier part of that quire. The main bulk of *Perceval*, making up most of quire K, is undecorated beyond plain Lombard initials in red ink. So despite its dialectal association with the first three romances, *Perceval* came in late during the construction of the romance booklet, and trailed into a subsection that Thornton never completed to the extent that he found it worthy to send out for professional decoration. In this case the dialect evidence cited by Hanna and the codicological evidence discussed here conflict; Thornton could have held onto *Perceval* for some unfulfilled purpose, such as the creation of a separate booklet; the minor texts which fill out the quire that contains the ending to *Perceval* (such as 'A charm for þe tethe werke', art. 22) also support the argument that Thornton included *Perceval* in his romance booklet as a later decision after the initial 'completion' and decoration of quires G and H. Taken together the evidence of *Octavian* and *Perceval* reveals that Thornton was making definite choices for his booklet collections, while his sense of closure for the booklets themselves was subject to spasms of *pentimento*.

Another version of these problems shows up in the lesser-known devotional booklet of the Lincoln manuscript (quires L–P, fols. 179–279).[17] As I mentioned above, the *Morte* and the *Privity* share Lincolnshire dialect forms, and this commonality suggests that Thornton intentionally set up two booklets for their separate genres from a single source. Evidence from the paper stocks supports this association since Thornton used the same paper (type v) to copy both works (although the *Morte* includes another paper stock as well).[18] This supporting evidence is somewhat compromised by two facts. First, the decoration of these two works is different: the *Morte* clearly was decorated separately from the rest of the Lincoln manuscript, while the *Privity* was decorated sparsely with a single style 1 initial at the opening and plain Lombards

[17] On this section also see G. R. Keiser, '"To Knawe God Almyghtyn": Robert Thornton's Devotional Book', in *Spätmittelalterliche geistliche Literatur in der Nationalsprache*, vol. 2, Analecta Cartusiana, ed. J. Hogg (Salzburg, 1984), pp. 103–29; Kennedy, 'The Evangelist', pp. 71–95.

[18] Here and in the discussion that follows I principally follow Thompson, *London Thornton MS*, pp. 71–3, plates 36–52, for full descriptions, illustrations and cross–references to C.-M. Briquet, *Les filigranes*, 4 vols. (Leipzig, 1923). Another useful account is given in Hanna, 'The Growth', pp. 51–61.

afterward. Second, a large cluster of devotional texts follow in quires L and M also using the same paper stock but not the same decoration: the same sparse style 1 decoration appears in quire L (fols. 179–198), but quires M and N (fols. 199–236) are decorated more fully in a variant York style that features short penwork sprays in brown ink;[19] the original style 1 penwork reappears sparsely in quires O–P (fols. 237–279). So neither paper stock nor dialectal evidence are sufficient to understand Thornton's compiling activities in this booklet, and the decorations suggest subdivisions with distinctive clusters of texts quire by quire that could come from individual pamphlets circulating in Yorkshire or York itself at the time. Whether or not the texts with Lincolnshire and Doncaster dialect remnants were copied by Thornton around the same time from the same exemplar, they were not always copied on the same paper or decorated together. Thornton seems to have had far more romance and devotional texts at his disposal from other exemplars around the time these clusters came into his hands, if indeed we can be sure that he did not get multiple exemplars from a similar source in either the Lincolnshire or the Doncaster case. The many subdivisions in Thornton's manuscripts, as indicated by the variety of decorative features, may be far more important in the archaeology of Thornton's compiling.

These subdivisions also further complicate the evidence of paper stocks. For instance, half the devotional booklet is built from the same paper stocks as the *Morte*, but so is a problematic cluster of texts in the romance booklet that include genre-challenging works such as the *Life of Saint Christopher* (art. 14), *The Wicked Knight and the Friar* (which follows *Christopher* in Quire H, art. 17) and *Lyarde* (art. 18 in Quire I). The outliers in terms of paper in this booklet are quires G (fols. 103–122, containing *Octavian*, *Isumbras* and *Earl of Toulouse*) using two other paper stocks, and quire K for the bulk of *Perceval*.[20] What seems to be happening is that Thornton copied *Awntyrs* around the time he copied the *Morte*. Thornton then refolded quire I (by reversing the fold so that *Awntyrs* began in the middle of the quire rather than the beginning) to accommodate the *Christopher* cluster along with the previously completed *Octavian* cluster at the beginning.[21] But then why would Thornton use different

---

[19]   These initials might be the work of Thornton, given the relatively unskilled spray lines and the use of a brown ink; see further below.

[20]   According to Thompson, *London Thornton MS*, p. 72, Thornton uses type iii paper in Lincoln quire G for all but one bifolio, a single sheet of type xii for fols. 110/115. Lincoln quire K, using Thompson i paper, may have been organized around the same time as London quires a–b (fols. 3–32, *Cursor Mundi* extracts), the other occurrence of this paper in the two manuscripts. See further Hanna, 'The Growth', pp. 53–4.

[21]   Hanna, 'The Growth', pp. 57–8, argues for this sequence, following the original theory about the copying of *Awntyrs* from Thompson, 'The Compiler in Action', pp. 113–24.

paper stocks for quire G if these three romances were copied in some continuous way, since *Octavian* and *Christopher* begin in the ends of previous quires? Thornton simply may have run out of these two stocks, but it is more likely that the change in paper indicates a gap in copying reflected in *Octavian*'s case by the shift in decoration as well. Thornton's use of his paper stocks may not have been orderly, but in most cases he employs a paper stock consistently throughout a quire unless he is reconfiguring a quire by inserting bifolia inside an existing quire or wrapping bifolia around an existing core. Thus the only subdivision of relatively standard romances in Thornton's two manuscripts, the *Octavian* cluster, is entangled with the decorating anomaly of style 2 and the most puzzling paper stock in Thornton's two anthologies.

It should be all too clear at this point that the evidence for Thornton's compiling activities is intimidating in its complexity, and our current understanding of it depends on a variety of evidence not always in harmony. Nonetheless, the decoration of the Lincoln manuscript offers a number of insights into Thornton's process of compiling and then establishing finished units; it identifies texts likely to be connected to York, and (in combination with other evidence) groupings of texts circulating together that constitute interesting cultural units on their own. My summary of the structure of the two manuscripts as we understand it at this point, presented more fully in the Appendix, divides Lincoln into four booklets and London into five booklets, within which are several subsections reconfigured into the larger collections that survive. In Lincoln, three substantial independent booklets offer the prose *Alexander*, the alliterative *Morte*, and the *Liber de Diversis Medicinis*;[22] smaller proto-booklets (that is, booklets which began with a substantial work from a distinct exemplar, and were completed with shorter works at a later time) contain the *Privity* and Hilton's *Epistle on the Mixed Life* (art. 76). Excepting the *Liber*, these works were likely to have come to Thornton as single texts (or, for the devotional works, with some attached short texts) since Thornton constructed booklets based on each. Similarly, in the London manuscript, the booklet organization argues that the *Cursor Mundi* excerpts (arts. 1, 3), the *Northern Passion* (art. 4), the *Four Leaves of the Truelove* (art. 21), *Richard Coer de Lyon* (art. 32) and the *Childhood of Christ* (art. 33) came to Thornton as single texts.[23] Other groupings, however, such as the trio of romances or the problematic sextet that follows in

---

[22]   *Octavian* begins after the *Morte* in quire F, and this opening piece of the poem is decorated in style 2 along with the full text of the *Morte* in quires D–F. Nonetheless, the remnant of *Octavian* in quire G is decorated in another style, and the dialects of the two works (which have prompted scholars' identification of separate 'Lincolnshire' and 'Doncaster' exemplars for the *Morte* and *Octavian*, respectively; see note 16 above) are quite different. Both facts argue that Thornton created an independent three-quire booklet for the *Morte* initially.

[23]   For a new argument, based on dialectical evidence, that Thornton derived both the

Lincoln, are more likely to have travelled to Thornton as pamphlet anthologies and represent some very interesting literary groupings before Thornton
imposed his own organization. The evidence (of quires G, H, I, K, M, O and
P in Lincoln and quires d, e, f and i in London) argues that most of Thorton's
subunits were built from small anthology-like exemplars, probably pamphlets
circulating in Yorkshire at the time and possibly from the book professionals
who decorated the manuscripts. The previous existence of these texts in such
groupings of a quire-sized pamphlet anthology simply is the best explanation
for the fact that Thornton reproduces them in individual quires himself before
combining them into a larger and more complex anthology.

For the sake of clarity, I should say here that I use the term 'booklet' quite
intentionally to suggest that it represents the final form of a self-contained unit
within the manuscript.[24] These units were formalized with decoration, though
in some cases that decoration helps to uncover an earlier 'proto-booklet' stage
(that is to say, a self-contained unit that was well-used by Thornton before
being integrated into a larger assembly); I call those earlier units 'subsections'
in the Appendix to distinguish them from the larger eventual booklets. By the
term 'pamphlet', I mean to identify small books of one or two quires circulating
independently. Thornton's booklets and subsections that may have started as
proto-booklets, then, are not themselves pamphlets because (as far as we know)
Thornton's copies did not circulate but were ultimately combined and decorated as sub-units in the books we have now.[25]

From the patterns of decoration, several important (and hopefully clear)
points do emerge for our understanding of Thornton's compiling activities.
First, the London manuscript was never sent out for professional decoration
comparable to the Lincoln manuscript.[26] London may be an overflow volume

---

Northern Passion and the *Siege of Jerusalem* from the same exemplar, see Johnston's chapter in
the present volume.

[24] On the large topic of the 'booklet', see most crucially P. R. Robinson, 'The "Booklet": A
Self-Contained Unit in Composite Manuscripts', *Codicologica* 3 (1980), 46–69; also see P. R.
Robinson, 'Booklets in Medieval Manuscripts: Further Considerations', *Studies in Bibliography*
39 (1986), 100–11; R. Hanna III, *Pursuing History: Middle English Manuscripts and Their Texts*
(Stanford CA, 1996), pp. 21–34; J. Boffey and J. Thompson, 'Anthologies and Miscellanies:
Production and Choice of Texts', in *Book Production and Publishing in Britain, 1375–1475*, ed. J.
Griffiths and D. Pearsall, Cambridge Studies in Publishing and Printing History (Cambridge,
1989), pp. 279–315; and J. Fredell, '"Go Litel Quayer": Lydgate's Pamphlet Poetry', *Journal of the
Early Book Society* 9 (2006), 51–74.

[25] For a recent discussion on the terminology for booklet production and usage see
E. Kwakkel, 'Late Medieval Text Collections: A Codicological Typology Based on Single-Author
Manuscripts', in *Author, Reader, Book: Medieval Authorship in Theory and Practice*, ed. E. Kwakkel
and S. Partridge (Toronto, 2012), 56–79.

[26] Two decorated initials, all in black ink, also appear in the London manuscript on fol. 33r
(opening the *Northern Passion*, a skillful foliate decoration with a number of drollery grotesques

with texts that finally did not meet Thornton's standard for thematic unity (a topic of enduring debate), prestige (the obscurity of the *Sege of Melayne* [art. 8], for instance), or completeness (many of the substantial texts are imperfect, such as *Wynnere and Wastoure* [art. 35] – which might also have met the obscurity standard) despite evidence that Thornton planned miniature programmes for one of the single-text booklets.[27] Again here the sub-units are instructive both in terms of Thornton's interests and the textual clusters in his sources. The use of undecorated Lombards throughout London is likely to be Thornton's own work, particularly given the fact that both Thornton manuscripts use red-ink Lombards throughout. Even here, though, one useful exception stands out: alternating red and green Lombards in fols. 104v–120r of London. John J. Thompson has shown that these alternating initials correspond with the first compiling stage of quire f, in which fols. 103–120 (*Virtues of the Mass, Rose of Ryse, Three Kings of Cologne* [arts. 24, 26, 27] and one Latin verse [art. 25]) constituted a separate unit first before Thornton wrapped another proto-quire containing the *Truelove* and some shorter texts (now fols. 98–102 and 121–124, containing arts. 21–3 and 28–31) around that stage 1 core.[28] This decorating anomaly, then, tells us that quire f represents an interesting devotional unit that Thornton probably received as a small anthology and then deliberately combined with a text different in kind (a maiden taught to seek divine love in the 'foure lefes' of the Trinity and the Virgin), reminding us that more than 'overflow' can be understood from this cluster.[29] Two of these three texts (*Virtues of the Mass* and *Three Kings of Cologne*) offer a fairly conventional vision of devotional literature; in fact, that conventional vision is quite dominant in terms of numbers in Lincoln's booklet 3 despite the fact that Thornton places affective texts that represent more contemporary devotional themes (such as the *Privity* and the *Truelove*) at the head of his devotional booklets in Lincoln and London.[30] The *Rose of Ryse* (art. 26), though labelled in the margin 'a Carole For Crystynmesse', is in fact a political poem about the superiority of the Tudor

---

and a king's head) and on fol. 50r (opening the *Siege of Jerusalem*, an initial with human profiles and a grotesque). Thompson, *London Thornton MS*, p. 58, argues for Thornton as the decorator for these initials. Based on the skill of these drolleries, I suspect the presence of another professional. However, these two initials do not support the fully developed programme of decoration we might expect if London was put into the hands of a professional for that purpose.

[27] On the pictorial spaces in the London manuscript, in the *Cursor Mundi* extracts and the space at the head of the *Northern Passion*, see Hardman, 'Reading the Spaces', pp. 254–62; on the *Sege of Melayne*, see further Thompson, *London Thornton MS*, p. 24.

[28] Thompson, *London Thornton MS*, p. 41.

[29] On Thornton's interest in Marian materials, see G. R. Keiser, 'More Light on the Life and Milieu of Robert Thornton', *Studies in Bibliography* 36 (1983), 111–19.

[30] Johnston, 'Robert Thornton', makes a similar point about London's booklet 2 (quires c–e, fols. 33–97), which contains the *Northern Passion* and the *Siege of Jerusalem*; however, the *Siege*

rose (a saviour of knights, no less) over the French fleur-de-lis.[31] Thus even this detail in the decoration allows us to tease out a pre-existing cultural artefact of some complexity before we observe Thornton's habit of combining this mini-anthology with visionary works.

Similarly, quire M in Lincoln opens with a continuation of the *Mirror of Saint Edmund* and a tract on the Lord's Prayer, but also includes short texts of remarkable variety, from a discussion of angel's song (art. 73) to the notorious political poem *When Adam Delved* (art. 69). Quire O combines two longer meditative works quite different in kind (the abridged *Psalter of Saint Jerome* and the *Abbey of the Holy Ghost* [arts. 84, 85]) with a short extract from the *Prick of Conscience* and a series of salutations to the Virgin, hymns and prayers. In both cases, the range of texts in Thornton's probable sources argues against the idea that such devotional mini-anthologies easily fit the model of spiritual instruction for the laity in any consistently affective or penitential way. His devotional booklets do follow familiar habits of the period: most such anthologies combine a wide range of works.[32] Nonetheless, in this diversity – both within small anthologies that would encourage reading multiple works in a single sitting, and in the larger thematic constructions that emerge from Thornton's compiling – we see the remnants of a sophisticated readership among the northern gentry who can absorb a variety of complex and contradictory discourses on Christian life, much like the kaleidoscopic perspectives found in the four poems of the Cotton Nero manuscript. Thornton clearly privileges mystical texts in his own organization, but he is quite willing to preserve the sheer range of his sources as well.

In the Lincoln manuscript, the style 1 decoration also tells us that Thornton organized the volume in at least four stages.[33] The paper stocks suggest that

---

was clearly added some time after Thornton copied *Passion*, using the last few pages of quire c for its opening, and using a different paper stock for the main remnant of the *Siege* in quire d.

[31]   On fol. 110v; first noticed by E. Rickert, *Ancient English Christmas Carols* (New York, 1915), p. 156.

[32]   J. Boffey, 'The *Charter of the Abbey of the Holy Ghost* and Its Role in Manuscript Anthologies', *Yearbook of English Studies* 33 (2003), 120–30 (p. 127), argues for a broad category of 'anthologies designed for spiritual instruction' in recognition that mystical texts since at least the Vernon manuscript (Oxford, Bodleian Library, MS Eng. poet. a. 1) and through early print often appear in association with a wide range of other devotional works. Thornton's anthologies would also fit within such a capacious category, as would the poems of Cotton Nero. The issue is the interaction between very different texts fitting into the omnibus term 'devotional', for which 'spiritually instructional' might as well be a definition. For thematic analysis of the Lincoln manuscript, see Kennedy, 'The Evangelist', pp. 75–86; for the London manuscript in terms of affective response and antisemitism, see Johnston, 'Robert Thornton', pp. 140–52.

[33]   Here I leave out the *Liber de Diversis Medicinis*, which is likely to have been copied either before or after the other sections, given its unique paper stock. But cf. Keiser's chapter in the present volume, which proposes a later moment of copying for the *Liber de Diversis Medicinis*.

the *Morte* and *Awntyrs* were copied first as independent booklets in a first stage, along with the first two quires of the devotional booklet in a period when Thornton was conceiving of a substantial anthology and acquired the first substantial batch of paper to produce it.[34] The ambition of its planned decoration suggests that the prose *Alexander* was copied from an independent exemplar some time afterward with a new stock of paper and many spaces for miniatures that were never completed. Possibly at this stage *Octavian* was acquired and copied, and the *Morte* subsection (quires D–F), now including *Octavian*, was sent out for its own distinctive, if lesser professional decoration as a trial run. In the third stage, quires G–I were completed, incorporating the partially empty quire holding *Awntyrs*; *Perceval* was either acquired or finally selected for inclusion; and quires A–C, G–I and O were sent out for style 1 decoration at a point when Thornton was more interested in unifying his larger book than distinguishing the *Alexander*.[35] The final stage for Thornton's copying in the Lincoln manuscript includes all the quires that remained undecorated (quire K), or had the variant style 1 initials in combination with plain Lombards (quires M–N).

The style 1 decoration, then, tells us that Thornton deliberately organized two booklets as anthologies where either romance or devotional texts dominated, and he organized the devotional section of the Lincoln manuscript in parallel with the romance section, though more uncertainty reigned over the hierarchy of decoration for the devotional section. The prose *Alexander* and the alliterative *Morte* have decorative features (an unfinished programme of miniatures and style 2 decoration, respectively) that make clear Thornton conceived of these two works as independent booklets at the start, unlike the rest of the Lincoln booklets. The details of the decoration, in combination with other codicological evidence, indicate that he copied from a number of small anthologies reshaped to some extent into his own larger grouping. The decoration thus is very helpful in understanding more about pamphlet anthologies that were circulating in Yorkshire, where some clusters (*Octavian*, *Isumbras*, *Earl of Toulouse*) may fit our standard histories, but others (the six texts beginning with the *Life of Saint Christopher*, the cluster beginning with the *Mirror of*

Also, London's booklet 2 looks to me to be a product of three sub-units, but since these sub-units are not distinguished by decoration, I will leave that topic to others.

[34] Also see the discussion above, p. 118 and note 21.

[35] Thompson, 'The Compiler in Action', p. 116, compellingly argues that the *Alexander* was decorated before it was combined with the *Morte*; he notes that after the extra leaves were taken out for quire C, the catchword on fol. 52v was added in the hand of the scribe. However, this would be the only occasion when Thornton sent out a manuscript for decoration before every folio was filled, even with the fragment of a poem he completes in a following quire separate from the decoration of the earlier materials, as in the case of *Octavian* and *Perceval*.

Saint Edmund [arts. 61ff.]) do not.[36] These groupings may look like a Thornton question, but they are in fact a Yorkshire question: how do we understand the relationship between saint's life, romance, Marian miracle and scurrilous fabliau in one anthology?[37] What does this grouping tell us about literary habits in late medieval Yorkshire, or its major city and book centre? We can look at this grouping as a broader manifestation of what we see in the Cotton Nero manuscript, and the literary interests of a single northern poet (as shaped by the choices of Cotton Nero's producer – who knows what part of the *Pearl* poet's work this single witness preserves?): the boundaries of romance and devotional narratives are so permeable as to render the generic terms deeply problematic. *Sir Gawain and the Green Knight* embeds a distinctly light-hearted allegory of the Fall in an Arthurian romance/sex comedy; *Patience* builds on the picaresque qualities of the Jonah narrative; *Cleanness* and *Pearl* adapt sermon and dream vision forms, respectively. Overall, Cotton Nero testifies to a flexible, open accommodation of themes and literary forms that, like the sophisticated range of devotional texts in Thornton's anthologies, argues for a wide familiarity with the range of narrative strategies witnessed not only by the Thornton manuscripts as a whole, but the pamphlet anthologies embedded within. The lay readership in this place and period in England, for which Cotton Nero and the Thornton manuscripts offer such eloquent testimony, were interested in an astonishing range of perspectives on Christian life and its relationship to an historical past, enough so that contradictory visions – *Cleanness* and *Sir Gawain*, *Lyarde* and a Marian miracle – are deliberately counterposed for those readers.

Thornton's two manuscripts do offer many examples of longer works that seem to maintain clear generic boundaries (such as *Octavian* or the *Privity*). Both manuscripts present booklets organized according to the broadest definitions of romance or devotional literature – and, in the case of London's quire i, political allegory. As Thompson has pointed out, the many apparent outlier texts in those booklets undercut our confidence that Thornton had pure intentions or even definitions for any generic organization.[38] Further challenging our

---

[36] Hanna, 'The Growth', p. 61, notes that this 'standard' cluster of three romances circulated together fairly widely, as in Cambridge, CUL, MS Ff. 2. 38; London, BL, MS Cotton Caligula A. ii; and Oxford, Bodleian Library, MS Ashmole 61. Hanna also notes there that the next cluster of texts is unique or rare.

[37] In London, quire e presents similar problems despite efforts to harmonize its elements, as in Johnston, 'Robert Thornton', pp. 152–7. For a recent edition of *Lyarde* and a discussion of its fabliau qualities, see 'A Minor Comic Poem in a Major Romance Manuscript: "Lyarde"', ed. M. Furrow, *Forum for Modern Language Studies* 32 (1996), 289–302.

[38] Thompson, *London Thornton MS*, p. 34. For other views on Thornton's approach to romance in his two manuscripts see J. Finlayson, 'Reading Romances in Their Manuscript: Lincoln Cathedral Manuscript 91 ("Thornton")', *Anglia* 123 (2005), 632–66; and J. Finlayson, 'The

hopes on this score are the many sub-genres needed to herd the complex record into single super-categories: Arthurian, Charlemagne and crusader romances; affective allegories, sermons, saints' lives, miracles, tracts and epistles, prayers. Neither Thornton nor his exemplars organize texts according to these sub-categories at all.

Apparently the only genre Thornton separates out is the epic, and the independence of the *Alexander* and the *Morte* as representatives of this genre may be a function of the sheer size of these works. The decoration in the Thornton manuscripts argues that these two epics may have come from distinct sources with distant roots. We could speculate that the *Morte*, decorated in style 2, followed its exemplar in that decoration, since the acanthus/oak leaf forms may be a Yorkshire attempt at an unfamiliar style. If so, the decorator would have had that exemplary model in hand. The *Alexander*'s planned programme of miniatures, an unusual design feature for any text in late medieval England, has no Yorkshire analogue for a literary work.[39] We have to assume that Thornton had access to a splendid model, whether that model served directly for the spaces Thornton left (and the three illuminated initials) or not. In both cases, though, the most likely source for such relatively deluxe exemplars would be a book centre such as York.

What influence, then, would York have had on Thornton's manuscripts if this line of argument is correct? We can assume that any decoration for the other exemplars, probably coming to Thornton in locally circulating pamphlets, was minimal enough that they influenced Thornton only in detail.[40] We can say that these pamphlets (like Thornton) had no apparent interest in organizing their texts by generic sub-categories, and in fact preferred to present texts with striking contrasts in theme and perspective in small-anthology groupings. The *Octavian* trio of romances and the devotional clusters do preserve the broader categories Thornton himself used to organize his major anthologies as a kind of unity-in-diversity. There can be little doubt that Thornton brought a mostly organized form of the Lincoln manuscript (quires A–M) to a York-trained decorator who sealed this unified form of the larger anthology with a consistent programme of decoration. Looking at this decoration, however, it is immediately clear that, while someone inserts Lombard initials throughout the romance and devotional sections, the decorator chooses to decorate every initial in the romance section (over one hundred folia that include numerous

---

Context of the Crusading Romances in the London Thornton Manuscript', *Anglia* 130 (2012), 240–63.

[39] Hardman, 'Reading the Spaces', 250–74, makes this argument for the Thornton *Alexander* specifically.

[40] Illuminated initials for the opening of *Isumbras* (fol. 109rb) and *Awntyrs* (fol. 154r), but not any other romances, may simply witness Thornton following his exemplar.

internal initials – seventy-three initials in the *Alexander* alone – and five illuminated initials, three in the *Alexander*) while leaving most initials undecorated in the devotional section. If we assume the variant initials in quires M and N were decorated later by a different hand (possibly Thornton's given the unskilled work), then it becomes clear that the decorator heavily privileged the romance texts over the devotional texts. The decorative hierarchy, in other words, reverses what we might expect to be the spiritual hierarchy for sacred and secular texts. Thornton, on the other hand, apparently added *Perceval* after the style 1 decoration, but no later decoration is added in this section, whereas even very short works in devotional quires M and N receive this attention. Similarly, one section in the London manuscript where Thornton may have distinguished texts with a higher order of decoration is in quire f, a cluster of shorter devotional texts with alternating red and green initials, along with a planned programme of miniatures for the *Cursor Mundi* extracts.[41]

Around the middle of the fifteenth century, then, we have evidence of a book professional located or associated with York who valorizes a romance anthology more than a devotional collection, rather like the way in which we have valorized *Sir Gawain and the Green Knight* over the other poems in Cotton Nero, and the romances over the devotional work in Thornton's manuscripts. At the same time Thornton makes some special efforts to valorize his devotional texts, even to the same extent as he is willing to decorate his epics. In all cases, though, this close association between Thornton's texts and York-associated decoration opens a window on literary traditions in the north of England that develop the complexities already apparent in the Vernon and Simeon anthologies from the Midlands half a century before, and the Cotton Nero collection from around the same time.

---

[41] The two decorated initials in London on fol. 33r (opening the *Northern Passion*) and on fol. 50r (opening the *Siege of Jerusalem*) emphasize the clearly mystical text in the anthology and a crusader poem that could at least arguably be devotional in the broader sense I argue for here. As noted above, Hardman, 'Reading the Spaces', pp. 254–62, argues for a substantial planned programme in London of miniatures for *Cursor Mundi* and a miniature at the opening of the *Northern Passion*.

Appendix
The structure and decoration of the Thornton manuscripts

Lincoln Cathedral Library, MS 91[42]

Booklet 1. Quires A–C, fols. 1–52: Prose *Life of Alexander*.

> *Paper:* A–B Thompson vi (sole of shoe) and xi (crossed axes); C Thompson xi.
>
> *Decoration:* Style 1 initials throughout; illuminated initials, fols. 19r, 19v, 27r; thorn/tun rebus, fol. 23v; *bas-de-page* practice display initials, fol. 33v.

Booklet 2. Quires D–K, fols. 53–178.

> **Subsection 2a.** Quires D–F, fols. 53–102: Alliterative *Morte Arthure* (in single columns), 'Lincolnshire exemplar'; *Octavian* (beginning, fols. 98v–102v) added later (in double columns), 'Doncaster exemplar'.
>
> *Paper:* Thompson ii (bull's head), v (fleur-de-lis/dolphin).
>
> *Decoration:* Style 2 initials throughout, including *Octavian* addition; bird with scroll and legend 'Robert Thornton' (fol. 93v).

> **Subsection 2b.** Quire G, fols. 103–122: *Octavian* (end), 'Doncaster exemplar'; *Isumbras*, 'Doncaster exemplar'; *Earl of Toulouse*, 'Doncaster exemplar'; *Life of Saint Christopher* (beginning, fol. 122v).
>
> *Paper:* Thompson iii (cart), xii (bull's head and cross).
>
> *Decoration:* Style 1 initials throughout; illuminated Style 1 initial, fol. 109rb (*Isumbras*).

> **Subsection 2c.** Quires H–I, fols. 123–163 (inserting a copy of *Awntyrs* from an earlier, independent quire): *Life of Saint Christopher*; *Degrevant*; *Eglamour*; *The Wicked Knight*; *Lyarde*; *Thomas of Erceldoune's Prophecy*; *Awntyrs off Arthure*; *Perceval of Gales* (beginning), 'Doncaster exemplar'.
>
> *Paper:* H Thompson v (fleur-de-lis/dolphin); I Thompson ii (bull's head).
>
> *Decoration:* Style 1 initials throughout up to fol. 158r; illuminated Style 1 initial, fol. 154r (*Awntyrs*).

> **Subsection 2d.** Quire K, fols. 164–178: *Perceval of Gales* (end), 'Doncaster exemplar'; three charms for toothache; *Epistola Sancti Salvatoris*; prayers.

⁴² For collation of the Lincoln manuscript, see *The Thornton MS*, intro. Brewer and Owen, p. xvi. On paper stocks for both manuscripts, see Thompson, *London Thornton MS*, pp. 71–3, plates 36–52, for full descriptions, illustrations and cross-references to Briquet.

Paper: Thompson i (bull).

Decoration: Plain Lombard initial, fol. 164r (*Perceval*); blank space, fol. 177v (opening *Epistola*); none for other short devotional texts.

Booklet 3. Quires L–P, fols. 179–279.

Subsection 3a. Quire L, fols. 179–198: *Privity of the Passion* (fols. 179–188v), 'Lincolnshire exemplar'; *Tractatus de Trinitate*; various short works; *Mirror of Saint Edmund* (beginning, fol. 197r).

Paper: Thompson v (fleur-de-lis/dolphin).

Decoration: Style 1 initials, fols. 179r (*Privity*), 219r (*Jesus Thy Sweetness*); Plain Lombard initials, fols. 181r–198v (*Privity, Tractatus,* various short works, beginning of *Mirror*).

Subsection 3b. Quire M, fols. 199–222: *Mirror of Saint Edmund* (end); *Tract on the Lord's Prayer*; various short works (two columns); Gaytryge's *Sermon*; various short works.

Paper: Thompson v (fleur-de-lis/dolphin).

Decoration: Plain Lombard initials, fols. 199r–209v (ending of *Mirror*), 211r–212v (short works in two columns), 222r (Rolle's *Thy Joy Be in the Love of Jesus*). Also some paraphs in red overwriting double virgules, but many double virgules in text without overwriting. Style 1 initial, fol. 219r (*Jesus Thy Sweetness*). Variant of style 1 initials (short sprays in brown ink), fols. 209v (inhabited by a face, *Tract on the Lord's Prayer*), 213r (*When Adam Delved*), 213v (Gaytryge's *Sermon*), 219v (*Of Angels' Song*).

Subsection 3c. Quire N, fols. 223–236 (missing opening to *Mixed Life*): Hilton's *Mixed Life* (fols. 223r–229v); various short works.

Paper: Thompson xiii (circle).

Decoration: Plain Lombard initials, fols. 223r–229r (inhabited, fols. 225r, 225v). Variant of style 1 initials (short sprays in brown ink), fols. 229v (*Epistle of Salvation*), 231r (*Of Saint John*), 233v (*On Prayer*).

Subsection 3d. Quires O–P, fols. 237–279: Various short works.

Paper: O Thompson viii (hammers), xiii (circle); P Thompson iii (cart), v (fleur-de-lis/dolphin).

Decoration: Style 1 initials, fols. 237r–250v, 258r–v (four in Vulgate Psalm 50, *Veni creator, Psalter of Saint Jerome*), 262r (*Psalter of Saint Jerome*), 267v–270v, 276v (*Prick of Conscience* extract). Plain Lombard initials, fols. 250v–258r (*Revelation*), 259r–261v (*Psalter of Saint Jerome*), 262v–267r, 271r (*Abbey of the Holy Ghost*).

Booklet 4. Quires Q–R, fols. 280–321: *Liber de Diversis Medicinis.*

Paper: Thompson xv (letter A and cross).

Decoration: None.

London, BL, MS Additional 31042[43]

Booklet 1. Quires a–b, fols. 3–32: *Cursor Mundi* extracts.
　　Paper: Thompson i (bull).
　　Decoration: Plain Lombard initials in red ink.
Booklet 2. Quires c–e, fols. 33–97 (copied in 3 stages by quire).
　　Quire c, fols. 33–53: *Northern Passion*; *Siege of Jerusalem* (beginning).
　　　Paper: Thompson ii (bull's head).
　　　Decoration: Plain Lombard initials in red ink.
　　Quire d, fols. 54–73: *Siege of Jerusalem* (end); *Sege of Melayne* (beginning).
　　　Paper: Thompson iii, iv, v (cart, crowned column, fleur-de-lis/dolphin).
　　　Decoration: Plain Lombard initials in red ink.
　　Quire e, fols. 74–97 (reorganized): *Sege of Melayne* (end); lyric by Lydgate;
　　　Roland and Otuel; verse by Lydgate; three Latin aphorisms; English
　　　lyric.
　　　Paper: Thompson vi wrapping vii (sole of shoe, serpent).
　　　Decoration: Plain Lombard initials in red ink.
Booklet 3. Quire f, fols. 98–124 (reorganized): *Four Leaves of the Truelove*; lyric
　　prayer; *Have Mercy of Me*; Lydgate's *Virtues of the Mass*; *Rose of Ryse*;
　　Three Kings of Cologne; lyric on wisdom; three lyrics on mercy.
　　Paper: Thornton vi wrapping viii (sole of shoe, hammer).
　　Decoration: Plain Lombard initials in red ink, fols. 98–103v; alternating
　　　red and green ink, fols. 104v–120r (corresponds with Thompson's
　　　stage 1 of quire f, which has fols. 103–120 as a separate unit first); red
　　　ink, fols. 121r–143v (original quire containing the *Truelove* wrapped
　　　around the stage 1 core).[44]
Booklet 4. Quires g–h, fols. 125–168.
　　Quire g, fols. 125–143: *Richard Coer de Lyon* (beginning).
　　　Paper: Thompson ix (crossed keys).
　　　Decoration: Plain Lombard initials in red ink.
　　Quire h, fols. 144–168: *Richard Coer de Lyon* (end); *Childhood of Christ*
　　　(beginning).
　　　Paper: Thompson x (crown).
　　　Decoration: Plain Lombard initials in alternating red and green ink.
Booklet 5. Quire i, fols. 169–181: *Parlement of the Thre Ages*; *Wynnere and
　　Wastoure* fragment.
　　Paper: Thompson x (crown).
　　Decoration: Plain Lombard initials in red ink.

---

[43] For the collation of London, see Thompson, *London Thornton MS*, pp. 19–34.
[44] Ibid., 41.

4

The Text of the Alliterative *Morte Arthure*: A Prolegomenon for a Future Edition

Ralph Hanna and Thorlac Turville-Petre

Editing Thornton's text

In one of the earliest publications of the nascent Early English Text Society, the alliterative *Morte Arthure* brought Robert Thornton's miscellany, Lincoln Cathedral Library, MS 91, to critical attention. It was the alliterative poem most frequently edited in the late nineteenth and early twentieth centuries, and it has retained its cachet as the poetic centrepiece of Thornton's scribal oeuvre. At this time, the *editio receptus* of this impressively moving work remains Mary Hamel's treatment of the poem, now thirty years old.[1]

Hamel's edition has been justly praised. She offers some important innovations in considering the poem's sources. However, her achievement is less happy as editorial work. As her statements about procedures indicate, Hamel conceptualizes her task as that of a person defending the plausibility of Thornton's transcription, not, as editors conventionally do, as one engaged in a critical investigation of that transcription.[2] Thus, the edition provides a good introduction to what Thornton copied, which is not necessarily what the poet wrote.

---

[1]   See *Morte Arthure, Edited from Robert Thornton's MS (ab. 1440 A.D.) in the Library of Lincoln Cathedral*, ed. G. G. Perry, EETS OS 8 (London, 1865). Perry's edition required nearly immediate retuning, undertaken by E. Brock, and was republished, under the same volume number, in 1871. It had actually been preceded by a limited, private-circulation edition: *Morte Arthure: The Alliterative Romance of the Death of King Arthur*, ed. J. O. Halliwell (Brixton, 1847). See now *Morte Arthure: A Critical Edition*, ed. Mary Hamel, Garland Medieval Texts 9 (New York, 1984). Other editions are: *Morte Arthure: An Alliterative Poem of the 14th Century, from the Lincoln MS*, ed. M. M. Banks (London, 1900); *Morte Arthure*, ed. E. Björkman (Heidelberg, 1915); *Morte Arthure*, ed. J. Finlayson (London, 1967) (selections); *The Alliterative* Morte Arthure: *A Critical Edition*, ed. V. Krishna (New York, 1976); as well as the student edition *King Arthur's Death: The Middle English Stanzaic* Morte Arthur *and Alliterative* Morte Arthure, ed. L. D. Benson, rev. E. E. Foster (Kalamazoo MI, 1994).

[2]   See *Morte Arthure*, ed. Hamel, pp. 21–2.

Although her commentary is valuable, explanations of the *received* text are not always provided.[3]

From this retrospect, furthermore, Hamel's edition suffers from its timing. Her work was produced prior to two important scholarly interventions which might have inspired her to offer somewhat differing results from those printed; these we intend here to examine in turn. The first of these was the publication of the broadest available conspectus of Middle English usage, in the Aberdeen dialect atlas; the second, Hoyt N. Duggan's important series of articles on those constraints governing alliterative metrics.[4] We begin by addressing the effects that these have on Hamel's presentation and on our understanding of the *Morte* more generally.

The *Morte*, as Hamel points out, has long been associated, not with the 'home of alliterative poetry' as conventionally recognized, the north and west, but with Lincolnshire. This view was first argued in 1962 by Angus McIntosh, who asserted that Thornton's forms overlay two other linguistic layers.[5] The oldest of these, in McIntosh's account, represents the language of somewhere near Louth (in Lindsey, northeast Lincolnshire). He localized the linguistic layer intermediate between this and Thornton's copying in Kesteven, in the south-west of the county, 'between Sleaford and Grantham'.

Hamel's edition assembles most of the evidence for the author's dialect and, following McIntosh, asserts the likelihood that the author came from Lincolnshire.[6] Such a conclusion, as Hamel sees clearly, must rely on features necessarily authorial, principally the evidence provided by alliteration. The subsequent appearance of the *Linguistic Atlas*, with much the largest data set of medieval scribal spellings ever assembled, offers some opportunities for further specification of the author's provenance.

On the basis of *LALME*'s evidence, a number of features Hamel mentions would appear general throughout Lincolnshire. For example, the poet's alliterative practice requires two forms for SHALL/SHOULD. His usage alternates

---

[3]   For example, line 539 'greet stones' does not, as Hamel's punctuation would suggest, mean 'big rocks', but 'gravel, pebbles' (a compound, as if a derivative of OE *grēot-stānas).

[4]   Respectively, *LALME* and H. N. Duggan, 'Alliterative Patterning as a Basis for Emendation in Middle English Alliterative Poetry', *Studies in the Age of Chaucer* 8 (1986), 73–105; H. N. Duggan, 'The Shape of the B-Verse in Middle English Alliterative Poetry', *Speculum* 61 (1986), 564–92; and H. N. Duggan, 'Final -e and the Rhythmic Structure of the B-Verse in Middle English Alliterative Poetry', *Modern Philology* 86 (1988), 119–45.

[5]   A. McIntosh, 'The Textual Transmission of the Alliterative *Morte Arthure*', in *English and Medieval Studies Presented to J. R. R. Tolkien on the Occasion of His Seventieth Birthday*, ed. N. Davis and C. L. Wrenn (London, 1962), pp. 231–40 (p. 233).

[6]   *Morte Arthure*, ed. Hamel, pp. 72–5. Hamel supplemented this finding in her further study, 'Arthurian Romance in Fifteenth-Century Lindsey: The Books of the Lords Welles', *Modern Language Quarterly* 51 (1990), 341–61.

between *sall/sulde*-types, alliterating on /s/, and *s(c)hall/s(c)holde* ones alliterating on /š/.[7] On the basis of *LALME*'s account, such variation might well be expected, since both forms are widely attested in Lincolnshire. In the *Atlas*, the *s*-forms appear generally typical of western Lincolnshire, and the *s(c)h*-forms of the east. Since the division between them falls along a line running north–south the length of the county, one can probably assume that most authors from this area would have been aware of both forms (although see our conclusions below).

A variety of further features mentioned by Hamel shows analogous results, and these establish the poet as probably representative of this county, but without offering evidence in support of any narrower placement. Thus, the form *agayn* AGAINST is ubiquitous in Lincolnshire (*LALME* Dot Maps 220–22 [I, 359–60]), as are also spellings of SUCH with initial *sw-* (usually a *swilk*-type, but *swiche* in southern Lincolnshire) (Dot Map 74 [I, 323; cf. II, 41]). Similarly, the Scandinavian form *kirk* represents CHURCH in general Lincolnshire usage (Dot Map 384 [I, 400; cf. II, 251]), although extreme southeast Lincolnshire and adjacent areas of west Norfolk display forms of the type *cherch(e)*, certainly present at some points in Thornton's archetype.[8] Additional items ignored in Hamel's account reflect equally general Lincolnshire linguistic practice. Duggan's rules for metrical b-verses, discussed more fully below, require that MUCH and THROUGH have disyllabic forms at lines 1382 and 3938, respectively. These, whatever Thornton has written, must reflect underlying forms of the types *mykel* and *thorow*, those usual in Lincolnshire generally (cf. *LALME*, II, 77 and 227, respectively).[9]

Two forms attested by the alliteration provide more decisive indicators. These two examples, if they accurately represent the author's dialect, would suggest a poet writing far to the south of the oldest level detected by McIntosh, and to the east of his 'intermediate' linguistic level underlying Thornton's copy. First, in addition to the conventional rhyming of /k/ with /kw/ and of /w/ with /hw/, the poet crossrhymes /w/ with /kw/ and /k/ with /hw/.[10] This feature indicates that the historically distinct sounds /hw/ and /kw/ have probably

---

[7]   Contrast, for example, line 514 'He **sulde** fore solempnitee hafe seruede þe hymseluen' with line 736 'Qwen all was schyppede that **scholde**, they schounte no lengere'; see *LALME* Dot Map 148 (I, 341) and cf. II, 95, 101, 107.

[8]   Analogous to the form *cherche*, see line 767 *schreede*, mishandled by Hamel, who fails to recognize that it is simply a reflex of OE *scrȳdan, here the past participle 'clothed'. The vocalism testifies to the same development that allows OE cyrice to have a reflex with stem-vowel *e* (OE *y* and *ȳ* as ME *e* and *ē*, respectively).

[9]   Although disyllabic representation of THROUGH becomes progressively more recessive throughout northern Lincolnshire, another point supporting our proposed provenance below.

[10]   For k/kw, see line 696; for w/hw, see lines 553, 948, 2668, etc.; but contrast line 1788 'So may þe wynde weile turnne, I **quytte** hym or ewyn'; similarly lines 1736 (although read

coalesced in the author's dialect – and thus, that /kw/ can participate in the traditional and widespread alliteration of /hw/ with /w/. In *LALME* materials, this feature should be indicated by spellings of the type *quare* WHERE. Evidence for this feature, spellings in *qu-* for earlier *wh-*, occurs recessively in a wide range of Lincolnshire scribal profiles, enough so for one to believe that forms of this sort may well have been recognizable across the medieval county. But in only two areas are *qu-* spellings for Old English *hw-* majority forms – through the northwest of the county, and extending into adjacent parts of the East Riding, Yorkshire, and in its southeastern corner around the Wash (*LALME* Dot Maps 270–3 [I, 372–3; cf. II, 189]).

This distribution corresponds with a second authorial feature recessive in Lincolnshire usage. In the *Morte*, the noun 'gift' and forms of the verb 'give', although usually alliterating on the voiced stop, must also alliterate with initial /j/ (cf. lines 1503, 2628). The spellings recorded in *LALME* for 'give' (see Dot Maps 425, 427 [I, 411]) show this as a recorded Lincolnshire form, e.g. *yive/ʒyve*, in precisely those areas that have majority *qu*-spellings for earlier *wh-*. Again, this feature is associated with the northwest and southeast. However, in this case, the form is restrictive; unlike *qu-* for *wh-*, it does not occur in adjacent areas of Yorkshire.

This last fact seems to us significant. The poem was more likely composed in southeast Lincolnshire than in northwestern parts of the county. Here one variation we have already noted, between the types *sall/s(c)hall*, is telling. Northwest Lincolnshire forms part of that large area of northern England and Scotland that routinely shows universal forms in *s-* for SHALL/SHOULD, and thus proves a less likely localization than its competitor. Yet further indirect confirmation of southeast Lincolnshire provenance is provided by various errors Robert Thornton made in transcribing the poem. He sometimes failed to understand the apparently frequent occurrence in his archetype of forms generally considered 'East Anglian', the reproduction of modern *-ght* as *-th*.[11] While these may have been introduced in the intermediate Sleaford/Grantham copying posited by McIntosh, they equally may represent authorial relicts.

We would conclude that the poem, if its forms reflect a natural dialect, would have been composed southeast of the Sleaford-Grantham area, around the Wash and the Lincolnshire/Norfolk border. Hamel argues that the poem

---

'[q]wellyde'?), 2103–4, 2189; 3503 "'Fro **qwyn** (OE hweþen) come þou, kene man", quod þe kynge than'; and overt crossrhyme of /hw/ and /kw/ at lines 3261, 3389.

[11] See, for example, Björkman's emendations in lines 1503, 2108, 2280. In the first example, Thornton presented 1503 as (the nonmetrical) 'may þou ʒeme now þeselfen', rather than the obvious 'ʒeme nowght'; the underlying archetypal 'ʒeme nowth' has fallen victim to haplography before the 'th' repeated at the head of the next word. See the *LALME* display for the spelling *myth* 'might', Dot Map 334 (I, 388; cf. II, 221).

was produced by a magnatial hanger-on (62). But given her equal demonstration that the poem concords a vast wad of chronicle material, other conclusions might be suggested. Access to materials of this sort, many of them learnedly Latinate, might equally imply access to a monastic library (although perhaps again composition for a magnatial patron of the house). If so, one might wish to consider (and investigate further) associations of the *Morte* with a Benedictine house situated within the preferred dialect area, the most plausible candidates being Crowland or its daughter-house at Spalding. Manuscripts containing chronicles survive from both, and there are references to additional copies in their surviving medieval booklists.[12]

Southeast Lincolnshire is an area far removed from those usually considered sites of alliterative composition. Such a provenance might provide one explanation for certain perceived peculiarities of alliterative practice in the *Morte*, deviations from a norm exemplified by the poets from further north and west. On the other hand, these deviations, or some of them, might be the responsibility of the scribes rather than the poet. Hamel as editor could not be aware of the full ramifications of these deviancies, since Duggan's impressive articles on alliterative metrical practice only appeared after her edition had been published.

One of Duggan's most persuasive showings concerns the rules for writing a metrical b-verse in an alliterative longline. On the basis of surveying a very large sample of lines from across the corpus, Duggan demonstrates that all b-verses are comprised of four elements, two lifts and two dips. These two dips, however, must display a complementary pattern, one of them strong (two or more syllables) and one weak (no more than a single syllable). Thus, the permissible syllabic patterns for b-verses follow one of only two forms:

$$x \, x \, (x \dots) \, C \, (x) \, C \, (x) \quad \text{OR} \quad (x) \, C \, x \, x \, (x \dots) \, C \, (x)$$

This observed codification of verse technique, when applied to the poem, may suggest some limitations on Thornton's *textus receptus*.[13]

Speaking generally, in quite a large number of instances, Thornton's graphemic representation offers perfectly fine (and widely attested) line types in an

---

[12] For surviving books, see N. R. Ker, *Medieval Libraries of Great Britain: A List of Surviving Books*, Royal Historical Society Guides and Handbooks 3, 2nd edn (London, 1964), 56, 181. For lost books, see R. Sharpe, J. P. Carley, R. M. Thomson and A. G. Watson, *English Benedictine Libraries: The Shorter Catalogues*, Corpus of British Medieval Library Catalogues 4 (London, 1996), B24.60, 75–7; B25.4–6; B95.2 (pp. 121, 123, 125, 126, 593). Cambridge, Magdalene College, MS 5, probably a Crowland book, contains a unique English translation of the French prose Apocalypse, and B24.93 (p. 125) had an English lapidary, both testimony to English writing in the house.

[13] Because Hamel wrote before Duggan published, her edition contains a number of ill-conceived emendations, none of them necessary, and revealed as such by their creation of unmetrical b-verses, e.g. lines 656, 2260, 2675.

overtly non-metrical guise. Thus, Thornton rather frequently fails to write out full plural verb inflections:

> ... and dredde ay schame (line 20)

where 'dredde[n]' is metrical (cf. line 168 'þey chaungen þeire wedes'). Similarly, while he usually writes -*ande* in these instances, a reader must understand that this termination of the present participle is disyllabic (< Old Norse -*andi*), e.g.

> ... in flammandë siluer (line 198)

More often, in the very frequent b-verse frame, conj/prep + adjective + noun plural, the -*e* that indicates the plural adjective, and that is required for a metrical verse, is not expressed graphemically:

> ... of diuers[ë] rewmes (line 66; cf. 'in dyuersë remmes' line 49)
> ... wyth sexten[ë] kynges (line 105)[14]

And similar oddments, e.g. '...thos erledom[e]s ryche' (line 42), occur with some frequency.

In contrast with these examples, all of which involve an accurately reported, if graphemically not very communicative, text, a relatively small number of lines violates those b-verse constraints Duggan outlines. In the main, these represent examples of Duggan's 'double dipping', instances where scribal padding has produced 'prosified' lines with two strong b-verse dips, rather than the single one required by the form. On the whole, these can be corrected relatively easily, by suppressing a syllable clearly otiose to the sense, e.g.

> ... to the pople þat them heres (line 11)

Here suppressing 'the' would provide a metrical form.[15] Similar examples, with suggested items to be suppressed noted parenthetically, include lines 60 (read 'be sent', cf. 1628), 115 ('his'), 415 ('þe'), 520 (elide or drop 'þe'), 1304 ('þe'), 1503 ('may þou'), 1870 ('sir'), 2057 ('thare', probably a scribal echo of the example in the a-verse), 3283 ('the'), 3807 (read 'postlys') and 3917 ('þe').[16]

The complementary form of unmetrical b-verses, a dearth of syllables, and thus a line with two weak dips, also occurs, e.g.

> þat sounde was neuere (line 932)

[14] On this basis, 'bryttenede' in line 2212 is an adjectival past participle, not the simple past Hamel reports, and the whole b-verse in parallel with 'Baneres'.

[15] And 'them' may be otiose as well, although still in a strong dip, since the antecedent 'worde' in line 9 is singular.

[16] In line 4215 Hamel misplaces the position of the caesura: 'bryghte' is part of the b-verse and 'euer' probably otiose and to be suppressed.

Here replacing 'was' with 'hadde be' (cf. 'þat sownde bese he neuer' line 4312) would solve the problem. Similar examples occur at lines 1160 (read 'þe flesche noght entamede'?), 1251 (read 'duchy men', i.e., fleeing people from the duchy of Burgundy, mentioned in 1241; but cf. 2653), 1347 (read 'and an erle'), 1659 (read 'erles'), 1796 and 1805 (read 'wounded many/fele'; the half-lines are identical), 2139 (read 'all thes'), 2653 (read 'Duché men'), 2840 (read 'are vndron be rongen'), 3021 (transpose to read 'wele es'), 3293 (read 'laide vnder'; cf. 4276), 3405 (transpose to read 'faye has', the normal locution, as in 1250, 2380), 3688 (read 'sall they'), 4249 (read 'the ventaile').[17] There are a few oddments that probably deserve more protracted attention; for example, line 4096 is only metrical on the assumption that 'steryn' is actually disyllabic, and line 4146, with 'beryn', may show a similarly disyllabic form (although in this instance reading 'opone lyfe' would resolve the problem, and the similar 'berynns' in line 3661 probably is a substitution for some variety of boat (e.g. 'balyngers', cf. Mannyng, *Chronicle* 1.5928).[18]

More challenging, however, is the *Morte*'s persistent marked departure from the norms of the full alliterative long line. In his study, Duggan demonstrates conclusively the truth of the ancient contention (it goes back at least to Thomas Warton in the eighteenth century) that the base form of the Middle English alliterative tradition is a four-stress line, divided by a caesura into a pair of half-lines, each of two stresses. In this form, the first three stresses must alliterate, and the fourth never does. This form includes the option that the first half-line may admit three stressed syllables, only two of which need alliterate,[19] and the poem's opening distich exhibits both forms:

    A   A   A   A   X
    Now grett glorious Godde, thurgh grace of hymseluen
        A   A   A X
    And the precyous prayere of hys prys modyr ...

But line patterning in the *Morte* proves unusually various, if not frequently deviant. This fact was readily apparent to Erik Björkman, whose 1915 edition undertook, so far as possible, to emend all lines in which alliteration fails to span the caesura.

However much he over-emended the text (and we do find many sugges-

[17]   Line 1503, discussed in another context in n.11 above, requires re-ordering as ' þou nowght ȝeme'.

[18]   See *Robert Mannyng of Brunne: The Chronicle*, ed. I. Sullens, Medieval and Renaissance Texts and Studies 153 (Binghamton NY, 1996).

[19]   See H. N. Duggan, 'Extended A-Verses in Middle English Alliterative Poetry', *Parergon* 18 (2000), 53–76.

tions here cavalier), Björkman did perceive the difficulty.[20] As transmitted, the alliterative verse in the *Morte* appears intractably different from that of any other poem, and certainly so from the 'core' (northern and western) tradition on which all statements about alliterative verse are predicated. The following cornucopia of examples from the first hundred-odd lines of the poem will give some taste of the problems and their frequency:[21]

26	Qwen that the **kynge** Arthur by **con**queste hade wonnyn
50	Mad of his **cosyns kyng**ys ennoyntede
64	Thane aftyre at **Car**lelele [sic] a **Crist**ynmesse he haldes
65	This ilke **kyde con**querour and helde hym for lorde
70	Bot on the **Crist**nymes-daye when they were all semblyde
77	**Mad** in **myd**wynter in þa weste **march**ys
78	Bot on the **New**-ȝere-daye at the **none** euyne
83	Ilke a **kynge** aftyre **kynge** and mad his en**clines**
86	Sir Lucius **Iberius** the **em**perour of Rome
90	Now in this **New**-ȝers daye with **no**taries sygne
92	That on **Lam**messe daye thare be no **lette** founden
95	At **pryme** of the daye in **payne** of ȝour lyvys
97	When he and his **sen**atours bez **sette** as them lykes
102	Thare schall thow gyffe **rek**kynynge for all thy **Round** Table
108	That thow ne schall **rowte** ne **ryste** vndyr the heuene **ryche**

All the lines cited are, in some measure or another, deviations from expected alliterative practice. Particularly striking are three examples (lines 77, 83, 108) where the poem avoids the practice nearly universal elsewhere and allows the last stress of the line to carry the alliteration.

One can certainly explain – or emend away – all these deviations. For example, line 26 might be construed, with stress on 'Qwen' (and not the somewhat intrusive 'Arthur'), as an example of the line-form AA | AX. Or lines 64, 70, 78, 86 and 92 might be taken as examples of an expected licence, poets

---

[20] The frequent excesses of Björkman's edition (which may underlie Hamel's stern non-interventionalism) were first (and conclusively) demonstrated in J. L. N. O'Loughlin, 'The Middle English Alliterative *Morte Arthure*', *Medium Ævum* 4 (1935), 153–68. O'Loughlin offers a good many salient explanations for a variety of apparently deviant lines, e.g. that certain staves, difficult to alliterate, e.g. /v/ and /dž/, might legitimately appear in lines with the apparently diminished form AX | AX or XA | AX. For recent discussion, see J. A. Jefferson and A. Putter, 'Alliterative Patterning in the *Morte Arthure*', *Studies in Philology* 102 (2005), 415–33; also A. Putter, J. A. Jefferson and M. Stokes, *Studies in the Metre of Alliterative Verse*, Medium Ævum Monographs n.s. 5 (Oxford, 2007), pp. 119–43.

[21] This truly represents only a sixty-odd line sample, since the prologue to the action and the list of Arthurian conquests (1–47), as with many set-pieces elsewhere in the poem, is largely unproblematic. Alliterating stressed syllables are marked in bold.

allowed reduced alliteration to incorporate proper names[22] – although one would then have to notice that the preceding catalogue of Arthurian conquests, with a prodigious list of place names and yet utterly regular patterning, never indulges in such a procedure. Following Björkman, one might replace 'they' in line 70 with a rhyming noun ('knyghtes'), just as 'Mad' in line 50 might be a substitution for 'Creat(e)' (potentially also the case at line 709, but cf. 649). At least two examples of the most unusual feature, alliteration on final stress, appear susceptible to easy transpositions that produce perfectly regular patterns: line 83 'and his en**clines** mad', line 108 'heuene-**ryche** vndyr'. But such a flurry of special pleading and editorial activity would indicate either that Thornton's *Morte* has been subjected to an unusually sloppy transmission, or that it is not always engaged in reproducing those patterns one expects from a tradition far removed from the area where this poem was composed.

Here there is a further consideration, first identified by J. L. N. O'Loughlin.[23] The text provides a huge amount of evidence suggestive of the view that alliterative patterning here answers imperatives very different from that visible elsewhere in the tradition. That is, the poet, frequently and ostentatiously, does not restrict a head-rhyme to the single line, but creates variously long leashes of successive lines rhyming on the same sound. Within these extended sequences linked on the letter, deviances like those surveyed above frequently occur. For example, at 2482–92, the poet writes an extended sequence of lines all alliterating on /f/. The great majority of these are perfectly regular, but the sequence also includes:

2482　One **Son**ondaye, be þe **soone** has a flethe ȝolden
2483　The kyng calles on **Florente** þat **flour** was of knyghttez
2486　For them wantes þe **flesche** and **fude** that them lykes
2491　Vs moste with some **fresche** mette re**fresche** oure pople

The first two lines, which open the passage, are fairly typical of the technique. The first shows the non-rhyming pattern AA | XX, but it follows upon 2481 'Settes vp sodaynly certayne engynes', also alliterating, in an unimpeachable pattern, on /s/. Thus, the a-verse in 2482 might be taken as the conclusion of an earlier sequence. Further, in its third-position noun 'flethe', it 'sets the sound' that will bind the remainder of the twelve-line passage. The whole 2482 thus might be perceived as a bridging line in which the b-verse is understood to allit-

---

[22]　Alternatively, that a number of lines through the poem involving the word 'day' or specific dates show similar deviations.

[23]　And see M. F. Vaughan, 'Consecutive Alliteration, Strophic Patterns, and the Composition of the Alliterative *Morte Arthure*', *Modern Philology* 77 (1979), 1–9, who estimates that about 75 per cent of the poem's lines are linked in ways described in this paragraph; so too Y. Moriya, 'Identical Alliteration in the *Alliterative Morte Arthure*', *English Language Notes* 38 (2000), 1–16.

erate with the following line. Its a-verse concludes one leash, while its b-verse anticipates the subsequent one.[24]

In terms of the full sequence, the following line, 2483, may be perceived as deviant, although closely resembling the third and fourth we have cited, but it is certainly also a regular example of A(A)B | BA.[25] In essence, an alliterative surround, partially echoed, but not echoed with formal exactitude, appears in many cases to obviate any need for exact adherence to the single-line AA | AX pattern ubiquitous elsewhere in the tradition. From such a perspective, one might accept nearly half the lines cited above from the poem's opening as plausibly unexceptionable; at least, lines 50, 64, 65, 70, 95, 102, 108 and perhaps 77 also occur in contexts where they might be construed as either anticipating or continuing a multi-line sequence of verses rhyming on the same stave. Yet the result remains perhaps as unsatisfactory as was our initial survey of these lines. There, only a considerable amount of thoroughly conjectural emendation would serve to reduce the anomalies in Thornton's presentation; here, even excluding the lines falling in continuous phonetic contexts, one is still left with a large residue of comparably inexplicable, and arguably poorly transmitted, instances. Examples like the two apparently deviant lines from the twelve-line leash on /f/ at lines 2481–92 might instill further doubts. These are capable, as are many lines cited by Jefferson and Putter (see note 20), of easy surgery that would create forms recognizable as those of the tradition at large:

> 2486 For them [fau]tes þe flesche and fude that them lykes[26]
> 2491 Vs moste with some fresche [fud]e refresche oure pople.

Evidence from Malory: Alliterative patterns

Without further guidance in the matter, the editor may well argue that the author of *Morte Arthure* wrote according to rules rather different from those followed by other poets, and consequently will supply conjectural emendations

---

[24] It is worth noting that such 'anticipatory' b-verses (as well as leashes of lines on the same sound) have been observed in another poet from (south)eastern England, also often perceived something of an alliterative 'sport'; see A. V. C. Schmidt, *The Clerkly Maker: Langland's Poetic Art* (Cambridge, 1987), pp. 38–40, 52–62.

[25] Notice that reading the line as if alliterating on a single stave /k/, although it does provide two rhymes in the a-verse and one in the b-verse, would involve the further anomaly already mentioned, the fourth and final stress of the line bearing alliteration (AA | XA). Again, this is readily transposable into an unexceptionable verse, 'of knyghttez was flour'.

[26] Or emend to the palaeographically more distant 'fayles þe flesche'; cf. *Cleanness* 1194, *Siege of Jerusalem* 881. A full conspectus of the editions from which we draw parallels appears in note 30.

only in order to correct evident nonsense. But, although Thornton's miscellany is the only surviving copy of the *Morte*, some check on its text can be derived from another source. With the discovery of the Winchester manuscript of Malory's work in 1934, it became apparent that Malory was an astute reader of the poem and followed it often very closely to line 3217 in his prose *remaniement*. Already in 1937, E. V. Gordon collaborated with Eugène Vinaver, the editor of the newly discovered manuscript (not to be published for another ten years) in a survey of the information the new version of Malory provided for the text of *Morte Arthure*.[27] This information was ignored by editors before Hamel, and, although she recognizes its significance, even she does her best to diminish its impact. She posits a 'Scribe E', envisioned as a not very competent redactor of the *Morte* familiar with the metre and vocabulary of alliterative verse, and taking a more conservative approach to alliterative patterning than the poet's.[28]

Such a reviser, though uncommon, is not entirely unknown elsewhere. For instance, among copies of *Piers Plowman* the redactor of the B version in Oxford, Corpus Christi College, MS 201, alters lines to increase alliteration, adds a few passages, and recasts the structure of the poem. Similarly, the prologue recorded in the Ilchester manuscript, University of London Library, MS S.L.V.88, is a scribal 'improvement' of a corrupt copy of Langland's work. Yet it is important to recognize that editors of *Piers Plowman* have little trouble in recognizing the scribal quality of these alterations. It seems unnecessary to involve such a complicating factor in the transmission of the *Morte* to Malory, who was clearly himself active in reshaping his source, in terms of both language and structure. We should recognize instead that Malory had access to a text of the poem that was at some points more accurate and more complete than Thornton's, but also should be attentive to the possibility that the prose writer was himself modestly adept at writing alliterative lines.

For example, one of the readings that Hamel attributes to Scribe E's intervention may instead illustrate Malory at work, substituting his own phrasing for that of the poem he had received, and yet creating a good alliterative line in the process.[29] Line 2371 reads: 'In the kalendez of Maye this caas es befallen'. The b-verse is a favourite of the poet's; there are precise parallels at lines 1892, 2371 and 3521. Malory has instead: 'For in the moneth of May this myscheff befelle' (226.20). However, there is no need to posit an intervening redactor

---

[27] E. V. Gordon and E. Vinaver, 'New Light on the Text of the Alliterative *Morte Arthure*', *Medium Ævum* 6 (1937), 81–98. Vinaver edited the text as *The Works of Sir Thomas Malory* (Oxford, 1947, 2nd edn 1967); all our citations come from the second edition and are by page/line.

[28] See *Morte Arthure*, ed. Hamel, pp. 9–13.

[29] Contrast what follows with Hamel's discussion, *Morte Arthure*, p. 10.

familiar with the alliterative a-verse 'In the month of May' (cf. *Parlement of the Thre Ages* 1 and 660, *Destruction of Troy* 625 etc.).[30] Almost inevitably, Malory would have simplified *kalendez* to *moneth*, using the same phrase in his famous passage at the beginning of the 'Knight of the Cart'. Furthermore, *myscheff* is rather a favourite word of Malory's,[31] and it would not take much alliterative prompting for Malory to use it here. The same may be said for a number of other lines in which Malory replaces one alliterating phrase by another (so *deme for His deth* [245.3] replacing *reuenge the Renke* in line 3217). Certainly the editor must exercise caution in adopting readings from Malory and judge each case on its merits, taking into account parallels elsewhere in the poem, as well as identifying the vocabulary characteristic of Malory as compared to that of the *Morte*.

Malory readily adopts from the poem vocabulary which is outside his usual range, and there is no reason to posit the involvement of any other writer. Hamel notes that the poet's lines

> And than the Bretons brothely enbrassez þeire scheldez,
> Braydes one bacenetez and buskes theire launcez (1753–4)

are replaced in Malory by

> And than they fruyshed forth all at onys, of the bourelyest knyghtes that ever
> brake brede. (214.31–2)[32]

In the poem *burliche* occurs frequently, and *frusche* is used as noun and verb (once each). It seems that the words appealed to Malory, for he uses them not only here but elsewhere, in contexts where the poet did *not* use them (*fruysshed* 208.14, cf. *Morte* 1376; *bowerly* 207.26 replacing the poet's *stelyn* in line 1354, and at 240.31 in a passage added by Malory). Lest it be thought that these words are exclusively from the vocabulary of alliterative verse, it should be observed that *frush* is in quite widespread use, but the only alliterative poem in which it is

---

[30] Editions of alliterative poems cited are: *The Awntyrs off Arthure at the Terne Wathelyn*, ed. R. Hanna (Manchester, 1974); *Cleanness*, ed. J. J. Anderson (Manchester, 1977); *The Destruction of Troy*, ed. H. Matsumoto, 3rd edn (Okayama-shi, 2011); *Piers Plowman: The A Version*, ed. G. Kane rev. edn (London, 1988); *Piers Plowman: The B Version*, ed. G. Kane and E. T. Donaldson, 2nd edn (London, 1988); *The Parlement of the Thre Ages* and *A Pistel of Susan*, in *Alliterative Poetry of the Later Middle Ages*, ed. T. Turville-Petre (London, 1989), pp. 67–100, 120–39, respectively; *The Siege of Jerusalem*, ed. R. Hanna and D. Lawton, EETS 320 (Oxford, 2003); *Sir Gawain and the Green Knight*, ed. J. R. R. Tolkien and E. V. Gordon, rev. N. Davis, 2nd edn (Oxford, 1967); *The Wars of Alexander*, ed. H. N. Duggan and T. Turville-Petre, EETS SS 10 (Oxford, 1989).

[31] See T. Kato, *A Concordance to the Works of Sir Thomas Malory* (Tokyo, 1974).

[32] See *Morte Arthure*, ed. Hamel, p. 11.

regularly found is *Destruction of Troy*.[33] The adjective *bourely* is predominantly a northern word, common in alliterative verse, and later very common in Scottish texts. So there is no reason to attribute these words to a redactor familiar with alliterative verse. As for Malory's alliterating phrase *brake brede*, its origin is of course the biblical *panem fregit*, familiar from the Consecration of the Mass, but apparently never occurring in an alliterative poem.[34] Hamel's characterization of it as 'a tag, reminiscent of popular traditions' is wide of the mark.

Hamel describes her treatment of Malory's readings as 'conservative, if not actively suspicious', and emends only in narrowly defined circumstances: 'Only when the line is defective by the poet's own rules – e.g., an *a a : x x* line in isolation without linkage to adjoining lines – may such a reading be accepted with some confidence'.[35] But this is to beg the question, since it assumes that the text as transmitted is equivalent to the practice of the poet, whose 'rules' remain to be determined. Usually Hamel's edition does not even supply a note to discuss a suspicious reading. Even if the editor adopts such a flexible attitude to the alliteration of the poem, it is surely important to accept the possibility of error in Thornton's text. Editors of alliterative verse are accustomed to recognize scribal error affecting the alliteration, as in this line, chosen at random from *Siege of Jerusalem*:

> For þer as fayleþ þe fode þer is feynt strengþe (line 881)

where the manuscripts offer the variants:

> fayleþ] fawtis A, lakketh C; fode] mete C; feynt] feble P, littill A; strengþe] herte E.

In this example, two synonymous substitutions in Manuscript C result in a line lacking alliteration. Equally, the similar error in MS A creates an AA | XX line, an error particularly germane to our discussion, for A is the sigil that here represents Robert Thornton's copy of *Siege* in London, BL, MS Additional 31042. The editors of *Siege* offer ample, if scattered, evidence of Thornton's faulted transmission of regular alliterative lines that, in the presence of the closely related Manuscript P, we can be certain were in his exemplar of the poem.

Hamel adopts Malory's readings in two lines that lack alliteration. For 'Gife it to thy sqwyere, fore he es wele horsede' (line 1179), Malory has 'geff hit to thy servaunte that is swyffte-horsed' (204.17). Hamel accepts *swyffte* with some

---

[33] *MED* cites it also from the partly alliterative *Joseph of Arimathea* and *Chevalier Assigne*.

[34] The closest parallel usage is *Awntyrs of Arthure* 548, 'He was þe burlokest blonke þat euer bote brede'.

[35] *Morte Arthure*, ed. Hamel, p. 14.

hesitation, commenting in her note that it 'may possibly be scribe E's'.[36] For 'Fifty thowsande men, wythin two eldes' (301), Hamel adopts Malory's *twenty* (188.24), though her edition fails to observe that he has *tyred men* for *men*, adoption of which would complete the alliterative pattern.[37] She accepts revision of the b-verse of an AA | XX line, 'Thay hade wonn that wone be theire awen strenghe' (2472), on the basis of Malory's 'the cité wonne thorow wyghtness of hondys' (227.29), with the reservation that this 'may be an example of Scribe E's tidying-up of the poet's unconventional versification'.[38] She might have pointed out that this emendation is confirmed by the same b-verse, 'by wyghtnesse of handes', in *Morte* line 516, and the b-verses 'by wyghtnesse of strenghte / horses' in lines 796, 1358 and 2214.

Elsewhere, however, Hamel rejects emendations Gordon and Vinaver had proposed on the basis of Malory's readings. In the following passage Malory closely reproduces his source:

> 3e are at the ferreste noghte passande fyve hunndrethe,
> And þat es fully to fewe to feghte with them all.
> Fore harlottez and hansemene sall helpe bott littill;
> They will hye theym hyen, for all þeire gret wordes! (lines 2741–4)

ye ar fraykis in this fryth nat paste seven hondred, and that is feythfully to fewe to fyght with so many, for harlottys and haynxmen wol helpe us but a lytyll, for they woll hyde them in haste for all their hyghe wordys. (235.24–8)

Supplying Malory's *fraykis* would improve the light a-verse of line 2741, and *hyghe* for *gret* seems an obvious improvement of the AA | XX patterning in Thornton's version of line 2744. Hamel adopts neither of these, making no comment on the former, remarking on the latter that the poet 'normally used *gret* (but never *hyghe*) in the sense "boastful"'.[39] In fact the adverb *heghe*, 'boastfully', appears in line 3715. The more important point is that b-verses consisting of alliterating adjective + *wordes* are very common (including *gret wordes* five times). Though the poet might be punning on *hye ... hyen ... hyghe*, we suspect that Malory's text points to further corruption, since the a-verse 'Fore they will hyde them in haste' is used in line 2886, with the preceding line, 'I hope that thees harlottez sall harme vs bot littill', a reminiscence of line 2743. In this

[36]   See p. 296. The line is still defective (X A | A X). Perhaps an alliterating adverb like *swythe* (cf. line 4273 etc.) or *sweperly* (cf. line 1465) should be inserted in the a-verse.

[37]   Malory does not use the form *tyred* elsewhere. Cf. 'tired in platis', *Wars of Alexander*, line 3731.

[38]   *Morte Arthure*, ed. Hamel, p. 334.

[39]   Ibid., p. 345.

passage Hamel makes one emendation, of *fully* to *feythfully* in line 2742, which is likely enough, although metrically unnecessary.

If we are right to conclude from such instances that Thornton's text is often corrupt, we must regard with considerable suspicion lines without b-verse alliteration, even if they occur in a run of lines alliterating on the same sound, and all the more so where Malory offers a more regularly alliterating alternative. Yet Hamel offers no comment on two more AA | XX lines, which she must regard as conforming to this poet's practice, rather than Thornton's misperceptions. Addressing the giant, Arthur says 'Thow has marters made and broghte oute of lyfe' (line 1066); the following line alliterates on /b/, and the subsequent 1068–9 on /m/. Malory has instead 'Thou haste made many martyrs by mourtheryng of this londis' (202.20–1). Thornton's b-verse is surely a scribal bowdlerization of Malory's much more powerful version, its verbal noun supported by line 4259, in which Arthur's army 'Mourtherys in the mowntaygnes'. Line 3215, 'Withe the rentes of Rome, as me beste lykes', is preceded by a line alliterating on /r/, but its vapid b-verse is much improved by Malory's 'with the rentys of Rome to rule as me lykys' (244.24–245.1). Lines ending in *lykes* are extremely common in the poem, and there are parallels for both versions.

Hamel never emends lines with single alliteration in the a-verse, and rarely comments, even to note Gordon and Vinaver's earlier suggestions. Line 2732 reads in Thornton's text 'Chiftayne of þis journee with cheualrye noble'. In the light of Malory's 'chyfften of this chekke' (235.12–13), one should conclude with Gordon-Vinaver that the scribe has substituted one synonym for another (both words, in this context, mean 'attack'). The word *journee* occurs thirteen times in the poem, always alliterating on /dž/ except here. Malory uses *chekke* only once elsewhere, at 239.16, reproducing the line 'This chekke hym eschewede [i.e. "achieved"] be chauncez of armes' (2956), so that emendation seems justified, despite a parallel in *Gawain* line 86 (voiced *joly* with voiceless *childgered*). No more doubtful is correction of 'Grete sommes of golde, sexti horse chargegid' (3136), a line surely composed in order to describe objects of silver, rather than gold. Malory's parallel rendition is 'grete sommys of sylver, syxty horsys well charged' (243.21–2); the error *golde* is perhaps an anticipation of the same word eight lines below. For 'Be than the Romaynez ware rebuykde a lyttill' (line 2153), Malory has 'Than the Romaynes reled a lytyl, for they were somewhat rebuked' (221.24–5), suggesting that *reled* should be included to make a much more satisfactory line: 'Be than the Romaynez [reled], ware rebukyde a litill'; cf. 'The renke relys abowte' (line 2794).

Hamel is frequently forced to offer strained explanations to preserve the transmitted text. Line 2883 reads '"Peter!" sais Sir Gawayne; "This gladdez myn herte"', but Malory's version of the same line begins 'Be God' (238.14). Noting that Priamus, whom Gawain is here addressing, had earlier sworn by Peter, Hamel suggests that 'perhaps Gawain is simply responding to the influence of his new friend'. Rather, reminiscence of the earlier line, '"Petire!" sais Priamus, "nowe payes me bettire"' (2646) is the source of Thornton's error here.[40]

On occasions where Malory replaces a non-alliterating word with a synonym, also non-alliterating, the editor should consider whether both represent the avoidance of a *difficilior lectio*. For 'And heyly his retenuz raykes hym aftyre' (line 2920), Malory has 'and streyte all his retynew folowed hym aftyr' (238.26–7), characteristically altering the northern verb *rayke* (he preserves it only once, at 226.9, reproducing line 2352). Neither *heyly* nor *streyte* completes the alliteration, and it is possible that both texts avoid the adverb *raply*, used in line 1763. Against this interpretation, it could be argued that *heyly* (cf. *hye*, 'haste' line 463 etc.) is equally difficult, since the adverb is only recorded in *Morte Arthure*.

On the whole, Malory's rendition is far more useful in suggesting corrections to the text of *Morte Arthure* than Hamel will credit. The conclusion must be that the text as transmitted by Thornton is often inaccurate. Either the exemplar available to Thornton, or his own particular predilections as copyist, has rendered a good deal of the original irrecoverable. This possibility needs careful pursuit by comparing (as we have done in passing earlier) Thornton's scribal behaviour here with his handling of comparable texts, especially the *Siege of Jerusalem* and the *Awyntyrs off Arthure*, where other manuscripts provide a check. For now we turn to additional Malorian evidence that indicates the limitations of the *textus acceptus* of *Morte Arthure* – which our analysis indicates is what Hamel's edition has provided, not the critical edition her title promises.

Evidence from Malory: Omitted passages

There are three possible sources of passages in Malory that are not represented in Thornton's copy of the alliterative *Morte*. Some of them may have been lost from the text as preserved by Thornton. Several, certainly, are added by Malory in his adaptation. The third possibility is that they had been added to the poem in the copy Malory followed, by Hamel's Scribe E. We shall consider each of these possibilities in the examples that follow.

As instances of the first category, Hamel inserts into her text nine passages from Malory, on the grounds that they supply information necessary to the

---

[40] For Hamel's discussion, see *Morte Arthure*, p. 348. Other emendations that should be adopted include: *venquiste* 325 > *venquiste with victorie* 189.11 (as line 1984); *In syngulere batell* 826 > *Boldely in batell* 197.21 (as line 1450); *dystroyede* 850 > *kylled* 198.11; *Proueste* 1889 > *pure Proueste* 216.32; *doo* 2322 > *meue on* 225.18; *proue todaye* 2751 > *prestly proue* 236.4; *sothely ... hade spede* 3016 > *trewly ... trauaillede (hade)* 240.24; *leue* 3063 > *sese* 242.7; *whills his lyffe lastis* 3147 > *all hir lyffe tymes* 244.1–2 (as line 4159); *þus wele tymede* 3150 > *he (for hym?) tyme semed* 244.4; *at þe Crystynmesse daye* 3213 > *comly þe Crystynmesse* 244.23.

sense, or that their vocabulary is typical of the poem but foreign to Malory.[41]
There are two likely cases in the description of the dragon of Arthur's dream,
which Malory paraphrases rather closely. Malory has 'his tayle was fulle of
tatyrs and his feete were florysshed as hit were fyne sable. And his clawys were
lyke clene golde' (196.15–17). The feet are described as in Thornton's text, and
the philosophers' interpretation of the dragon in line 821 implies that its tail
also had been mentioned previously. On the basis of that line, Gordon-Vinaver
suggest the form 'His tayle was totaterd, with tonges ful huge'. Hamel, as is her
practice, makes no attempt to recreate an alliterative line, inserting 'And his
tayle was fulle of tatyrs' after line 768, though her predecessors would more
convincingly place the line after 769, since the next line also alliterates on /t/.
Malory's description of the claws was surely also in his source, perhaps in some
such form as 'His clowez were like clene golde, colourede full faire' (cf. lines 217,
197). There is no obvious reason for the loss of the lines from the poem.

Another two lines seem convincingly the poet's style and vocabulary. Lines
2576–7, in which Priamus mocks the injured Gawain, are transmitted faithfully
by Malory. But between these lines he has 'for thou all bebledis this horse and
thy bryght wedys' (230.15–16; cf. *Beblede … bryghte mayles* line 2250), which
improves the sense. Hamel is obviously right to add the line, and the simple
substitution of *blonke* for *horse* would produce a more authentic alliterative
line. The line was lost in a run of /b/, with the next two lines also beginning
For. After line 2273 Hamel adopts 'that thousandis in an hepe lay thrumbelyng
togedir' (224.13–14) on the grounds that the verb *thrumblen* does not appear
elsewhere in Malory's vocabulary. In fact it is only elsewhere recorded in *Piers
Plowman* in this form, though the related verb *thrublen* occurs in several alliterative poems. The phrase in *Cleanness* line 504, 'þrublande in þronge', suggests
the reading *thrange* (as in line 2217) to replace *an hepe*. The placement of this
material in Malory suggests that Hamel should probably have inserted it after
line 2275; on the other hand it is easier to account for its loss at the end of the
paragraph two lines above.

Hamel admits two lines on the grounds that they are part of a list which
Malory is unlikely to have extended: after line 603, she would insert 'and of
Calabe and of Catelonde bothe kynges and deukes' (193.16–17), and after line
2296, 'of Ethyope the kyng and of Egypte and of Inde two knyghtes full noble'
(225.3–4). The latter obviously requires some adjustment to construct a good
alliterative line or two. Arthur's address to his men (lines 2121–2) lacks the note
of exhortation in the sources and provided by Malory's 'Fayre lordys, loke youre
name be nat loste' (221.4–5); in her note Hamel suggests improving to 'Fayre
lordys loke ȝe lese noghte ȝour name', but an AA | AA line ending 'ȝour loos

41 *Morte Arthure*, ed. Hamel, pp. 79–80.

be noghte loste' is suggested by the imitation of the line in *Awntyrs* 402.[42] Line 2664, beginning 'For they are my retenuz', evidently requires a plural subject, which is supplied by Malory in a line lost from the poem; 'For here hovys at thy honde a hondred of good knyghtes' (233.13) can therefore be inserted with confidence, although *of* should be dropped in accord with the poet's usual syntax.

The longest of the passages Hamel inserts into her text follows line 2740, where Malory's words, if rearranged as verse, would amount to three or four lines in the poem. Malory has:

> 'Now, fayre lordys', seyde sir Pryamus, 'cese youre wordys, I warne you betyme; for ye shall fynde in yondir woodys many perellus knyghtes. They woll putte furth beystys to bayte you oute of numbir'. (235.21–4)

Hamel notes that something is necessary to introduce a new speaker, and surmises that the passage has been invented by Malory or Scribe E to fill the gap, since she thinks the language is not that of the poem. Yet in her note she offers 'a plausible pair of lines',[43] and not much rewriting would be needed to turn the whole passage into lines entirely characteristic of the poet:

> 'Swete Lordes', said sir Priamūs, 'cessen 3owr wordys; (cf. line 371 etc. *lystynnys þise wordez*)
>
> 3e wynne no wyrchip, I warne 3ow before. (as line 965)
>
> There houys in 3one hare wode harageous knyghtes; (cf. 1260 *Hufes thare*; 3544 *hare wode*, 1645, 1878 etc. *harageous knyghttez*)
>
> They wyll putte furthe bestes to baite 3ow owte of nombre'. (or *brynge furthe*, cf. 1381, or *buske furthe as*. For knights described as animals, cf. *blodhondes* 3640.)

More frequently than inserting material, Hamel discusses possible additions in her notes, reluctant to admit them to her text, even when the argument for doing so might seem unimpeachable. In a note to 271–5 she agrees that Malory's 'Therefore counceyle me, my knyghtes, for Crystes love of Hevyn' (188.4–5) reflects the poet's sources at this point.[44] Here, at the end of Arthur's speech, Malory is closely following the poet, though he has more detail at several points. Hamel finds 'no discernible gap', although the line would fit well after

---

[42] Ibid., p. 320. For the influence of the *Morte* on the *Awntyrs off Arthure*, see Hanna's edition, pp. 38–43.

[43] *Morte Arthure*, ed. Hamel, pp. 344–5.

[44] Ibid., p. 265. Wace has 'Cunseil illuec prendre vuleit' (10731). See *Wace's Roman de Brut: A History of the British*, ed. J. Weiss, 2nd edn (Exeter, 2002).

the current line 274. Furthermore its b-verse repeats exactly those of lines 3980 and 4324.

Similarly, a few lines later, Hamel notes that Malory's information that Belin and Brennius were born in Britain is supported by Wace's testimony. Malory's 'of my bloode elders that borne were in Bretayne' (188.7), might be reversed and inserted after line 277 as 'That born were in Bretayne, of my blode elders'. She makes no reference to Malory's 'thus was the Empyre kepte be my kynde elders' (188.12), which would appropriately follow line 285, altering *empyre* to *kyngryke*, though there is no close parallel elsewhere in the poem, despite the b-verses 'alle oure/his bolde elders' in lines 1698 and 4345.

It can hardly be doubted that something is lost between line 2559, in which Gawain cleaves Priamus's shield, and the next lines, at which point Priamus's liver is visible. The intervening passage in Malory (230.5–7) has alliterating phrases and the vocabulary of the poem, and there is nothing to suggest the rewording of the poem was not Malory's work, though Hamel is inclined to attribute it to Scribe E.[45] In lines 2981–2 Gawain slays Sven of Sweden, who has killed the child Chastelain:

> And with a swerde swiftly he swappes him thorowe,
> That he swyftly swelte and on þe erthe swounes.[46]

Following this distich, Gawain's words have been dropped, as Malory's text shows:

> And swyfftly with his swerde he smyttyth hym thorow. 'Now and thou haddyst ascaped withoutyn scathe, the scorne had bene oures'! (240.1–4)

Hamel regards this 'as an alternative rather than an addition' to 2982, and ascribes the line to Scribe E.[47] However, both the vocabulary and the b-verse pattern are the poet's (cf. 'þe fawte sall be owrs', line 2737; 'þe felde sall be owres', line 3740). Furthermore, the *Awntyrs off Arthure* imitates this line with 'if he skape skaþelese, hit were a foule skorne' (472). The line should be inserted after 2982 as 'Had þou skaped without skathe the skorne had been owres'.

The cases discussed so far demonstrate beyond doubt that considerable material has been lost from Thornton's text, and that, furthermore, Malory's text often remedies the loss. There is no need to have recourse to an interfering

---

[45] *Morte Arthure*, ed. Hamel, pp. 338–9. P. J. C. Field, '"Above Rubies": Malory and *Morte Arthure* 2559–61', in *Malory: Texts and Sources*, ed. P. J. C. Field (Cambridge, 2001), pp. 196–8, discusses the passage, emending *rubies* to *ribbes*.

[46] An edited text would, of course, transpose the b-verse here to read metrical 'and swounes on þe erthe'.

[47] *Morte Arthure*, ed. Hamel, p. 350.

Scribe E. Between lines 2472 and 3221 Malory follows the poem particularly closely, and consequently his apparent additions in this part of the text should be considered carefully as evidence for a fuller text than that Thornton transmitted. Lines 2875–77, describing a gleeful assault by the British knights, constitute a three-line run on /dž/, beginning 'Was neuer siche a justynge at journé in erthe'. Malory's 'they jowked downe with her hedys many jantyll knyghtes. A more jolyar joustynge was never sene on erthe' (238.7–9), suggests an additional line to begin the set. While Gordon-Vinaver propose such an insertion, Hamel does not mention their suggestion;[48] yet Malory's unusual verb *jowked* deserves some discussion. Although not in the *Morte*, or at least not in this form, it is used in several alliterative poems, in the senses 'roost' (*A Pistel of Susan* 82 var.), 'lurk' (*Wars of Alexander* 4331) and 'rest, dwell' (*Siege of Jerusalem* 304 var., *Piers Plowman* B.16.92) (*MED*, s.v. *jouken* (v.)). Malory's sense, perhaps 'strike and bring to a standstill', is not exemplified elsewhere, although the editors of *Siege of Jerusalem* emend line 823 of that poem to 'Io[u]ken Iewes þroȝ' where copytext has meaningless *Iolken*. For the sense, compare *MED chokken* (v.), 'thrust, strike' (from OF *choquier* rather than *jochier*) which is found as *chokkes* in *Morte* line 2955. On the basis of Malory's version, line 2875 should be emended to 'Was neuer a jolyere justynge at journé in erthe', supported by 4110, 'A jolyere journé ajuggede was neuer'.

In line 2931 the soldiers of the duke of Lorraine, disgruntled because they have not been paid, switch sides, saying 'We maye with oure wirchipe weend whethire vs lykes'. Malory adds to this, with: 'for we may with our worshype wende where us lykys, for garneson nother golde have we none resceyved' (239.3–4). The last clause is not essential to the sense of the passage, but it adds concrete detail to the soldiers' complaint, and, though Hamel does not discuss it, the vocabulary is the poet's, not Malory's (cf. line 1729: 'Gifen vs gersoms and golde'). It seems evident that Malory signals an omission in the poem, which might be restored as 'For gersom nothyre golde geten have we none'. A standard AA | AX line in Malory, describing the flight of the Roman ambassadors to the coast, presents something of a puzzle: 'and by the sonne was sette at the seven dayes ende they com unto Sandwyche ...' (191.13–14). The poem has: 'By þe seuende day was gone þe citee þai rechide' (line 488). There is no place for Malory's line in the received text of the *Morte* without rewriting, although he has constructed a better line than that in the Thornton text, and both the a- and b-verses have structures familiar from alliterative poems. There is nothing strikingly similar in *Morte Arthure*, but for the a-verse cf. (for example) *Parlement of the Thre Ages* 658 'Than the sone was sett', and for the b-verse *Piers Plowman* A.2.69, 7.42, 11.227 'at one ȝeris ende'.

---

[48] Ibid., p. 87.

Though the editor should dispense with Scribe E, Hamel is right to exercise caution in adopting passages from Malory. We have examined sections where Malory follows the poem closely, but often his source is no more than a basis for his re-imagining and reshaping. One such passage is 221.12–26, describing the battle with the giant warriors in the Roman army, which is inspired by *Morte* lines 2131–52. Malory begins with a list of Arthur's knights assembled from widely dispersed parts of the poem, as Vinaver points out (1391). These 'grymly knyghtes' kill fifty of the giants, and then proceed to a devastating slaughter of the Romans. Though the outline of the action is the same in the two accounts, Malory drops some of the poet's most vividly brutal descriptions, as is his usual squeamish practice. Even Arthur's sardonic invitation to the giant he has cut off at the knees, '"Come down", quod the kynge, "and karpe to thy ferys"' (line 2126), is jettisoned. To a considerable degree the vocabulary and alliterative phrases are those of the poet, but mostly they are drawn not from this passage but from elsewhere in the poem. Malory has:

> They leyde on with longe swerdys and swapped thorow braynes. Shyldys nother no shene armys myght hem nat withstonde tyll they leyde on the erthe ten thou-sand at onys (221.21–4)

The last phrase is based on line 2152, 'a thosande at ones', which conforms to a very common b-verse consisting of a numeral followed by 'at ones' (also lines 179, 281, 930, 2160, 2945, 3705, 3756). Both *layes one* and *lange swerde* are used in lines 2226–30; the verb *swappe* is frequent (nine times), and brains are constantly lacerated, though the closest to 'swapped thorow braynes' is the b-verse 'cruschede braynez' in line 2114. So, too, there are some familiar phrases: *scheldys* and *schene* alliterate in lines 3747 and 4116 (for *schene wedys*, 'armour', see lines 2429 and 4235). Buried in Malory's redaction is a decent alliterative line: 'by the dyntys were dalte and the dome yoldyn', with the sentence completed by 'they had felled hem starke dede of fyffty all to the bare erthe' (221.17–18). There is no place for this in the *Morte Arthure* passage, which has in its stead: 'Whylls sexty ware seruede soo, ne sessede they neuer' (line 2132), ending a run of /s/ alliteration. There follow runs on /r/, /f/, /w/ and /f/ again, but none on /d/. The commonplace collocation 'dynntys they dalte' is used in line 3749 (and cf. 332, 1277, 2183),[49] but, rather surprisingly, the noun *dome* does not occur in the *Morte* except in the compound *Domesday*, and *ȝelde* has only the sense 'surrender'. Presumably Malory's 'dome yoldyn' is an ironic way of saying 'sentence of death meted out'.

---

[49] J. P. Oakden, *Alliterative Poetry in Middle English*, 2 vols. (Manchester, 1930, 1935), II, 277, records the phrase in eleven alliterative poems; it is also common in metrical romances.

Malory's handling of this passage shows how he had absorbed the vocabulary and formulas of the alliterative poem, to the extent of creating, perhaps unconsciously, an acceptable (if unadventurous) alliterative line. This is really not surprising, in view of his evident admiration for the poem. But the consequence is that such lines in Malory cannot be assumed to be clear evidence of omissions in *Morte Arthure*. The situation is more complicated than that, and so each instance needs to be argued on its merits.

Some of the examples we have discussed are rather trivial in themselves, yet cumulatively editorial choices have a major impact upon our assessment and interpretation of the poem. For example, there is one instance where a major interpretative issue hangs upon acceptance or rejection of additional passages in Malory. The single combat between Gawain and Priamus (*Morte* lines 2513–3083) is imported from the story of Fierabras in the Charlemagne cycle. The pagan knight Fierabras, son of the emir Balan, challenges Charlemagne's knights to a duel, which Oliver accepts, pretending to be a knight of no consequence. Fierabras carries a healing balm 'Hwych ys ful of þat bame cler þat precious ys & fre, / þat ȝoure god was wiþ anoynt' (lines 510–11).[50] The two warriors fight at great length and are both seriously wounded. Fierabras demands to know his opponent's name, and Oliver confesses his true identity. Finally Oliver has Fierabras at his mercy, and the latter asks for baptism and promises to restore the holy relics. Subsequently Fierabras and his men fight valiantly for Charlemagne.

In the *Morte*, Gawain encounters Priamus on a river bank. They fight furiously and are both seriously wounded. Gawain eventually admits he is not the squire of the chamber he had pretended to be, and Priamus gives him a vial containing precious water from the rivers of Paradise, with which he and Gawain are healed of their dreadful wounds. Priamus is so pleased to learn the true identity of his opponent that he decides to switch sides, and he and his men take a major part in Arthur's fight for Metz. The handling and significance of this episode in the *Morte Arthure* is the subject of a fine intertextual study by Lee Patterson.[51]

Both Hamel and Patterson accept Thornton's text as it stands, where there is no reference to Priamus asking for baptism. However, they differ sharply in their interpretation of this alteration of the Fierabras story. Hamel argues that Priamus is Greek Orthodox, so a schismatic Christian.[52] But this view ignores

---

[50] *Sir Ferumbras*, ed. S. J. Herrtage, EETS ES 34 (London, 1879).

[51] L. Patterson, 'The Romance of History and the Alliterative *Morte Arthure*', in his *Negotiating the Past: The Historical Understanding of Medieval Literature* (Madison WI, 1987), pp. 197–230.

[52] M. Hamel, 'The "Christening" of Sir Priamus in the Alliterative *Morte Arthure*', *Viator* 13 (1982), 295–307.

the text, in which Priamus claims ancient pagan ancestry: his father is 'of Alex-andire blode' (line 2602), whose grandfather's uncle was Hector of Troy, and, moreover, he is related to the Jewish Worthies Judas and Joshua. Obviously his name Priamus proclaims his Trojan origins and status. The point of this display of ancestry is certainly not to suggest that Priamus is a post-Schism Greek, but rather to mark him as a knight of an ancestry as noble as Arthur's, descended from two of the pagan Worthies and related to two of the Jewish Worthies, of whose rise and fall Arthur dreams before the final battle. For Patterson, Priamus is a pagan, who 'embodies, in short, the virtue of the non-Christian world as is later to be manifested in the figure of the Nine Worthies'.[53] Priamus, who offers Gawain healing for his wounds on condition that Gawain gives him opportunity to make his confession before death 'for sake of thy Cryste' (2587–8), is one of the many 'Sarazenes', 'ethyns' and 'paynyms' in the Emperor's army.

Supposing Priamus to be Christian already, Hamel must dismiss as the work of Scribe E the two passages in Malory that have Priamus ask for baptism, just as Fierabras does. In Malory's version of lines 2587–8, when Gawain asks for a remedy for his wounds, Priamus replies:

> That may I do, and I woll, so thou wolt succour me that I myght be fayre crystynde and becom meke for my mysdedis. Now mercy I Jhesu beseche, and I shall becom Crysten and in God stedfastly beleve, and thou mayste for thy manhode have mede to thy soule. (230.24–231.4)

Remnants of alliterative lines seem to survive in Malory's passage; indeed the last clause has the poet's vocabulary in a perfect alliterative line, its b-verse paralleled at lines 666, 3455 and 4018.

In the *Morte*, Gawain then asks Priamus who he is and 'whate laye thow leues on' (line 2593). Priamus describes his ancestry, as we have seen, but does not answer Gawain's question directly. In Malory, Priamus says: 'yet woll I beleve on thy Lorde that thou belevyst on, and take the for thy labour tresour inow' (231.16–17). Two good alliterative lines perhaps lie behind this:

> ʒit wyll I leue on þi [or þe] Lorde that þow leues on
> And take þe for þi trauayle tresour ynowe.

In also rejecting this second passage from Malory, Hamel argues that it would not be appropriate for Priamus to give Gawain treasure, but at this point Priamus is ignorant of Gawain's identity; if Gawain were the servant he pretends to be later, a reward would be fitting. In the ensuing battle against the Duke of Lorrayne and his allies, Priamus switches sides to fight against the Saracens, and his men join him, complaining they have not been paid by the

---

53 Patterson, *Negotiating the Past*, p. 220.

Duke. In the poem, we hear no more of Priamus, which is surprising since he has played such a prominent part. In Malory, however, Gawain brings him to Arthur after the great victory, singing his praises and requesting that he may be baptized. The king has him christened and makes him a knight of the Round Table. Malory is apparently diverging from his source at this point; there are no traces of alliterative verse in his version, and in the poem it is not Gawain and Florent who come to report the victory to Arthur, bringing the heroic Priamus with them, but a messenger, who could not appropriately have introduced Priamus to the king.

For Patterson, the pagan Priamus represents the passing of the old order, in a cyclical model of history foreshadowing Arthur's dream of Fortune's Wheel. Patterson regards the absence of baptism as significant, in that 'classical heroism is transferred but not transformed'.[54] Yet given that the christening is so prominent in the poet's source, Malory's two passages in which Priamus asks for baptism almost certainly go back to the poem, though omitted in Thornton's text. And surely this makes for a far more satisfactory interpretation? It is a mark of the Emperor's impiety that he summons to his aid 'Sowdanes and Sarazenes owt of sere landes' as well as sixty giants 'engenderide with fendez' (lines 607, 612). Arthur's struggle with the Emperor is a religious as well as a nationalist one, and to switch to Arthur's side, Priamus, the noble pagan, must adopt the True Faith.

Hamel's is the only edition of *Morte Arthure* to pay serious attention to the relationship between the poem and Malory's adaptation. Her treatment is discriminating, and she is prepared to introduce a few readings and passages where she is persuaded by the evidence. Yet her notion that Malory's source was mediated by Scribe E allows her to dismiss, often without discussion, much of the evidence for readings which probably, sometimes certainly, are those of the poet. To bolster her support for the received text, she expresses a high regard for Thornton as a scrupulous copyist, which he may indeed have been.[55] Certainly, like many scribes, he corrected his text when he realized he had miscopied. However, the editor cannot conclude from this that Thornton was not capable of mistranscriptions and misunderstandings, and more importantly, it says nothing about the quality of his exemplars, and so nothing about the accuracy of his text.[56] We have argued that Thornton's *Morte* is at least a

---

[54] Ibid., p. 222.

[55] See M. Hamel, 'Scribal Self-Corrections in the Thornton *Morte Arthure*', *Studies in Bibliography* 36 (1983), 119–36.

[56] A point made by H. N. Duggan, 'Scribal Self-Correction and Editorial Theory', *Neuphilologische Mitteilungen* 91 (1990), 215–27. Duggan qualifies Hamel's argument, and extends it to consider other alliterative poems copied by Thornton. See further J. I. Carlson, 'Scribal Intentions

third-generation copy with numerous erroneous accretions. Undoubtedly many authorial readings cannot be recovered, but even so we believe it is possible, with critical scrutiny of the traditions, to establish a more satisfactory text of *Morte Arthure* than any so far published.[57]

in Medieval Romance: A Case Study of Robert Thornton', *Studies in Bibliography* 58 (2007–8), 49–71.

[57] R. H. expresses his gratitude to the Radcliffe Institute for Advanced Study for its fellowship support during 2011–12, when this paper was composed.

5

'The rosselde spere to his herte rynnes': Religious Violence in the Alliterative *Morte Arthure* and the Lincoln Thornton Manuscript

Mary Michele Poellinger

Much can and has been said regarding Robert Thornton's awareness of genre distinctions, and rightly so: the careful division of Lincoln Cathedral Library, MS 91 into three fairly clear sections for romance, sacred and medicinal pieces is remarkable for a household book of the fifteenth century.[1] Yet his selection of pieces, whether by plan or by accident, indicates something even more remarkable: how medieval readers such as Thornton appreciate not only genre distinctions but also genre cohesion. By recognizing generic tropes and signals across the manuscript's texts, we may begin to understand the literary experience of its readers. A careful examination of the evocative language used in the alliterative *Morte Arthure* (Lincoln art. 8) illustrates not only the anonymous author's skill in weaving a litany of medieval traditions together, but also Thornton's ability, as compiler, to incorporate the individual text into the context of the manuscript – allowing further illumination on the ambiguous *Morte* itself.[2] In order to understand this context, I will examine the variety of

---

[1] See J. J. Thompson, 'The Compiler in Action: Robert Thornton and the "Thornton Romances" in Lincoln Cathedral MS 91', in *Manuscripts and Readers in Fifteenth-Century England: The Literary Implications of Manuscript Study. Essays from the 1981 Conference at the University of York*, ed. D. Pearsall (Cambridge, 1983), pp. 113–24; G. R. Keiser, 'Lincoln Cathedral Library MS. 91: Life and Milieu of the Scribe', *Studies in Bibliography* 32 (1979), 158–79; and *The Thornton Romances*, ed. J. O. Halliwell, Camden Society 30 (London, 1844).

[2] T. H. Crofts, in his study of the illustrations in the Lincoln manuscript, argues that the unique profusion of marginal drawings in the *Morte* sets it apart from the rest of the manuscript's texts, and that the use of helmeted bird-man hybrids may indicate Arthur's growing pride; however, it is very difficult to ascertain the meaning of the figures (if any) with any certainty, and he acknowledges himself that 'the more we try to systematize the hybrids, the more slippery they tend to get' ('The Occasion of the *Morte Arthure*: Textual History and Marginal Decoration in the Thornton MS', *Arthuriana* 20 (2010), 5–27 [p. 20]). Furthermore, J. Finlayson places the *Morte* into context within Lincoln's romance section, arguing that Thornton organized his romances into 'sub-sections' which begin with the 'heroic' *Alexander* and *Morte*, proceed

devotional items found in Thornton's religious collection. In particular, I will focus on the centrality of the Passion narrative in both of Thornton's volumes, the Lincoln manuscript and London, BL, MS Additional 31042, providing close readings of *Jesus Thy Sweetness* (Lincoln art. 72), the *Privity of the Passion* (Lincoln art. 38) and the *Northern Passion* (London art. 4) to gain an understanding of how they deploy an imagery of violence. By examining the graphic language used to describe heart, chest and head wounds, I will explore the relation between Passion violence and the secular violence of the alliterative *Morte Arthure*, before focusing on the close relationship between chivalric sacrifice and the Passion, evident in the *Morte* and the *Siege of Jersusalem* (London art. 6). In the identification of a shared language of violence between genres, exemplified by the *Morte*, we can begin to understand the sympathies and judgements passed upon the knights who are encountering the affective language.

'Mixed' items in Lincoln Cathedral Library, MS 91

It is not my intention to analyse the composition of the Lincoln manuscript, but its arrangement of texts is of importance to the *Morte*'s use of religious imagery and language. It is clear that Thornton wished to demarcate genre by section. However, the religious and secular works in his volume are also inseparable; they speak to each other's language and tropes. Many of the texts occupy the edges between 'romance' and 'religious', borrowing from secular narrative to discuss spiritual issues or vice versa. For example, the Marian miracle *The Wicked Knight and the Friar* (Lincoln art. 17) links the secular closely with the religious; it is a tale of the reformation of an errant knight, a man saved from demons by a friar and the Virgin Mary. When a knight prone to greed, envy, anger and pride hears the friar preaching, he is enraged at being chastised for his sins and attacks the holy man, but is stopped by the friar's prayer to Mary. Mary drives away the knight's demonic spirits, and the friar gives the remorseful knight absolution. Thornton also took some interest in warfare and the redemption of a warrior's sins: the *Morte*'s detailed battle sequences are accompanied by the destruction of Arthur's reign and cautions against greed and pride. It is not surprising that the knight's redemption occurs through a prayer to Mary, given the appeals to Mary's mercy found throughout the Lincoln manuscript.[3] The

to the adventure and Christian-warrior romances of *Octavian* and *Sir Isumbras*, continue with the 'courtly romances' of *Sir Degrevant*, *Sir Eglamour of Artois* and *Earl of Toulouse*, and finish with the 'unreal' and improbable fantasies of the *Awntyrs off Arthure* and *Sir Perceval of Gales*; 'Reading Romances in Their Manuscript: Lincoln Cathedral Manuscript 91 ("Thornton")', *Anglia* 123 (2005), 632–66 (p. 666).

3   The Lincoln manuscript contains several Marian lyrics, including *Lady for Thy Joys Five*,

poem neatly bridges the gap between Thornton's romance adventures and the Marian lyrics. Pieces of religious work giving moral guidance for secular life can be found throughout the Lincoln manuscript, such as Walter Hilton's *Epistle on the Mixed Life* (art. 76), which offers advice for living a spiritual secular life.[4] *Epistle* is a spiritual code of conduct for those who govern land and people, such as Thornton. It advises those in a role of power to prepare their souls for God through the performance of charitable deeds and the careful guidance of their tenants and servants. Hilton's spiritual advice for the proper behaviour of secular leaders parallels Thornton's personal interest in both the practical and the devotional. It teaches the reader how to be a good Christian as well as how to conduct oneself appropriately in secular society. Hilton believes that, through a balance between active (secular) and contemplative (spiritual) life, governors find the key for success, and the mixture of religious and romance texts in the composition of Lincoln reflects this. Jonathan Hughes interestingly comments that 'the importance of "mixed life" as a practical reality was such that the distinctions between the two genres of secular romance and religious literature almost disappeared'.[5] It is, indeed, with this philosophy in mind that we should view the interests of the *Morte* poet.

Religious material in Thornton's manuscripts

It is important before analysing the language of the *Morte* to establish Thornton's religious concerns. What areas of devotion did Thornton take interest in? How might he have practised his religion? The contents of his manuscripts indicate a preference for Marian lyrics, Passion narratives, hagiography and the works of the Yorkshire hermit Richard Rolle.[6] The numerous Marian lyrics in the Lincoln manuscript have already been highlighted: lyrics that praise the Virgin's virtues and appeal to her role as mediator, reflecting her function as an instrument of forgiveness. Thornton, like other Christians of the fifteenth

---

Father and Son and Holy Ghost, Gaude flore virgenali and *Gaude virgo mater Cristi* (arts. 29, 64, 88, 89).

⁴ Other Hilton inclusions, such as *Of Angel's Song* (Lincoln art. 73), are more theoretical than *Epistle of the Mixed Life*, but they still lend themselves to understanding proper devotional practices. *Of Angels' Song* cautions against false ecstasies, and the extract from *The Scale of Perfection* (Lincoln art. 77) assures that one does not need to have mystical experiences to be given salvation.

⁵ J. Hughes, *Pastors and Visionaries: Religion and Secular Life in Late Medieval Yorkshire* (Woodbridge, 1988), p. 282.

⁶ For further analysis of the devotional material in the Lincoln manuscript, see J. J. Thompson, 'Another Look at the Religious Texts in Lincoln, Cathedral Library, MS 91', in *Late-Medieval Religious Texts and Their Transmission: Essays in Honour of A. I. Doyle*, ed. A. J. Minnis (Cambridge, 1994), pp. 169–87.

century, took great comfort in the cult of the Virgin.[7] The Lincoln manuscript also contains a number of instructional programmes for the study of basic Christian elements, such as the Ten Commandments, the Gifts of the Holy Ghost and the Passion of Christ (arts. 57, 58, 77), all of which intend to educate the medieval reader on how to understand and practise his or her faith. Thornton's large selection of Richard Rolle's mystical treatises may derive from the wide circulation of Rolle's devotional material, but it may also indicate Thornton's interest in a local Yorkshire religious figure.[8] Many of the texts in the Lincoln manuscript 'do not seem to show signs of having come from other dialects', implying a thriving local literary culture.[9] Given Thornton's favouring of local subjects and compositions, it seems likely that he was not simply using the easiest items to obtain, but also choosing some out of personal interest in his own regional society. His impressive selection of Rolle treatises and lyrics is testament to this: Rolle was born in Thornton le Dale, not far from Thornton's East Newton residence, and he settled just south of it in Hampole.[10] Although a mystic, Rolle incorporated the practical side of theology into both his writings and his way of life. Despite being a hermit, he became famous for preaching to and counselling those in need of spiritual guidance.[11] Many of Rolle's *exempla* and treatises offered a simple, accessible spiritual pathway for secular readers such as Thornton. Rolle's treatises on the Gifts of the Holy Spirit and the Ten Commandments have already been mentioned. In addition to these, Thornton's Rolle collection in the Lincoln manuscript includes four *exempla – A Tale of Hampole's Temptation, Imperfect Contricion, True Contrition* and *A Woman Enclosed for Love of Christ* (arts. 47, 51, 52, 54) – which demonstrate how to live a devout life. The Rolle collection also includes *The Bee and the Stork* (art. 53), which uses natural metaphors to clarify the nature of the soul. The Lincoln manuscript also provides the reader with mystical and contemplative writings. In addition to *Of Angels' Song* and *Epistle on the Mixed Life*, the Hilton tracts also include *Epistle of Salvation* (art. 77). This piece instructs the reader in the contemplation of the Passion, summoning the image of the suffering Jesus to focus on intense feelings of sorrow, remorse and penitence, and stressing the importance of sensory feelings in achieving direct communication with God.

---

[7] See E. Duffy, *The Stripping of the Altars: Traditional Religion in England 1400–1580* (New Haven, 2005), pp. 256–65.

[8] For more information on local interest in Rolle's works, see M. Vale, *Piety, Charity and Literacy Among the Yorkshire Gentry, 1370–1480*, Borthwick Papers 50 (York, 1976).

[9] R. Hanna III, 'The Growth of Robert Thornton's Books', *Studies in Bibliography* 40 (1987), 51–61 (p. 61).

[10] For further reading on Thornton's interest in Rolle and northern material, see Hughes, *Pastors and Visionaries*, pp. 93, 295–6.

[11] M. Glasscoe, *English Medieval Mystics* (London, 1993), pp. 64–5.

Hilton's treatise highlights a larger interest found in Thornton's religious material and across medieval devotional literature: Christ's wounds and Mary's suffering.

Affective piety in Thornton's Passion texts

A particularly popular subject in vernacular lyrics, the Passion was crucial to private devotional practices in late medieval England. The theological reformations of the Cistercians and Franciscans, primarily interested in meditation and Christ's humanity, created an increasingly emotional devotion that expressed itself in a growing literary interest in Christ's wounds.[12] Passion texts were composed to 'teach their readers, through iterative affective performance, how to feel';[13] to stimulate the senses, graphic descriptions of the Passion commonly gave account of the breaking of bones, profuse bleeding, ripped skin, driving in the nails and piercing with thorns through Christ's head and with a spear through Christ's heart. The popularity of the Passion narrative is clear in both of Thornton's manuscripts, which contain Crucifixion literature in Latin and English. The London manuscript includes two extracts from the *Cursor Mundi*, providing a meditation on the life of Christ, and the *Northern Passion* (arts. 1–4). It is possible that London was in fact intended to be a Passion-centric narrative in which the *Cursor Mundi* extracts act as a prequel to the *Northern Passion*, whilst the *Siege of Jerusalem* acts as a sequel and prayers to Mary and the Cross provide concluding meditation (arts. 9, 11, 14).[14] This theory is certainly plausible, given that Thornton clearly demonstrated care in organizing his manuscripts, and that London strongly encourages meditation on the images of Christ's suffering. Many of the seventy-three religious works in Lincoln are also devoted to Mary or Christ: eight of these focus solely on the Passion, such as *Adoro te piissime Ihesu*, *O crux frutex* and *Tuam crucem adoramus Domine* (arts. 66, 67, 91). Some, like the Latin prayer on fol. 278v that begins 'Crucem coronam spiniam' (art. 94), engage in the *arma Christi* tradition and use simple descriptions to list the instruments of the Passion. Others, such as *Salva plaga lateris* (art. 96), beginning 'A Preyere to þe wounde in Crystis syde', focus specifically on the spear wound to Christ's side. Affective material portrays Christ's wounded heart as a 'symbol and proof of His love' as well as a 'resting-place, in

---

[12] T. H. Bestul, *Texts of the Passion: Latin Devotional Literature and Medieval Society* (Philadelphia, 1996), p. 35.

[13] S. McNamer, *Affective Meditation and the Invention of Medieval Compassion* (Philadelphia, 2010), p. 2.

[14] P. Hardman, 'Reading the Spaces: Pictorial Intentions in the Thornton MSS, Lincoln Cathedral MS 91 and BL MS Add. 31042', *Medium Ævum* 63 (1994), 250–69 (pp. 263–4).

which a man may hide enveloped in Christ's love'.[15] Highlighted as a physical symbol of the suffering Jesus undertook for the salvation of humankind, the spear wound is viewed as a place of refuge. The piercing of Christ's heart is depicted vividly in *Jesus Thy Sweetness*:

> His sydes full bla and bludy ware,
> That sum-tyme ware full brighte of blee;
> *His herte was perchede with a spere;*
> His bludy woundes was reuthe to see.
> My raunsone, I-wys, he payede þare
> And gaffe his lyfe for gylte of me.
> His dulefull dede burde do me dere
> *And perche myne herte for pure petee.* (lines 57–64; emphasis added)[16]

The image is cyclic – Jesus's pierced heart figuratively pierces the reader's, moved to compassion and grief. The devout Christian can enter Christ's heart through his wound by participating in his suffering, and Mary's sorrow should be emulated by the reader. In Wynkyn de Worde's edition of Pseudo-Bonaventure's *Meditationes vitae Christi*, Mary is 'wounded in her herte wyth a new wounde of sorowe', and 'the swerde of this spere hath perced bothe the body of the sone and the soule of the moder'.[17] The spear that has pierced Christ's body should also enter the Christian's heart and soul.[18]

The *Privity of the Passion*, one of the Lincoln manuscript's Passion narratives and a Middle English translation of the Pseudo-Bonaventure *De mysteriis passionis Iesu Christi*, is of particular interest in examining the relationship between the *Morte* and religious violence. Angus McIntosh argues persuasively that the alliterative romance was taken from the same Lincolnshire exemplar as the *Privity* and that they were both copied down quite early in Thornton's collecting career.[19] Thornton was certainly interested in these two pieces of liter-

---

[15] R. Woolf, *The English Religious Lyric in the Middle Ages* (Oxford, 1968), p. 186.

[16] The image of the viewer's heart being pierced with pity by the sight of Christ's wounded body is a common trope in Passion lyrics, one which conjures tangible physical pain so that the reader may 'feel' and understand Christ's suffering. See *Jesus Thy Sweetness*, in *Yorkshire Writers: Richard Rolle of Hampole and His Followers*, ed. C. Horstmann, 2 vols. (London, 1895–6; repr. Cambridge, 1999), I, 368–70 (cited by line number in the text).

[17] Pseudo-Bonaventure, *Meditationes vitae Christi* (or *Our lorde god stronge and myghty, and myghty in battayle, he is kynge of glorye*), trans. Nicholas Love (London, 1507), in *Early English Books Online*, http://o-eebo.chadwyck.com.wam.leeds.ac.uk/home (image 109).

[18] For an intriguing discussion of the political and social symbolism of Christ's body, see S. Beckwith, *Christ's Body: Identity, Culture and Society in Late Medieval Writings* (London, 1993).

[19] See A. McIntosh, 'The Textual Transmission of the Alliterative *Morte Arthure*', in *English and Medieval Studies Presented to J. R. R. Tolkien on the Occasion of His Seventieth Birthday*, ed. N. Davis and C. L. Wrenn (London, 1962), pp. 231–40; and Keiser 'Lincoln Cathedral Library MS. 91', pp. 177–9.

ature: the Lincoln manuscript was shaped around them. Thornton's awareness of genre was sharp enough for him to place the texts in separate sections of his manuscript, and he and those who read his manuscripts were likely sensitive to their connections in tone and language. The Pseudo-Bonaventure piece stresses Christ's human suffering. The Middle English translation in Lincoln asks the reader to 'make hym-selfe present in his thoghte as if he sawe fully with his bodily egne all the thyngys þat be-fell abowte þe crosse'.[20] The author encourages the evocation of strong sensory pictures, utilizing gory details for Christ's wounds: Longinus, with his spear, 'ffersely and with a fell herte … thriste oure lorde thorow-owte his swete herte, & made a greuose wonde'.[21] The pierced heart, although central to Passion violence, is not the only bloody image that can be drawn upon; the *Privity* author also makes use of the injury to Christ's head: 'his heued was thurge-prikked with scharpe thornes thurghe his blesside brayne, and ofte-tyme þey smote hyme with þe septure one þe heued … and beholde his blyssede face all rynnande with rede blode'.[22]

The vivid and gruesome nature of the head injury features also in the *Morte*, where heads are struck and smashed often to the point of brain damage, and streaming blood accompanies many wounds. The use of violent rhetoric to remind the reader of Christ's suffering fulfils a dual purpose. Evocation of the holy wounds serves to both compare and contrast: an awareness of the language for Christ's pains in chivalric literature allows a reader to draw sympathetic parallels for victims of violence and to make negative comparisons for those who fail to fulfil Christian moral expectations. A closer analysis of the language of violence in the *Morte* reveals a use of images that feeds on readers' knowledge and awareness of Passion tropes and manipulates their affective sympathies – images which were likely recognized by Thornton in the composition of the Lincoln manuscript.

Thornton did not compile the Lincoln manuscript in isolation. Ralph Hanna has demonstrated that Lincoln's *Awntyrs off Arthure* (art. 20) and London's *Northern Passion* were probably copied around the same time as the *Morte*,[23] further implying that Thornton had an early and simultaneous interest in Arthurian and Passion narratives. The incomplete copy of the *Northern Passion* in the London manuscript – still the largest piece on the Crucifixion in Thornton's second compilation – demands attention if one is to understand the role of Passion violence in Thornton's texts. Thornton's version contains a much shorter segment on the Crucifixion than is found, for example, in the version

---

[20] *The Privity of the Passion*, in *Yorkshire Writers*, ed. Horstmann, I, 198–219 (p. 198).

[21] Ibid., I, 208.

[22] Ibid., I, 204.

[23] The *Awntyrs off Arthure* and the *Northern Passion* both use B paper stock, the main stock Thornton used for copying the *Morte*. See Hanna, 'The Growth', p. 56.

extant in London, BL, MS Harley 4196, but it still conveys the essential importance of the Passion to medieval Christian devotion. It describes how the holes
in the Cross have not been bored correctly, and it emphasizes Christ's agony
as the soldiers 'dide a rope one the ryghte hande / that the blode braste owte
for strenghe strange', and 'drewe his arms than full faste' so that 'the synowes
braste alle in twaa' as they nail his hands.[24] Mary demonstrates the correct way
to respond to the sight of Jesus's body on the Cross. Her son's wounds become
her own as she cries bloody tears:

> Oure lady herde thies wordis swete
> and teris of blode scho gane downe lete
> all was hir face by rowne with blode
> whene scho by helde Ihesu one the rode. (lines 1747–50)

Longinus's spear-thrust to Christ's side is given the longest description of the
wounds:

> longeus putt the spere hym fra
> To Ihesus herte it gune ga
> the blode by gane owt to sprynge
> and þe water owte to thrynge
> ffra deuylls we ware with his blode boghte
> and with þe water waschede fra euyll thoghte. (lines 1877–80b)

Once again, the poet specifically identifies the heart as being pierced by the
spear. Blood and water stem directly from the heart and bear spiritual qualities.
Christ's spilt blood has purchased the redemption of humankind, warding off
devils, and the water has cleansed Christians of their sins. The divine quality
of this heart-blood has the power to heal both physically and spiritually. Blind
Longinus, unaware of what he has done, regains his sight when he touches
Christ's blood.

This scene is not unique to the *Northern Passion*. Making a direct connection between Christ's pierced heart and absolution is a common concept in
late medieval Passion literature. The spear-thrust and the injury received are
followed immediately by forgiveness of sins and protection from evil. Blood and
water flowing from Jesus's side were commonly seen as symbols for baptism and
the Eucharist.[25] Passion writers highlighted this connection through detailed
descriptions of Christ's bleeding and disfigured body, which allow the reader to
imagine Christ's wounds. The visualization of the Crucifixion was an important
devotional tool used to develop a personal love for Jesus through the excitement

---

[24] *The Northern Passion*, ed. F. A. Foster, EETS OS 145, 147 (London, 1913–16), I, lines
1614–15, 1617, 1619. All subsequent references to the *Northern Passion* will be by line number in
parentheses in the body of the work.

[25] Bestul, *Texts of the Passion*, p. 39.

of human emotions. The sight of Christ's body was powerful and memorable, able to be recalled time and time again to commemorate God's love for human-kind.[26] The *Northern Passion* closes with a passage that reminds the reader that the Passion is not limited to the past:

> Send vs thi strange pynynge
> *To hald it stabilly in oure menynge*
> agayne þe deuyll oure warant it be. (lines 2081–83; emphasis added)

The recollection of Christ's wounds is vital for redemption in the future. The image of the Passion must be 'sent' to the reader so that he/she may 'hald it stabilly' in his 'menynge' (understanding, memory) and keep him/herself from sin. Indeed, the poet offers a very tangible benefit for reading his poem (and other Passion literature): all who have heard the narrative 'sall haue a thowsande 3eris to pardone' (line 2090).

Affective language in the alliterative Morte Arthure

The vivid detail of Christ's wounds, which in the Passion narratives evokes sensational and sympathetic images of Christ's suffering, is reflected in the graphic violence of the *Morte*. As the poet tells the story of Arthur's war with the Holy Roman Emperor, he fills his lines with gruesome bodily violence that is often similar to what is found in Crucifixion lyrics, and which produces a similar reader response of shock and grief. Injury to internal organs is commonly implied in Arthurian warfare, and the damage done to a particular organ is often made fully clear – whether to lungs, intestines, bowels or guts. The *Morte*'s violence focuses largely on injuring the heart (and central organs), the head and the sword-arm. The first two areas – the heart and the head – have religious overtones paralleled in devotional material within and outside of the Lincoln manuscript, and so demand attention. The breast contains almost all of the body's spiritual organs, of which the heart is foremost. It is 'the instrument of alle þe vertues of þe body and þe ful oonhede of þe soule'.[27] Grotesque heart injuries are the most explicit in their spiritual parallels. In several instances, the sword or lance 'rynnys' or 'glodes' to the heart. When Sir Bedivere is killed in battle, his breast is 'thyrllede / With a burlyche brannde' so that 'The ryall rannke stele to his herte rynnys' (lines 2238–40).[28] Similarly, Round Table

---

[26] See C. Whitehead, 'Middle English Religious Lyrics', in *A Companion to the Middle English Lyric*, ed. T. G. Duncan (Cambridge, 2005), pp. 96–119.

[27] *The Cyrurgie of Guy de Chauliac*, ed. M. Ogden, EETS OS 265 (London, 1971), p. 55.

[28] *Morte Arthure: A Critical Edition*, ed. M. Hamel, Garland Medieval Texts 9 (New York, 1984). All subsequent references to the *Morte* will be by line number in parentheses in the body of the work.

knight Sir Richard thrusts through the shield of the pagan Raynold of Rhodes so that 'the rosselde spere to his herte rynnes' (line 2793).

The image of the heart pierced by a spear has already been seen in the Passion narratives found in Thornton's manuscripts, and these follow the patterns found in the affective lyrics so popular in the fourteenth and fifteenth centuries, all of which elaborate on the wound in Christ's side. Whilst John 19. 34 simply states that 'one of the soldiers with a spear pierced his side, and forthwith came there out blood and water',[29] Middle English literature recounting the Passion is much more graphic, claiming that the spear has struck deep into Christ's body, reaching the heart and sometimes even the liver and lungs. The fourteenth- and fifteenth-century *Long Charter of Christ* paints a vivid picture of the power of the invasive spear and of the outpouring of sacred blood:

> With a spere my hert they stonge
> Þrow my lyuyr and my longe
> Vpon my syde they made a wownde
> That my hart blode ran to grownde. (B-text, lines 221–24)[30]

The heart is still the main recipient of the thrust, but the liver and lungs are also damaged. This manner of wounding also occurs in the *Morte* during the battle with the Holy Roman Emperor. Kay, spotting an enemy king, 'thirllez his sydez' with a lance so that 'the lyuer and þe lunggez on þe launce lengez' (lines 2167, 2168). The poet's purpose in using such images, wherein Arthur's knights 'hewe thorowe helmes hawtayne biernez / Þat þe hiltede swerdes to þaire hertes rynnys' (lines 2910–11), can be understood through an awareness of their use in Passion lyrics. As in the Crucifixion narratives, the reader is expected to feel the agony and despair of the hero (Christ or knight) through the emotional experience triggered by the vivid images. Strongly sensory in nature, the detailed visual images both heighten and intensify emotions. The violent images also act to create a vocabulary for affective devotion, one which – through the images' ability to engrave themselves onto the reader's memory – is able to trigger certain feelings and reactions. That is, the poignant description of Christ's mutilated body – the colour of his skin, the blood on his body, the horror of his wounds – makes Christ's suffering unforgettable, just as the knights' gory injuries in the *Morte* are to be recalled and remembered after the story has finished. The author asks the reader to consider the virtues and sins of the Arthurian knights in light of the ultimate sacrifice Christ made, to view the knights' faults as a reflection of their own humanity. The *Morte* poet wants

---

[29] *The Douay-Rheims Catholic Bible*, www.drbo.org.

[30] *The Middle English Charters of Christ*, ed. M. Spalding (Baltimore, 1914), in *Corpus of Middle English Prose and Verse*, http://quod.lib.umich.edu/c/cme/.

his tale of Arthur's death to be remembered by making allusions to Passion violence, indicating the sacrificial nature of knightly deeds.

It can also be argued that injuries to the brain and head in the *Morte* carry spiritual overtones. The head is not only the site of one of Christ's five wounds, received through the crown of thorns and beating, but it is also the 'dwellynge of þe resonable soule', according to the *Cyrurgie of Guy de Chauliac*.[31] The head was considered the most important member of the body, according to Guy, for it held wit, imagination, thought and memory.[32] The neck provided the link between the head and the other major spiritual members (heart, liver, lungs), and the blood circulating amongst them altered the spiritual state of each organ as it passed through. As the centre of one's spirit and soul, the head and the heart were targeted and vulnerable to attack. Crushed skulls, pierced brains and beheadings are prominent in the Arthurian romance. Knights are beheaded, removing the source of intellect from the rest of the body (lines 2129, 2959, 2993, 3709), or the source of thoughts itself is destroyed by a blow to the head. Arthur's knights 'craschede doun crestez and cruschede braynez' whilst the brains of Roman nobles 'forebrusten thurghe burneste helmes' (lines 2114, 2272). Christ's head is 'thurge prikkede with scharpe thornes thurghe his blesside brayne' in the *Privity*,[33] whilst Sir Florent 'thurghe [Sir Feraunt's] bryghte bacenette his brayne has he towchede' (*Morte*, line 2770). Whilst there is not always a direct correlation between chivalric injuring and Christ's Passion, the *Morte* poet is clearly aware of the affective vocabulary of the popular religious lyrics, and he borrows from their language to describe the secular combat of Arthur's wars.

Given the prominence of affective piety in the Lincoln manuscript, in addition to the general popularity of Passion lyrics, it is likely that Robert Thornton himself would have recognized the familiar and repetitive images of violence the devotional material and the *Morte* have in common. We do not know how much control Thornton had over the selection of items, but we may begin to understand Thornton's experience as a reader when he had finished his manuscripts. The graphic iconography and spiritual connotations of bodily violence in the *Morte*, when read in the context of devotional texts found in the Lincoln manuscript, gain an intensity from the Passion transferable to the secular violence distributed and endured by Arthur's knights. The worth of their inju-

---

[31] *The Cyrurgie*, ed. Ogden, p. 37. It is not specified that Jesus was struck on the head during the Crucifixion in the Bible; it says simply that the soldiers placed the crown of thorns on his head and 'gave him blows' (John 19. 3). It is clear, however, that by the Middle Ages it was certainly believed that he was, as indicated by the passage in *De mysteriis passionis Iesu Christi* quoted earlier in this discussion.

[32] *The Cyrurgie*, ed. Ogden, p. 41.

[33] *The Privity*, in *Yorkshire Writers*, ed. Horstmann, I, 204.

ries is paralleled to and measured by Christ's ultimate sacrifice on the Cross. As the reader of the Arthurian romance recollects the vocabulary of Passion, he/she is able to judge the protagonists by comparing knightly sacrifices to that of Christ.

Considering the importance and popularity of Passion lyrics in the daily devotional life of middle- and upper-class laymen in the fourteenth and fifteenth centuries, it is not surprising that the poet of a secular romance would want to make use of religious vocabulary. The rhythm and images of Passion lyrics were used to engage readers' feelings. These devices serve the same function in the *Morte*, where the author requests a sympathetic and complex response to the war-torn end to Arthur's golden reign. The violence in which a knight engages during war can itself be viewed as a sacrificial act, and the *Morte* poet certainly seems keen for the reader to view his Arthurian heroes in this way. The knights in the romance enter into a sacrifice of blood when they agree to fight for Arthur to remain free of the Emperor's oppression, submitting their bodies to physical jeopardy as Christ does on the Cross. By exposing their bodies to injury and suffering, the knights both reveal their inner virtues and create a unity of fellowship. The engagement of the knight's body with another in combat allows each knight to prove his own courage and worth. Once the knights have tested their opponent's worth, resolution is possible, for after chivalric combat participants can ideally join in a bond of brotherhood.[34] This reconciliation is rarely allowed to take place in Arthur's wars, however; instead of seeking peace and granting mercy to defeated enemies, Arthur often slays the opposing ruler or destroys and ruins his lands as he continues his dangerous quest for conquest across the continent. It is perhaps this lack of reconciliation that forecasts Arthur's downfall, as no wholeness is achieved after sacrifice.

The chivalric 'sacrifice' of Gawain and Priamus

The *Morte* poet does provide the reader with an example of knightly sacrifice ending in fellowship in the episode between Gawain and Priamus. Gawain's forest adventure has been seen as a confusing inclusion in a romance otherwise concerned with politics, conquest and warfare, but its presence acts as an *exemplum* when viewed through a sacrificial and religious lens. When Gawain ventures into the woods and encounters Priamus, they test each other with their bodies and demonstrate their prowess – signifying their inner worth – ripping into one another until both are near death. Their injuries are not in vain. They choose to end the fight and make a peace, which involves Priamus

---

[34] See J. Mann, 'Malory: Knightly Combat in *Le Morte D'Arthur*', in *The New Pelican Guide to English Literature: 1. Medieval Literature. Part One: Chaucer and the Alliterative Tradition*, ed. B. Ford (Harmondsworth, 1982), pp. 331–9.

converting to Christianity and joining Arthur's army. After the sacrifice of the body, the ensuing unity of fellowship is physically symbolized by the healing of the two knights, with Priamus's salves containing water from the springs of Paradise. Gawain and Priamus are helped down from their horses, stripped of their clothes and laid out on the ground, where their wounds are bathed in the holy water:

> They laide [Priamus] down in the lawndez and laghte of his wedes,
> And he lened hym on lange or how hym beste lykede.
> A fyole of fyne golde they fande at his gyrdill:
> 'Þat es full of þe flour of þe four well
> Þat flowes owte of Paradice when þe flode ryses,
> That myche froyt in fallez þat feede schall vs all;
> Be it frette on his flesche þare synues are entamede,
> The freke schalle be fische-halle within fowre howres'.
> They vncouere þat cors with full clene hondes;
> With [the] clere watire a knyghte clensis theire wondes,
> Keled theym kyndly and comforthed þer hertes,
> And whene þe carffes ware clene þay clede them aȝayne.
>
> (lines 2702–13; emphasis added)

Their injured and naked bodies are revived by the application of the holy balm; the process cleanses their physical, spiritual and chivalric wounds. The words 'clene', 'clere' and 'clensis' implies that the treatment physically clears the injuries of Priamus' poison and 'comfort[s] þer hertes', providing a greater, inner cleansing. While not religious, the *Morte* offers something of a sacrificial parallel in the language used by the poet and the images he conjures. Both knights have undertaken a physical sacrifice wherein they have endured 'stokes at þe stomake with stelyn poyntes' (line 2554). Gawain has pierced Priamus so that 'with þe lyghte of þe sonne men myghte see his lyuere' (line 2561), and Gawain's blood 'voydes … violently' after Priamus severs a vein (line 2571).

Gawain's sacrifice is not for God, however, but for Arthur and chivalry. Nevertheless, the wounding ultimately leads to a physical healing that can be accomplished only through spiritual salvation. The two knights must be bathed in a holy salve and Priamus converted to Christianity. Priamus, before allowing access to the curing waters from Paradise, specifically asks to be converted so that he can gain absolution for his sins and prepare for the afterlife ('suffre me, for sake of thy Cryste / To schewe schortly my schrifte and schape for myn ende' [lines 2587–88]). The reader, aware of these familiar images, is even instructed how to react to the knights' suffering. Upon seeing Gawain's wounds, his followers are full of woe, and one of them goes to him 'wepand and wryngande his handes' (line 2679). Having been treated with and healed by the holy salve, the knights partake in a feast that symbolizes their new fellowship, after which Priamus not only converts but also agrees to help Gawain's men and join Arthur's force.[35] The physical sacrifice that the two knights have gone through leads to peace and brotherhood because of the mercy they have shown one another and the healing powers of Christianity.

In contrast, Arthur and his army are never ultimately given this redemption. Whilst it has been argued that the *Morte Arthure* is an anti-war poem,[36] the glorification of the heroes and their deeds of prowess in the poem seem to indicate a more complex response. It is certainly a cautionary tale; the poet is interested in wartime behaviour and the governance of kings, the pride of the victors and the despair of the fallen. It is a romance illustrating the excesses of war and warning against the greed of conquest. Arthur's army frees Britain from the yoke of the Holy Roman Empire but then continues to ravage the Italian countryside, killing innocents and burning towns and buildings. In Metz they destroy churches, hospitals, inns and houses (lines 3038–43); in Como they kill villagers and force them to flee into the forest (lines 3108–15); and in Tuscany their plundering is so destructive that word reaches Spain and Prussia (lines 3153–63). Whilst Arthur's atrocities do not result in any immediate punishment, and the citizens' submission to the king acknowledges his power, the author is aware of the immorality of Arthur's now excessive and merciless behaviour: after being chastised by his philosophers, Arthur dreams of being cast down by Lady Fortune from Fortune's Wheel, an event mirrored in Mordred's usurpation of Arthur's throne and the subsequent downfall of the Round Table.

The knight in combat can be a religiously approved figure provided he fights

[35] L. Patterson sees the episode as representing an inability to transition from past to present, from Priamus's classical ancestry to Arthur's rule, and that the conversion of Priamus to Arthur's cause is an appropriation of Alexandrian values to the new order; *Negotiating the Past: The Historical Understanding of Medieval Literature* (Madison WI, 1987), pp. 217–30. Whilst Patterson believes this episode to indicate the failure of Arthur to avoid Alexander's fate by its own lack of success, I would argue that it is the very success of the episode which is used as a contrast to highlight the flaws of the Arthurian characters in the remaining war narrative, in which Christian morality is overshadowed by secular desires.

[36] Plenty of scholarship has been written on this debate. See W. Matthews, *The Tragedy of Arthur* (Berkeley, 1960); G. R. Keiser, 'The Theme of Justice in the Alliterative *Morte Arthure*', *Annuale Mediaevale* 16 (1975), 94–109; K. Göller, 'Reality versus Romance: A Reassessment of the Alliterative *Morte Arthure*', in *The Alliterative* Morte Arthure: *A Reassessment of the Poem*, ed. K. Göller (Cambridge, 1981), pp. 15–28; L. D. Benson, 'The Alliterative *Morte Arthure* and Medieval Tragedy', *Tennessee Studies in Literature* 11 (1966), 75–87; J. Finlayson, 'The Concept of the Hero in *Morte Arthure*', in *Chaucer und seine Zeit: Symposium für Walter F. Schirmer*, ed. Arno Esch (Tübingen, 1968), pp. 249–74; R. Moll, *Before Malory: Reading Arthur in Later Medieval England* (Toronto, 2003), pp. 97–122; L. Johnson, 'The Alliterative *Morte Arthure*', in *The Arthur of the English*, ed. W. R. J. Barron (Cardiff, 2001), pp. 90–99; and A. Mueller, 'The Historiography of the Dragon: Heraldic Violence in the Alliterative Morte Arthure', *Studies in the Age of Chaucer* 32 (2010), 295–324.

for a morally just cause. In *Jesus Thy Sweetness*, Christ, after suffering the pain of the Crucifixion, returns as a triumphant victor fighting for the sinner:

> Whene he hade venqwyste his bataile
> His banere full brade displayede es,
> When so my faa will me assaile. (lines 74–6)

The vocabulary of banners and battles is clearly borrowed from secular chivalric literature. Arthur, however, clearly overstepping the boundaries of spiritually acceptable physical sacrifice, has put his entire kingdom in jeopardy because of his secular desires. The chivalric wounding is no longer God's cause but Arthur's. His knights have supplanted their devotion to Christ with a devotion to Arthur, and the excessively violent imagery highlights this disparity. Readers' sympathies are roused with affective vocabulary, but the fall of the realm reminds them that the knights are *not* Christ, nor are they fighting for a religious cause. It is not the poet's intention to condemn Arthur and his knights, but the language of violence is used to punish the sins of chivalric power and glorify its virtues, as well as to lament the loss of chivalry's power and virtues.

Affective language in the Siege of Jerusalem

The alliterative *Morte Arthure* is not the only chivalric poem copied by Thornton that displays an interest in the Passion. The *Siege of Jerusalem* demonstrates a clear link between mourning Christ's wounds and chivalric sacrifice. The *Siege* follows the *Northern Passion* in London and provides an interesting postscript to the Crucifixion of Jesus. It, like many of Thornton's texts, straddles the world of religious meditation and chivalric violence, providing a gory but detailed vision of the first Jewish-Roman war. Michael Johnston argues that the texts that proceed the *Siege* in the London manuscript – the *Cursor Mundi* and the *Northern Passion* – emphasize the Jews' responsibility for the death of Christ and, thus, set the *Siege of Jerusalem* up as a 'narrative of revenge for the deicide encountered in the Northern *Passion*'.[37] Indeed, the *Siege's* opening reference to Christ's suffering establishes the poem as a direct response to the Passion:

> A pelare pyghte was thare down appon the plate erthe
> his bow body bownden ther to and betyn with scourges
> withe whippes of qwereboyle abowte his whitte sydis
> Till alle one rede blode rane als rayne in the strete
> …

---

[37] M. Johnston, 'Robert Thornton and *The Siege of Jerusalem*', *Yearbook of Langland Studies* 23 (2009), 125–62 (p. 129).

and sythen a kene crown of thorne thay thrange one his heuede
vmbykeste hym with a crye and one crosse sloughe

(lines 9–12, 17–18)[38]

Although there is no mention of the wound to Christ's side in this version, it contains many graphic images of Christ's broken and beaten body, a reference to the crown of thorns upon his head, and flowing blood.

After the poet reminds readers of Christ's suffering, he introduces them to Titus, son of the Roman general Vespasian. Titus is soon converted by means of an explanation of the nature of the Trinity and an enumeration of Christ's miracles. In portraying this conversion, the poem serves an educational and devotional purpose. While we can assume the medieval reader is already familiar with the life of Christ and with the Trinity, the poet offers these stories in another (and perhaps simpler) context. The *Siege* serves as a reminder to the audience of the purpose of the tale's war and the reader's own emotional responses, a purpose reiterated by the reciting of biblical stories before the Romans besiege Jerusalem (lines 477–84). The lamentation over Christ's death is transformed into a physical battle of vengeance. Titus himself exhibits the sacrificial vengeance already demonstrated by the Christian knights in the *Morte Arthure*, vowing himself to Christ's cause: 'Sende me helpe of my hurte and hally I a vowe / To be dede for thi dede …' (lines 200–01).

Scholars such as Suzanne Yeager and Maija Birenbaum have discussed the role of penitential revenge in Vengeance of Our Lord texts such as the *Siege* and *Titus and Vespasian*, highlighting the portrayal of the Jewish-Roman wars as a path to salvation. Violence against Jews is legitimized in these texts because of the Jews' rejection of Jesus's love. The purging of Christ's foes becomes a form of active penitence: 'Within the context of *Titus and Vespasian*, those who commit violence against the remorseless Jews perform charity both personally, in the penitential act of risking death for love of Christ, and communally, by purging the Holy Land of the faithless deicides.'[39]

In addition, the unrepentant Jews are both sympathetic and despicable to the late medieval reader fearful of divine vengeance. Contemporary readers, concerned for their own sins, may compare themselves with the remorseless Jews and are instructed to avoid the fate of the Jews through penitence. This penance, according to the *Siege* poet, can be achieved through an empathetic response to Christ's suffering and an expression of this love through vengeance

[38] All quotations from the London Thornton text of the *Siege of Jerusalem* are taken from *The Siege of Jerusalem Electronic Archive*, ed. T. J. Stinson, www.siegeofjerusalem.org. I am greatly indebted to Tim Stinson for allowing me pre-publication access to the database. All subsequent references to the *Siege* will be by line number in parentheses in the body of the work.

[39] M. Birenbaum, 'Affective Vengeance in *Titus and Vespasian*', *Chaucer Review* 43 (2009), 330–44 (p. 332).

towards his foes. The *Siege* is a warning to its contemporary Christian readers to repent of their sins, and the experience of penitential vengeance sanctioned by God – physically or vicariously through reading tales of the Jewish-Roman wars – is a road to salvation. Vespasian continues this connection between chivalric combat and the Passion in his battle-speech before they begin the siege, asking his men (and the audience) to visualize Christ's suffering for their inspiration:

> 'Be holdis to the hethynge and to the harde wondis
> the bufffetynge the betynge that he one body hade
> late neuer ӡone laweles ledis laughe at hir harmes
> that dere boghte vs fra bale with bolde of his herte' (lines 477–80)

It is the blood 'of [Christ's] herte' that is emphasized as the ransom Christ gives to redeem humankind. Like Passion narratives, the *Siege* draws on affective piety to move its audience, offering them the opportunity of salvation refused by the Jews in the poem. Yeager notes that readers of the *Siege* 'would have had a vested interest in noting how other social groups had dealt with inexplicable failures and crises which would have been historically interpreted as the result of divine wrath'.[40] The poet encourages readers to avoid this fate by repenting of their sins, going through this penitence by experiencing the grief of the Passion and transferring this grief to vengeance.

How does this vengeful warfare express itself in the language of violence in the *Siege*? As in the *Morte*, the *Siege* describes warfare in gruesome detail. It describes battle formations and siege machines, beautifully rich armour and horrible deaths. The *Siege* does not have the same emphasis on injuries to the heart that is so prominent in the Arthurian romance, but it does contain numerous wounds to the head and to brains. Titus 'with a bryghte brande brittynes one harde / that the blode and the brayne appon the bent lefte' (lines 523–24), and Sir Sabyn of Syria is given his death stroke in the last battle when he is hit with 'ane vn mete dynt / that the braynes owte braste at bothe his nesse thirles [nostrils]' (lines 1172–73). The poet graphically describes head wounds. One knight attacked with a stone sustains a remarkable injury: 'a barne with a balghestone was the hed clouen / a grete pece of the [brain] pane the stone owte strake / that it fleghe in to þe felde a furlonge and more' (lines 802–4). The emphasis in all of these cases is upon how the force of the knight's blow is so strong that it pierces through the head armour and the skull strikes into the brain. The gruesome details of this violence heighten readers' emotions as they envisage the battlefield.

---

[40] S. Yeager, 'Jewish Identity in *The Siege of Jerusalem* and Homiletic Texts: Models of Penance and Victims of Vengeance for the Urban Apocalypse', *Medium Ævum* 80 (2011), 56–84 (p. 59).

The wonders that the Christian army can achieve are contrasted sharply with the fate that the inhabitants of Jerusalem now face. The only wound received by Vespasian – an injury that nails his foot to his horse's flank – acts as a perverse parallel to the nailing of Christ's foot:

> waspasyane was wondyde wondirly sore
> thorowe the harde of the hele with ane hande darte
> It *bate* thorowe the *bote* and the bone *naylede*
>
> (lines 792–94; emphasis added)

The leader of the siege of Jerusalem and the Christian army is given an injury that, although not exact, allows him to experience one of the wounds of Christ. While the wound is to the heel not the foot, the proximity of the injury is highlighted by the use of 'bate' (pierced) and 'naylede', and it provides an excellent example of the sacrificial nature of the venture the knights have embarked upon. The injury is seen as 'heroic ... but unsettling' by David Lawton, who argues that the poet is developing the topos of 'Vespasian as hero', reflected in Vespasian's desire to go hunting and hawking – knightly pursuits which establish the honour of Titus and his father.[41]

The *Siege* only mentions pierced hearts once, when Roman soldiers strike through the hearts of the Jewish soldiers: 'they schoke owte of schethis þat schrape were Igrounde / and melyn metalle thorowte maltyn hertis' (lines 539–40). In a reverse parallel to the piercing of Christ's heart, the Romans gain their vengeance by punishing the Jews in the same way; as Johnston points out, Christ's suffering is 'subsequently transmogrified into the suffering of Jewish and Saracen bodies' in the *Siege* and in the Charlemagne romances which follow it in the London manuscript.[42] In the parallel passage in Oxford, Bodleian Library, MS Laud Misc. 656, the text of the *Siege* claims that the Jewish hearts are 'vnmylt',[43] which can mean 'fierce, savage or cruel'.[44] The author offers a comparison; the 'cruel' hearts of the Jews, contrasted with Jesus's compassionate heart, justify the Romans' brutality. The *Siege* offers an affective language of violence for warfare with penitential properties. When this affective language is applied to the secular (and excessive) chivalric sacrifice of Arthur and his knights in the *Morte*, the reader both sympathizes with and questions their motives.

---

[41] D. Lawton, 'Titus Goes Hunting and Hawking: The Poetics of Recreation and Revenge in *The Siege of Jerusalem*', in *Individuality and Achievement in Middle English Poetry*, ed. O. S. Pickering (Cambridge, 1997), pp. 105–18 (pp. 106, 108).

[42] Johnston, 'Robert Thornton', p. 128.

[43] See *The Siege of Jerusalem*, ed. R. Hanna and D. Lawton, EETS OS 320 (Oxford, 2003), line 560.

[44] *MED*, s.v. *unmilde* (adj.).

John J. Thompson notes, interestingly, that mystical items 'tend not to get copied by compilers who were interested in ME romances' and that manuscripts containing both romances and mystical material tend not to separate them.[45] This raises an interesting question about the organization of the romances in Thornton's manuscripts and the nature of their readers. The *Morte Arthure* and its descriptions of violence may well shed light on the interests of the audience of Thornton's compilations. The alliterative romance has epic, chronicle and religious associations. It is possible that the emphasis on the mystical and emotional aspects of Christianity in Thornton's manuscripts, particularly in the Lincoln manuscript, which devotionally highlights the Passion, is an indication of a compilation tailored in part for female readers,[46] but the affective material is not limited to a female audience;[47] the *Morte Arthure* and many of the epic romances within Thornton's two volumes would certainly appeal to both genders. The collection of literature that he created uses an awareness of genre not just for separation but also for cohesion. The manuscripts would have catered to a wide audience. His material speaks to a relatively prosperous secular society, one that desired to hear tales of war as well as understand spiritual matters. By portraying religious emotion through physical sacrifice, not just in Passion narratives but also in popular secular literature such as the alliterative *Morte Arthure*, violent images and the language of injuring become ways to borrow and share generic tropes, and, by their means, the secular protagonists of romance are both glorified and judged.

---

[45] Thompson, *London Thornton MS*, p. 4.

[46] See Thompson, 'Another Look', pp. 179–80.

[47] While McNamer argues that the emotive response to the Passion originated in the affective meditative traditions of medieval women, she rightly points out that this compassion was also harnessed for male devotion in the late Middle Ages. The compassion that is so frequently encouraged in Middle English meditations on the Passion may be seen as 'largely a function of gender performance: to perform compassion is to feel like a woman'; the reader is often cast in the feminine role of spouse, mother or feminized man, a technique used to elicit an empathetic response to Christ's suffering (*Affective Meditation*, pp. 119–20).

6

Constantinian Christianity in the London Manuscript: The Codicological and Linguistic Evidence of Thornton's Intentions*

Michael Johnston

Of late, scholars have expressed an increased interest in the activities of scribes as interpreters of literary texts and as co-participants, along with authors, in the creation of meaning. No longer are such author-centric views of literary culture, like George Kane's, taken as *a priori* truths, with both errors and conscious emendations on the part of scribes mere white noise to be filtered out in the act of recovering the words of the author:

> To sentimentalize such scribal response or to dignify it by calling it 'criticism' is unrewarding. … At the level of style it is the response of mediocrity to distinction. By nature as variation it damages the work of art that evoked it. Scribal variation from the text of such a work cannot have 'intrinsic' value. The scribal variant is a deplorable circumstance of the manual transmission of texts. It has value only as evidence for the authorial reading it supplanted.[1]

Of course, Kane is writing from the perspective of a critical editor, for whom recovering the words of the author is, by definition, paramount, and hence his Platonic view of textuality makes sense. But those Aristotelians among us, whose interests are in historicizing medieval literary-cultural practice, have turned to scribal activity, seeing scribes as exhibiting cultural agency – to varying degrees – and seeing it as the scholar's job to retrieve that agency, which is rendered opaque by the critical edition.[2] Studies have shown the diversity and creativity

* I wish to thank Simon Horobin and Robyn Malo for their insightful comments on this essay.

[1] G. Kane, 'The Text', in *A Companion to 'Piers Plowman'*, ed. J. A. Alford (Berkeley and Los Angeles, 1988), pp. 175–200 (p. 194).

[2] J. Dagenais, *The Ethics of Reading in Manuscript Culture: Glossing the 'Libro del buen amor'* (Princeton, 1994), pp. 3–29; D. Pearsall, 'Editing Medieval Texts: Some Developments and Some Problems', in *Textual Criticism and Literary Interpretation*, ed. J. McGann (Chicago, 1985), pp. 92–106; and T. W. Machan, *Textual Criticism and Middle English Texts* (Charlottesville VA, 1994). But cf. the cautionary remarks registered by D. Wakelin, 'Writing the Words', in *The*

of scribal responses to Middle English religious literature,[3] Chaucer's *Troilus*[4] and *Canterbury Tales*,[5] Gower's *Confessio amantis*,[6] *Piers Plowman*,[7] the work of John Lydgate,[8] and Middle English romance.[9] In particular, commonplace

Production of Books in England 1350–1500, ed. A. Gillespie and D. Wakelin (Cambridge, 2011), pp. 34–58, who notes the general fidelity scribes of Middle English held for their exemplars.

[3] J. J. Thompson, 'Textual Instability and the Late Medieval Reputation of Some Middle English Religious Literature', *TEXT: Transactions of the Society for Textual Scholarship* 5 (1991), 175–94.

[4] B. A. Windeatt, 'The Scribes as Chaucer's Early Critics', *Studies in the Age of Chaucer* 1 (1979), 119–41.

[5] B. Kennedy, 'Cambridge MS Dd.4.24: A Misogynous Scribal Revision of *The Wife of Bath's Prologue*?' *Chaucer Review* 30 (1996), 343–58; B. Kennedy, 'Contradictory Responses to the Wife of Bath as Evidenced by Fifteenth-Century Manuscript Variants', *Canterbury Tales Project Occasional Papers* 2 (1997), 23–39; and S. Schibanoff, 'The New Reader and Female Textuality in Two Early Commentaries on Chaucer', *Studies in the Age of Chaucer* 10 (1988), 71–108.

[6] K. Harris, 'John Gower's "Confessio amantis": The Virtues of Bad Texts', in *Manuscripts and Readers in Fifteenth-Century England: The Literary Implications of Manuscript Study. Essays from the 1981 Conference at the University of York*, ed. D. Pearsall (Cambridge, 1983), pp. 27–40; and A. W. Bahr, 'Reading Codicological Form in John Gower's Trentham Manuscript', *Studies in the Age of Chaucer* 33 (2011), 219–62.

[7] S. Horobin and A. Wiggins, 'Reconsidering Lincoln's Inn MS 150', *Medium Ævum* 77 (2008), 30–53; S. Horobin, 'The Scribe of Bodleian Library, MS Digby 102 and the Circulation of the C Text of *Piers Plowman*', *Yearbook of Langland Studies* 24 (2010), 89–112; C. J. Grindley, 'Reading *Piers Plowman* C-Text Annotations: Notes toward the Classification of Printed and Written Marginalia in Texts from the British Isles 1300–1641', in *The Medieval Professional Reader at Work: Evidence from Manuscripts of Chaucer, Langland, Kempe, and Gower*, ed. K. Kerby-Fulton and M. Hilmo, English Literary Studies 85 (Victoria BC, 2001), pp. 73–141; and K. Kerby-Fulton and D. L. Despres, *Iconography and the Professional Reader: The Politics of Book Production in the Douce 'Piers Plowman'*, Medieval Cultures 15 (Minneapolis, 1998).

[8] M. Nolan, 'Lydgate's Worst Poem', in *Lydgate Matters: Poetry and Material Culture in the Fifteenth Century*, ed. L. H. Cooper and A. Denny-Brown (New York, 2008), pp. 71–87.

[9] Regarding compilers and scribes of romance manuscripts, M. J. Evans, *Rereading Middle English Romance: Manuscript Layout, Decoration, and the Rhetoric of Composite Structure* (Montreal and Kingston, 1995), p. xvi, comments that 'Some scholars take the extreme view that there are no patterns of shaping in manuscript compilation and others, the opposite view that manuscript compilations provide irrefutable evidence of medieval literary-critical sensibility. I believe the truth as it can now be ascertained lies on a continuum between these two poles and will vary according to the manuscript under discussion'. For discussions of particular romance manuscripts, see P. Hardman, 'The Unity of the Ireland Manuscript', *Reading Medieval Studies* 2 (1976), 45–62; A. Wiggins, 'A Makeover Story: The Caius Manuscript Copy of *Guy of Warwick*', *Studies in Philology* 104 (2007), 471–500; and L. S. Blanchfield, 'The Romances in MS Ashmole 61: An Idiosyncratic Scribe', in *Romance in Medieval England*, ed. M. Mills, J. Fellows and C. Meale (Cambridge, 1991), pp. 65–87.

books formed a locus for copyists to tailor texts to the ends of their own, often idiosyncratic, compilations.[10]

It is in relation to this larger turn towards scribal agency that I wish to place Thornton and his efforts as literary copyist and compiler.[11] As I will argue here, when we examine the opening series of texts in the London manuscript, we find mixed evidence about how much agency Thornton exhibited in the creation of his codex. In general, if modern scholars find a textual pairing or sequence of texts within a given manuscript to be of significance, we then need to ask who created it. If it was the scribe of the manuscript under consideration, then he/she can rightly be said to exhibit a good deal of agency, operating as what Saint Bonaventure called a *compilator*, one who 'writes material composed by others, joining them together but adding nothing of his own'. If, by contrast, the pairing was in the scribe's exemplar, and he/she merely replicated it, then the agency belongs to the scribe of the exemplar, and the scribe under consideration would be a Bonaventuran *mere scriptor*, one who 'writes material composed by other people, adding or changing nothing'.[12] In Thornton's case, at least as regards the opening sequence in the London manuscript, we find him straddling the border between *scriptor* and *compilator*, sometimes gathering texts from disparate exemplars into unique – and meaningful – combinations, sometimes replicating pairings from his exemplar, while, on a few occasions, he gestures towards the even more creative role of *commentator*.

---

[10]   D. Parker, *The Commonplace Book in Tudor London: An Examination of BL MSS Egerton 1995, Harley 2252, Lansdowne 762, and Oxford Balliol College MS 354* (Lanham MD, 1998); U. Frost, *Das Commonplace Book von John Colyns: Untersuchung und Teiledition der Handschrift Harley 2252 der British Library in London*, Europäische Hochschulschriften 14, vol. 186 (Frankfurt, 1988); C. Meale, 'The Compiler at Work: John Colyns and BL MS Harley 2252', in *Manuscripts and Readers*, ed. Pearsall, pp. 82–103; *The Commonplace Book of Robert Raynes of Acle: An Edition of Tanner MS 407*, ed. C. Louis (New York, 1980); and A. G. Rigg, *A Glastonbury Miscellany of the Fifteenth Century: A Descriptive Index of Trinity College, Cambridge, MS O.9.38* (London, 1968).

[11]   For analyses of Thornton's scribal habits, see M. Hamel, 'Scribal Self-Correction in the Thornton *Morte Arthure*', *Studies in Bibliography* 36 (1983), 119–37; J. A. Jefferson and A. Putter, 'Alliterative Patterning in the *Morte Arthure*', *Studies in Philology* 102 (2005), 415–33; J. I. Carlson, 'Scribal Intentions in Medieval Romance: A Case Study of Robert Thornton', *Studies in Bibliography* 58 (2007–8), 49–71; P. R. Robinson, 'A Study of Some Aspects of the Transmission of English Verse Texts in Late Medieval Manuscripts' (unpublished B.Litt. thesis, University of Oxford, 1972), pp. 66–9; D. Lawton, 'Gaytryge's Sermon, "Dictamen", and Middle English Alliterative Verse', *Modern Philology* 76 (1979), 329–43; and H. N. Duggan, 'Alliterative Patterning as a Basis for Emendation in Middle English Alliterative Poetry', *Studies in the Age of Chaucer* 8 (1986), 73–105.

[12]   Quoted in *The Idea of the Vernacular: An Anthology of Middle English Literary Theory, 1280–1520*, ed. J. Wogan-Browne, N. Watson, A. Taylor and R. Evans (University Park PA, 1999), p. 3. For a discussion of Bonaventure's terminology, see A. J. Minnis, *Medieval Theory of Authorship*, 2nd edn (Philadelphia, 2010), pp. 94–103.

To make the case about Thornton's cultural agency, I will present linguistic evidence showing that, in this opening series, he drew upon four distinct exemplars across a lengthy period of time, out of which he crafted a Salvation History that posits hard and fast and stable distinctions between Christians and Jews/Muslims. The opening sequence of texts in the manuscript is as follows:

Two selections from *Cursor Mundi* (arts. 1–3)

Northern Passion (art. 4)

Siege of Jerusalem (art. 6)

Sege of Melayne (art. 8)

O Florum Flos, a Marian lyric by John Lydgate (art. 9)

Duke Roland and Sir Otuel of Spain (art. 10)

The chronological development underwriting this sequence is unmistakable: first, the selections from *Cursor Mundi* that Thornton preserved narrate the birth and life of Christ, right up to his death. The *Northern Passion* then follows, which tells of Christ's crucifixion. This is followed by the *Siege of Jerusalem*, in which the Jews are annihilated for being Christ-killers. Finally, Thornton copied two Charlemagne romances, which show the Church triumphant defeating its contemporary rivals, Muslims. I and others have previously examined the opening series of texts and argued, based on literary-critical readings and codicological analyses, that Thornton has here intentionally created a Salvation History.[13] But none of the preceding readings of the London manuscript draws upon the linguistic evidence, which is essential in establishing whether this salvation-historical sequence was in Thornton's exemplar, or whether he himself compiled it from disparate sources and thus can be said to have exerted some cultural agency. Readings attributing this sequence to Thornton, as mine did, depend upon the conclusion that Thornton himself was responsible for the sequence – which I now hope to demonstrate was the case.

---

[13] M. Johnston, 'Robert Thornton and *The Siege of Jerusalem*', *Yearbook of Langland Studies* 23 (2009), 125–62; P. Hardman, 'The *Sege of Melayne*: A Fifteenth-Century Reading', in *Tradition and Transformation in Medieval Romance*, ed. R. Field (Cambridge, 1999), pp. 71–86; P. Hardman, 'Reading the Spaces: Pictorial Intentions in the Thornton MSS, Lincoln Cathedral MS 91, and BL MS Add. 31042', *Medium Ævum* 63 (1994), 250–74 (pp. 267–9); and J. Finlayson, 'The Context of the Crusading Romances in the London Thornton Manuscript', *Anglia* 130 (2012), 240–63. For briefer comments to the same effect, see *The Northern Passion*, ed. F. A. Foster, 2 vols., EETS OS 145, 147 (London, 1913–16), II, pp. 12–13; G. Keiser, 'Review of *Robert Thornton and the London Thornton Manuscript*, by J. J. Thompson', *Envoi* 2 (1990), 155–60 (p. 159); and S. C. Akbari, 'Incorporation in the *Siege of Melayne*', in *Pulp Fictions of Medieval England: Essays in Popular Romance*, ed. N. McDonald (Manchester, 2004), pp. 22–44 (pp. 37–9).

Thornton as compilator

The touchstone study for understanding Thornton's dialect and the amount of translating he did to his exemplars remains Angus McIntosh's brief 1962 essay in the *Festschrift* for Tolkien, in which he argues that 'Robert Thornton was not by habit a scribe who transformed or "translated" his exemplars so thoroughly as to obliterate all those characteristics in them which were alien to his own', a statement that has been accepted by subsequent scholars.[14] In short, my own analysis bears out McIntosh's observations about Thornton's scribal behaviour. Thornton drew from the following four exemplars for his five texts:[15]

A manuscript from Lancashire, from which he copied *Cursor Mundi*

A manuscript from the East Riding, from which he copied the pairing of the *Northern Passion* and the *Siege of Jerusalem*

A manuscript from the border between the West Riding and northern Lincolnshire, from which he copied the *Sege of Melayne*

A manuscript from roughly the same place as the *Sege of Melayne* (possibly, but not likely from the same manuscript), or from slightly further south, from which he copied *Roland and Otuel*

Before summarizing the linguistic evidence that led me to identify these separate exemplars, I must first outline those forms Thornton used regularly

---

[14]   A. McIntosh, 'The Textual Transmission of the Alliterative *Morte Arthure*', in *English and Medieval Studies Presented to J. R. R. Tolkien on the Occasion of His Seventieth Birthday*, ed. N. Davis and C. L. Wrenn (London, 1962), pp. 231–40 (p. 231). For subsequent scholars who have built upon McIntosh's thesis, see, in particular, G. R. Keiser, 'Lincoln Cathedral Library MS. 91: Life and Milieu of the Scribe', *Studies in Bibliography* 32 (1979), 158–79; *Morte Arthure: A Critical Edition*, ed. M. Hamel, Garland Medieval Texts 9 (New York, 1984), pp. 5–14; and R. Hanna, 'The Growth of Robert Thornton's Books', *Studies in Bibliography* 40 (1987), 51–61. For a pointed critique, see J. I. Carlson, 'The Alliterative *Morte Arthure*: A Hyper-Critical Edition' (unpublished Ph.D. dissertation, University of Virginia, 2006), 5.3.2. Carlson takes issue with McIntosh's and Hamel's localizations of the authorial dialect of the *Morte Arthure*, not the dialect of Thornton's immediate exemplar, which is at issue here.

[15]   Here, and in what follows, when I write 'a manuscript from …', this does not mean that Thornton actually acquired the manuscript from there or that it was even physically copied there. Rather, it simply means that the scribe's dialect shows him to have learned to write there. The key point in what follows is that the various dialects I have identified show that Thornton is drawing from different manuscripts. Whether he actually acquired the manuscript from the place to which I localize the scribal dialect is immaterial – and, unless further evidence surfaces, ultimately unrecoverable. On the issue of scribal mobility and its effect on dialectal analysis, see R. Beadle, 'Prolegomena to a Literary Geography of Later Medieval Norfolk', in *Regionalism in Late Medieval Manuscripts and Texts: Essays Celebrating the Publication of A Linguistic Atlas of Late Mediaeval English*, ed. F. Riddy (Cambridge, 1991), pp. 89–108.

across all five texts: these features comprise his own idiolect, into which he translated, with nearly perfect consistency, the various forms he encountered in the exemplars. These forms appear regularly in all five texts, making it almost certain that they were part of Thornton's own native North Yorkshire dialect, what McIntosh, Samuels and Benskin call his 'active repertoire' in copying:[16]

4. She: scho	137. Give (pt. sg. and pt. pl.): gaf(f)e
5. Her: hir	139. Good: gud(e)
8. Them: þam (thaym)	145. Heaven: heuen(e)
13. Many: many	147. Hell: helle
14. Man: man (mane)	149. High: heghe
15. Any: any	157. Hundred: hundrethe
21. Was: was	170. Little: littill
24. Will: will	172. Lord: lorde
34. As: als	173. Love (sb.): luf(f)e
40. Yet: ȝitt	180. Mother: modir
49. Think: th(þ)ynk(e)	182. Name (sb.): name
63. Weak ppl: -ed, -ede	195. Now: now(e)
70. All: alle	205. Pray: pray(e)
84. Blessed: blyssed(e)	218. Six (card.): sex(e)
91. But: bot(e)	218. Six (ord.): sexte
93. Call (ppl.): called(e)	220. Some: som(e)
101. Day: day(e)	222. Sorrow: sorow(e)
103. Die (pt.): dyede	230. Ten: ten(e)
107. Earth: erthe	237. Three (card.): thre
112. Eleven: elleuen	239. True: trew(e)
115. Eye (sg.): eghe	240. Twelve: twelue
115. Eye (pl.): eghne	241. Twenty: twent(t)y
116. Far: ferre	244. Upon: appon(e)
124. Fire: fyre, fire	245. Way: waye
125. First: firste, fyrste	247. Well (adv.): wele
127. Flesh: flesche	258. Without: with-owtten
130. Four (ord.): ferthe	260. Worship: wirchip(p)e
132. Friend: frende	264. Year: ȝer(e)

---

[16] *LALME*, I, p. 14. In this, and all subsequent linguistic analyses, I present the data in the format used in *LALME*: viz., the number from *LALME*'s questionnaire, the modern English word or suffix followed by a colon, followed by the predominant form used by Thornton, followed by subsidiary forms, if any, within parentheses. On the methodology of using *LALME*, see M. Benskin, 'The "Fit-Technique" Explained', in *Regionalism in Late Medieval Manuscripts*, ed. Riddy, pp. 9–26. For an overview of the limitations in using *LALME*, which has guided much of my thinking on the linguistic analyses I have undertaken here, see S. Horobin, 'Mapping the Words', in *The Production of Books*, ed. Gillespie and Wakelin, pp. 59–78.

266. Young: ȝong(e)
272. -dom: -dom(e)
274. -est: -est(e)

275. -ful: -full(e)
277. -less: -les
278. -ly: -ly

Of course, some of the forms listed here may coincidentally have been in all of Thornton's exemplars and thus may not have been the result of his translation.[17] Additionally, many of these forms are widely attested across numerous Middle English dialects and hence do not offer us much insight into the particular contours of Thornton's translation habits. But until further study of all the texts in both Thornton manuscripts can establish a sounder picture of his own *usus scribendi*, Occam's razor is the best we can do here, and hence I have excluded these forms in my analysis of the dialect of each text Thornton copied. Morever, each of these forms is consonant with the dialectal features of the English found in the south-central North Riding, where Thornton lived, thus making it plausible that these are part of his idiolect.[18] As McIntosh elsewhere notes, 'Robert Thornton can be shown to have added a Yorkshire veneer to a number of texts he copied', an assertion borne out by my findings here.[19] When trying to recover the dialect of the exemplars lying behind Thornton's copy, one must disregard these forms, since Thornton has almost certainly translated these features into his own dialect. He is not, then, a purely *literatim* copyist, preserving his exemplar verbatim; however, on the continuum from *literatim* to total translator, Thornton falls much closer to the former, as McIntosh suggests.[20]

[17] See Jefferson and Putter, 'Alliterative Patterning', p. 425, who show that in his copy of the alliterative *Morte*, Thornton translates the various forms of *without* as *with-owtten*, even at the expense of metrical regularity.

[18] *LALME* provides two Linguistic Profiles of texts located close to Thornton's home of East Newton. Comparison of these LPs shows that the forms I have identified as Thornton's own are indeed standard for this part of the North Riding. See LP 190, a copy of *Northern Homily Cycle* from London, BL, MS Additional 30358 in *LALME*, III, pp. 577–8; and LP 203, a copy of *Chastising of God's Children* from Cambridge, St John's College, MS 128 (E.25) in *LALME*, III, pp. 579–80. The identification of this scribe as Robert Thornton of the North Riding has been soundly made by Keiser, 'Lincoln Cathedral Library MS. 91', pp. 158–79; G. R. Keiser, 'More Light on the Life and Milieu of Robert Thornton', *Studies in Bibliography* 36 (1983), 111–19; M. Johnston, 'A New Document Relating to the Life of Robert Thornton', *The Library* 7th ser. 8 (2007), 304–13; and M. Johnston, *Romance and the Gentry in Late Medieval England* (Oxford, forthcoming 2014), chapter 5.

[19] A. McIntosh, 'A New Approach to Middle English Dialectology', *English Studies* 44 (1963), 1–11 (p. 9).

[20] McIntosh, 'The Textual Transmission', pp. 231–40. But cf. the cautionary remarks of S. Horobin, '"In London and opeland": The Dialect and Circulation of the C Version of *Piers Plowman*', *Medium Ævum* 74 (2005), 248–69, who suggests that *literatim* copying may have been more common than contemporary scholarship has yet accounted for.

The first text in the manuscript as it now stands is *Cursor Mundi*, a text drawn from a different source than the others in this opening series. The following features help us to localize Thornton's exemplar of *Cursor Mundi* to an area near the Lancashire/West Riding border:[21]

> 3. Those: thase (Dot Map 616)
> 10. Such: swilke (Dot Map 66)
> 11. Which: whilke (Dot Map 84)
> 28. From: fra (Dot Map 173)
> 85. Both: bathe (Dot Map 366)
> 109. Eight: aught (Dot Map 741)
> 155. Holy: haly (Dot Map 805)
> 164. Law: laughe, lawe (Dot Map 817)[22]
> 177. Mon (for shall): mon (Dot Map 831)
> 242. Two: twa (Dot Map 548)
> 257. Witen: infinitive with *-e* in stem vowel (Dot Map 581)

Further attestation of the Lancashire connections of Thornton's exemplar can be gleaned from Sarah Horrall's stemmatic analysis of the surviving manuscripts of *Cursor Mundi*: she demonstrates that Thornton's copy and Oxford, Bodleian Library, MS Fairfax 14 alone share unique readings and thus comprise a unique branch of the textual tradition (though neither descends immediately from the same exemplar). The Fairfax manuscript has demonstrable linguistic ties to Lancashire, thus lending further support to my analysis here.[23]

The second and third texts in the manuscript, the *Northern Passion* and the *Siege of Jerusalem*, were likely together in the same exemplar, for they have a nearly identical set of linguistic forms in Thornton's copy – although there are a few exceptions.[24] The similarities in linguistic forms between these two texts are strong enough, on balance, to make a good case for a single exemplar. (The

---

[21] I analysed *Cursor Mundi* from the appendices in *The Southern Version of* Cursor Mundi: *Volume II*, ed. R. R. Fowler (Ottawa, 1990), pp. 151–92; and *The Southern Version of* Cursor Mundi: *Volume III*, ed. H. J. Stauffenberg (Ottawa, 1985), pp. 165–210, who provide diplomatic transcriptions of Thornton's text. I analysed the following three 500-line sections from the beginning, middle and end: 10630–11130, 12525–13025 and 14225–14925.

[22] Thornton only uses *laughe* in the opening 500 lines, while *lawe* is the main form attested in the other texts analysed below, suggesting that *laughe* is the form in his exemplar and he was slowly working-in to his native dialectal form of *lawe*. Note that *laughe* is from the NW Midlands and is rarely attested in the North Riding.

[23] S. M. Horrall, 'The Manuscripts of *Cursor Mundi*', *TEXT: Transactions of the Society for Textual Scholarship* 2 (1985), 69–82 (pp. 75–6). See also J. J. Thompson, *The Cursor Mundi: Poem, Texts and Contexts*, Medium Ævum Monographs n.s. 19 (Oxford, 1998), pp. 80–7. For a dialectal analysis of Fairfax 14's copy of *Cursor Mundi*, see LP 6 in *LALME*, III, pp. 200–1.

[24] For example, in the *Northern Passion* Thornton consistently uses 189. Never: neuir, while

exceptions may be due to multiple scribes with slightly different dialects at work on the exemplar Thornton was using.) The following forms help localize this exemplar to the region of the East Riding or Northern Lincolnshire, between York, Hull and Grimsby:[25]

> 3. Those: those (thase) (Dot Map 616). Thornton translates to his usual form *those* predominantly, but enough uses of *thase* survive to indicate that it must have been in his exemplar, and thus I have mapped *thase*.
> 10. Such: swylke (Dot Map 66)
> 28. From: fra (Dot Map 173; Item Map 28, Region 3). From: fra, within this region, only occurs north of the Humber. *Fra* occurs as a secondary form south of the Humber, but it is never a primary form south of the Humber, with the exception of one LP, on the south bank of the Humber. Thus, this example is likely from the northern part of Lincolnshire or southern part of the East Riding, near the Humber.
> 33. If: ȝif(f) (Dot Map 212)
> 242. Two: twa (Dot Map 548)

Allen Bond Kellogg's analysis suggests that Thornton's copy of the *Siege of Jerusalem* belongs among a group descended from an East Midlands archetype, and Kellogg furthermore concludes that of this group, Thornton's copy is the most northern, which would put it near my suggested home, the York-Hull-Grimsby triangle.[26]

As Thornton's Salvation History progresses from the fight against the Jewish Other to the fight against Muslims, he turns to yet a different exemplar. That is, he drew the *Sege of Melayne* from an exemplar that came from the border of the eastern West Riding and northern Lincolnshire, roughly an area triangulated

---

in *Siege* it is *neuer(e)*. In the *Northern Passion* Thornton frequently ends the third-person object pronoun with an *-e* (*þame, þayme*), something he never does in *Siege*.

[25] I analysed the *Northern Passion* from *The Northern Passion*, ed. Foster, I, who uses the London manuscript as one of four parallel texts. For this selection, I analysed the entirety of Thornton's text. As Foster notes, 'Robert Thornton of East Newton, Yorkshire, who transcribed [the London manuscript], wrote in Northern dialect, and since the poem is also Northern, we should expect the dialect to be fairly uniform. The presence of many Midland and a few Southern forms, however, indicates that Thornton was copying from a MS. written by a Midland scribe.' (II, p. 28). I analysed the *Siege of Jerusalem* from *The Siege of Jerusalem Electronic Archive*, ed. T. J. Stinson, www.siegeofjerusalem.org, which presents a diplomatic transcription of all surviving copies of this poem. For this analysis, I analysed the entire text. I wish to thank Tim for generously allowing me pre-publication access to this site.

[26] A. B. Kellogg, 'The Language of the Alliterative *Siege of Jerusalem*' (unpublished Ph.D. dissertation, University of Chicago, 1943), pp. 57–62.

by Doncaster, Grimsby and Hull. The following features allow us to narrow it down to this region:[27]

> 7. They: þay (þey) (Item Map 7, Region 3). *Þay* is Thornton's dialectal form, while he never uses *they* in the *Northern Passion* or *Siege*, and uses it only once in *Cursor Mundi*. Therefore, *they* must be in his exemplar and I have thus mapped it. As Item Map 7 shows, *they* occurs only sporadically in the southern East Riding and then more commonly throughout Lincolnshire.
> 9. Their: þaire (theire) (Item Map 9, Region 3). *Þaire* is Thornton's dialectal form, while he never uses *theire* in *Siege* and only once in the *Northern Passion*. Therefore, *theire* must be in his exemplar and I have thus mapped it. As Item Map 9 shows, *theire* only occurs once north of the Humber in the region of the East Riding, while it is common in central and southern Lincolnshire.
> 10. Such: slyke (Dot Map 72; Item Map 10, Region 3). Note that the Item Map here demonstrates that Doncaster represents the approximate western-most boundary of the use of *slyke*.
> 11. Which: whilk (Dot Map 83)
> 12. Each: ilk (Dot Map 84)
> 38. Ere: or (Dot Map 234)
> 65. About: abowte (Dot Map 667)
> 71. Among: a-mange, a-manges (Dot Map 685)
> 96. Cast: keste (Dot Map 717)
> 98. Church: kirke (Dot Map 388)
> 102. Death: dede (Dot Map 728)
> 223. Soul: saul (Dot Map 887)
> 259. Worse: wars (Dot Map 593)
> 276. -hood: -hode (Dot Map 950)

This finding accords with McIntosh's suggestion that Thornton drew the *Sege of Melayne* as well as numerous texts that he copied into both the Lincoln and London manuscripts (though no others that he placed in this opening series) from a single exemplar that 'may be said to be basically in a kind of Middle English which belongs somewhere not very far from where the counties of Yorkshire, Lincolnshire, and Nottinghamshire meet' – roughly, that is, the

---

[27] I analysed the *Sege of Melayne* from *The English Charlemagne Romances, Part II. 'The Sege off Melayne' and 'The Romance of Duke Rowland and Sir Otuell of Spayne'*, ed. S. J. Herrtage, EETS ES 35 (London, 1880). I analysed the entire text. See also R. Purdie, *Anglicising Romance: Tail-Rhyme and Genre in Medieval English Literature* (Cambridge, 2008), pp. 227–9, who locates this text to the border of the North and North Midlands dialects, likely the West Riding. Note that Purdie is analysing the authorial dialect, and thus focuses predominantly on rhyme words, which I exclude in seeking to localize the immediate exemplar Thornton used.

same region I found for the *Sege of Melayne* and what Ralph Hanna refers to as 'the Doncaster exemplar'.[28]

The case of *Roland and Otuel* is more ambiguous. In general, Thornton's copy of this text employs very similar forms to what we meet in his copy of the *Sege of Melayne*. However, there are a few important differences that consistently mark dialectal variation between these two texts as Thornton preserved them:[29]

10. Such: siche (Dot Map 68; Item Map 10, Region 3). He used *slyke* in *Sege*.

11. Which: wiche (Dot Map 79). He used *whilk* in *Sege*.

12. Each: iche (Dot Map 87). He used *ilk* in *Sege*.

16. Much: miche (Dot Map 102, Item Map 16, Region 3). Thornton initially alternates between *miche* and *mikell* here but has worked into *mikell* by the end of the text. Since *mikell* is his preferred dialectal form, *miche* must come from the exemplar and I thus mapped *miche*. He used *mekill* in *Sege*.

142. Have 3rd sg: hath, hase (Dot Map 646). Thornton alternates between the typically northern 3rd-person singular ending *-s(e)* and the typically southern *-th*, but only on the verb *has*. Elsewhere, he follows his expected Yorkshire usage of *-s*. Note that the Doncaster-Grimsby-Hull triangle lies just to the north of the attested usage of 3rd sing. *-th* endings, suggesting that this is a relict form of a previous copy by a Southern scribe.

All of these forms, used here and not in the *Sege of Melayne*, must be accounted for in attempting to assess whether Thornton acquired these two texts from the same exemplar. Each of these forms argues for an exemplar from further south than the *Sege of Melayne*'s exemplar, or, alternatively, a more southerly scribe responsible for the copying at some point in this romance's history.[30] One possible explanation for these particular points of dialectal divergence is that Thornton's exemplar contained texts by two different scribes from similar regions, with the *Roland and Otuel* scribe being more southerly. Or Thornton may have had access to a single library in the Doncaster-Grimsby-Hull triangle, which library might have housed numerous texts from local scribes with some

---

[28] McIntosh, 'The Textual Transmission', pp. 231–2; and Hanna, 'The Growth', n. 8. Among the texts from this same exemplar, McIntosh lists *Octavian*, *Sir Isumbras*, *Earl of Toulouse*, *Sir Perceval of Gales* and the *Abbey of the Holy Ghost* (all of which Thornton placed in the Lincoln manuscript), and *Parlement of the Thre Ages*, *Wynnere and Wastoure* and *Sege of Melayne* (which he placed in the London manuscript).

[29] I analysed the entire text of *Roland and Otuel* from *The English Charlemagne Romances*, ed. Herrtage.

[30] Purdie, *Anglicising Romance*, pp. 176–8, notes relict forms of Southern Middle English in this text, attributing this to a layer of scribal copying several stages removed from Thornton's copy. Purdie also notes a preponderance of Northern Middle English forms and vocabulary in this text, suggesting that its author was perhaps from Northumberland.

dialectal variation among them. Perhaps Hanna's admittedly hesitant conjecture is as close as we can come to disambiguating the exemplars of these two romances: 'The *Siege of Milan* shows the same dialect forms as the other romance texts [from the Doncaster exemplar]; presumably, given the paucity of Charlemagne materials in Middle English, the adjacent romance *Roland and Otuel* reflects a common exemplar (even though it lacks distinctively Doncaster spellings)'.[31]

Although the dialectal origin of Thornton's exemplar for the *Northern Passion-Siege* pairing resembles that which he must have used for the *Sege of Melayne* and *Roland and Otuel*, there are enough substantial differences to point to a different exemplar for the Charlemagne romances, this one from slightly further south. For example, in the former, Thornton freely alternates between *þame* and *thaym* for the plural object pronoun, whereas the latter consistently attests only *þam*. Likewise, the former uses Such: *swylke*, where the latter reads Such: *slyke* in *Sege* and Such: *siche* in *Roland and Otuel*, with one lone use of *swilke* in *Sege* (likely a moment when Thornton translated into his own dialect). The former regularly attests Is: *es*, while *Sege* alternates freely between *is* and *es* for the copular verb. The former has Two: *two* (*twa*), while the latter only uses *two*, with one lone use of *twa* near the end of *Roland and Otuel*. Finally, the exemplar for the *Northern Passion* and the *Siege of Jerusalem* likely represented Old English <sc> as <sch>, for the opening 500 lines of the *Northern Passion* contain a preponderance of Shall: *schall*, but by about line 500 Thornton has made the shift to *salle*, which one would expect in his own dialect. Likewise, with his copy of *Siege*, he begins alternating between *solde* and *scholde* for *should*, but after about 500 lines his own dialect has been 'worked in' and he regularly copies *solde*.[32] By contrast, in Thornton's copy of *Sege*, he consistently spells these forms with an initial <s>. The lack of 'working in' here suggests that the initial <s> was in his exemplar – a further piece of evidence that the exemplar for the *Northern Passion* and *Siege* was different from that upon which Thornton drew for *Sege*.[33]

This distribution of exemplars accords well with what has previously been established about the codicological makeup of the opening quires.[34] The *Cursor*

---

[31]   Hanna, 'The Growth', p. 57.

[32]   See *LALME*, IV, pp. 37–43; and R. Jordan, *Handbook of Middle English Grammar*, trans. E. J. Crook, *Janua Linguarum* Series Practica 218 (The Hague, 1974), p. 171. Note that *LALME* shows *salle* to be common in northern counties, including the North Riding, but only localizes *solde* to a general Northern Middle English dialect without specifying particular counties.

[33]   In *Roland and Otuel*, Thornton uses <s> and <sch> in random combinations with no discernible pattern.

[34]   See, in particular, 'Hs. Brit. Mus. Additional 31042', ed. K. Brunner, *Archiv* 32 (1914), 316–27; Thompson, *London Thornton MS, passim*; R. Hanna, 'The London Thornton Manuscript:

Mundi, for example, was almost certainly copied much later in Thornton's compilation process than the *Northern Passion*, which now follows it. Presumably, Thornton came upon this exemplar later and then added it as a prequel to the *Northern Passion*. The *Cursor Mundi* survives as a discrete booklet of two quires, with its ending corresponding with the end of quire b, marked by a catchword. It was copied on a stock of paper that appears only here and in Thornton's copy of *Sir Perceval* in the Lincoln manuscript, which was copied late in the process, as well.[35] Such a state supports my findings that Thornton drew *Cursor Mundi* from a different exemplar than the rest of the opening series and then placed it, in a self-contained set of quires (i.e., a booklet), at the head of the London manuscript.

Likewise, the codicological evidence supports my finding that Thornton drew the *Northern Passion-Siege* pairing from a single exemplar and that he compiled this section of his manuscript at an earlier point in time than the *Cursor Mundi*, originally intending these two as the opening texts. Phillipa Hardman notes that Thornton commences the *Northern Passion* with fourteen lines of blank space, presumably intended for a large illustration of the Crucifixion, which was never executed. Such would make sense for a text originally intended to serve as the head of a compilation.[36] The outside of quire c, which begins with the *Northern Passion*, shows particularly heavy wear, indicative of a quire that was unbound, with nothing else compiled in front of it, for some period of time.[37] Moreover, the transition between the *Northern Passion* and the *Siege of Jerusalem* occurs in the midst of quire c, all of which is on a single stock of paper. Thus, Thornton must have copied these two texts seriatim, filling quire c and spilling over into d, presumably because he had the exemplar containing both texts in front of him at one time. Moreover, Thornton's ruling pattern on fol. 50r accounts for the transition between the *Northern Passion*'s couplets and the alliterative long lines of the *Siege of Jerusalem* in a manner indicating both texts were in front of him when he set up the page. In this case, Thornton ruled the top half of the page for the double-column format of the *Northern Passion* (with its couplets) and the bottom half for the single-column format of the *Siege of Jerusalem* (with its alliterative long lines), something he does not elsewhere do at transitions between single- and double-column formats.[38]

A Corrected Collation', *Studies in Bibliography* 37 (1984), 122–30; Hanna, 'The Growth', pp. 51–61; S. M. Horrall, 'The London Thornton Manuscript: A New Collation', *Manuscripta* 23 (1979), 99–103; and K. Stern, 'The London "Thornton" Miscellany: A New Description of British Museum Additional Manuscript 31042', *Scriptorium* 30 (1976), 26–37, 201–18.

35   Hanna, 'The Growth', p. 60.

36   Hardman, 'Reading the Spaces', pp. 261–2.

37   Thompson, *London Thornton MS*, p. 53.

38   Ibid., p. 48; for a reproduction of this folio, see plate 9.

Thornton's ad hoc procedures indicate that he was having to make impromptu decisions about how to incorporate the *Sege of Melayne* and *Roland and Otuel* into the existing quires and that they thus came from a different source than the *Northern Passion-Siege* pairing. He did not, that is, initially construct his quires with these two Charlemagne romances in mind, and thus seems not to have had them in front of him when folding the paper. This state indicates that he came upon them later and worked to accommodate them by adding to each quire. The distribution of paper stocks indicates that Thornton planned to end quire d with the *Siege of Jerusalem* but then added leaves to the quire to extend it – presumably when he came upon a copy of the *Sege of Melayne*.[39] Likewise, the codicological evidence may imply that Thornton drew the *Sege of Melayne* and *Roland and Otuel* from different exemplars: the *Sege of Melayne* spills over from quire d into quire e. As Thornton originally constructed it, this text would have ended right in the centre of quire e. But Thornton subsequently nested a small quire of six bifolia inside the centre of quire e (a common practice by Thornton) in order to enlarge this quire, likely because he realized, after copying of the *Sege of Melayne* had commenced, that he needed more leaves. On these inserted bifolia Thornton inscribed the Marian lyric *O Florum Flos* immediately after the *Sege of Melayne* and only then began his copy of *Roland and Otuel*, leading John Thompson to postulate 'a delay of some kind between the time when Thornton copied *Melayne*, the time when he inserted the batch of paper containing *O Florum Flos*, and the time when he returned to the newly-expanded gathering to add *Otuel*'.[40] Thus, my linguistic findings in general accord with what we know about the makeup of these quires.

Thornton as commentator

Returning to Bonaventure's famous discussion of the 'fourfold' ways of making a book – I earlier suggested that Thornton's acts of bringing together texts from different exemplars into a unique series showed him oscillating between the roles of *scriptor* and *compilator*. But I now wish to turn to a few moments in this opening series when he flirts with the role of *commentator*, which Bonaventure defines as one who 'writes both materials composed by others and his own, but the materials composed by others are the most important materials, while his

---

[39] As Hanna, 'The Growth', p. 57, conjectures, 'Quire 4 may have begun as fourteen leaves, largely on stock C, originally a size calculated to handle only *The Siege of Jerusalem*. Thornton would have produced a larger quire by suppletion, inserting into the original leaves extras which extend the writing area; this extension involves the unique examples of stock D and enabled Thornton to continue on with the Charlemagne materials.'

[40] Thompson, *London Thornton MS*, p. 47.

own are added for the purpose of clarifying them'.[41] In these three cases – in which he exhibits his greatest creative agency – we see Thornton undertaking unique tasks: first, he composes a set of lines to form a transition between two different selections of *Cursor Mundi*; second, he composes presumably original colophons foregrounding the larger thematic concerns of his compilation; and third, he makes a few small, but resoundingly important, emendations to his copy of the *Northern Passion* that amplify the Jews' responsibility for Christ's death, thereby drawing attention to this narrative's central place in the Salvation History which this textual sequence traces.[42]

Thornton's copy of the *Cursor Mundi* is intentionally selective. This compendious verse history runs, as its title suggests, over the whole history of the world, from Creation to Doomsday, but only two relatively small sections of this text survive in the London manuscript: the first comprises lines 10630–14915, containing the story of the Annunciation, Christ's youth and early ministry, and his Passion.[43] Near Christ's death, the *textus receptus* of the *Cursor Mundi* has a metrical shift, from octosyllabic couplets to a septenary metre with stanzas of varying length (lines 14916–17110). But Thornton omits these lines in a different metre, picking up again at line 17111, when the text has returned to octosyllabic couplets. The second section, which he appends to the first, is known as the *Discourse between Christ and Man*, wherein, in the tradition of affective piety, Christ points to his wounds and instructs the reader to meditate on the Passion. The text that follows, the *Northern Passion*, is written in octosyllabic couplets, and, as Thornton had already copied the *Northern Passion* into the manuscript when he decided to add *Cursor Mundi* as a prequel, it is almost certain that he selectively edited the *Cursor Mundi* to end near the Passion and let the *Northern Passion* stand as the literary exploration of Christ's death, thereby creating a pendant to the life of Christ narrated in the *Cursor Mundi*.

---

[41] Quoted in *The Idea of the Vernacular*, ed. Wogan-Browne et al., p. 3.

[42] See J.-P. Pouzet, '"Space this werke to wirke": Quelques figures de la complémentarité dans les manuscrits de Robert Thornton', in *La complémentarité: Mélanges offerts à Josseline Bidard et Arlette Sancery à l'occasion de leur depart en retraite*, ed. M.-F. Alamichel (Paris, 2005), pp. 27–43 (p. 39), who remarks that in such moments, 'il semblerait que Robert Thornton ait multiplié les signes d'une certain "possession" scribale qui déborderait assez fréquemment vers l'auctorial' [it would seem that Robert Thornton multiplied the signs of a certain scribal 'possession' which rather frequently spilled over into the authorial].

[43] Thornton may initially have copied much more of the *Cursor Mundi*: the first quire is now fragmentary and the text begins acephalously, so some amount is certainly missing. For discussions of how much he may have originally copied, see Thompson, *London Thornton MS*, p. 22; G. Keiser, Review of *Robert Thornton*, p. 157; P. Hardman, 'Windows into the Text: Unfilled Spaces in Some Fifteenth-Century English Manuscripts', in *Texts and Their Contexts: Papers from the Early Book Society*, ed. V. J. Scattergood and J. Boffey (Dublin, 1997), pp. 44–70 (pp. 54–5); and Keiser's chapter in this volume.

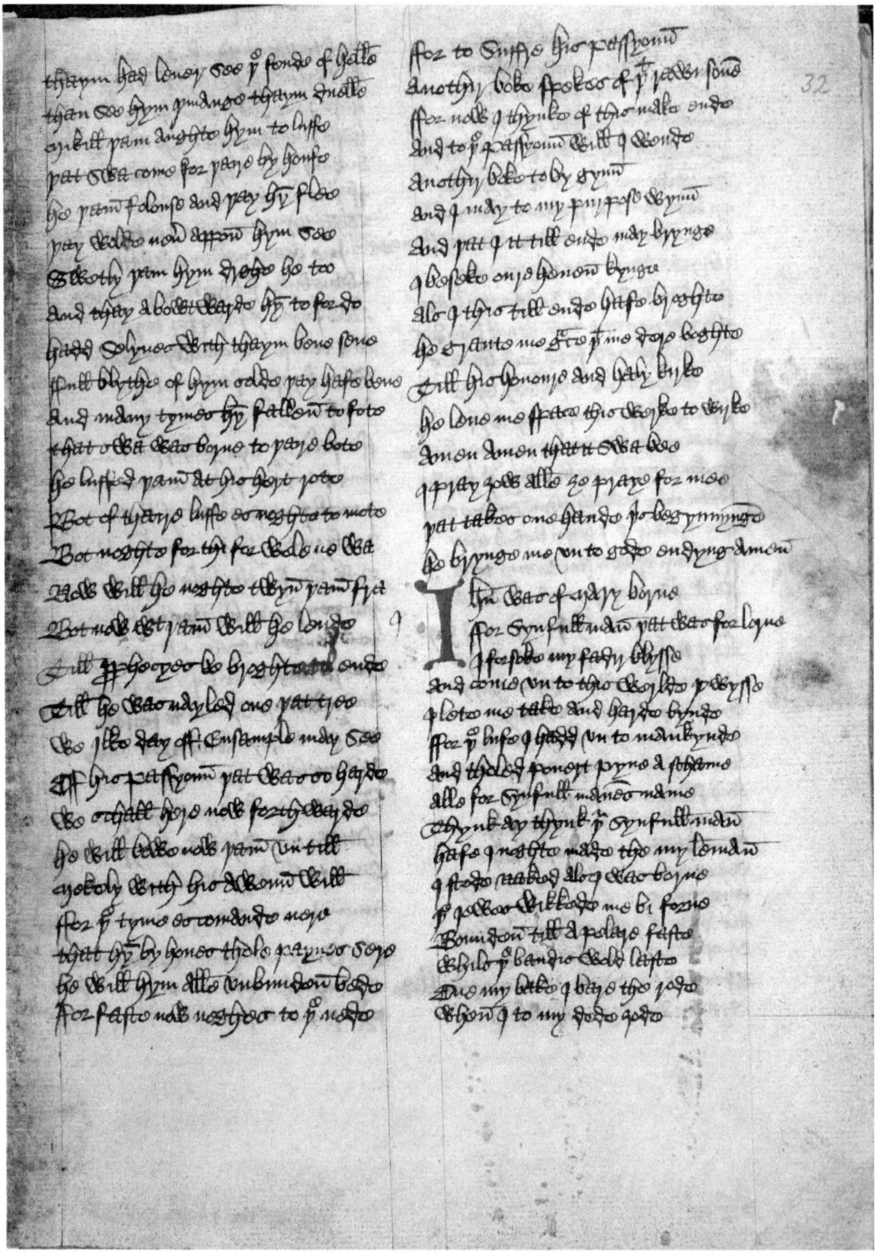

Figure 1. London, BL, MS Additional 31042, fol. 32r (*Cursor Mundi* bridge)

By this intelligent editorial decision, Thornton reduced narrative redundancy and smoothed out the experience for the reader, placing two texts written in octosyllabic couplets in sequence – and eliminating the parts of the first text in the sequence that were not in this metre. As Jean-Pascal Pouzet rightly remarks, 'c'est le *Cursor Mundi* qui *signe* l'affleurement le plus symptomatique de l'activité scribale de Thornton' [it is the *Cursor Mundi* that signals the most obvious evidence of Thornton's scribal activity].[44]

Such still simply makes Thornton a *compilator*, one who brings together the words of others, 'joining them together but adding nothing of his own', to quote Bonaventure. But we do see Thornton adding something of his own when he composes a bridge to unite the two metrically disparate sections of the *Cursor Mundi* (see Figure 1):

> For now I thynke of this make ende
> And to þe passyoun will I wende
> Anothir boke to bygynn
> And I may to my purpose wynn.
> And þat I it till ende may brynge
> I beseke oure heuen kynge,
> Als I this till ende hafe broghte,
> He grante me grace þat me dere boghte;
> Till his honoure and haly kirke
> He leue me space this werke to wirke.
> Amen. Amen. That it swa bee
> I pray ȝow alle ȝe praye for mee
> Þat takes one hande þis begynnynge
> He brynge me vnto gode endyng. Amen.[45]

Of course, there is no way to establish for certain that these lines were not in Thornton's now-lost exemplar and that he merely transcribed them wholesale. However, the language here accords with what one would expect of something composed in North Yorkshire, Thornton's own dialect.[46] Thus, coupled with

---

[44] Pouzet, '"Space this werke to wirke"', p. 32.

[45] Fol. 32r; *The Southern Version of* Cursor Mundi: *Volume III*, ed. Stauffenberg, pp. 208–9. Rate, the scribe of Oxford, Bodleian Library, MS Ashmole 61, presents an analogous case: he selectively omitted the conclusion of the *Northern Passion* because he already had a copy of *The Legend of the Resurrection* to hand. In place of the omitted passages, Rate, as Thornton did here with the end of *Cursor Mundi*, composed a short textual supplement to link to the following text. See *Codex Ashmole 61: A Compilation of Middle English Popular Verse*, ed. G. Shuffelton (Kalamazoo MI, 2008), pp. 514–15. See also Thompson, *London Thornton MS*, p. 54, who discusses the copy of *Cursor Mundi* in Göttingen University Library, MS Theol. 107, whose scribe has similarly composed a unique conclusion to the text.

[46] These lines present a very small sample size for analysis. Every form that appears here is attested both in the North Riding, Thornton's home, and in Lancashire, the likely dialectal origin of the exemplar. See *LALME*, IV. Thus, these lines offer inconclusive dialectal analysis as to their

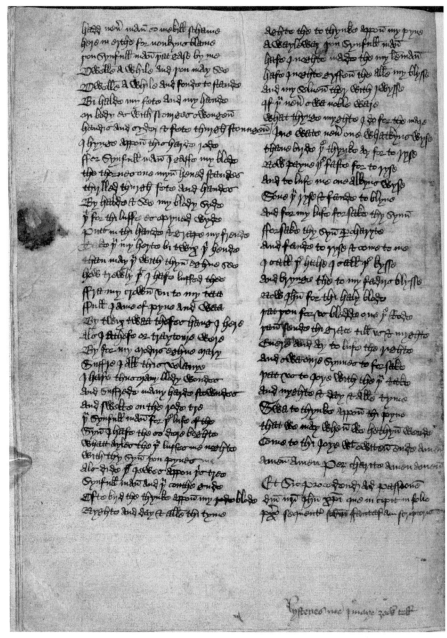

Figure 2. London, BL, MS Additional 31042, fol. 32v (Thornton's explicit to booklet 1, introducing booklet 2: 'secundum *Fantasiam scriptoris*')

the fact that the lines missing from this copy of the *Cursor Mundi* afford it metrical concord with the subsequent *Northern Passion*, it seems almost certain that Thornton is the one responsible for this change – acting, that is, as a *commentator* of sorts.

In these lines, we see Thornton drawing particular attention to his role in the creation of meaning. Note, for example, the numerous uses of the first-person singular pronoun (subject and object case) and the possessive adjective *my*: in these fourteen lines, he uses one of these forms thirteen times. In particular, he speaks of 'my purpose', foregrounding the significance of his own role as manuscript compiler. At the conclusion of the *Cursor Mundi*, Thornton continues this emphasis on his own importance in this collection when he authors an explicit announcing the thematic connections between this text and the following text, the *Northern Passion*: 'Et Sic procedendum ad passionem domini nostri Ihesu Cristi que in-cipit in folio proximo sequente secundum ffantasiam scriptoris et cetera' [And thus we must proceed to the Passion of our Lord Jesus Christ, which begins on the following leaf, according to the fancy of the writer, etc.] (fol. 32v) (see Figure 2). Here he notes that this textual pairing is 'secundum ffantasiam scriptoris' – the result of his own literary-critical decisions as manuscript compiler. Thompson aptly paraphrases Thornton's explicit as, 'according to the whim of a writer who has brought two very different things together', further remarking that Thornton uses this phrase 'to describe the technical process of bringing together diverse material in different quires to form part of a single manuscript collection'.[47] Thornton also composes an incipit to the *Siege of Jerusalem*, one which makes patent the salvation-historical connections between the death of Christ – as narrated in the immediately preceding *Northern Passion* – and the revenge upon the Jews to follow: 'Hic Incepit Distruccio Ierarusalem Quomodo Titus & Vaspasianus Obsederunt & distruxerunt Ierusalem et vi[n]dicarunt mortem domini Ihesu Cristi' [Here begins the destruction of Jerusalem, in which Titus and Vespasian besiege and destroy Jerusalem and avenge the death of our Lord Jesus Christ] (fol. 50r) (see Figure 3). In such moments,

---

origin. However, given the rest of the evidence discussed here, I remain confident in ascribing these lines to Thornton's quill.

[47] Thompson, *The* Cursor Mundi, pp. 82–3. See also Pouzet, '"Space this werke to wirke"', pp. 36–7, who first noticed the 'et cetera' at the end of the colophon. Pouzet remarks that these lines 'pourrait bien functionner tout entier comme une reference capital à l'activité du *scriptor*, entendue à la fois comme l'inscription ou la transcription des texts, leur mise-en-page et leur ornamentation éventuelle, ainsi que la compilation générale et détaillée du recueil: en un mot, l'*écriture* en tant qu'activité littéralement *fantastique*, ou *fantasmatique*' [could function almost entirely as a basic reference to the activity of a *scriptor*, understood at the same time as the inscription or transcription of texts, their *mise-en-page* and their possible ornamentation, together with the general and detailed compilation of the collection: in a word, *writing* as an activity which is literally *fantastic* or even *phantasmal*].

we can see Thornton foregrounding his role as literary mediator, celebrating the creative agency that could be exploited by medieval scribes.

Returning to the *Northern Passion*, we also find Thornton acting like a *commentator*, bringing together the words of others and adding some of his own – exhibiting perhaps his greatest agency by altering the words of the text he copied. Here, we find a set of unique emendations in Thornton's version, each of which transfers culpability for deicide from the Romans and Jews in combination – as the Bible would have it – to the Jews alone. These particular lines occur at the *ecce homo* moment, as Pilate asks the Jews what they would have him do with Jesus. The four lines in question read (see Figure 4):

> Alle thay sayde with o voice
> Gyffe hym *vs* to hange on croyce.
> Pilate graunted thayme thayre will
> He gaffe *thaym* Ihesu for to spill.[48]

Subtle word changes here present some startling variation from what survives in all other copies of this text, suggesting again that Thornton's creative agency is at work. In the other versions, the Jews ask Pilate to give Christ *dome* (judgment/verdict) to die, whereas here Thornton has the Jews ask Pilate to hand Christ directly over to them – so that they may lynch him being the obvious implication of these lines.[49] In the final line of the passage cited here, Pilate accedes to the crowd and gives Jesus to *thaym*, whereas in the other versions, he gives the *dome* that Jesus must die. In this case, then, the Jews ask for, and are given, the privilege of putting Jesus to death.[50] Again, we cannot know for certain that Thornton was the one responsible for these emendations, but it seems likely, especially given the other moments of creative agency in which he engaged, as outlined above. Thornton's decisions do not do great violence to the text's logic, it must be noted, for the text itself makes several anti-Jewish changes from the biblical narrative: for example, in lines 1187–98 the Jews are the ones to scourge Christ, not the Roman soldiers acting on Pilate's command,

---

[48] Fol. 40v; lines 1275–6 (emphasis mine). I discuss these emendations, along with other ways in which Thornton's version heightens the Jewish culpability for Christ's death, in greater detail in 'Robert Thornton', pp. 147–51.

[49] See *MED*, s.v. *dom* (n.).

[50] See J. Cohen, *Christ Killers: The Jews and the Passion from the Bible to the Big Screen* (Oxford, 2007), pp. 190–209, who analyses the late medieval Christian iconographical trope of depicting Jews as directly and solely responsible for executing Christ. See also C. Hourihane, *Pontius Pilate, Anti-Semitism, and the Passion in Medieval Art* (Princeton, 2009), pp. 296–370, who discusses artistic and literary depictions of Pilate in the fourteenth and fifteenth centuries across Europe, demonstrating how variable and malleable Pilate's character was in the hands of late medieval writers and artists.

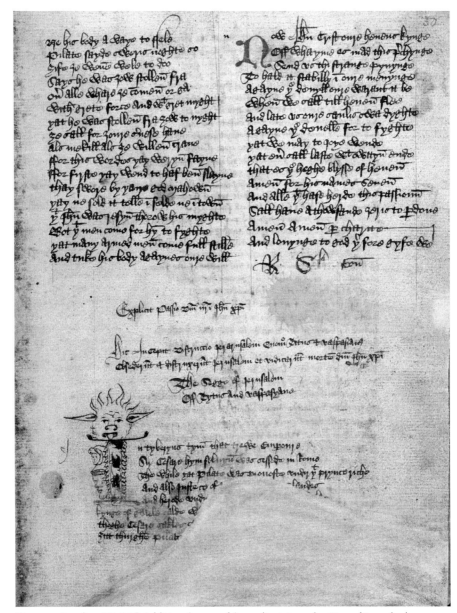

Figure 3. London, BL, MS Additional 31042, fol. 50r (incipit to the *Siege of Jerusalem*)

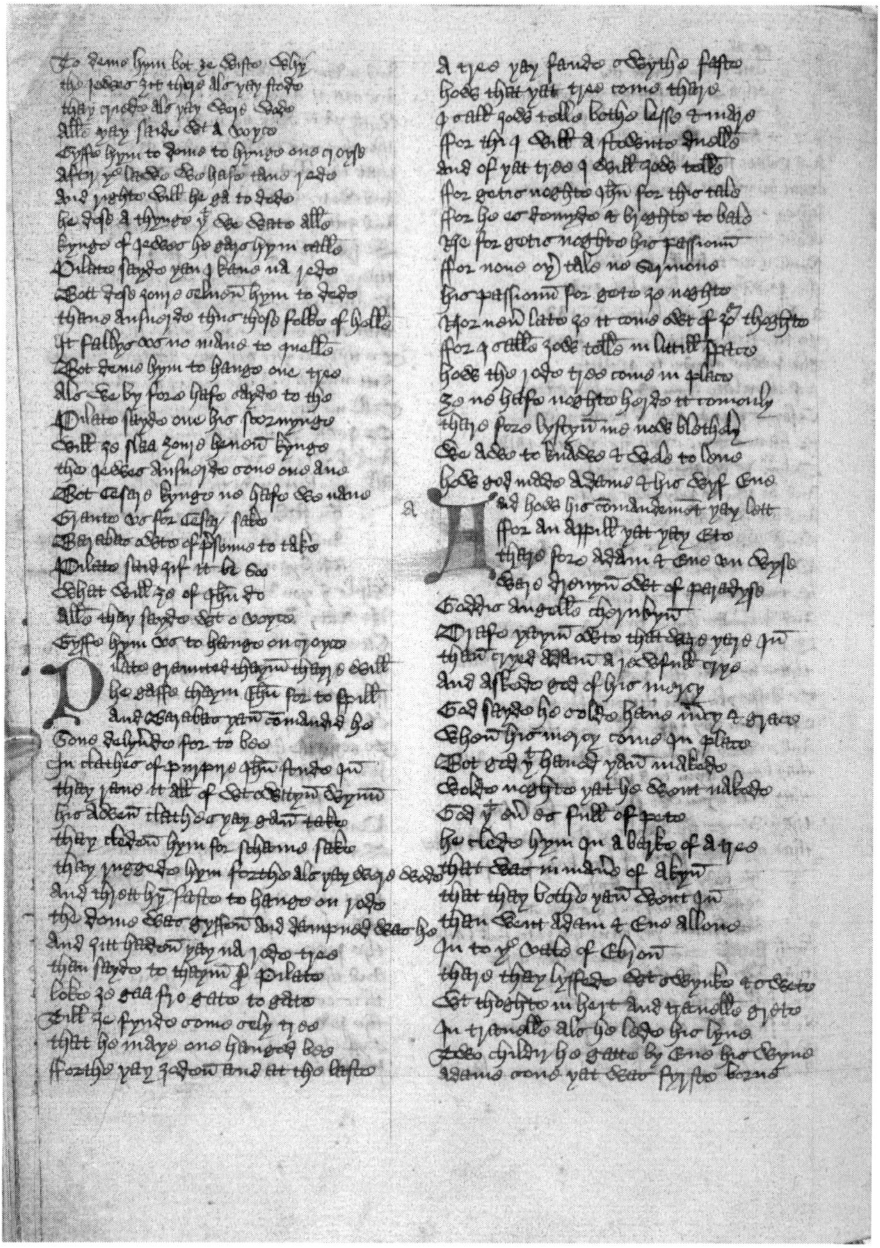

Figure 4. London, BL, MS Additional 31042, fol. 40v (unique lines from the *Northern Passion*)

as Mark 15. 15 and Matthew 27. 26 would have it. It should also be noted that Thornton was not a careful or thorough textual emender, for shortly before the lines in question, the Jews in Thornton's version – as in all the other surviving versions – insist that Pilate give a death sentence to Christ (lines 1253–4, 1262–3). Thus, Thornton's subsequent emendations create some inconsistency, having the Jews first ask Pilate to execute Christ and then, a few lines later, having them ask for the right to do the deed themselves.

In the appendix, I present my transcription of these two couplets as they appear in the other thirteen surviving manuscripts of this poem – showing how unique Thornton's efforts are in these four lines. But he was not the only copyist/compiler to alter the *Northern Passion* in order to heighten the anti-Jewish sentiment. As Lynne S. Blanchfield shows, Rate, the copyist of the *Northern Passion* in Oxford, Bodleian Library, MS Ashmole 61, also emended his text frequently to this end – though not these particular lines.[51] Thus, although there can be no 'smoking gun' proving Thornton is the one responsible for these lines, I believe that Pamela Robinson's dictum makes good sense when applied here: 'When a compiler's selection of material is governed by a particular interest or criterion and when the nature of the variants found in each of the texts within his compilation illustrates the same criterion one may argue that he is the copyist responsible for introducing the variants.'[52] These lines, by amplifying Jewish culpability for Christ's death, fit into the goals of the Salvation History Thornton has created in this sequence of texts.

Conclusion: Contextualizing Thornton's Salvation History

In sum, by examining the opening of Thornton's London manuscript and attending in particular to how many exemplars he was using and what this tells us about Thornton's creative agency, a picture begins to emerge. By and large, Thornton crafted his own unique combination of texts, one that speaks to the very worst impulses of medieval Christianity: the denigration of the non-Christian Other, the unadulterated embrace of violence as a means to underline Christianity's doctrinal superiority, a belief that the state's and the Church's

---

[51] L. S. Blanchfield, 'Rate Revisited: The Compilation of the Narrative Works in MS Ashmole 61', in *Romance Reading on the Book: Essays on Medieval Narrative Presented to Maldwyn Mills*, ed. J. Fellows, R. Field, G. Rogers and J. Weiss (Cardiff, 1996), pp. 208–20.

[52] Robinson, 'A Study of Some Aspects', p. 60; see also P. Hardman, introduction to *The Heege Manuscript: A Facsimile of National Library of Scotland MS Advocates 19.3.1*, Leeds Texts and Monographs n.s. 16 (Leeds, 2000), pp. 1–57 (p. 41), who invokes the same principle to examine the emendations in the Heege manuscript.

power rightly underwrite one another – in short, an exemplification of what Cornel West calls 'Constantinian Christianity':

> As the Christian Church became increasingly corrupted by state power, religious rhetoric was often used to justify imperial aims and conceal the prophetic heritage of Christianity. ... The corruption of a faith fundamentally based on tolerance and compassion by the strong arm of imperial authoritarianism invested Christianity with an insidious schizophrenia with which it has been battling ever since. This terrible merger of church and state has been behind so many of the church's worst violations of Christian love and justice – from the barbaric crusades against Jews and Muslims, to the horrors of the Inquisition and the ugly bigotry against women, people of color, and gays and lesbians.[53]

Given the lengths Thornton went to in order to gather together this series from numerous sources, the amount of time over which he compiled these texts, the efforts he undertook to make additions to this series, and the sheer amount of labour that went into copying so much text, one has to admire his dedication, even while recognizing the morally retrograde product that resulted from these efforts. Steven Pinker's recent words ring true with regard to Thornton. We must, Pinker says,

> ask whether our recent ancestors can really be considered morally retarded. The answer, I am prepared to argue, is yes. Though they were surely decent people with perfectly functioning brains, the collective moral sophistication of the culture in which they lived was as primitive by modern standards as their mineral spas and patent medicines are by the medical standards of today. Many of their beliefs can be considered not just monstrous but, in a very real sense, stupid. They would not stand up to intellectual scrutiny as being consistent with other values they claimed to hold, and they persisted only because the narrower intellectual spotlight of the day was not routinely shone on them.[54]

Yet at the same time, one must recognize that in the moral world we have gained, there is a cultural world we have lost. That is, this admittedly repellent compilation was only made possible by the technological and cultural conditions pertaining in late medieval manuscript culture – conditions that reached their zenith in Thornton's day and soon receded in the wake of the commodification of literary production under print. Only at this moment in history did numerous laymen like Thornton find themselves in a world where they could create numerically unique and unreproducible textual artefacts in the vernacular. The conditions at this time were just right: only a generation or two before Thornton, literature in Middle English had begun to proliferate; likewise, paper

---

[53] C. West, *Democracy Matters: Winning the Fight against Imperialism* (New York, 2004), pp. 148–9.

[54] S. Pinker, *The Better Angels of Our Nature: Why Violence Has Declined* (New York, 2011), p. 658.

was becoming more readily available, affording a cheap alternative to animal skins for those who wanted to make their own books;[55] and literacy was on the rise, at least among gentry landowners, like Thornton, and merchants.[56] From this heady mix arose a brief period of what Curt F. Bühler memorably calls the "'every man his own scribe" movement' – when any individual with the leisure time, access to exemplars, and interest in literature could yoke together texts into unique combinations for his and his family's entertainment and edification.[57] By the time Caxton had imported Gutenberg's invention to England, the die was cast: literature was to become a commodity, produced by someone else and rendered unto the reader in a finished form.[58] The decisions about what to commit to print, in what order, alongside what, with what illustrations, and in what format, were to be made by others, in far-away Westminster and London. But Thornton worked during the efflorescence of local vernacular manuscript production, moving effortlessly between the roles of *scriptor, compilator* and *commentator*. For that, he merits our study, if not our celebration.

[55] R. J. Lyall, 'Materials: The Paper Revolution', in *Book Production and Publishing in Britain, 1375–1475*, ed. J. Griffiths and D. Pearsall, Cambridge Studies in Publishing and Printing History (Cambridge, 1989), pp. 11–29; E. Kwakkel, 'A New Type of Book for a New Type of Reader: The Emergence of Paper in Vernacular Book Production', *The Library* 7th ser. 4 (2003), 219–48; and U. Neddermeyer, *Von der Handschrift zum gedruckten Buch: Schriftlichkeit und Leseinteresse im Mitterlalter und in der frühen Neuzeit: Quantitative und qualitative Aspekte*, 2 vols. (Wiesbaden, 1998), II, 644.

[56] A. Truelove, 'Literacy', in *Gentry Culture in Late-Medieval England*, ed. R. Radulescu and A. Truelove (Manchester, 2005), pp. 84–99; M. B. Parkes, 'The Literacy of the Laity', in *Scribes, Scripts and Readers: Studies in the Communication, Dissemination and Presentation of Medieval Texts* (London, 1991), pp. 275–97 (pp. 291–7); J. B. Trapp, 'Literacy, Books and Readers', in *The Cambridge History of the Book in Britain: Volume 3, 1400–1557*, ed. L. Hellinga and J. B. Trapp (Cambridge, 1999), pp. 31–43; and H. S. Bennett, *The Pastons and Their England: Studies in an Age of Transition*, 2nd edn (1922; repr. Cambridge, 1970), pp. 102–10.

[57] C. F. Bühler, *The Fifteenth-Century Book: The Scribes, the Printers, the Decorators* (Philadelphia, 1960), p. 22.

[58] Of course, compiling *Sammelbände* offered late medieval and early modern book-owners something akin to manuscript compilation. However, one was constrained in one's choices by what texts printers chose to devote their capital to, and the investment required for printing thus resulted in a smaller selection among which an interested *Sammelband*-compiler could choose. On this question, see A. Gillespie, 'Poets, Printers, and Early English *Sammelbände*', *Huntington Library Quarterly* 67 (2004), 189–214, who is rather more sanguine about the freedom afforded by *Sammelbände* than am I.

Appendix
Readings of the *Northern Passion*, lines 1273–6, from all surviving manuscripts[59]

MS G₁: Cambridge, CUL, MS Gg. 1. 1, fol. 129va

> Alle þai seiden at one woiȝ
> Yef him dom to henge on croiȝ
> Pilat graunted hem her wille
> He yaf dom him to spille

MS D: Cambridge, CUL, MS Dd. 1. 1, fol. 12v

> Alle þei cride wiþ on voys
> ȝeue him doom to hange on croys[60]

MS G₅: Cambridge, CUL, MS Gg. 5. 31, fol. 179v

> All þai answerd with a voice
> Gyff hym dome to hyng croice
> Pilate grauntid þaime þair will
> ffor he gaf dome Ihesu to spyll

MS F: Cambridge, CUL, MS Ff. 5. 48, fol. 29v:

> Alle þei seid *with* avoyce
> Gif hym dome to heng on croyce
> Pilate graumtid to her will
> he gaf he dome ihesu to spill

MS I: Cambridge, CUL, MS Ii. 4. 9, fol. 26r

> Alle they seyden seyden wyth on woyse
> ȝeue hym dome to hange on crosse
> Pylate grauntyd hem her wylle
> he ȝafe the dome Ihesu to spylle

---

[59] Note that the manuscript sigla for the *Northern Passion* refer to those found in Foster's edition, with the exception of Cambridge MA, Harvard University Houghton Library, MS Eng. 1031, about which Foster did not know.

[60] These are the last two lines on fol. 12v, and fol. 13 is lacking in this manuscript; hence, the final couplet does not survive.

MS A: Oxford, Bodleian Library, Ashmole MS 61, fol. 99r

> All þei seyd wi*th* o voys
> Gyff hy*m* dome to hong o*n* cros
> Pylat gra*u*ntyd hem þ*eir* wyll
> Than gafe he dom Ih*es*u to spyll

MS R: Oxford, Bodleian Library, MS Rawlinson C. 86, fol. 19v

> All they answerid with one voice
> And seide he shulde dye on crosse
> Pilate gra*u*ntid hem with out delay
> ffor to slee Ih*es*u thatt ilke day

MS C: Oxford, Bodleian Library, MS Rawlinson C. 655, fol. 32v

> Alle hii saied wiþ a vois
> gif him [ ]
> Pilate graunted he*m* her wille
> He ʒaf dom Ih*es*u to spille[61]

MS H₂: London, BL, MS Harley 215

The lines in question have not survived in this version.

MS V: London, BL, MS Cotton Vespasian D. ix

The lines in question have not survived in this version.

Cambridge MA, Harvard University Houghton Library, MS Eng. 1031

The lines in question have not survived in this version.

The Expanded version:[62]

MS T: London, BL, MS Cotton Tiberius E. vii, fol. 174v

> [hi]s state he tok no tent vntill
> [b]ot demid al efter þaire will

---

[61] Note that the second line here had been omitted and the scribe has copied it in the margin, running perpendicular to the rest of the text. However, as it is in the margin, most of this line has faded and is no longer legible.

[62] These texts form a different textual tradition of the *Northern Passion*; however, I offer the readings from the relevant sections here as further proof that Thornton did not derive his inspiration for his variations from any surviving copy that he might have encountered. On the relationship between the so-called Shorter Version and Expanded Version, see *The Northern Passion*, ed. Foster, II, 45–7.

and all efter þaire wordes wrang
he demid hi*m** on rode to hang[63]

MS P: Oxford, Bodleian Library, MS Rawlinson Poetry 175, fol. 65r

His state he toke no tent vntyll
Bot demed all efter þair will
And all ef*ter* þair wordes wrang
He demed him on rode to hang

MS H: London, BL, MS Harley 4196, fol. 76v

His state he toke tent untill
Bot demid al efter þaire will
And all efter þaire wordes wrang
He demid him on rode to hang

---

[63] * = corrected, written in superscript, in red. Note that this manuscript was severely damaged in the Cotton Library fire, so the outside edge of each leaf has undergone much repair work. Hence, the initial letters of lines 1–2 are conjectural.

7

Apocryphal Romance in the London Thornton Manuscript

Julie Nelson Couch

'Here Bigynnys the Romance of the childhode / of Ihesu Criste þat clerkes callys Ipokrephum'. So begins the *Childhood of Christ* found in London, BL, MS Additional 31042 (see Figure 1). Robert Thornton's incipit, unique to this attestation of the Middle English stanzaic *Childhood*, flaunts the romance and apocryphal status of a poem that is in other manuscripts treated as a more authentic rendering of Jesus's life on earth. It is instructive to note the contrast between Thornton's presentation and the two other extant redactions of this poem, also found in fifteenth-century manuscripts. Those renditions gird the poem with Latin and thereby maintain an illusion of verity for the narrative. The poem in London, BL, MS Harley 3954 includes both a Latin incipit – 'Hic incipit infancia saluatoris' – and explicit – 'Explicit infancia saluatoris'; in addition, Latin subtitles appear throughout the poem, introducing episodes.[1] The version found in London, BL, MS Harley 2399 is also framed by a Latin incipit – 'Pueritia vel Infancia Christi' – and explicit – 'Et sic finitur pueritia domini nostri Jesu Cristi'.[2]

---

[1] 'Kindheit Jesu. A) aus Ms Harl. 3954, fol. 70 (14. Jhdt.)', in *Sammlung altenglischer Legenden*, ed. C. Horstmann (Heilbronn, 1878), pp. 101–10. Henceforth, all citations from Harley 3954 will be from this edition; line numbers will be supplied parenthetically.

[2] 'Kindheit Jesu. B) aus Ms Harl. 2399, fol. 47 (15. Jhdt.)', in ibid., pp. 111–23. Henceforth, all citations from Harley 2399 will be from this edition; line numbers will be supplied parenthetically. Moreover, the Harley 2399 poem is generally presented in a scholarly context: the text is signed by the scribe, John Archer, a canon of the Benedictine priory of St Petroc in Cornwall, and the manuscript contains medical, theological and classical texts in Latin in addition to the few texts, including the *Childhood* poem, in Middle English. See *British Library Catalogue of Illuminated Manuscripts*, www.bl.uk./catalogues/illuminatedmanuscripts/record,asp?MSID=3666&CollID =8&NStart=2399. Additionally, in the earliest extant Middle English *Infancy of Christ* poem (a unique text), found in Oxford, Bodleian Library, MS Laud Misc. 108 (*c.* 1300), the incipit reads, 'Jci comence le enfaunce ih'u crist', which does not indicate any sense of a romance or even apocryphal nature. In fact, a French title suggests a degree of authoritative credibility; 'Kindheit Jesu aus Ms Laud 108', in *Altenglische Legenden*, ed. C. Horstmann (Paderborn, 1875), pp. 1–60. Henceforth, all citations from Laud 108 will be from this edition; line numbers will be supplied parenthetically.

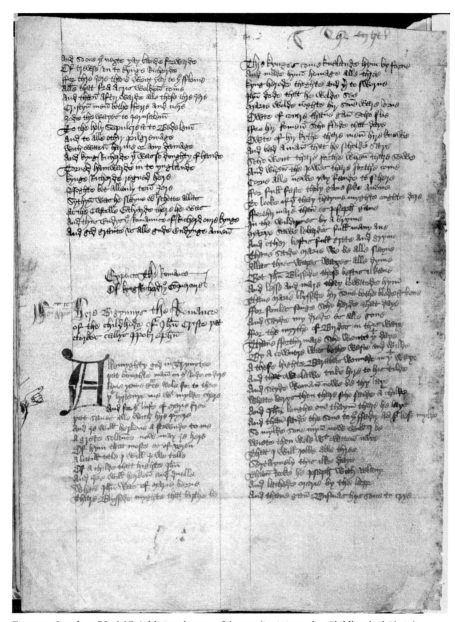

Figure 1. London, BL, MS Additional 31042, fol. 163v (incipit to the *Childhood of Christ*)

In this chapter I consider the function of the *Childhood* poem and its remarkable incipit in the context of the London Thornton manuscript. A story of Jesus's childhood is already present as part of the *Cursor Mundi* text that appears as the first item in London (arts. 1–3). In that verse narrative, the divine childhood folds into a greater sacred history, one that commences the spiritual and historical focus of the London anthology.[3] With *Childhood* (art. 33), Thornton returns to the subject of Jesus's childhood, this time as a separate entity – outside historical time and space – presenting it explicitly as an apocryphal narrative through the use of the narrative structures and fabulous content of romance.

Thornton's admission of the poem's apocryphal status is not meant to subtract from its spiritual authority. While structuring the divine childhood as a romance, *Childhood* also amplifies the role of Mary and explicitly ties events in the childhood to Christ's Passion. These emphases, I contend, reveal an intentional correlation with the manuscript's preoccupation with the Passion and Mary.[4] Additionally, I will show that the poem's vengeance-and-conversion mentality ties it to the particular romance world found in the manuscript, where the enemy is always an enemy of Christ and the hero is always Christ's special avenger. A sense of a Christian kingdom perpetually at war emerges in the *Siege of Jerusalem* (art. 6), the *Sege of Melayne* (art. 8), *Duke Roland and Sir Otuel of Spain* (art. 10) and *Richard Coer de Lyon* (art. 32). *Childhood* participates in the exciting narrative world within which the Passion and its after-battles live in this manuscript. Thornton's *Childhood* thus emerges as a singular, context-specific and entertaining recollection of the Passion. This referential narrative enacts the dialectic at play within and among the manuscript's texts between affective devotion to and righteous indignation for Christ's sacrifice.

---

[3] The *Cursor Mundi* is acephalous in the London manuscript. For different conjectures on the possible amount of text missing, see Thompson, *London Thornton MS*, pp. 22, 53; P. Hardman, 'Reading the Spaces: Pictorial Intentions in the Thornton MSS, Lincoln Cathedral MS 91, and BL MS Add. 31042', *Medium Ævum* 63 (1994), 250–74 (p. 257); G. Keiser, 'Review of *Robert Thornton and the London Thornton Manuscript*, by J. J. Thompson', *Envoi* 2 (1989), 155–60 (p. 157); and Keiser's chapter in the present volume. The complete *Cursor* constitutes a lengthy and popular verse history that spans seven ages of the world. See J. J. Thompson, *The Cursor Mundi: Poem, Texts and Contexts* (Oxford, 1998). Contrary to Thompson in *London Thornton MS*, Hardman contends that the missing leaves would not have contained the full history but would have begun with the fifth age, forming, with the extant section, a 'Life of Mary and Jesus' (p. 257).

[4] Hardman, 'Reading the Spaces', pp. 260–7, discusses Thornton's focus on the Passion and Mary that, she contends, is evident in both manuscripts.

The textual tradition

The Thornton *Childhood* is a late medieval instance of the apocrypha-based vernacular tradition of *Infancy of Christ* poems.[5] This textual tradition reflects the larger practice of depicting biblical and apocryphal stories in verse, prose narratives, manuscript illustrations and church art.[6] Oscar Cullmann and J. K. Elliott locate inquisitiveness about the *enfances* of Christ within the gospels' brief references to Jesus's birth and childhood.[7] For example, stories of the child Jesus going to school and astounding (and, in the apocryphal accounts, periodically killing) his teachers, sprouted from Luke's story of twelve-year-old Jesus in the temple.[8] Likewise, Luke's mention of the Holy Family's sojourn in Egypt spurred stories about the child Jesus's adventures in Egypt. Apocryphal infancy stories remained popular through the Middle Ages despite patristic and papal condemnation.[9]

---

[5] The most thorough discussion of the medieval vernacular tradition of the *Infancy of Christ* texts remains M. Dzon, 'The Image of the Wanton Christ-Child in the Apocryphal Infancy Legends of Late Medieval England' (unpublished Ph.D. dissertation, University of Toronto, 2004), esp. Chapter 3. Dzon has subsequently published much of her analysis of these poems in various articles; see, e.g., her discussion of the late medieval reception of the apocryphal legends in M. Dzon, 'Boys Will Be Boys: The Physiology of Childhood and the Apocryphal Christ Child in the Later Middle Ages', *Viator* 42 (2011), 179–225; and M. Dzon, 'Joseph and the Amazing Christ-Child of Late-Medieval Legend', in *Childhood in the Middle Ages and the Renaissance: The Results of a Paradigm Shift in the History of Mentality*, ed. Albrecht Classen (Berlin, 2005), pp. 135–57. These analyses focus on the common features of the vernacular poems rather than their distinctive functions as texts in particular manuscripts.

[6] On this tradition, see J. H. Morey, *Book and Verse: A Guide to Middle English Biblical Literature* (Chicago, 2000), pp. 1–86. See also D. R. Cartlidge and J. K. Elliott, *Art and the Christian Apocrypha* (London, 2001).

[7] Matt. 1. 18–2. 23; Luke 2.

[8] O. Cullmann, 'Infancy Gospels', in *New Testament Apocrypha: 1. Gospels and Related Writings*, ed. W. Schneemelcher, trans. R. McL. Wilson, rev. edn (Louisville KY, 1991), pp. 414–69 (pp. 416–19, 425); and J. K. Elliott, 'Birth and Infancy Gospels', in *The Apocryphal New Testament: A Collection of Apocryphal Christian Literature in an English Translation Based on M. R. James*, ed. J. K. Elliott (Oxford, 1993), pp. 46–122 (pp. 47, 68). The apocryphal narrative tradition grew concentrically as legends from divergent sources coalesced into larger cycles. Many of the episodes are repetitive in nature, so that multiple episodes of 'Jesus versus a teacher' or of 'Jesus and playmates sit on a sunbeam' can accrue in the same narrative. For example, *Cursor* includes two versions of the pools episode wherein Jesus fatally curses a playmate and three school episodes (see Appendix and note 15 below). Two school episodes and two sunbeam-related episodes appear in the *Childhood* (see Appendix).

[9] On the childhood episodes extant in church art and in manuscripts, see Cartlidge and Elliott, *Art and the Christian Apocrypha*, pp. 74–8, 99–116. On the condemnation, see Cullmann, 'Infancy Gospels', p. 418.

Episodes from the childhood of Jesus are found initially in the late second-century apocryphal *Infancy Gospel of Thomas*, which presents Jesus as a particularly fearsome child prodigy; Elliott calls him an *'enfant terrible'*.[10] The characterization of the God-child combines his omniscience and divine power to curse (kill) and resurrect with play and laughter, resulting in a sort of scary, slightly Gnostic child Jesus.[11] For example, one of the most frequently retold episodes of the *Infancy Gospel of Thomas* finds the child Jesus playing with other boys at a stream, making dams or pools. Jesus collects water into ponds, and then, by speaking one word, he makes the water pure. Another boy, the son of Annas the scholar, drains Jesus's pools. Jesus becomes angry, saying, 'Damn you, you irreverent fool! What harm did the ponds of water do to you? From this moment you, too, will dry up like a tree', and with that the boy withers away. Only later after Jesus has killed another boy who bumped into him, blinded his accusers, and deflated his teacher with his knowledge does he laugh and reverse his curses – presumably the boy is resurrected, but it is not narrated.[12]

The *Infancy* stories were made known in Western Europe largely through the eighth- or ninth-century Latin *Pseudo-Matthew*.[13] In *Pseudo-Matthew*, the child Jesus is slightly less malevolent than in the *Infancy Gospel* and, in line with the rising devotion to Mary, the text expands her maternal role.[14] In the pools episode, for example, the child Jesus, as in the *Infancy Gospel*, fatally curses the boy who spoils his seven pools. In this version, the parents are immediately on the scene: Joseph asks Mary to scold Jesus, and she begs her son not to do such things. Jesus, 'not wishing to grieve His mother', kicks the backside of the boy and bids him rise: he does, and Jesus continues playing.[15]

---

[10] 'Jesus is an *enfant terrible* who seldom acts in a Christian way!' (Elliott, 'Birth', 68). Speaking of the *Infancy Gospel of Thomas* and its influence, Elliott suggests that 'The Gnostic nature and origin of the infancy narratives is seen by some to exist not only in the stories themselves in which Jesus the *Wunderkind* is possessed of complete knowledge and wisdom and power *ab initio* and thus as a Gnostic revealer, but also in the [condemnatory] reaction of early fathers to a Gospel of Thomas' (pp. 69–70). See also Cullmann, 'Infancy Gospels', pp. 442–3.

[11] On the possible Docetism in the *Infancy Gospel of Thomas* and the deliberate turning from this characterization in later adaptations, see Dzon, 'Boys Will Be Boys', pp. 200–2.

[12] *The Infancy Gospels of James and Thomas*, ed. and trans. R. F. Hock (Santa Rosa CA, 1995), pp. 105–23.

[13] The *Pseudo-Matthew* was extremely influential, with more than 130 manuscripts extant (Elliott, 'Birth', pp. 84–6).

[14] Cullmann, 'Infancy Gospels', pp. 457–8; and Elliott, 'Birth', pp. 84–6.

[15] Chapter 26 of *Pseudo-Matthew*, in *Apocrypha of the New Testament*, trans. A. Walker, in *The Ante-Nicene Fathers*, ed. A. Roberts and J. Donaldson, rev. C. Coxe, 10 vols. (New York, 1903), VIII, 368–83 (p. 378). For the Latin edition, see *Evangelia Apocrypha*, ed. C. Tischendorf (Leipzig, 1853), pp. 50–105 (pp. 88–9). Chapter 26 forms part of the last section of the *Pseudo-Matthew* (chapters 25–42), referred to as *Pars altera* by Tischendorf. This section of childhood

Pseudo-Matthew and other ancient infancy narratives were adapted into multiple medieval vernacular *Infancy of Christ* texts, including narratives written in German, Irish, Welsh, Italian, Provençal, Czech, Old French and Anglo-Norman.[16] In addition to the Thornton text, there are five extant Middle English *Childhood* accounts, including the early and unique octosyllabic couplet version found in Oxford, Bodleian Library, MS Laud Misc. 108, and the two additional redactions of the Thornton version (in MSS Harley 3954 and 2399).[17] These four versions are self-contained *Infancy* poems that begin with an orthodox telling of the birth in Bethlehem and commonly end with the biblical wedding miracle.[18] The two additional Middle English versions form part of larger poems with a grander narrative scope; these include *Cursor* and the *Life of Saint Anne* found in Minneapolis, University of Minnesota Library, MS Z822 N 81.[19]

episodes based on the *Infancy Gospel of Thomas* was appended to some *Pseudo-Matthew* texts beginning in the twelfth century. The latest editor of the text does not include it in his edition: *Libri de nativitate Mariae: Pseudo-Matthaei evangelium, textus et commentarius*, ed. J. Gijsel, vol. 1 (Turnhout, 1997). For a concise textual history of *Pseudo-Matthew*, see P. Sheingorn, 'Reshapings of the Childhood Miracles of Jesus', in *The Christ Child in Medieval Culture: Alpha es et O!*, ed. M. Dzon and T. Kenney (Toronto, 2012), pp. 254–92 (pp. 256–7). See also Dzon, 'Boys Will Be Boys', p. 202. The first *Cursor* pools episode closely matches this *Pseudo-Matthew* one; the second includes the withering found in the *Infancy Gospel of Thomas* episode (lines 11931–82, 12015–28). All line references to the Thornton *Cursor* are from *The Southern Version of Cursor Mundi: Volume II*, ed. R. R. Fowler (Ottawa, 1990), pp. 151–92 (for lines 10630–12710); and *The Southern Version of Cursor Mundi: Volume III*, ed. H. J. Stauffenberg (Ottawa, 1985), pp. 165–208 (for lines 12713–14915). Subsequent line references from these editions will be supplied parenthetically.

[16] T. N. Hall, 'The Miracle of the Lengthened Beam in Apocryphal and Hagiographical Tradition', in *Marvels, Monsters, and Miracles: Studies in the Medieval and Early Modern Imaginations*, ed. T. S. Jones and D. A. Sprunger (Kalamazoo MI, 2002), pp. 109–39, esp. pp. 120–2 and nn. 18–26. For the German tradition, see P. Sheingorn, 'Joseph the Carpenter's Failure at Familial Discipline', in *Insights and Interpretations: Studies in Celebration of the Eighty-Fifth Anniversary of the Index of Christian Art*, ed. C. Hourihane (Princeton, 2002), pp. 156–67. For the Old French and Anglo-Norman texts, see, respectively, *The Old French Evangile de L'enfance*, ed. M. Boulton (Toronto, 1984); and *Les Enfaunces de Jesu Crist*, ed. M. Boulton, ANTS 43 (London, 1985).

[17] For a listing and survey of the extant Middle English *Infancy* poems, see Dzon, 'The Image of the Wanton Christ-Child', pp. 102–28.

[18] The shorter poem found in Harley 3954 is the exception to this characterization, ending with the Infancy miracle of the lengthened beam instead. The Thornton *Childhood* also adds a short account of Jesus's baptism by John the Baptist after the wedding miracle. Dzon, 'Image of the Wanton Christ-Child', p. 114, notes the reverse order of these two biblical events in the Thornton version.

[19] The tail-rhyme version that has been edited as the *Life of Saint Anne* includes the childhoods and lives of Anne (Mary's mother), Mary and Jesus. See *The Middle English Stanzaic Versions of the Life of Saint Anne*, ed. R. E. Parker, EETS OS 174 (London, 1928). Henceforth, all citations from the *Life* will be from this edition; line numbers will be supplied parenthetically.

The section of the Thornton *Cursor* that covers the birth and childhood of Christ (lines 11233–648) parallels some of the episodes found again in *Childhood*, including the flight to Egypt, the miraculous fruit tree and the miracle of the clay sparrows. In contrast to the more fast-paced, forward movement of the *Childhood* narrative, the *Cursor* narrator often pauses to sermonize. For example, in the telling of the presentation of infant Jesus in the temple, the narrator preaches the moral value of poverty: the narrator first explains the law of Moses commanding one to bring a lamb or, if poorer, two turtledoves with the infant. The speaker notes that God does not disdain the poor since he bids us to live in poverty but be rich in good thoughts (lines 11301–12).[20] In *Cursor*, Jesus's childhood folds into the larger history of the lives of Mary and Jesus and is not meant to stand as an isolated adventure narrative, an *Ipokrephum*. An example of *Cursor's* larger scope occurs in the middle of the narration of Jesus's infancy: between the idols falling in the temple in Egypt and the pools episode, the narrator states that he will take leave of Jesus in Egypt and speak of King Herod. For the next 112 lines, he berates King Herod and details his wretched fall after the Slaughter of the Innocents. Only after much detail concerning the political, divine and malicious machinations that result in Herod's murderous demise does the narrator tie this history back to the Holy Family's journey, by way of the biblical account of Joseph's dream of the angel who informs them they can now safely return home (lines 11797–908). The tone of the long, leisurely paced *Cursor* is thus homiletic and expository, in contrast to the more action-packed *Childhood*.

The Childhood of Christ *as romance*

The self-contained *Childhood*, explicitly framed as *Ipokrephum* and *Romance*, embraces the implausibilities of a romance structure, complete with a streamlined adventure pace, knights and kings as characters, and even emperors with beautiful daughters vying for Jesus as a son-in-law.[21] John Thompson conjec-

---

[20] Likewise, the *Cursor* narrator dwells on the humble accoutrements of the birth itself by emphasizing what did not surround the infant: 'In symple cloutes scho hym layde / Was thare no riche wedes graythede / Was thare no pride of couerlite / Chambrere curtyns ne no tapite' (lines 11237–40).

[21] *Childhood* is reduced to about half the size of the earlier Laud Misc. 108 version: 925 lines compared to 1854 lines. The birth and childhood section of *Cursor* runs to 1416 lines. Additionally, *Childhood* is told as one continuous story rather than being divided into discrete, disparate episodes as it is in the Laud 108 poem, where episodes are headed by boxed prose précis. On this layout, see J. N. Couch, 'Misbehaving God: The Case of the Christ Child in Ms Laud Misc. 108 "Infancy of Jesus Christ"', in *Mindful Spirits in Late Medieval Literature: Essays in Honor of Elizabeth Kirk*, ed. B. Wheeler (New York, 2006), pp. 31–43 (pp. 40–1).

tures that the incipit likely reflects a deliberate linking of the 'romance' of *Child-hood* to 'The Romance of Kyng Richerd'; this title for *Richard* occurs in the poem's explicit with the incipit for *Childhood* following directly.[22] The juxtaposition is suggestive and draws attention to their commonalities. Like *Richard*, *Childhood* presents a series of adventurous episodes, all forwarding the idea of the inimitable greatness of the Christ(ian) hero.

Superficial romance features – including the increase of individual names with the knightly honorific of *Sir* and an addition of derivative marital entreaties – distinguish *Childhood* from other ancient and vernacular versions, including, to an extent, the other Middle English poems.[23] For example, the child Jesus's enemies are named as knights: Sir Jokere, Sir Melchi, Sir Abia-kare.[24] Other versions are not as generous with the knightly monikers or with names in general. For example, in the Laud poem, the father who imprisons his son in a tower to keep him away from Jesus is simply another enraged 'giv' whose child 'louede Jh>m' (lines 695, 680); in *Childhood*, the imprisoned child is Jesus's good friend Osepe whose father is 'Sir Jokere ... þat was thare Empe-rour' (lines 400–1).[25] Several of the children's fathers (and Jesus's contenders) are emperors, despite the illogic of having several emperors floating around: in addition to Sir Jokere, there is Emperoure Sir Leefede (line 763) and Sir Sadoke, 'Emperour of that countre' (lines 585–6). The Thornton narrative even inserts an entire episode wherein two noblemen (landed knight Sir Melchy and Emperor Sadoke) contend to give their daughters and land to Jesus. Emperor Sadoke introduces his daughter as the 'fayreste may of this contree' and insists that Jesus will wed her and have all the emperor's lands (lines 587–91). In turn, Sir Melchy claims his daughter is 'fayrere than swilke fyve' and if Jesus weds her, Melchy will give him tools and lands (lines 593–600). When he rejects them

---

[22] Thompson, *London Thornton MS*, pp. 47–8. Thompson explains 'that the part of the incipit which describes the text as a "romance" was Thornton's later addition (in red)'. He contends that Thornton's label 'seems a determined effort on his part to create in his reader's mind some limited sense of continuity, despite the unlikely pairing of the blood-thirsty Richard with a story about the childhood of Christ'. As I show in this chapter, the two texts are more compatible than Thompson imagines.

[23] The exception is Harley 2399, which includes the marital entreaties (lines 509–539) and one entreaty in the *Life of Saint Anne* version (see note 26 below). Neither the Harley 2399 nor the Harley 3954 redaction use the moniker *Sir* nor have as many emperors as the Thornton version.

[24] Lines 401, 487, 654. All line references to *Childhood* are from 'Nachträge zu den Legenden: I. Kindheit Jesu, aus Ms. Addit. 31,042', ed. C. Horstmann, *Archiv* 74 (1885), 327–39. Henceforth, all citations from *Childhood* will be from this edition; line numbers will be supplied parenthetically. The names *Abakor* and *Melchy* are also found in Harley 2399, though without the *Sir*. I cannot find other instances of the name *Jokere*. Even the dyer is referred to as *Sir Awye* (line 674).

[25] See below for further discussion of Osepe.

both, they insist that he choose one, threatening him with death by stoning if he does not, so that the child Jesus flees the land (lines 605–11)![26]

The child Jesus and his family are constantly fleeing from one land to another, which not only typologically repeats the flight to Egypt but also creates the small, interconnected world typical of romance, wherein travelling from one country to another is the work of a moment. True to romance, Jesus, in every country, is playing with the children of emperors (although his father is a carpenter). The Thornton Jesus's special friendship with Osepe adds to the nonrealistic interconnectedness of the narrative's romance world while simultaneously lending to the logical continuity of the narrative. Osepe is Jesus's friend from almost the beginning of his childhood: Jesus keeps Osepe from leaping over the hills like the other children who die in the attempt, and then enlists Osepe – 'my frende' Jesus calls him – to call the slain children by name to resurrect them (lines 286, 312–15). Osepe is also the child who responds wisely when the children's water pitchers break after they attempt to hang them on the sunbeam like Jesus did: Osepe names who Jesus is – 'kynge of alle pouste' (line 356) – and tells Jesus he can make the pitcher whole with one breath; Jesus restores the pitchers 'for [Osepe's] sake' (line 360). Later in the poem – and in a different country – the apocryphal episode of Jesus sowing the barleycorn that yields a miraculous harvest is connected to Osepe: When Mary tells Jesus to have compassion for the hungry, she adds that those starving are 'Of Osepe kyne that thou wele knewe' (line 576).

This logical continuity is also evident in Thornton's linear narration of the child Jesus's exploits. For example, one long series of his exploits moves the narrative forward from Jesus's day at school, to making the clay sparrows, to hill-leaping, to hanging pitchers on sunbeams (lines 193–363).[27] In logical response to the accumulation of traumatic and miraculous events surrounding Jesus playing with their children, the parents decide to keep their children from Jesus, which leads to the children being hidden in an oven (and turned into swine [lines 364–99]).[28] Again, logically, it is after this trial that Osepe's father conceals his son in a tower (lines 400–11). In contrast, in *Cursor*, the episodes

---

[26] In the Harley 2399 redaction, the child Jesus adds that the insistent fathers are 'wolde' and that his mother is fairer than their daughters and ten like them! (lines 526–8). In the *Life of Saint Anne* version, one emperor offers his kingdom and daughter to Jesus; Jesus rejects the offer, saying no one shall 'part my moder & me'. In this instance, the emperor and his men do not dare to say any more but let Jesus 'do als he wold' (lines 2599–2608).

[27] Transitions, such as 'Bot thane' and 'Bot sone ther-aftire appone anothire daye', move the narrative immediately to Jesus's next exploit (lines 268, 280). In other versions these episodes are interrupted by additional school days and section titles. See Appendix for the order of episodes found in the Thornton *Childhood*. This version collects the childhood exploits into clusters with each cluster bookended by Jesus's expositions on creedal points, such as the virgin birth.

[28] In the Laud 108 poem, the swine episode occurs directly (and not as logically) after Jesus

are not only set apart from each other by section headings, but the child Jesus simply does not play as much as he does in *Childhood*: the *Cursor* Jesus does not leap over hills or sit on sunbeams; he only plays in the water, makes the sparrows and otherwise goes to school or achieves helpful tasks.[29]

'Helpful' is not the word one associates with the child Jesus of *Childhood*.[30] Beyond the superficial construct of the romance world, *Childhood* is tied to romance, and particularly *Richard*, by its very Richard-esque divine child. The Thornton child Jesus has more in common with the jovial and violent King Richard than with the sweeter, more helpful child Jesus of the *Cursor*. The similarity of Jesus to Richard emerges as the most significant and striking parallel between the two narratives: the child Jesus is an outlandish protagonist who, like Richard, enjoys his power and laughs in the face of his enemy. Richard begins his reign with disguise and jest: he orders all his men to face off in a tournament to which he himself enters disguised – three times – to defeat them all. When his two knights who withstood his blow complain to the king of the unknown knight, Richard laughs and says, 'that was I!'[31] Richard also laughs with shocking and triumphant glee when he discovers that the flesh he has just eaten is from a dead Saracen rather than a swine: '"What deuyl is þis?" þe kyng cryde, / And gan to lauȝe as he were wood' (lines 3214–15).[32] In Richard's world, accidental cannibalism of the enemy becomes a badge of triumph – he is thrilled to know he will never be defeated by hunger since he can always cook the enemy.[33] Richard uses this stunt later to terrify and mock

helps the hungry by sowing oats in a field (lines 985–1050). For more on the swine episode, see below.

[29] See Appendix for the order of Infancy and Childhood episodes in *Cursor*.

[30] When discussing Thornton's reasons for labelling *Childhood* a romance, Thompson, *London Thornton MS*, p. 48 n. 25, erroneously describes the poem as one that 'celebrat[es] the virtues of obedience and mercy'. These are not the qualities associated with the apocryphal boy Jesus, better known for his anger and absence of concern.

[31] 'Kyng Richerde sat righte still & loughe / And seyd frendis nowe sekirly / Takes noghte to grefe I prey for that was I' (fol. 128v; lines 584–6). Unless otherwise noted, all citations from *Richard* come from the London Manuscript, as no critical edition is based on Thornton's text. Line references are to the parallel passages in *Der mittelenglische Versroman über Richard Löwenherz*, ed. K. Brunner, Wiener Beiträge zur englischen Philologie 42 (Vienna, 1913).

[32] Citation here is from *Der mittelenglische Versroman über Richard Löwenherz*, as the leaves containing these lines are wanting in the London Manuscript. On Richard's 'extravagant laughter' in this romance, see G. Heng, 'The Romance of England: Richard *Coer De Lyon* and the Politics of Race, Religion, Sexuality, and Nation', in *Empire of Magic: Medieval Romance and the Politics of Cultural Fantasy* (New York, 2003), pp. 63–113 (p. 64).

[33] On cannibalism in this romance, in addition to Heng, see S. Akbari, 'The Hunger for National Identity in *Richard Coer de Lion*', in *Reading Medieval Culture: Essays in Honor of Robert W. Hanning*, ed. R. Stein and S. Pierson Prior (Notre Dame, 2005), pp. 198–227; A. Ambrisco, 'Cannibalism and Cultural Encounters in *Richard Coeur de Lion*', *Journal of Medieval and Early*

Saracen messengers by serving them their own princes' heads hot on a platter. Understandably, they quake with fear and will not eat, even when the heads are replaced with conventional food. Richard taunts them: 'oh, don't be squeamish; this is our custom, to serve hot Saracen heads first; your custom I know not!'[34]

In *Childhood*, the child Jesus approaches the frequent deaths and subsequent resurrections of his friends and teachers with a similar jovial nonchalance. In one instance, for example, the children want to leap hills with Jesus; Jesus successfully leaps over the hill but the children fall and die (lines 280–327). In these instances Jesus never gasps, mourns or even sympathizes with the grieving parents, but is either absent from the narrative until Mary calls him to redress the situation or simply continues playing.[35] For example, when the children fall and die from attempting to sit on a sunbeam like Jesus, 'Jhesu loughe and made hym playe' (line 478). This relentless image of an impervious, gleeful Jesus is sandwiched between the falling of the children and the graphic depiction of their injuries:

> Some brake þe haulse & some þe thee,
> Some þe schanke & some þe arme,
> Some þe bakke & some the knee:
> Þare skapede nane with-owttene harme. (lines 480–3)

Laughter, mocking and play in response to others' destruction binds Richard and Jesus.[36] Both protagonists are distinctively characterized by a certain charmed joyousness. Richard's exuberance erupts in frequent hearty celebrations and in unleashing his dark humour on his enemy.[37] Likewise, the child Jesus lives large by playing and carrying out pranks on unwitting adults. The dyer episode in *Childhood* exemplifies Jesus's penchant for play and pranking.

Modern Studies 29 (1999), 499–528; L. Cordery, 'Cannibal Diplomacy: Otherness in the Middle English Text *Richard Coer de Lion*', in *Meeting the Foreign in the Middle Ages*, ed. Albrecht Classen (New York, 2002), pp. 153–71; and N. McDonald, 'Eating People and the Alimentary Logic of *Richard Coeur de Lion*', in *Pulp Fictions of Medieval England: Essays in Popular Romance*, ed. N. McDonald (Manchester, 2004), pp. 124–50.

[34] 'Ffrendes, beþ nouȝt squoymous, / þis is þe maner off myn hous, / To be seruyd ferst, God it woot, / Wiþ Sarezyns hedes al hoot: / But ȝoure maner j ne knewe!' (lines 3509–13). Citation here is from *Der mittelenglische Versroman über Richard Löwenherz*, as the leaves containing these lines are wanting in the London Manuscript.

[35] The parents, in contrast, 'ffule grete sorowe þane þay alle gane make,/ And grete mournynge bathe daye & nyghte' (lines 302–3).

[36] Dzon, 'Boys Will Be Boys', pp. 179–80, 210–11, notes that the child Jesus laughs more in the later apocryphal adaptations. See also I. Bejczy, 'Jesus' Laughter and the Childhood Miracles: The *Vita Rhythmica*', *South African Journal of Medieval and Renaissance Studies* 4 (1994), 50–61.

[37] On the use of humour in the romance, see Heng, 'The Romance of England', p. 67. For examples of Richard's hearty – and with Margery, his enemy's daughter, sexual – celebrations, see lines 1050, 1788.

The dyer, angry that Jesus did not follow instructions to place cloths in three different dyes but instead threw them all in one vat, hurls a firebrand at Jesus (it lands and flowers instead of harming Jesus). After this miracle, the dyer discovers that the clothes have miraculously been dyed properly despite being thrown into one vat. In response, 'fast [Jesus] loughe' (line 694). Jesus forgives the dyer and wife when they beg mercy, but *immediately* gets back to playing: 'sone he wente hym to playe' (line 701). It was because Jesus wanted to play ball with his friends in the street in the first place that he had thrown all the clothes into one vat: 'And went to playe hym at the balle / With his felawes, walde he noghte lette' (lines 672–3).

One episode fully embraces the idea of the divine child-trickster who cares not for men's souls but only wants to have fun with his power.[38] In this long episode, a boy, Arnold, invites Jesus to play in the forest with the children. For fear of wild animals, the children leave Jesus and climb a tree that stands in water; bears and wolves come and shake the tree and the children drown. Jesus slays the wild animals to avenge their deaths. The grieving parents take their dead children home in carts. When the parents are asleep, Jesus resurrects the children who sneak back with him to the forest to play; and Jesus replaces the children's corpses with the dead bodies of bears and wolves, to (of course!) the great dismay of the awakened parents (lines 702–809). Both Richard and the child Jesus share a particularly playful, devil-may-care attitude in their conquests for God – laughing, mocking and playing to show their supremacy against their (human and animal) foes. The outlandish child Jesus thus proves an amiable companion to the outlandish, feisty Richard.[39]

What keeps the childhood romance from being too detached from religious sincerity is its tenacious redirection of such fabulous childhood incidents perpetrated by a rash, divine child toward creedal paradigms. Even the trite episode of the noblemen offering their daughters and estates to Jesus affords an opportunity for the divine child to ask them why they offer him such things 'When alle this werlde it es myne awenne?' (line 604). These recurrent manoeuvres gloss the romance/apocryphal narrative, enlisting it in the service of a responsible didactic end.

---

[38] The episode is also included in the Harley 2399 redaction of this poem (lines 629–730) and in the *Life of Saint Anne* poem (lines 2485–2592). On the child Jesus functioning as a trickster figure, see K. M. Ashley, 'The Guiler Beguiled: Christ and Satan as Theological Tricksters in Medieval Religious Literature', *Criticism* 24 (1982), 126–37.

[39] Like Richard who likes to eat his enemy, Jesus toys with, or at least alludes to, the idea of eating his enemy in the swine episode. Similarly, the forest episode also enacts a replacement of humans with animals.

In fact, this version of the divine infancy marries an entertaining, outlandish structure to an equally exuberant typology. This poem's version of the apocryphal fruit tree episode exemplifies its overt typology. In this scene, Mary and Joseph have halted in their journey to Egypt due to Mary's hunger and Joseph's thirst. In the more traditional rendering of this episode, found in *Cursor*, after the child Jesus commands the tree under which Mary sits to bend down and offer its fruit, Jesus then has the tree make a well from its roots so that they may drink water to their fill (lines 11657–730). In *Childhood*, wells of water *and wine* spring up from the tree's roots, a conscious link to the biblical miracle at the wedding at Cana.[40] The longstanding apocryphal tradition of Jesus commanding the tree to provide water has been overlaid with an explicit biblical allusion.

The wedding at Cana, which, as in other versions, comes toward the end of the Thornton poem, not only recalls the childhood miracle of the fruit tree but also ties the tree and the wedding miracles explicitly to the Passion. When asked why the wine is so good, Jesus explains it as a figuration of the Eucharist: 'Thus salle be delyd my flesche & blode / To cristene men in ilke a lande' (lines 900–1). As discussed in the next section, this poem's preoccupation with the Passion is its most representative use of typology and forges a clear connection to the manuscript context.

The Childhood of Christ *as the Passion*

The first two lines of the poem immediately link the text to the London manuscript's devotion to the Passion of Christ: 'Allemyghty god in Trinytee / Þat bought mane on þe Rode so dere' (lines 1–2).[41] It is well established that the Passion emerges as a central focus in the manuscript.[42] The second item in London is an affective meditation on Jesus on the cross, excerpted from *Cursor* (lines 17111–88) and given the title *Discourse between Christ and Man* (art. 3). The crucified Jesus speaks, detailing the abuses he has suffered, all for 'synfull man', admonishing him to 'Thynk ay think þou synfull man / Hafe I noght made the my leman' (lines 17119–20). The poem is both graphic with details of the Passion – 'see my blody syde' – and affective – 'Þat for thi luffe es opyned wyde':

---

[40] The water and wine reference also appears in the two Harley redactions. To my knowledge this addition of wine is unique to this Middle English poem.

[41] The second personage referred to in the prayer, Mary, is also in keeping with the manuscript's focus on the Holy Virgin: 'And for the lufe of Marie free' (line 5).

[42] See, e.g., Hardman, 'Reading the Spaces', pp. 262–8.

Putt in thi hande & grape my frende,
Take þou my herte bitwix þi hende;
Than may þou with thyn eghne see
How trewly þat I hafe luffed thee. (lines 17139–44)

This graphic meditation on the cross prepares the devout reader for the detailed verse retelling of the Passion found in London's fourth item, the *Northern Passion*.[43] As Thompson explains, the *Northern Passion* continues the aborted *Cursor* to provide a 'premeditated sequence of texts dealing with events in the life of Christ'.[44] Thompson notes that not only does Thornton omit the Passion section of *Cursor* (exchanging it for the *Northern Passion*), but he also never returns to the rest of the *Cursor*, thus omitting the rest of its world history that continues to Judgement Day.[45] This omission, I contend, can be seen as lending focus to the Passion and, ultimately, with the crusade romances, its militant ramifications.[46] Instead of placing the Passion in a larger history, the Passion *is* the beginning and end of history. The Passion's omnipresence is manifest in this manuscript: it is the past, present and future. In the context of Christ's birth in *Cursor*, for example, the Passion (and the accompanying sense of vengeance) is there: during the presentation at the temple, Simeon prophesies, as he does in the Bible, that a sword of sorrow will strike Mary's heart; the *Cursor* Simeon adds the explicit reason: 'when his [her] sone hange one þe rode' (line 11372).[47] This immediate placement of the Passion alongside the birth, along with Mary's prophesied grief, encapsulates the manuscript's narrative parameter, that is, its Passion focal point. The notion of the Proleptic Passion, 'that is, the future Passion represented as already occurring or accomplished in the Christ Child',

[43] Hardman, 'Reading the Spaces', p. 262, suggests this idea of the *Discourse* serving as a 'preparatory exercise before reading this most solemn part of the gospel narrative', that is, the Passion. This idea accords with her conjecture of an intended picture of the Crucifixion in the empty space at the top of the first page of the *Northern Passion* (pp. 261–2). See Thompson, *London Thornton MS*, p. 52, on the order of these texts; he notes that the *Discourse* typically comes after the account of the Passion in *Cursor*.

[44] Thompson, *London Thornton MS*, p. 49.

[45] Ibid., p. 49; see pp. 49–55 for possible literary and codicological reasons Thornton exchanged the *Cursor* version of the Passion for the *Northern Passion* text.

[46] Hardman, 'Reading the Spaces', p. 263, also contends and explains how the first texts in London, from *Cursor* to (at least) the *Sege of Melayne* 'form a coherent historical and thematic sequence ... centred on the Passion narrative'.

[47] Simeon, similar to the Bible passage, also prophesies that the baby will be the downfall and damnation of many and the uprising and salvation of others. The biblical passage is more cryptic, unlike *Cursor* which explicitly ties the prophesy to the Passion. In Luke 2. 34b–35, Simeon says, 'Behold this child is set for the fall and for the resurrection of many in Israel, and for a sign which shall be contradicted; And thy own soul a sword shall pierce, that, out of many hearts, thoughts may be revealed'.

appears in this Simeon episode in *Cursor* and, as I discuss below, in *Childhood*.[48] The birth of Jesus is the Passion of Christ; the childhood of Jesus is the Passion of Christ. All narrative, finally, is meant to recollect and remind, and ultimately direct a reader toward the Passion. In addition to the numerous references to the Passion found throughout London's texts, Thornton returns to the Passion explicitly in his two versions (one incomplete) of Lydgate's *Complaint That Christ Makes of His Passion*, another affective, graphic retelling of the Passion (arts. 11, 14). Like the *Discourse*, Christ on the cross is the speaker, drawing attention to his suffering and wounds and reminding the listener at the end of each stanza to 'thynke one my passioun' (fol. 94v; line 16).[49]

A preoccupation with the Passion distinguishes the Thornton version of the apocryphal childhood. The first words the child Jesus speaks in *Childhood* refer to his Passion.[50] Jesus does not speak directly in the wilderness episode as he does in *Cursor*; instead Jesus first speaks after the abductors Barabbas (yes, that one) and his son Dismas have spared the Holy Family, and Mary has asked Jesus to acquit the abductor's son: 'And he [Jesus] sayde: "modire, on my right syde salle he dye / And come with me in-tille my blysse"' (lines 63–4). With this precocious speech, the image of the child Jesus is immediately superimposed with the image of the Christ Jesus on the cross. Including the abduction scene signals the Passion focus of this poem: this scene, for example, is not in the *Cursor* or Laud versions of the poem.[51] Its introduction of criminals – the biblical Barabbas and his son, the now-named thief on Christ's right side – at the very beginning of the childhood episodes immediately thrusts the child Jesus into the antagonistic setting of the Passion.

---

[48] M. Dzon and T. Kenney, 'Introduction: The Infancy of Scholarship on the Medieval Christ Child', in *The Christ Child in Medieval Culture*, ed. Dzon and Kenney, pp. xiii–xxii (p. xvi). The analyses of the Proleptic Passion found in their book centre on literary and artistic representations of the infant Christ (rather than the childhood episodes). See esp. Part One of the collection, 'The Christ Child as Sacrifice', pp. 3–114.

[49] All citations from Lydgate's *Complaint* come from the London manuscript, as no critical edition is based on Thornton's text. Line references are to the parallel passages in John Lydgate, 'Cristes Passioun', in *The Minor Poems of John Lydgate I*, ed. H. N. MacCracken, EETS ES 107 (London, 1911), pp. 216–21.

[50] In *Cursor*, the child Jesus first speaks when he tames the wild beasts on their flight to Egypt. In his long speech, an adaptation of the speech originally found in the *Infancy Gospel of Thomas* and *Pseudo-Matthew*, Jesus smoothly proclaims his perfection and power and tells Mary not to be afraid (lines 11623–28, 11637–40).

[51] An analogous abduction scene is found in the ancient *Arabic Infancy Gospel* ('The Arabic Gospel of the Infancy of the Saviour', in *Apocrypha*, trans. Walker, VIII, 405–15). In that one the two criminals are Titus and Dumachus: Jesus prophesies that both will hang with him when he is crucified but that the kind one (Titus) will be saved. See Cullmann, 'Infancy Gospels', 460. For other accounts of the robbers episode, see Dzon, 'The Image of the Wanton Christ-Child', pp. 92–100.

Tying the outlandish childhood exploits of the apocryphal child Jesus explicitly to the actors and events of Christ's Passion validates them via the medieval meditative practice of affective, spiritual recollection, a practice provided
for throughout the manuscript.[52] Unlike most previous accounts of Jesus's
childhood, typology becomes an *unambiguous* device in the Thornton version.
Those who, like the thieves, contend with the child Jesus in the Thornton poem
turn out to be future persecutors in the Passion drama. For example, the boy
who messes up Jesus's pools? In *Childhood*, he is Judas: after Jesus makes two
dams, 'one Judas putte his stafe þer-in / And swythe vndide þat he [Jesus] had
done' (lines 155–6). In *Cursor*, in contrast, he remains an unnamed boy who is
described as 'full … of Sathane' and possessing 'wanttones of witt' (lines 11940–
1).[53] The *Cursor* child Jesus is angry that this boy messed up his dam and decries
him as 'full of felony' as he is resurrecting him (line 11977). In *Childhood*, the
child Jesus's specific prophecy explicates precisely the nature of the boy's 'felony'.
After Jesus derisively raises him – 'Judas, why lies þou stylle? / My modir walde
þou hade resyne are' (lines 187–8) – Jesus tells his mother:

> 'This traytour es fulle of felonye
> Vn-to the Jewes he salle me selle
> Ymanges my faamene for to dye'. (lines 190–2)

[52] Lydgate's *Complaint* provides the explicit terminology used to instruct a supplicant in
the practice of affective meditation: Christ bids those who sleep all night to awaken and with
'*Inward sight* / Looke on my tormentis, of equyte and resoun' (line 45; my emphasis) and later
instructs: 'Alle these tokenys *enprente* hem *in þi mende*' (line 75; my emphasis) (*The Minor Poems*,
ed. MacCracken, I, 218–19). 'Inward sight' and imprinting in the mind are key terms in the
instruction and conceptualization of affective meditation. On the medieval practice of affective
meditation, see S. McNamer, *Affective Meditation and the Invention of Medieval Compassion*
(Philadelphia, 2010) and L. LeVert, "'Crucifye Hem, Crucifye Hem'": The Subject and Affective
Response in Middle English Passion Narratives', *Essays in Medieval Studies* 14 (1997), 73–90.
Hardman, 'Reading the Spaces', pp. 259–60 and *passim* also discusses affective meditation in
relation to London.

[53] In the Laud 108 version, the pool-breaker is also not named, simply being referred to as
'giw' by the narrator and 'feondes sone of helle' by the child Jesus (lines 315, 318). Similarly, in *The
Old French Evangile de L'enfance*, ed. M. Boulton, lines 555, 558, he remains an unnamed and
insulted Jew: 'un Juïf' and 'fix de Sathenas'. These renditions lie close to Chapter 26 of *Pseudo-
Matthew* in which the pool-breaker is repeatedly referrred to as a 'son of' iniquity, death, devil,
Satan. See *Evangelia Apocrypha*, ed. Tischendorf, pp. 88–9; and *Pseudo-Matthew*, in *Apocrypha*,
trans. Walker, VIII, p. 378. In *Pseudo-Matthew* he is not referred to as a Jew, however. There is
a child Judas mentioned in the *Arabic Infancy Gospel* who is said to be 'possessed of the devil'
when he 'smites Jesus'; as a result, the devil transforms him into a dog (Elliott, 'Birth', p. 103). In
the *Life of Saint Anne*, lines 2401–53, the child Jesus also prophesies about Judas who appears as
one of the several children who dies (and is then resurrected) leaping on a sunbeam.

Jesus's prophecy is concise and clearly redirects the pools episode to Christ's Passion.[54]

Two subsequent episodes are redirected in a similar manner. A teacher who strikes Jesus and is thus killed but then resurrected by Jesus is Cayface, the high priest Caiaphas who arrests and beats the adult Jesus in the biblical accounts.[55] Again, Jesus prophesies:

> 'Modire, one mee he [Cayface] salle halde mote
> And do bete my body alle bare,
> So þat a flye sall nott mowe sette hir fote
> Neuer nowrewhare one my body for sare'. (lines 260–3)

These specific associations, and graphic recounting of a Passion scene, are not found in *Cursor* (nor the Laud version), where Jesus's enemies, both child and adult, are labelled more generically as 'evil Jews'. The graphic detail of beating Christ's body so severely that a fly cannot land on it recalls the graphic depictions of Jesus being beaten found in *Discourse*, Lydgate's *Complaint* and the *Siege of Jerusalem*.

In another episode, the Thornton child Jesus explains to his mother Mary that the children who falsely accuse him of killing a child who fell from a loft will be the very adults who will bear false witness against him, beat and strip him, put a crown of thorns on his head and hang him on the cross (lines 521–72). Characteristically, the Laud version refers to the children as Jews who are fighting with each other 'With wraþþe and with wicke dede' (line 893). In Laud and *Cursor*, the accusers are simply referred to as the 'frendes' of the killed boy (lines 902 and 12281, respectively).[56] In Thornton, the apocryphal childhood is used to retrace the graphic story of Jesus's Passion, keeping the reader spiritually 'busy' reading the acts of the child Jesus as surface images that point to the truth of the Passion.

---

[54] This episode in *Childhood* also exemplifies the close relationship between Jesus and Mary that is elaborated in the poem. Mary scolds Jesus here in a very intimate, mother-son way. See below, p. 228. In *Cursor*, as in *Pseudo-Matthew*, Mary speaks to Jesus only because Joseph did not dare to.

[55] The other Middle English versions follow *Pseudo-Matthew* in depicting Zaccheus and Levi as Jesus's teachers. Caiaphas thus provides another clear link between this poem and other Thornton texts. Caiaphas appears as Christ's nemesis in the *Northern Passion* and in the *Siege of Jerusalem*, where he is killed as part of the vengeance for the Passion: Caiaphas is drawn, flayed alive and hung upside down with cats and dogs attached to his thighs. See *Siege of Jerusalem*, ed. M. Livingston (Kalamazoo MI, 2004), lines 697–708.

[56] Fowler notes that changing to 'friends' instead of parents in 12281 and omitting the context of a generally bratty Jesus so that the parents would of course immediately suspect him 'softens' the portrayal of Jesus here (*The Southern Version II*, p. 140,). This softening continues in the *Cursor* childhood account as the child Jesus is seen as progressively more helpful and compassionate and less mischievous.

The Childhood of Christ *as* Vengeance of Our Lord

These typological moments retell the Passion as a personal attack on Jesus by his would-be playmates and teachers. In this way, *Childhood* prolongs the antagonistic context that emerges in Thornton via the romances that participate in the Vengeance of Our Lord tradition. This tradition includes narratives that depict the taking of the Holy Land, specifically Jerusalem, as the rightful revenge of Christians for the Jews' 'murder' of Jesus.[57] In this rhetorical world the Passion appears as the initial manoeuvre in the ongoing war between Christ and his Christians and 'heathen' Others. Immediately following *Discourse* and the *Northern Passion*, the *Siege of Jerusalem* continues the Passion drama by enacting the vengeance of the Lord upon the actual perpetrators of the crucifixion. What Thompson says about one cluster of texts can be said for the manuscript as a whole:

> In gathering **c** the juxtaposition of *The Northern Passion* and *The Siege of Jerusalem* stresses for Thornton's readers the continuous nature of the links between Christ's life and Passion and the repercussions of these events on the lives of both Christian knights and wicked Jews.[58]

The *Siege*, in fact, begins with a very graphic retelling of the Passion. Immediately – in the very next line after the image of an as-yet-unspecified 'they' slaying Christ on the cross – Christ is portrayed as contemplating revenge (rather than, for example, redemption), although he will delay vengeance to give 'them' time to 'convert' (*tourne*):

> For alle those harmys þat he hade he hastede hym noghte
> One thaym that velanye to venge þat his veynes braste
> Bot aye taryede he the tym if thay torne wolde
> and lent thaym space þat hym spilt þofe it spede littill
> Fourty wynter als I fynde and na faere ʒeris
> Or he oghte put at that prynce of þat pepill þat hym þose
>   paynes wroghte. (fol. 50v)[59]

---

[57] On the Vengeance of Our Lord Tradition, see M. Livingston, 'Introduction', in *Siege of Jerusalem*, pp. 1–40 (pp. 5–7). See Heng, 'The Romance of England', p. 80, on the medieval elaboration of the death of Christ as a murder perpetrated by the Jews.

[58] Thompson, *London Thornton MS*, p. 49, who also notes how the incipit of the *Siege* explicitly links the romance to the Passion of Christ (pp. 48–9). Hardman, 'Reading the Spaces', pp. 263–4, also discusses the *Siege of Jerusalem*, *Sege of Melayne* and *Roland and Otuel* as sequels to the Passion.

[59] Citations from the *Siege* are from *The* Siege of Jerusalem *Electronic Archive*, ed. T. J. Stinson, www.siegeofjerusalem.org, which provides transcriptions of the *Siege* from each manuscript copy. See also *Siege of Jerusalem*, ed. Livingston, lines 19–24.

This episode puts forth the assumption that Christ will ultimately avenge his death rather than simply suffer it. The *Siege* then narrates the story of Titus besieging Jerusalem as Christ's vengeance.

Related primarily to the Fall of Jerusalem narratives, the Vengeance of Our Lord tradition can also refer to the larger, Augustinian conception of history, wherein historical events mark the progressive triumph of God, manifested in the superiority of the Christian Church over the Old Law and religion of the Jews and over the religion of the other crusade enemy, Saracens (Muslims).[60] In this scenario, every crusade battle is a matter of vengeance for the Passion and a manifestation of Christ's (and Christians') triumph over infidels. For example, while the enemy shifts to Saracens in the unique Charlemagne romance, the *Sege of Melayne*, which follows directly after the *Siege*, this Thornton romance rewrites the Charlemagne story as 'a religious struggle rather than a glorification of the military prowess of the French king and his warriors'.[61] The war against the Saracens is depicted explicitly as a holy war, through numerous divine signs, including an angel giving a sword to Charlemagne. Even more notably, Bishop Turpin re-enacts the suffering of Christ through his own wounds, for which he will not accept treatment until the city of Milan is won.

Richard and *Childhood* continue in this mode of history being a matter of the Passion and its vengeance. Immediately preceding *Childhood*, *Richard* continues both the recounting of the Passion, with frequent allusions, and the vengeance conceit as Richard crusades mightily against the ever-present heathens.[62] For example, when Richard relates to his subjects the call to crusade against the infidels in the Holy Land, the Thornton version adds a thirty-line sermon to his appeal, in which Richard exhorts his men to 'Wynne the holy Crosse agayne'. He explicitly paints the Saracens as *Jesus's* enemies: his men will travel to where 'god was borne ... To sla vp thase false Sarazenes, / þat are oure lordes Jhesu

[60] See Livingston, 'Introduction', pp. 28–30. Heng discusses how 'medieval modalities of thought made it possible to slide, ideologically, from one religious target to another' ('The Romance of England', p. 78,). See also M. Hamel, 'The *Siege of Jerusalem* as a Crusading Poem', in *Journeys toward God: Pilgrimage and Crusade*, ed. Barbara N. Sargent-Baur (Kalamazoo MI, 1992), pp. 177–94; and R. Mills, 'The Early *South English Legendary* and Difference: Race, Place, Language, and Belief', in *The Texts and Contexts of Oxford, Bodleian Library, MS Laud Misc. 108: The Shaping of English Vernacular Narrative*, ed. K. K. Bell and J. N. Couch, Medieval and Renaissance Authors and Texts 6 (Leiden, 2011), pp. 197–221.

[61] A. Lupack, 'Introduction' to the *Siege of Milan*, in *Three Middle English Charlemagne Romances*, ed. A. Lupack (Kalamazoo MI, 1990), pp. 105–8.

[62] Hardman, 'Reading the Spaces', p. 268, also notes that *Richard* functions as yet another 'episode in the continuing story of Christian champions taking vengeance on the enemies of Christ: a fitting companion piece for the other romances of Christian revenge in the same manuscript'.

wethirwyns' (fol. 133r; lines 23, 29–30).[63] Later, the narrator explicitly states that Richard went into the Holy Land 'To wreke Jhesu j vndirstonde' (fol. 135r; line 1676).

The juxtaposition of retellings of the Passion and violent vengeance tales creates a strong, antagonistic presence in the manuscript, one that, with the child Jesus's hostile relationship with almost everyone around him and specifically the Jews, *Childhood* fully participates in. In this framework, Jesus's killing of Judas or Caiaphas functions as a sort of pre-vengeance of the Passion. The most telling addition to the Thornton *Childhood* – the violently forced mass conversion of the Egyptians to infant Jesus – confirms its link to *Richard* and settles *Childhood* in the Vengeance of Our Lord tradition that saturates the manuscript. As Geraldine Heng puts it, *Richard* is 'obsessive' in its 'description of the forcible mass conversion of Saracens'.[64] Richard orders his men to slay all – husband, wife, boy, girl – detailing how everyone should be killed everywhere – in town, city, castle – for seven lines, 'Bot if þay will take Cristundome' (fol. 145r; line 3828).[65] In *Childhood*, after the presence of infant Jesus causes the *mawmettes* to fall in the temple of Egypt, the 'lorde of that contree', Froudeus, angry and crazy, hits himself so hard that he gives himself a bloody face – his 'nesse and mouthe braste alle one blode' (line 135) – and is so afraid (*for-drede*) of infant Jesus that he begs mercy and converts (lines 127, 133–42). Subsequently, Jesus receives all of his men, 'grete' and 'smalle' who ask for mercy, 'And thase þat wolde noghte, þay were slayne / Or done in presone, thare to dye'! (lines 144–8). The graphic and extreme violence of this forced conversion in *Childhood* is unique to this rendition and strikingly recalls the forced conversions of Saracens in the preceding *Richard* rather than the accounts of this episode in other infancy poems.[66]

---

[63] *Der Mittelenglische Versroman*, ed. Brunner, prints these variant lines from the London manuscript at the foot of pp. 153–4.

[64] Heng, 'The Romance of England', p. 82. Heng discusses how conversion of the enemy to Christianity, synonymous with imperial conquest, becomes the romance's objective, contrary to historical accounts of conversion obstruction (pp. 82–3). Conversions also form part of the plots of the *Siege of Jerusalem*, the *Sege of Melayne* and *Roland and Otuel*.

[65] Richard gives another such order to slay all: 'Bot 3if þay grawnte *with* mylde mode / To bene Cristenyde in the fownte stane' (fol. 146r; lines 3968–9).

[66] While this scene is repeated in the Harley 2399 redaction, it is not included in Harley 3954. In *Cursor*, there is also no mass, violent conversion. Instead, as in *Pseudo-Matthew*, the ruler hears of the destruction of the *mawmettes* and comes to the temple with an army, ready to avenge. However, when he sees infant Jesus in Mary's arms, he falls down and proclaims Jesus God above all. He continues with a long speech in which he refers to the unbelief of Pharaoh and that all should be afraid of God's vengeance. The conversion in the Laud 108 version is written as a personal, thoughtful conversion on the part of one Herodous, whose repentance and conversion to the infant Jesus after the idols fall explicitly serve as a model for the reader (lines 209–300).

The converted Saracens in *Richard* ultimately function, as Heng argues, as 'virtual Jews' in the narrative's linking of Saracens to stereotypical anti-Jewish associations with swine and wells.[67] Notably, in *Childhood*, the forcibly converted Egyptians *literally* transmute into Jews in the next episode: the child Jesus goes to play with '*thaire* childre', and, as it happens, one of their children is Judas. After Jesus kills his playmate, those who were previously referred to as Froudeus's men are now 'Jewes' who threaten to slay Jesus and his family (lines 149, 167–8, 175). The replacement of historical Jews by a fantastical rendition of converted Muslims in *Richard* is thus mirrored in the linguistic shift in *Childhood* from Egyptians to Jews. *Childhood's* relentless antagonism against the Jews as Jesus's nemesis continues the manuscript's demonizing and dehumanizing of Jews, from the oppressive slaughter of Jews narrated in the *Siege* to the virtual Jews (Saracens) of the crusade romances.[68] In the London manuscript, the Jews, along with other 'pagan' enemies – Saracens, even the traitorous French in *Richard* – overlap and blur, becoming finally the undifferentiated Other against which a communal Christian identity defines itself.[69] This conflation functions at the meta-level, across the texts in the manuscript: an erasing of ethnic and religious differences raises the spectre of the non-Christian Other – be he Jew or Muslim, Herod or Caiaphas – against which Christianity is incessantly avenged. *Childhood's* extension of the manuscript's Othering, via Jesus's antagonistic antics, brings this version into the Holy War zone of the London manuscript's texts. Like Richard, the child Jesus exists in this post-Passion antagonistic world and faces it with the violent power of remorseless glee. Thus, *Childhood* continues the vengeance mentality of the 'siege' romances.

The Childhood of Christ *as Mary's story*

Mary's participation in Jesus's antics highlights her roles as cohort, intercessor and agent. Like the emphasis on the Passion, Mary and Marian devotion emerge as central aspects of the London manuscript. For example, in addition to the role Mary plays in the Passion retellings, the Marian prayers found in the romance narratives, and the life of Mary in *Cursor*, the manuscript contains

[67] Heng, 'The Romance of England', pp. 78–91.

[68] For medieval anti-Judaism in general, see J. Cohen, *The Friars and the Jews: The Evolution of Medieval Anti-Judaism* (Ithaca NY, 1984). For the specific medieval anti-Judaism of the apocryphal childhood tradition, see Dzon, 'Image of the Wanton Christ-Child', pp. 288–99.

[69] On this ideological operation, see Heng, 'The Romance of England', esp. pp. 76–7, 87; and Mills, 'The Early *South English Legendary*'.

a Lydgatian song of praise to Our Lady (*O Florum Flos* [art. 9]). In the *Four Leaves of the Truelove* (art. 21), Mary is the intercessor for the penitent sinner. *Childhood* is a key Thornton text for developing Mary as a three-dimensional character who is on a par with the child Jesus not only via her affective role but also in the elaboration of her agency and – like the child Jesus and King Richard – her joy. Beginning with *Pseudo-Matthew*, Mary began to play a greater role in the apocryphal infancy tradition, with her intercessory relationship to the child Jesus becoming the only one with efficacy.[70] For example, in the pools episode Mary must speak directly to Jesus before he resurrects the cursed child.[71]

In *Childhood*, Mary assumes an additional layer of narratorial agency; actions that in orthodox and other apocryphal accounts belong to others, such as Joseph, Herod and even God, are enacted by Mary. The initial events of the poem quickly establish Mary's narrative domination: after Jesus is 'of Mary born' (line 13) and Herod demands his death (lines 17–18), it is Mary who does not wish to lose her son, so 'out of the country did *she* flee / from *her* fomene *she* fled that day' (lines 19–21; my emphasis).[72] The reader follows her through the narrative and sees events through her point of view. In *Cursor*, the flight is spurred, as it is in the Gospel of Matthew, by Joseph's dream, wherein the angel details the need for Joseph to flee to Egypt with Mary and her son because of Herod's intent; it is Joseph who gets ready and flees in the night 'With marie and þaire menȝe' (line 11597).[73] Omitting the angel's message to Joseph, the *Childhood* narrator assumes that Mary (inexplicably) discerns that Herod wants to kill Jesus.[74] Five lines detail Mary fleeing the country (neither

---

[70] For the interest in Mary from the earliest apocryphal accounts that narrate her life, see Elliott, 'Birth', pp. 47–51; and Cullmann, 'Infancy Gospels', pp. 423–5. In the *Infancy Gospel of Thomas*, the central relationship occurs between Joseph and Jesus; for the text and translation, see *The Infancy Gospels*, ed. Hock, pp. 104–43.

[71] See discussion of this episode above.

[72] In contrast, in the Laud 108 version, it is God who knows the wicked scheme of Herod, and because *God* 'Nolde he nouȝt þat þe maistrie / Hedde heroude with his enuie', God sends his angel to Mary and Joseph to warn them. Then 'huy' left as the angel bid them (lines 39–54).

[73] In this way, the *Cursor* version adheres more closely to the *Infancy Gospel of Thomas* and *Pseudo-Matthew* versions where Joseph plays a more agential role. Joseph is the one who complains to Jesus directly, for instance, when he tells Jesus they need to find another way to Egypt because the route is so long and hot, and Jesus responds by shortening their way (lines 11732–46). In *Childhood*, after they learn from an 'Olde Jewe' that Egypt is still thirty days' journey away, Mary begins to weep and sits down for weariness (lines 113–8). It is Mary's actions that trigger Jesus's miraculous response: 'Modere ... be mery & wele ȝowe lete! / loo here the walles of Egipte townne!' (lines 119–20).

[74] *Childhood* also does not elaborate the story of the Three Kings (wise men) and their dealings with King Herod as narrated in *Cursor*. *Childhood* simply states in two lines that Three Kings came and kneeled and paid homage (lines 15–16), and then that Herod swears to see Jesus

Joseph nor Jesus are mentioned).[75] This rendition makes it appear as if it is only Mary who is escaping; she alone keeps Jesus safe. Mary as agential heroine thus comes to the fore. In fact, the child Jesus himself as a character in the tale is not mentioned until line 11, and Joseph, who plays a much larger role in the ancient and early vernacular accounts, is not mentioned until line 29, and then only in passing: Joseph and Mary have gone into a wilderness where *Mary* sees leopards and 'other bestis full grete and gryme' (line 32). Mary is the only parent who speaks in the next two episodes: the wild animals episode and the abduction episode.[76] From a narrative standpoint, it is as if she is the only one who is experiencing the events: even though the events are happening to all three, *Mary* sees the leopards, the thief takes *her* to his tent, and Mary's experience and words draw out the child Jesus's saving words and actions. A typical transition sentence in the Thornton reads: 'And fforthir-mare thane oure lady wente' (line 65).

Mary is at once entertaining protagonist and intimate intercessor. When, for example, the Holy Family stops for Mary to rest under the fruit tree, she remarks, 'he ware fulle slye / That any of this froyte myghte gette' (lines 75–6), her light-hearted words interceding with the child Jesus and setting up the miracle of Jesus ordering the tree to bow down. Instead of Joseph replying as in *Cursor* and *Pseudo-Matthew* (which *Cursor* follows closely here), Jesus 'wiste whate was hir [Mary's] wille' and performs the miracle (line 78).[77] Mary's intimate and intercessorial access to Jesus gives the poem its emotional heft, its affective valence. Both Mary and Jesus frequently bless one another. For example, the narrator elaborates the wild beasts episode as a fond and, literally, a springtime Jesus/Mary moment: Mary sees leopards; Jesus blesses (and thereby tames) the animals, so Mary blesses him

---

dead (lines 17–18) without even connecting his intent to the Three Kings' deceit of him. The focus thus remains on Mary's thoughts and actions.

[75]   Lines 20–4. Mary also instructs a man to give a message to her pursuers. A generic group of Jews are then presented as looking around to harm someone. In contrast to *Cursor* and Laud 108, the Slaughter of the Innocents is not narrated. The narrative does not stop to contemplate such a tragedy but rather moves forward quickly, with Mary, like a romance rather than a reflective recounting.

[76]   In *Cursor*, both parents fade into the background as Jesus gives a speech telling Mary and Joseph not to fear because he, Jesus, is perfect and can make beasts wild or tame (lines 11624–8).

[77]   In contrast, in *Cursor*, Mary first addresses Joseph about getting dates from the tree. When Joseph balks at the height of the tree, Jesus commands the tree to bow down. When Jesus sends the tree to paradise via an angel, *Cursor* focuses on the reaction of an 'all' and on Jesus's speech to them. Joseph and Mary both seem to have disappeared from this scene; the focus is on a self-contained, articulate, divine Jesus.

> bothe blode & bone,
> ffor foules songe scho herde that daye,
> And sayde: 'my drede es alle gone
> ffor the myrthe of Birdes in this waye'. (lines 37–40)

Her delight in the birds epitomizes the affective, emotional aspect of her inter-action with Jesus.

When her son Jesus prophesies the dark events of the Passion, Mary experi-entially feels grief. Prophesying in the loft episode about the children who will be false witnesses against him as adults, the Thornton child Jesus paints the future event as an intimate, gruesome experience that *Mary* shares with him: 'And ʒour face salle be with blode by-wefede / Was neuer womane so sory in mode' (lines 567–8; my emphasis). At these moments, Mary is deeply moved by the prophecies and often tells Jesus that he need not let them (the future perpe-trators) live so long. In this instance, her emotional response to the (future) loss of her son is poignant:

> Whene scho that herde, hir liste no sange,
> That þay hire dere sone so solde spille.
> 'The thare noghte late þame lefe so lange,
> My dere sone, it if be thi wille'. (lines 569–72)

While the salvific narrative of the future adult Jesus justifies the rash actions of the child Jesus, these exchanges with his mother also redirect the reader to their affective, intimate relationship.

The mother/son nature of their relationship affords many scenes where Mary's interceding with the child Jesus takes the form of affectionate scolding. For example, in the pools episode, Mary confronts Jesus, 'lefe sone, whate does þou here?' (line 178). When he begins explaining literally what he is doing – making dams – rather than explaining the death of Judas, she interrupts him by saying 'lefe son ... me liste not playe' (line 179–81). Mary is exasperated with her divine son. When the children try to sit on the sunbeam like Jesus and fall down and die, Mary exclaims, 'dere sone, this foly late þou cesse!' (line 506). Her six-line speech tacks between scolding – 'late vs somewhare lyfe in peese' – and intercessing – 'I pray the, if it be thi wille' – until Jesus resurrects the dead, maimed children by blessing them (lines 506–14). Mary becomes the reader's direct access to the child Jesus, putting the reader on the front lines with his divinity in a direct, experiential, affective (but certainly not senti-mental) manner.

The Childhood of Christ *as the priesthood of Christ*

Jesus's blessing of each child in the sunbeam episode exemplifies how the Thornton child Jesus prefigures not only his own Passion but also his subsequent Christian priesthood.[78] Even when the Passion is not explicitly invoked, the mischievous child Jesus is, at the end of episodes, regularly superseded by an orthodox Jesus, so that every outlandish act of Jesus directly or inadvertently killing his friends is translated into an institutionally oriented, teachable moment. In the hills episode, for example, Jesus keeps his friend Osepe from leaping. Jesus queries his friend: 'Why wenys þou, Osepe, þay felle so sare? / ffor þay wende alle to be my pere' (lines 288–9). Osepe then preaches this word of Jesus's inimitability to the parents, and by the end of the scene, the resurrected children are repeating the lesson: 'With hym to leppe, we tyne [forfeited] oure blys, / We will hym loue and trowe his lare' (lines 326–7). Jesus effects orthodox conversion to 'his lare'.

In *Childhood*, with its explicit typology and didacticism, historical difference and linearity are collapsed, so that the childhood episodes perpetually migrate to the level of typological, figurative reading. In the swine episode, for example, the child Jesus explicitly serves a priestly role, carrying out an institutional-style ritual of conversion to himself, or more accurately, his future self. When parents attempt to hide their children from Jesus by putting them in an oven, the man they leave to watch the oven dissimulates and tells a querying Jesus that there are only swine in the oven. When the children have actually turned into pigs, the parents are (understandably) upset. In *Childhood*, as in the ancient apocryphal *Arabic Infancy Gospel* episode of the children being turned into goats, the child Jesus restores them, but in the Thornton version, the restoration is carried out as a sacrament:

> And Jhesu *calde thaym forthe ilkane*
> And blyssede þame *with his hande*:
> And whene þay hade his blyssnge tane,
> Als þay ware firste [that is, human], þay gane vp stande.
> (lines 396–9; my emphasis)

Rather than simply narrating the swine episode as yet another instance of Jesus's omniscient mischief, this poem redirects attention to Jesus in a priestly role, providing individualized attention – naming and blessing each child via the laying on of hands, a sacred ceremony of blessing.[79] This scene dramatizes

---

[78] As E. B. Vitz, 'The Apocryphal and the Biblical, the Oral and the Written, in Medieval Legends of Christ's Childhood: The Old French *Evangile de L'enfance*', in *Saturna: Studies in Medieval Literature in Honour of Robert R. Raymo*, ed. N. M. Reale and R. E. Sternglantz (Donington, 2010), pp. 124–49 (p. 127), says in her discussion of the French *Evangile de L'enfance*, 'the narrator cannot imagine the world before Christ and Christianity'.

[79] The imposition of hands was used in sacramental ceremonies, including baptism, confirmation and conferral of Holy Orders. Significantly, it was also part of the conversion of faith outliers: at 'the reception of schismatics, heretics, and apostates into the Church, hands

conversion: Jesus converts his friends from being pigs to being 'believers', before there is a salvational creed to believe in.[80]

Conclusion: *The* Childhood of Christ *as narrative play*

The child Jesus's routine conversion of his friends to his 'lore', the redrawing of childhood events as prefigurations of the Christ, and Jesus explaining creedal doctrine typify how, in the Thornton version, Jesus's childhood serves, like the *Northern Passion* or the *Siege* do, as another figuration and remembrance of Christ and his Passion, making the childhood itself a figurative, rather than

---

were formerly, and still are, imposed' (P. Morrisroe, 'Imposition of Hands', in *The Catholic Encyclopedia*, vol. 7, http://www.newadvent.org). Upon baptism and confirmation, the recipient was traditionally given a new name (H. Thurston, 'Christian Names', in *The Catholic Encyclopedia*, vol. 10).

[80] Harley 2399 retains this scene of Jesus blessing 'all with his holy hand' but omits the line that states his *calling forth each one* (which implies a naming), stating instead, 'Jesus toke the swyne everychone' (line 393). The Harley 3954 version omits any depiction of Jesus restoring each child sacramentally, focusing instead upon the restoration as an instance of the efficacy of Mary's intercession. When the parents find their children are pigs, they say they will ask Mary for help because 'Jesus grantyt sekerly' her will; imploring Mary 'for well we wyte' they tell her 'that Jheus wyl done / thi wyl boht in bours and halls'. As predicted, 'He grantyd here wyl ful sone / the chylder of wo weren unbounde' (lines 524–5). In the earlier Laud 108 poem and in the two French versions, the pigs are never changed back to children; instead, the narrator portrays the episode as an origin story – this is why Jews do not eat pork. The depiction of Jews as pigs in a conversion narrative connects this apocryphal poem to the disturbing tradition of the dehumanizing of Jews by associating them with swine in medieval texts, including *Richard*. In the earliest known version (the *Arabic Infancy Gospel*), the children are turned into goats, not swine, and, as mentioned above, are restored (after the appeal of their mothers) (*Apocrypha*, trans. Walker, VIII, pp. 405–15). In relation to the medieval association of Jews with swine, see D. H. Strickland, 'The Jews, Leviticus, and the Unclean in Medieval English Bestiaries', in *Beyond the Yellow Badge: Anti-Judaism and Antisemitism in Medieval and Early Modern Visual Culture*, ed. M. Merback (Leiden, 2007), pp. 203–32 (pp. 226–8). Heng explains that 'In the thirteenth century the ideological reduction of Jews to animality found hideous expression in the *Judensau*, the conflation of Jews with swine, tabooed animals in *Judensau* as much as Islam' ('The Romance of England', p. 80). She finds this correlation evident in the cannibal scenes in *Richard*: the 'polemical equation of Jews with carnality, animal senses, and the body, and the *Judensau*'s conflation of Jews with swine make Richard's desire for swine's flesh, and his eating of humans as if they were animals, grotesquely meaningful' (p. 81). In the London Thornton manuscript, the analogical signifying occurring in *Richard* is doubled by the swine episode in *Childhood*. This poem adds to this building portrait of the subhuman Other with the child Jesus's actual transformation of Jewish children (which also invokes the blood libel directed toward Jews) into swine. The Jews, the worst of (medieval) God's enemies, are perceived as swine, who only become human after conversion to Christ.

a biographical or developmental, entity.[81] In this way, while the poem retells the childhood of Jesus as an entertaining romance, it confirms that the childhood is but a surface image of the real, the true story, an image that overlays the kernel of truth that is the real Lord, the Christ, the adult biblical Jesus. The Thornton *Childhood* serves a circumscribed function of reflecting Jesus's scriptural adulthood.

Nevertheless, the elements of violence, play and gleeful attitude, which keep the child Jesus anchored to *Richard* via narrative pleasure, also keep the proscribed reader response in flux. For example, no moral redeems the prank Jesus plays on the devastated parents who drag the bodies of their dead children home in carts only to find animal bodies in the morning. When the parents ask, 'Where are our children?', *Mary* laughs heartily and that is it – no lesson follows.[82] Such an episode confirms the poem's view of the divine childhood as simply a diverting surface illusion – a 'Romance', an 'Ipokrephum' – meant ultimately to direct the entertained reader to the truth of salvation.

At the end of the poem the narrator informs us that 'now es [Jesus's] Barnehede redde & done, / But his manhede lastes aye' (lines 918–19). Christ's *barnehede*, that is, his childhood, is neatly cropped, limited and ultimately superseded by Christ's eternal *manhede*. The wildness of the childhood, like the cannibalism of King Richard, is safely cordoned off in a textual space, a finite narrative. The finitude of narrative is contrasted to the infinity of Christ.

Though the final verses resolutely shift the reader's attention away from Jesus's childhood toward Christ's eternal, saving existence in heaven, the last word of this remarkable poem is *play*. While all three redactions of this version end with a prayer, the Harley poems end on a sombre note that points the reader toward the afterlife: Harley 2399 calls on Father and Son and Holy Ghost and Mary to 'Grante vs your blys par cheryte' (line 841), while Harley 3954 begs Christ to shield us 'Fro þe peyne of helle' (line 694). In contrast, the Thornton *Childhood* ends, distinctively, on a lighter image of heaven: the narrator asks the 'Swete lord' (line 921) that we may dwell with you without end 'Thare Joyes are euer & myrthe & playe' (line 925).

---

[81] In the Laud 108 version, in contrast, the divine childhood comes across as a more historic entity and a theological conundrum. See Couch, 'Misbehaving God'; and D. T. Kline, 'The Audience and Function of the Apocryphal *Infancy of Jesus Christ* in Oxford, Bodleian Library, MS Laud Misc. 108', in *The Texts and Contexts*, ed. Bell and Couch, pp. 137–55. See further Dzon, 'Boys Will Be Boys', on the *Infancy* poems as developmental narratives.

[82] 'Marye stode and faste scho loughe' (line 790). The parents ask Mary if she is crazy, and she said she just saw their children gathering nuts under a tree. The (or rather, an) emperor sighs and says if his son is truly alive, 'ffaire womane', I will give you a hundred pounds. She refuses the money and guides them to their children (lines 791–809).

Childhood reflects, in a strikingly distilled manner, the manuscript's embedded negotiation between affective and humble response to Christ's sacrifice and the fervent, inflammatory call to and narrative indulgence of vengeance for this heinous act against all Christendom past and present. Nevertheless, in the *Romance of the childhode*, negotiations always reflect the essence of narrative: play.

Appendix
Comparative chart of the childhood of Christ in two versions

1. *Cursor Mundi* childhood of Christ, by episode and line number

[acephalous, begins in the middle of Mary's childhood]

11177–11286:	Birth of Jesus
11287–11372:	Jesus offered at the temple
11373–11550:	Three Kings make offering
11551–11576:	Slaughter of the Innocents
11577–11606:	Flight to Egypt
11607–11654:	Jesus tames animals in wilderness
11655–11730:	Miracle of fruit (palm) tree
11731–11748:	Jesus shortens way to Egypt
11749–11926:	Fall of idols in Egypt; King Herod
11927–11982:	Pools episode I
11983–12014:	Miracle of clay sparrows
12015–12028:	Pools episode II (withering)
12029–12078:	Boy struck dead; resurrected by Jesus
12079–12268:	School day I
12269–12302:	Boy falls from loft and dies; resurrected by Jesus
12303–12322:	Jesus fetches water by shaping it into a ball
12323–12332:	Miracle of wheat
12333–12386:	Lioness and two cubs honour Jesus
12387–12414:	Miracle of lengthened beam
12415–12448:	School day II
12449–12486:	School day III
12487–12516:	Jesus resurrects burgher named Joseph
12517–12542:	Jesus heals James's hand from viper bite
12543–12574:	Jesus's family reverences him
12575–12658:	Jesus in temple
12659–12712:	Genealogy of Jesus

2. The London Thornton *Childhood of Christ*, by episode and line number

1–12:	Opening prayer and address
13–18:	Birth of Jesus (including Three Kings and Herod)
19–29:	(Mary's) Flight to Egypt
30–40:	Jesus tames animals in wilderness
41–64:	Abduction scene [Jesus prophesies Passion]
65–112:	Miracle of fruit tree
113–124:	Jesus shortens way to Egypt

125–148: Fall of idols in Egypt; Foudreus and his men convert

149–192: Pools episode

193–267: School day I: Jesus kills and resurrects Caiaphus [Jesus prophesies Passion]

268–279: Miracle of clay sparrows

280–327: Jesus leaps from hill to hill

328–363: Jesus hangs pitcher on sunbeam

364–399: Children in oven turn into swine

400–411: Boy in tower

412–443: Jews question Jesus and his parents; Mary asserts her virginity; Jesus explains the Immaculate Conception; Jews think they should be flayed as witches

444–471: School day II: Jesus stumps teacher with question and answers it himself; teacher tells of prophecy of Savior from maiden but says Jesus is too wild to be that Savior; Jesus proclaims, 'It is I'

472–520: Jesus sits on sunbeam

521–572: Boy falls from loft and dies; resurrected by Jesus [Jesus prophesies Passion]

573–584: Miracle of barleycorn

585–616: Two men offer daughters to Jesus

617–701: Miracle of dyer who asks Jesus about star that shone over Bethlehem

702–809: Forest prank: Jesus resurrects children slain by wild animals and replaces their bodies with animal corpses

810–833: Miracle of lengthened beam

834–845: Jesus creates rivers Jor and Dane

846–857: More questions for and answers from Jesus

858–905: Wedding feast at Galilee (Cana)

906–917: John the Baptist and Jesus's baptism

918–925: Closing address and prayer

8

Thornton's Remedies and the Practices of Medical Reading*

Julie Orlemanski

Robert Thornton's Lincoln manuscript, Lincoln Cathedral Library, MS 91, falls into three distinct sections, constituted respectively by romances and other narratives, moral and devotional materials, and medical and pharmaceutical knowledge. In the pages that follow, I consider the medical section of Thornton's book. At present it consists of a Middle English remedy collection known as the *Liber de Diversis Medicinis* and six paper fragments that are the vestiges of a Middle English herbal in Thornton's hand (arts. 99, 100). The inclusion of these two works of practical and therapeutic knowledge in Thornton's book takes on its full significance only in light of late medieval trends in reading, writing and book production in England, especially the efflorescence of medical textuality. In the pages that follow, I place Thornton's medical writings within this broader context to determine how they relate to contemporary genres of scientific and practical knowledge. I also seek to characterize how typical, or exceptional, was Thornton's inclusion of a remedy collection and herbal alongside Middle English romances. Vernacular literature, like medicine, was a category in formation and in flux in the fifteenth century. Both discourses were reaching new readers and evolving to meet altered conditions of reception. Under what circumstances did they appear together, and what might this tell us about secular reading practices?

A third piece of medical writing in Thornton's hand further aids me in answering these questions. A copy of John Lydgate's versified regimen, the *Dietary*, survives imperfectly on fol. 97r–v of London, BL, MS Additional 31042 (Thornton's London manuscript, art. 16). The poem is a close translation of the anonymous fifteenth-century Latin poem the *Dietarium*, itself based in part on the popular thirteenth-century medical poem the *Regimen sanitatis Salernitanum*, also known by the title *Flos medicinae*.[1] While Thornton's copy of

*   I would like to thank George Keiser for his thoughtful advice as I began work on this chapter.

[1]   M. Förster provides an edition of Lydgate's poem and the *Dietarium*, in 'Kleinere mittelenglische Texte', *Anglia* 42 (1918), 145–224 (pp. 176–92). The Latin and English poems appear

Julie Orlemanski

Lydgate's poem has been noticed and identified, it has not been considered in conjunction with the *Liber de Diversis Medicinis* – perhaps because Thornton's scribal treatment of the *Dietary* assimilates it to the moralistic and didactic poems around it. Among the questions the latter part of this chapter will take up is whether categorizing the *Dietary* as a medical text is appropriate, and if so, what is to be gained from such a categorization.

Robert Thornton's versions of the *Liber*, the herbal and Lydgate's *Dietary* together constitute a case study in the circulation of medical writings in the fifteenth century. As I detail below, readers and writers like Thornton, who were not medical specialists, nonetheless sought out and produced works of regimen, diagnosis, prognosis, pharmacopeia and cure. In so doing, they helped to shape the fields of practical and scientific knowledge for English audiences. As is generally the case with Robert Thornton, his writings register significant trends in late medieval textuality and do so in a singular manner.

Medical knowledge in late medieval England

In a 2005 essay George Keiser brought Thornton's practice of medical writing into sharper focus. Keiser had made a felicitous discovery: one of the other seventeen surviving copies of the *Liber de Diversis Medicinis* shares a common exemplar with Lincoln's *Liber*.[2] Both Thornton's text and Oxford, Bodleian Library, MS Rawlinson A. 393, which is dated by its scribe John Rede to 1529, appear to have descended from a manuscript associated with the Pickering family of Oswaldkirk.[3] Both Thornton and Rede had ties to the Pickering family, and so their common source makes sense. The most distinctive feature shared by the two descendants of the lost Pickering manuscript is the high number of *probatur* statements attributing verification of recipes to the Rector of Oswaldkirk: 'Secundum Rectorem de Oswaldkirk'.

Through detailed comparison of the two versions, Keiser was able to isolate what Thornton contributed to the *Liber*'s manuscript tradition – namely, a certain amount of confusion. Although Thornton set about copying the remedy book with some thoughtfulness, evidenced by his organization of the

together, in alternating stanzas, in London, BL, MS Sloane 3534, fols 1–3v; it is the unique witness of the *Dietarium*. See J. W. Morrissey, '"Termes of Phisik": Reading Between Literary and Medical Discourses in Geoffrey Chaucer's *Canterbury Tales* and John Lydgate's *Dietary*' (unpublished Ph.D. dissertation, McGill University, 2011), pp. 223–6.

[2] The relationship is first reported in G. R. Keiser, 'MS. Rawlinson A.393: Another Findern Manuscript', *Transactions of the Cambridge Bibliographical Society* 7 (1980), 445–8.

[3] G. R. Keiser, 'More Light on the Life and Milieu of Robert Thornton', *Studies in Bibliography* 36 (1983), 111–19 (p. 114).

page layout for ease of reference, comparison with Rede's version indicates that Thornton transmitted the text clumsily. His perplexity is evident, for instance, in his numerous misreadings and the resultant corruption of ingredients' names, as well as in his dutiful preservation of nonsensical portions of the exemplar. A number of eye-skip errors likewise attest to the relative lack of precision in copying. Keiser concludes, 'the text of the Lincoln MS *Liber* is replete with evidence that Thornton frequently did not understand the medical material he was copying', which was 'perhaps because of his unfamiliarity with the technical language – a common problem in the copying of vernacular medical books in 15th-century England'.[4] To the scholar of medieval English medicine, however, this misunderstanding and unfamiliarity are themselves of interest.

The 'very problematic'[5] exemplar, which already had a number of errors sedimented into its text, and Thornton's own inexpert transmission attest to practices of recording medical information that was to varying degrees opaque to those who copied or owned it. How should the 'practicality' of such writings be understood? The *Liber* came into Thornton's hands in a version bearing the imprint of local and individual practice, in the personal efficacy statements of the Oswaldkirk rector. Yet to what extent and in what manner were Thornton's copy and similar scribal productions involved in, say, bedside care? When medical texts appear alongside widely varying discourses, as they do in the Lincoln manuscript, and when they are known not to have been produced for medical professionals, how is the modern scholar to understand their evident desirability and perceived utility in the later Middle Ages?[6]

England was the scene of a particularly vibrant 'vernacularization – or laicization, or popularization' of medical and scientific writing.[7] The accelerated pace of scientific writing began in the last quarter of the fourteenth century and continued for about a hundred years. As Faye Getz observes, 'the greatest growth was seen in the number of medical and surgical texts written in medieval English. The increase was nothing less than explosive.'[8] The dramatic

---

4   G. R. Keiser, 'Robert Thornton's *Liber de Diversis Medicinis*: Text, Vocabulary, and Scribal Confusion', in *Rethinking Middle English: Linguistic and Literary Approaches*, ed. N. Ritt and H. Schnedel (Frankfurt, 2005), pp. 30–41 (pp. 35, 33).

5   Ibid., p. 33.

6   For a general consideration of these questions, see L. R. Mooney, 'Manuscript Evidence for the Use of Medieval Scientific and Utilitarian Texts', in *Interstices: Studies in Middle English and Anglo-Latin Texts in Honour of A. G. Rigg*, ed. R. F. Green and L. R. Mooney (Toronto, 2004), pp. 184–202.

7   L. E. Voigts, 'Multitudes of Middle English Medical Manuscripts, of the Englishing of Science and Medicine', in *Manuscript Sources of Medieval Medicine: A Book of Essays*, ed. M. R. Schleissner (New York, 1995), pp. 183–95 (p. 183).

8   F. M. Getz, 'Charity, Translation, and the Language of Medical Learning in Medieval England', *Bulletin of the History of Medicine* 64 (1994), 1–17 (p. 3).

increase is evidenced by the calculations of Peter Murray Jones, based on Dorothea Waley Singer's handlist of scientific manuscripts in the British Isles from before the sixteenth century – which deals with an estimated 30,000 to 40,000 texts in several languages. Jones estimates that the proportion of texts surviving from the fifteenth century compared to those surviving from the fourteenth is of the order of six to one.[9]

Despite its scale, this accelerated dissemination of medical knowledge appears to have been decentralized and eclectic. The most significant difference between English medicine and its continental counterparts lay in England's lack of centralizing regulatory institutions for medicine. Oxford and Cambridge had only very small medical faculties: 'At Oxford ... fewer than 100 men left any record of medical study. This was about one percent of recorded students. Cambridge's body of medical students was about half the size of Oxford's.'[10] Despite the efforts of a group of elite physicians in 1421 and again in 1423, university-trained physicians were unable to secure even a nominal monopoly on practices of healing, nor to claim any broad licensing authority. Instead, patients in England continued to seek healthcare within a heterogeneous network encompassing physicians, apothecaries, astrologers, members of barber-surgeon guilds, itinerant 'leeches' without formal education, midwives, tooth-drawers, parish priests, monastic communities, saints' shrines and members of their own households. Since 'leechcraft' was practised by many, the authority to care and cure did not reside in a single stratum of society nor in a single set of authoritative texts or textual practices.

Clerics appear to have played an important part in medical care within provincial communities. Healing bodies, as well as souls, was understood as part of pastoral duty.[11] Because they were literate, clerics were especially likely to bring practices of reading and writing together with their medical care, as the *probatur* statements of the Rector of Oswaldkirk exemplify. Keiser has observed that 'of the few bequests of medical books' in late medieval Yorkshire wills, 'all are in the wills of clergymen'.[12] Documentary traces of other rural healers are more difficult to recover, since these practitioners relied less on written medical knowledge, or the medical writings they did possess were less likely to survive.[13]

[9]   P. M. Jones, 'Medicine and Science', in *The Cambridge History of the Book in Britain, Vol. 3: 1400–1557*, ed. L. Hellinga and J. B. Trapp (Cambridge, 1999), pp. 433–48 (p. 434).

[10]   F. Getz, 'Medical Education in Later Medieval England', in *The History of Medical Education in Britain*, ed. V. Nutton and R. Porter (Amsterdam, 1995), pp. 76–93 (p. 86).

[11]   See Getz, 'Charity'.

[12]   G. R. Keiser, 'Lincoln Cathedral Library MS. 91: Life and Milieu of the Scribe', *Studies in Bibliography* 32 (1979), 158–79 (p. 176).

[13]   However, see London, BL, MS Harley 1735, the commonplace book of a fifteenth-century

Much provincial medical care likely went on within the household itself. One brief letter from Sir John Paston II attests to the role of gentry women in both medical practice and medical writing. He writes to his wife:

> Mastress Margery, I recomand me to yow, and I prey yow in all hast possybyll to send me by the next swer messenger that ye can gete a large playster of *your flose ungwentorum* for the Kynges Attorney Jamys Hobart; for all hys dysease is but an ache in hys knees. ... But when ye send me the playster ye must send me wryghty*ng* hough it shold be leyd to *and* takyn from hys knee, and hough longe it shold abyd on hys kne unremevyd, and hough longe the playster wyll laste good, and whethyr he must lape eny more clothys a-bowte the playster to kepe it warme or nought.[14]

It is striking that Paston writes from his location among more elite court circles to seek out the medical expertise of his Norfolk home. In this, he perhaps echoes the perspective of his mother, who wrote to John Paston I in 1464, 'fore Goddys sake be ware what medesynys ye take of any fysissyanys of London. I schal neuer trust to hem.'[15] John Paston II requests from his wife not only the poultice itself but also written instructions of considerable detail. Thus, the letter shows how, in one case at least, the medical knowledge of a gentry woman would have found occasion to be written down. Medical expertise also took a more bookish form in the Paston household. The 'litel boke of fisik' written by the professional scribe William Ebesham, most likely for the Pastons, consists of Middle English texts about uroscopy, the plague and astrology juxtaposed with roughly equivalent Latin versions.[16] This book, with its doubling of Latin and Middle English expertise, poses interesting questions about how it might have found its place among the literate interests and healing practices of the Paston family.

While there are no entirely Latin medical texts in the Lincoln manuscript, Thornton's version of the *Liber* does incorporate a number of Latin recipes as well as the text of a Latin mass for the treatment for epilepsy and Latin charms

---

bailiff and medical practitioner in Essex, named John Crophill. For an account of Crophill, see J. K. Mustain, 'A Rural Medical Practitioner in Fifteenth-Century England', *Bulletin of the History of Medicine* 46 (1972), 469–76.

[14] The letter was written between 1487 and 1495: *Paston Letters and Papers of the Fifteenth Century*, ed. N. Davis, R. Beadle and C. Richmond, 3 vols., EETS SS 20, 21, 22 (Oxford, 2004–5), I, 628.

[15] Ibid., I, 291.

[16] The manuscript is Boston, Countway Medical Library, MS 19. For the link to the Paston family, see C. Jones, 'Discourse Communities and Medical Texts', in *Medical and Scientific Writing in Late Medieval English*, ed. I. Taavitsainen and P. Pahta (Cambridge, 2004), pp. 23–36 (p. 33). For more on the manuscript, see M. P. Harley, 'The Middle English Contents of a Fifteenth-Century Medical Book', *Mediaevalia* 8 (1982), 171–88.

'for the tethe' and for childbirth.[17] Such mixing of Latin and vernacular was very typical of medical texts in late medieval England. The Lincoln *Liber* is also typical in the spectrum of medical authorities to which it refers. In addition to the twenty *probatur* statements attributed to the Rector of Oswaldkirk, another is ascribed to 'Magistrum William de Excestre', and still another to 'Ser Apilton', plausibly supposed by Margaret Ogden to be William Appleton (d. 1381), a Minorite friar who served as physician to John of Gaunt.[18] The recipe attributed to 'Apilton' is indeed of the most complicated and expensive variety, bearing out differences between elite care for the aristocracy and the more workaday remedies that fill most of the *Liber*. Two other remedies are proved by 'Ypocras' (Hippocrates), and 'Ypocras' and 'Plinius' are each mentioned in the fragments of the herbal found after the *Liber*.[19] The evidence of the Paston household and Thornton's *Book* together confirms that – in the eyes of provincial patients – local clerics, classical authorities, urban physicians and surgeons, and household practitioners occupied distinct positions in the constellation of medical authority.

Medicine's new popularity in the course of the fifteenth century generated relatively little 'meta-discourse' – that is, little theoretical or polemical comment on the spread of medical information and expertise.[20] It is correspondingly difficult to locate medicine's changing accessibility within a precise matrix of social, cultural or intellectual significance. Unable to draw on explicit statements of value, scholars have looked instead to records of behaviour and practice and to attitudes expressed implicitly in textual and material artefacts. Another challenge facing the field is the overall heterogeneity of medical writings, which means that comprehensive attempts to explain medicine's dissemination have tended to be overly general or to address only one aspect of medicine's textualization. The most effective approaches to understanding the late medieval valuation of medical knowledge – valuation expressed for instance in Thornton's decision to copy the *Liber* and include it in his Lincoln codex – would

---

[17] For references, see *The 'Liber de Diversis Medicinis' in the Thornton Manuscript (MS. Lincoln Cathedral A.5.2)*, ed. M. S. Ogden, EETS OS 207 (Oxford, 1938), p. xxiii n. 1.

[18] Ibid., p. xiv. For more on Appleton, see R. F. Green, 'Friar William Appleton and the Date of Langland's B Text', *Yearbook of Langland Studies* 11 (1997), 87–96.

[19] *The 'Liber de Diversis Medicinis'*, ed. Ogden, p. xvi.

[20] For instance, it provoked much less meta-discourse than Middle English devotional and theological writings, the object of extensive comment, debate and polemic. English medicine also seems to have been less frequently discussed than its continental counterparts: in Paris, for instance, a medical faculty eager to defend its authority found numerous occasions to articulate academic ideals and disparage vernacular rivals. The best sources for medicine's 'meta-discourse' in England are translators' prologues; the 1421 physicians' petition to Parliament and the records of the short-lived 1423 'comminalte' of London physicians and surgeons; and original English surgical writings, particularly when they discuss deontology, or the behaviour proper to a surgeon.

seem to be piecemeal, examining different 'families' of texts, readers and institutions. For instance, there has been excellent scholarship on insular surgery,[21] on the transmission and translation of guides to blood-letting[22] and on medieval English hospitals.[23] Much remains to be done, however, before these respective areas of medical learning and practice are placed accurately in their relations to one another. In the meantime, localizing strategies for the study of English medicine register the fact that patients, practitioners and readers sought out medical knowledge according to an especially wide range of expectations and needs.

The Lincoln manuscript's three text-types

There are perhaps three models of late medieval medical writing relevant to Thornton's Lincoln codex: remedy books; 'medical and scientific books'; and household miscellanies. I discuss each of these in turn below, along with the hypothetical position of each in the sequence of the manuscript's production.

It is reasonable to suppose that Thornton's *Liber* was originally intended to be a self-contained textual object. As John J. Thompson has shown, the nineteen bifolia that originally constituted the full remedy collection were all gathered together into one out-size quire, and its first half was foliated with roman numerals according to its stand-alone status. The high number of pages in the quire is remarkable, and no other gathering in Thornton's two books is so large. Its original length of thirty-eight pages suggests that Thornton thought differently about the *Liber* than he did about the narrative and religious materials he was copying. This part of the manuscript also lacks the red ink Thornton used for rubrication and emphasis within the literary and devotional portions of the Lincoln manuscript. The *mise-en-page*, with marginal headings for the remedies and headlines (used irregularly) to designate ailments, contributes to the visual distinctiveness of the *Liber* (see Figure 1).

Thompson notes that the paper constituting the *Liber*'s gathering was 'manufactured on a single pair of moulds, whose watermark type … does not appear

---

[21] For instance, see any of P. M. Jones's excellent articles on the English surgeon John of Arderne, e.g., 'Four Middle English Translations of John of Arderne', in *Latin and Vernacular: Studies in Late-Medieval Texts and Manuscripts*, ed. A. J. Minnis (Cambridge, 1989), pp. 61–89. See also T. R. Beck, *The Cutting Edge: The Early History of the Surgeons of London* (London, 1974).

[22] L. E. Voigts and M. R. McVaugh, 'A Latin Technical Phlebotomy and Its Middle English Translation', *Transactions of the American Philosophical Society* 74 (1984), 1–69.

[23] C. Rawcliffe, *Medicine for the Soul: The Life, Death and Resurrection of an English Medieval Hospital, St Giles's, Norwich, c. 1249–1550* (Stroud, 1999); and C. Rawcliffe, *The Hospitals of Medieval Norwich* (Norwich, 1995). See also S. Sweetinburgh, *The Role of the Hospital in Medieval England: Gift-Giving and the Spiritual Economy* (Dublin, 2004).

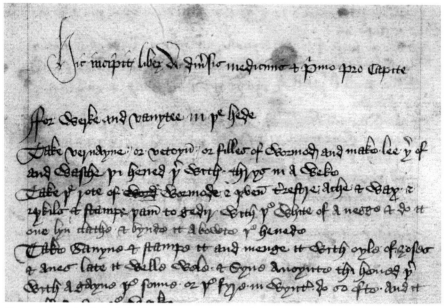

Figure 1. Lincoln Cathedral Library, MS 91, fol. 280r (incipit to the *Liber de Diversis Medicinis*)

elsewhere in either the Lincoln or the London MS'.[24] Ralph Hanna III observes that this paper stock 'is of a type which would have been available from 1413 on; in contrast, the remainder of Thornton's papers, insofar as they are datable, suggests that the scribe's main work was in the period roughly 1430–49 or perhaps slightly later'.[25] This leads Hanna to speculate that Thornton's medical writing 'may well be much older than the remainder of the manuscript and indeed Thornton's first essay at copying'.[26] All in all, it appears that Thornton copied the *Liber* at some remove from his romance and devotional materials, most likely before them, and that the large quire originally formed a distinctive entity – 'tailor made', as Thompson puts it, 'for the purpose of containing a single medical compilation'.[27]

[24] J. J. Thompson, 'Textual *Lacunae* and the Importance of Manuscript Evidence: Robert Thornton's Copy of the *Liber de Diversis Medicinis*', *Transactions of the Cambridge Bibliographic Society* 8 (1982), 270–5 (p. 273).

[25] R. Hanna III, 'The Growth of Robert Thornton's Books', *Studies in Bibliography* 40 (1987), 51–61 (pp. 58–9).

[26] Ibid., p. 58. But cf. Keiser's chapter in the present volume, which argues that the *Liber* may have been copied 'at about the same time as [Thornton] was copying works that appear in the latter part of the London manuscript' (p. 92).

[27] Thompson, 'Textual *Lacunae*', p. 273.

In this stage of its production, when Thornton's *Liber de Diversis Medi-cinis* can be plausibly supposed to be self-contained, the most relevant model for understanding its textual and codicological identity would seem to be the remedy book. For the purposes of this chapter, I use 'remedy book' to designate an assemblage of smaller textual units focused on the treatment of symptoms, the largest portion of which are medical recipes; it may also include prognostic aids, simple surgical instructions, charms, prayers and the like – as the *Liber* does.[28] England is notable for having what is probably Europe's oldest tradi-tion of vernacular remedy books. The Anglo-Saxon *Leechbook of Bald* survives from the first half of the ninth century, and Anglo-Saxon recipes and charms were still being copied in the early twelfth century. Anglo-Norman remedy collections appeared in the mid twelfth century and became more prevalent in the thirteenth century.[29] Meanwhile two important and enduringly popular Anglo-Latin medical compendia were assembled, both of which were later vernacularized: Gilbertus Anglicus's *Compendium medicinae* (c. 1240) and John of Gaddesden's *Rosa medicinae* (1305–1317). In the fourteenth century, Middle English collections began to be seen, taking off with alacrity in the latter half of the century.

Because remedy books are by their nature modular and accretive, their contents changed according to the needs and interests of copyists, even as particular recipes circulated with stability over centuries. The earliest known version of the Middle English *Liber de Diversis Medicinis* is from around 1330, roughly a hundred years before Thornton made his copy.[30] It is unsurprising that Thornton's copy has numerous elements not found in the earliest version. For instance, by the time Thornton transcribed the *Liber*, the text of a Latin mass had been incorporated among the treatments for epilepsy (fol. 296r–v), and the Middle English translation of John of Burgundy's plague treatise was interpolated among other cures (fols. 300v–302r). John of Burgundy's was by far the most frequently copied plague text in medieval England, and its shorter Middle English version survives in 'more than forty' manuscripts.[31] The pres-

---

[28] I use 'remedy book', 'remedy collection' and 'recipe collection' interchangeably.

[29] T. Hunt, *Popular Medicine in Thirteenth-Century England* (Cambridge, 1990), p. 25. Also see M. Green, 'Salerno on the Thames: The Genesis of Anglo-Norman Medical Literature', in *Language and Culture in Medieval Britain: The French of England, c. 1100–c. 1500*, ed. J. Wogan-Browne, with C. Collette, M. Kowaleski, L. Mooney, A. Putter and D. Trotter (York, 2009), pp. 220–33.

[30] Keiser, 'Robert Thornton's *Liber de Diversis Medicinis*', p. 39. The text appears in Cambridge, Corpus Christi College, MS 388, fols. 36r–48v, and printed in *Three Receptaria from Medieval England: The Languages of Medicine in the Fourteenth Century*, ed. T. Hunt and M. Benskin, Medium Ævum Monographs n.s. 21 (Oxford, 2001), pp. 159–92.

[31] L. M. Matheson, '*Médecin sans frontières?* The European Dissemination of John of Burgundy's Plague Treatise', *American Notes and Queries* 18 (2005), 17–28 (p. 22).

ence of the plague treatise no doubt helped to bolster the *Liber's* desirability for a late medieval household like Thornton's.

Remedy collections proliferated alongside other medical writings during the period of medical vernacularization, but the genre also appears to have occupied a somewhat different position than did other medical text-types. The remedy book has strong connections to genres like commonplace books and household *Fachprosa*, including culinary instruction, estate management and courtesy books. Remedy books' porousness to instructions that are not strictly medical meant that they sometimes lost their focus on healing in the process of their transmission.

At some point, Thornton brought together his copy of the *Liber* with the vernacular herbal that follows it. Little evidence survives for determining when this happened: no watermarks are recoverable from the fragments,[32] and although no red ink of the sort used in Lincoln's romance and devotional sections is visible, it is not possible to conclude it was entirely absent from the lost text. Nonetheless, since the *Liber's* exceptional quire size suggests that it was meant to stand alone, one suspects that the herbal joined it at a moment subsequent to the remedy book's original construction. The Rawlinson copy of the *Liber de Diversis Medicinis*, written by John Rede from the common Pickering exemplar, does not include the same herbal – which at least does not contradict the hypothesis that Thornton copied the herbal at a different time, from a different exemplar.

By way of some ingenious detective work, Keiser has identified the basic text of Thornton's herbal. It is a hybrid made up of parts of the versified *Tretys of Diverse Herbis* together with elements of a prose translation of the Macer herbal. While it is impossible to know the original scale of Thornton's text, Keiser speculates that his source may have approached the comprehensiveness of the Macer translation in London, BL, MS Sloane 1571, 'which has more than two hundred entries'.[33] While its scale is uncertain, the herbal's 'likely comprehensiveness'[34] indicates that it might have been a substantial counterpart to the *Liber*. In uniting these two texts, Thornton had the makings of a 'litel boke of fisik' not dissimilar from the one likely made for the Paston household and the sort owned by many others in late medieval England.

At this (admittedly hypothetical) phase of Thornton's book production,

---

[32] Though Hanna states that both the *Liber* and the subsequent herbal are 'on a single unique paper-stock', his summary of the manuscript's production data in fact does not indicate an identifiable paper stock for quire 17 (the herbal) ('The Growth', pp. 58, 54). I have been unable to find other references positing or assuming the identification of the fragments' paper stock.

[33] G. R. Keiser, 'Reconstructing Robert Thornton's Herbal', *Medium Ævum* 65 (1996), 35–53 (p. 49).

[34] Ibid., p. 50.

when the *Liber* and herbal were brought together as an autonomous codicological unit, the most relevant model for the resulting text would seem to be that of the 'scientific and medical book'. Expertly documented by Linda Voigts, this is perhaps the most important 'family' of manuscripts relevant to understanding medicine's popularization in the fourteenth and fifteenth centuries. Voigts describes a pattern of late medieval English book-making that is thematically and codicologically distinct from 'belletristic, theological, philosophical, chronicle, legal, pedagogical and household manuscripts'.[35] These compendia began to appear around 1375 and drew from a common set of discourses both in Latin and the vernacular – most notably, medicine, astrology, pharmacology, alchemy, geometry, weights and measures and, occasionally, agriculture. Voigts estimates that 'more than 1,000 manuscripts that fit the definition ... survive from late medieval England'.[36] In addition to the distinctive time frame of their production (1375–1500) and their standard range of textual materials, these books share a number of other features: 'compilation from booklets; dependence on visual materials; and common use of English'.[37]

However, in a further stage of Thornton's treatment of his medical writings, he overrode the model of the medical book. In deciding to bring the remedy book and herbal together with narrative and devotional texts, Thornton abandoned the modest booklet form of the remedy collection as well as the ascendant model of the 'medical and scientific book'. What he made instead is something closer to an ambitious household miscellany. In his analysis of the manuscript of Humphrey Newton (1466–1536), a Cheshire gentleman, Hanna notes that the oldest segment of Newton's miscellany is a quire of professionally copied medical texts. Hanna adduces Thornton's Lincoln manuscript as 'the best analogy' for Newton's, and on the basis of these two manuscripts as well the 'codicology of several prominent examples', Hanna offers a more general 'theory of the production of domestic manuscripts'. Namely, he writes, 'the impulse to book production begins with the thoroughly practical. ... And literary production seems to be superadded upon that practical basis'.[38] In Thornton's case, the literary production that perhaps grew from his medical writings was especially organized and ambitious.

Julia Boffey and John J. Thompson characterize such collections of *domestitia* as typical of provincial book producers, whose efforts are 'directed either wholly

---

[35]   L. E. Voigts, 'Scientific and Medical Books', in *Book Production and Publishing in Britain, 1375–1475*, ed. J. Griffiths and D. Pearsall, Cambridge Studies in Publishing and Printing History (Cambridge, 1989), pp. 345–402 (p. 351).

[36]   Ibid., p. 353.

[37]   Ibid., p. 386.

[38]   R. Hanna III, 'Humphrey Newton and Bodleian Library, MS Lat. misc. C.66', *Medium Ævum* 69 (2000), 279–91 (p. 283).

or in part by the suitability of the material available for family readership'.[39] As a rule, the miscellaneous composition of these books is an index both of the sundry desires of household audiences and of the unpredictable availability of texts for copying. As Hanna writes, 'a combination of happenstance acquisition and variously motivated selection is quite typical of a large range of Middle English manuscript books'.[40] Thornton, however, shows himself to have been capable of accessing a remarkably large number of texts. The thoughtfulness with which the texts are arranged is distinct from the accidental ordering of many commonplace books. Moreover, Thornton's decision to separate secular and devotional materials from the outset indicates his confidence in having had such ready access to texts.[41] In Thornton's case, then, the broad swathe of contents would seem to have less to do with any erratic austerity of textual circulation and more to do with a specific vision for the scope of knowledge a codex might hold.

Medicine in mixed manuscripts

How idiosyncratic was Thornton's vision for his book? When I first embarked on my research for this chapter, I planned to gather a set of contemporary manuscripts that, like the Lincoln manuscript, included secular narratives in Middle English alongside remedy collections. I would compare these manuscripts with Thornton's to isolate what was distinctive in Thornton's treatment of different genres and discourses. I assumed it would not be hard to populate such a set of manuscripts because of the remarkably high number of recipe collections that survive from the fifteenth century. It is by far the most common genre among informational texts in the vernacular.[42] Moreover,

---

[39] J. Boffey and J. J. Thompson, 'Anthologies and Miscellanies: Production and Choice of Texts', in *Book Production*, ed. Griffiths and Pearsall, pp. 279–315 (p. 297).

[40] R. Hanna III, 'Miscellaneity and Vernacularity: Conditions of Literary Production in Late Medieval England', in *The Whole Book: Cultural Perspectives on the Medieval Miscellany*, ed. S. G. Nicholas and S. Wenzel (Ann Arbor, 1996), pp. 37–51 (p. 47).

[41] Keiser, 'Lincoln Cathedral Library MS. 91', p. 177.

[42] The catalogue of Old and Middle English scientific and medical writings prepared by L. E. Voigts and P. D. Kurtz, which includes entries from more than 1200 surviving codices, allows for proportional comparisons across genres. Instances of recipe groupings (minimally three recipes in the same hand) number 2500. The next most numerous category, 'alchemy', has well fewer than half the witnesses (about 1000). See Voigts, 'Multitudes', pp. 191–2. The database is available as a CD-ROM, *Scientific and Medical Writings in Old and Middle English: An Electronic Reference* (Ann Arbor, 2000) and in an expanded version online at *Voigts-Kurtz Search Program*, University of Missouri-Kansas City, http//cctr1.umkc.edu/cgi-bin/search. The total number of codices (1200+) is cited from the introduction to the CD-ROM.

as I noted above, recipe collections tend not to have the discursive exclusivity of other medieval medical genres and instead shade into works of household management. If, as Hanna suggests, 'household necessity involves gentry with books' and literary production perchance follows,[43] remedy collections would sometimes have acted as the seeds for more literary compilations. I supposed that with a little sifting through catalogues and handlists, I would have an ample stock for comparison.

Thus, one of the surprising aspects of my research has been the discovery of how rarely surviving compendia from late medieval England include both romances and medical texts – or at least medical texts of any real scope. There are plenty of examples of small groups of recipes appearing in the margins and fly-leaves of manuscripts with literary materials, or as filler at the ends of pages or quires – as with the three charms for toothache that Thornton records on fol. 176r–v at the end of Lincoln's romance section (arts. 22–4). These can hardly be said to play a role similar to that of the *Liber* and the herbal, however. Given the paucity of similar contemporary books, might there be something rather old-fashioned about the capaciousness of Thornton's compilation? Household miscellanies from a century and a half earlier, like Oxford, Bodleian Library, MS Digby 86, do include similar ranges of contents. MS Digby 86 includes the Anglo-Norman remedy collection *Lettre d'Hippocrate*, of twelve folios, along-side romances, fabliaux and devotional texts. The Digby manuscript, however, does not show anything like Thornton's self-consciousness regarding generic and discursive distinctions.

One promising foil to Thornton's book appeared to be Aberystwyth, NLW, MS Brogyntyn II.1 (*olim* Porkington 10), completed around the year 1470.[44] The household miscellany contains an especially diverse range of materials, including literary texts like the romance *Syre Gawene and the Carle of Carelyle*, the prose *Siege of Jerusalem* and religious and love lyrics. It also encompasses such medical materials as a guide to blood-letting, prognostication and calendric aids and medical recipes. However, the phlebotomy and prognostication texts appear only in the first quire, a gathering of ten folios featuring ten hands that appear nowhere else in the manuscript. This first quire, it seems, was tacked on to the twenty-six quires that follow, which were planned and edited by a single scribe who managed and directed others.[45] The only medical materials that appear within these quires are eighteen recipes in two hands, added as filler at the end of the eleventh quire. In other words, what looked like it might indeed

---

[43] Hanna, 'Humphrey Newton', p. 283.

[44] D. Huws, 'MS Porkington 10 and Its Scribes', in *Romance Reading on the Book: Essays on Medieval Narrative Presented to Maldwyn Mills*, ed. J. Fellows, R. Field, G. Rogers and J. Weiss (Cardiff, 1996), pp. 188–207 (p. 202).

[45] Ibid., pp. 198–9.

be a deliberately organized household miscellany with substantial medical writings turns out to have a more contingent and cursory relation to its texts of healing. Gisela Guddat-Figge notes another apparently incidental conjunction of romance and remedy: in Cambridge, Trinity College, MS O.2.13, a collection of Middle English medical tracts and recipes, a fragment of *Bevis of Hampton* was copied on the final, originally blank leaves: 'After six pages, however, the scribe grew weary of his task and left the last leaf unused'.[46]

Despite my difficulty in identifying manuscripts similar to Thornton's, at least one fifteenth-century book *does* appear to echo the deliberate planning, the thematic divisions and the inclusion of substantial medical and literary materials that characterize the Lincoln manuscript. In a 2003 essay Keiser notes the fact that the medical texts found in London, BL, MS Sloane 3489 belonged to the fifteenth-century English manuscript partially reconstructed in 1966 by Kathleen L. Smith (now Kathleen L. Scott).[47] Subsequent to Keiser's article, Scott provided a revised reconstruction and re-evaluation of this manuscript, which she judged to have been commercially produced by a team of at least three scribes. The scribes followed 'an obvious plan from the outset to make the miscellany of texts look as much alike as possible'.[48] The contents are entirely in Middle English and secular in content, leading Scott to suppose that 'the volume was originally made up to suit the needs of a household, some of whose members were literate, if not clerical', and that this household, as Keiser had previously suggested, was of the provincial gentry.[49] The book is now divided among ten different manuscripts held in the Bodleian Library and the British Library. For convenience I will here refer to the original compendium as the 'Rawlinson-Sloane' manuscript.[50]

The similarities between the Lincoln manuscript and the Rawlinson-Sloane manuscript are striking. Both compendia are relatively long (at least 237 folios in Rawlinson-Sloane, at least 321 in Lincoln) and were written on paper in the middle of the fifteenth century. They may have shared an audience, the provincial gentry household. Both manuscripts are thematically organized and thereby register in their physical structure an awareness of generic and

[46] G. Guddat-Figge, *Catalogue of Manuscripts Containing Middle English Romances* (Munich, 1976), p. 25.

[47] G. R. Keiser, 'Two Medieval Plague Treatises and Their Afterlife in Early Modern England', *Journal of the History of Medicine* 58 (2003), 292–324. For the original reconstruction, see K. L. Smith, 'A Fifteenth-Century Vernacular Manuscript Reconstructed', *Bodleian Library Record* 7 (1966), 235–41.

[48] K. L. Scott, 'Newly Discovered Booklets from a Reconstructed Middle English Manuscript', in *Regional Manuscripts 1200–1700*, ed. A. S. G. Edwards, English Manuscript Studies 1100–1700, vol. 14 (London, 2008), pp. 112–29 (p. 120).

[49] Ibid., p. 122.

[50] See ibid., p. 115, on Thomas Rawlinson's likely dismantling of the original manuscript to make part of it available to Sir Hans Sloane.

discursive distinctions. In Rawlinson-Sloane, these thematic sections are as follows: a didactic and moralistic unit; a historical unit ('Here beginneth a tretis compiled oute of diuerse cronicles'); a sequence of narrative and literary works; a sequence of 'functional and informative' texts, first on hunting and hawking and then on medicine; and finally a religious text, the confessional guide *Manuale curatorum*. Rawlinson-Sloane shares two texts with Lincoln: the *Awntyrs off Arthure* (art. 20) and John of Burgundy's plague treatise;[51] it shares one text with the London manuscript: Lydgate's *Dietary*.

In Rawlinson-Sloane, the medical materials fill fifty-one folios and include five items: a compilation of recipes for medicines, plasters and salves, entitled 'the tretees of Phisik that ffrere Randolf made' (fols. 1r–5v); a collection of sundry medicinal waters as well as an incomplete regimen (fols. 7–10); a version of the *Agnus castus* herbal in Middle English (fols. 12r–28r); a surgical text written in the form of a dialogue, largely translated from the *Practica chirurgica* of Roger of Parma (fols. 29r–42r); and a Middle English translation of the longer version of John of Burgundy's plague tract, attributed to 'A master of diuinite of the ordre of ffrere prechoures, Master Thomas Multon of diuerse Doctours of Phisik' (fols. 44r–51r).[52] At a glance, it is clear that the medical writings of Lincoln and Rawlinson-Sloane share interests in medicinal recipes, herbal lore and the plague.

The medical portion of the Rawlinson-Sloane manuscript is exceptional in its searching attitude toward the status of medical knowledge itself. Keiser has drawn attention to the uniquely moralistic bent of the plague treatise attrib- uted to 'Master Thomas Multon', which alone among Middle English medical texts begins by designating 'plague as divine retribution for sin'.[53] The redac- tion's unusual mingling of religious and medical explanations has a parallel in the dialogue on surgery that precedes it. The dialogue, unfolding between two 'brothers', is an engaging device to present the translated surgery, but at its outset it deviates from its straightforwardly informational content. One 'brother' asks the other about the very idea of medicine's usefulness:

> Brother, seth thou sayst that God sendeth men syknes and helth hem aftirward
> when Hym liketh, wherto shuld eny man studien in lechecraft syth God, yf Hym

---

[51] However, Rawlinson-Sloane contained the long version of the plague treatise, and Lincoln the shorter version. On the different versions, see Matheson, '*Médecin sans frontières?*', pp. 19–24.

[52] 'Thesaurus Pauperum: An Edition of B.M., M.S. Sloane 3489, a Fifteenth Century Medical Miscellany, with Introduction, Notes and Glossary', ed. P. A. Cant (unpublished Ph.D. dissertation, University of London, 1973), pp. 250–1.

[53] 'This cultural construction of plague was common in moral writings and sermons from the time of the Black Death. It is, however, unprecedented in the various forms of the John of Burgundy treatise, the only vernacular plague treatise in circulation through most of fifteenth- century England'; Keiser, 'Two Medieval Plague Treatises', p. 301.

liketh, may hele a man wythout leches, and yf He wyl that a man be nat heled, trauayle of leches nys but in vayne?[54]

In effect the speaker is asking what is the purpose, what is the good, of medical knowledge. In light of God's omnipotence, how is one to understand the utility of 'lechecraft'? More broadly, how does one resolve the differing accounts of knowledge and agency offered by medicine and religion? These questions asked explicitly in the dialogue are raised implicitly by the very shapes of Lincoln and Rawlinson-Sloane. Their wide-ranging contents would have required readers to decide when and how to use their different generic sections. As a practical matter, what are the distinctions in how one interprets and uses such a book's several parts? Do romance, religion and medicine have anything to say to one another? Their material unity in these manuscripts suggests that they do.

The Rawlinson-Sloane texts wrestle more explicitly and directly than those in Lincoln with the uncertain place of medicine in late medieval England. Yet both manuscripts manifest exceptional sensitivity to a system of knowledge encompassing literary, religious and practical discourses. Modern scholars, in trying to reconstruct the specific desires that motivated the production of vernacular medical texts for non-specialist audiences, run up against the same sort of puzzle embedded in John Trevisa's well-known translator's prologue, a dialogue between lord and clerk. The clerk argues that there is little point in translating Ranulf Higden's *Polychronicon* into English because 'Hit nedith not that alle siche know the cronicles'. The lord answers that, while it is not neces-sary in the strict sense that 'mete and drinke nedith for kepyng and sustynaunce of lyf', nonetheless, in a broader sense, 'al that is profitable nedith, and so for to speke all men nedith to knowe the cronicles'.[55] The modern reader is left wondering precisely what being 'profitable' entails. Similarly, one wonders about the 'profit' of the *Liber* within the Lincoln codex. Thornton's book-making real-izes a singular vision for how the resources of practical knowledge and literary imagination could serve a community of readers. Among the tasks facing the modern scholar is recovering the fullest sense of the utility and interest, the 'nede' and the 'profit', that motivated such labours of textual production.

[54] 'Thesaurus Pauperum', ed. Cant, p. 159.

[55] John Trevisa, 'Dialogue Between the Lord and Clerk on Translation', in *The Idea of the Vernacular: An Anthology of Middle English Literary Theory, 1280–1520*, ed. J. Wogan-Browne, N. Watson, A. Taylor and R. Evans (University Park PA, 1999), pp. 132–3.

Lydgate's Dietary[56]

My final contribution to a consideration of Thornton's medical writings is to reflect on his inclusion of John Lydgate's *Dietary* among the contents of the London manuscript, where it survives as a fragment. The poem begins imperfectly on fol. 97r with the line 'Be noghte hasty nore sodanly vengeable', apparently lacking the first seventeen lines. Lydgate's *Verses on the Kings of England* (art. 15) ends in the middle of a stanza on fol. 96v, and Thompson plausibly concludes that one leaf is missing between them.[57] The *Dietary* is followed by three Latin aphorisms and then the first four lines of a unique poem that also ends abruptly (arts. 17–20), another leaf apparently lacking.[58] As mentioned above, the *Dietary* is Lydgate's translation of an anonymous fifteenth-century Latin poem, the *Dietarium*, which is based in part on the widespread thirteenth-century medical poem the *Regimen sanitatis Salernitanum*.[59]

It turns out that Lydgate's *Dietary* was remarkably appealing to late medieval and early modern readers. It survives in fifty-six manuscript copies – 'topping everything in popularity', as A. S. G. Edwards writes.[60] Rossell Hope Robbins notes that among Middle English verse texts, only the *Prick of Conscience*, the *Canterbury Tales*, *Piers Plowman* and the *Confessio Amantis* survive in more copies.[61] The poem's wide circulation is indeed worth querying. While I do

---

[56] It was not until the present chapter was in revision that I encountered J. W. Morrissey's learned and extremely helpful 2011 Ph.D. dissertation '"Termes of Phisik"' (see note 1 above). My understanding of the *Dietary*'s circulation benefitted from being checked against Morrissey's 'Working Handlist of the Manuscripts Containing Lydgate's *Dietary*' (pp. 261–301).

[57] Thompson, *London Thornton MS*, p. 25. The *Dietary* frequently circulated adjacent to Lydgate's historical poem *Verses on the Kings of England*. (*Stans Puer ad Mensam* was another frequent companion.) Including Thornton's copy, the *Dietary* appears next to or close by *Verses* in twelve manuscripts: Oxford, Bodleian Library, MS Bodley 686, MS Bodley 912 and MS Lat. Theol. d. 15; Oxford, Jesus College, MS Q. G. 8; London, BL, MS Additional 31042, MS Additional 34360, MS Cotton Titus D. xx and MS Harley 2251; Nottingham University Library, MS Mellish Lm 1; and Dublin, TCD, MS 516. Morrissey speculates that *Dietary* and *Verses*, along with *Stans Puer*, perhaps 'were available in fascicular collections for sale at commercial scriptoria' ('"Termes of Phisik"' 219).

[58] Thompson, *London Thornton MS*, pp. 25–6.

[59] Thornton's copy of the *Liber* includes two Latin lines from the *Regimen sanitatis Salernitanum*, with an interpolated line between them; see *The 'Liber de Diversis Medicinis'*, ed. Ogden, p. 11 and notes.

[60] A. S. G. Edwards, 'Lydgate Manuscripts: Some Directions for Future Research', in *Manuscripts and Readers in Fifteenth-Century England: The Literary Implications of Manuscript Study. Essays from the 1981 Conference at the University of York*, ed. D. Pearsall (Cambridge, 1983), pp. 15–26 (p. 15). The number of copies is cited from Morrissey, '"Termes of Phisik"', pp. 199–200.

[61] *Secular Lyrics of the XIVth and XVth Centuries*, ed. R. H. Robbins (Oxford, 1964), p. 251.

not have the space here to explore the full manuscript tradition, I offer some preliminary observations.

There are no codicological indications that Thornton considered the poem a work of medical writing. Unlike Thornton's distinctive treatment of the *Liber*, the *Dietary* is undifferentiated from the didactic poetry around it. However, the poem's transmission history makes clear that medicine *was* one of the discourses to which it belonged, or might belong, depending on manuscript context. The present chapter's analysis of Thornton's medical writing has sought thus far to describe medicine's distinctive role in a single codicological object. The *Dietary*, in a sense, reverses the operation: Lydgate's poem blends into its literary-didactic environs in the London manuscript, but its multiple manuscript versions attest to its potential to be recognized as distinctly medical. I show below that the *Dietary*'s circulation – sometimes as medicine, sometimes as moral exhortation, sometimes as literary art – illustrates medicine's discursive instability in fifteenth-century England, when its textual forms were available to be read and understood along alternative vectors of reception simultaneously. Just as Thornton's book instantiates recognition of both medicine's difference from other discourses and its place alongside them, Lydgate's poem helps to constitute and to blur the category of Middle English medicine.

The *Dietary* was copied and read as a representative of at least three different genres of Middle English writings. Two of these are familiarly Lydgatian. First, it was treated as a work of literary art and is frequently found in literary anthologies centred on Lydgate's writings or Lydgate's and Chaucer's.[62] Although its authorship is attested in only two witnesses,[63] the poem's regular company with other Lydgatian verse indicates that its authorial association was firm in the minds of contemporary audiences. The poem also circulated as a piece of moralistic didacticism, accompanying, for instance, Benedict Burgh's rendering of the *Distichs of Cato* – as it does in Rawlinson-Sloane.[64] In London, Lambeth Palace Library, MS 853, the *Dietary* appears among didactic texts apparently meant for children. In Oxford, Bodleian Library, MS Bodley 48, the *Dietary* was added in a later hand to a collection of moral prose and verse. It is the 'moralistic' atti-

[62] These manuscripts include Oxford, Bodleian Library, MS Bodley 686; MS Laud Misc. 683; MS Rawlinson C. 48; MS Rawlinson C. 86; Oxford, Jesus College, MS Q. G. 8; London, BL, MS Additional 34360; MS Harley 2251; MS Lansdowne 699; and Leiden University Library, MS Vossius Germ. Gall. Q. 9.

[63] Oxford, Bodleian Library, MS Bodley 686 and MS Rawlinson C. 48.

[64] The *Dietary* is found adjacent or close to Burgh's *Cato* in London, BL, MS Arundel 168; MS Harley 116; MS Royal 17 B.xlvii (just one stanza of *Cato*); Glasgow University Library, MS Hunterian 259; and Rome, English College, MS 1306.

tude toward the poem that best characterizes Thornton's treatment of it in the London manuscript, where it is followed by three Latin aphorisms.

The third tradition of the poem's circulation is within medical compilations. Thirteen of the poem's fifty-six witnesses appear within coherently medical and scientific manuscripts.[65] Lydgate's poem there appears in the company of Latin, Anglo-Norman and English medical writings, in verse and in prose. Neighbouring medical texts include recipes, charms, phlebotomies, uroscopies, prognostication aids, astrological charts, alchemical instructions, herbals, a treatise on the virtues of rosemary, a lapidary, plague tracts, mnemonics for the four humours and a Middle English poem on embryology.

Lydgate's poem itself cannily performs the passage of medical knowledge from a specialized sphere into a more generalized realm of moral didacticism and poetic wisdom. The first stanza provides a kind of medical 'hook', seeming to establish the poem on straightforwardly medical grounds:

> For helth of body kover from cold thyne hede;
> Ete non rawe mete, – take gode hede therto;
> Drynk holsom wyne; fede þe on lyght brede;
> And with thyne appetite ryse from thy dyner also;
> With women aged fleschely haue not a-do;
> Vppon thy slepe drynke not of the kuppe;
> Gladde toward bedde, at morow both two,
> And vse neuer late for to suppe. (lines 1–8)[66]

The *Dietary* invites its audience into the poem for the sake of 'helth of body', and the reader embarks amid the typical precepts of medical regimens. These tend to advise thoughtfulness and moderation in managing the quotidian factors that influence health, systematized in medieval medical theory as the six 'non-naturals': 'the first is the air which surrounds the body. Then follow food and drink, exercise and rest, sleep and waking, fasting and fullness, and finally affections of the mind.'[67] These elements of everyday life were the proper territory of *physic*, or learned medicine, and elite physicians would tailor their advice

---

[65] The medical manuscripts are: Oxford, Bodleian Library, MS e Musaeo 52; MS Additional B. 60; Cambridge, Fitzwilliam Museum, MS 261; Cambridge, Trinity College, MS O.2.13; London, BL, MS Harley 5401, MS Sloane 775, MS Sloane 989, MS Sloane 3534; London, Lambeth Palace Library, MS 444; London, Wellcome Library, MS 406, MS 411, MS 8004; Edinburgh, NLS, Advocates' MS 23. 7. 11; Bethesda MD, U.S. National Library of Medicine, MS 514; and Dublin, TCD, MS 537.

[66] I cite the poem's first two stanzas from Sloane 3534 ('Kleinere mittelenglische Texte', ed. Förster, pp. 182–4), because the *Dietary*'s first stanzas are unfortunately missing from the London manuscript. H. N. MacCracken prints an expanded twenty-one-stanza version that survives in only two manuscripts; see J. Lydgate, *The Minor Poems of John Lydgate I–II*, ed. H. N. MacCracken, 2 vols., EETS OS 107, 192 (London, 1911–34), II, 702–7.

[67] Quoted from the *Isagoge* of Johannitius, a foundational text in medieval medical education,

to the humoral disposition of each patient. However, the *Dietarium*, which is the basis of Lydgate's poem, seeks to be generally applicable, for instance by leaving aside even the broad humoral distinctions of the *Regimen sanitatis Salernitanum*, which tailors its advice for sanguine, choleric, phlegmatic and melancholic types, respectively. The poem's generality might have contributed to the 'mass' appeal of the Middle English version.

While the first stanza is focused on physical factors with physical effects, the second stanza opens the poem to wider discursive territory:

> Yff so be, that leches don the faile,
> Than take hede to vse thynges thre:
> Moderat diet, moderat trauayle,
> Not malicious for non aduersite;
> Meke in troubull, gladde in poverte,
> Ryche with lityll, content with suffisaunce,
> Neuer grucchyng, myry like thy degre.
> Yff phisik lakke, make þis þi gouernaunce. (lines 9–16)

If 'leches', or medical practitioners, fail you, make this poem your rule. The second stanza promises to replace specialized medical expertise with the poem's own guidelines for self-govern . The advice here turns blandly proverbial, encompassing such truisms as   kness in adversity, cheer in poverty and so on. The *if/then* syntax of the stanza's first two lines and last line emphasizes the verses' ability to fulfil the function of learned medicine, despite the fact that the poem's subject matter wanders away from a focus on the body.[68]

The remaining eight stanzas continue this pattern, oscillating from primarily physical advice, with physical consequences, to ethical and spiritual precepts:

> Fyre at the morne and towarde bede at even,
> Agayne mystes and blake ayere of pestylence
> Be tymly at messe þou schall the bettir cheve
> Firste at thi rysynge to do to God reverence. (fol. 97r; lines 129–32)[69]

Rising early for Mass will dispense with the mists, miasmas and pestilential air thought to cause fever and plague. Numerous witnesses of Lydgate's poem survive in manuscripts that also include the *Doctrine of Pestilence* (Lydgate's short poem on the plague) or a version of John of Burgundy's plague tract. Such

excerpted and translated in *A Source Book in Medieval Science*, ed. E. Grant (Cambridge MA, 1974), pp. 705–15 (p. 711).

[68] On the occasional antagonism between vernacular poetry and vernacular medical expertise, see J. Orlemanski, 'Jargon and the Matter of Medicine in Middle English', *Journal of Medieval and Early Modern Studies* 42 (2012), 395–420.

[69] Citations here are directly from the manuscript. Line numbers refer to the parallel passages in Lydgate, *The Minor Poems*, ed. MacCracken, II, pp. 702–7.

textual neighbours recall the context of actual medical urgency and physical need in which these verses exercised their appeal. Plague tended to be treated very differently in medical and religious writings respectively, but Lydgate's poem effaces the distinctions between them (not unlike the plague treatise of 'Master Thomas Multon', discussed above). It does not separate the priorities of body and soul, much less set them into hierarchical opposition. Instead, it articulates an account of self-governance in which physical, social and spiritual goods are inseparable from one another. The final stanza makes the point explicitly:

> Thus in two thynges standes alle the welthe,
> Of soule and Body who so liste thaym sewe
> Moderate fude ȝeuethe to a man his helthe,
> And alle surfettes dothe fro theym remewe
> And charite to þe soule es dewe.
> This resceyte boehte es of no poticarye,
> Of maister antonye ne of mayster hughe.
> To alle in-deferent recheste is dyetarye. (fol. 97v; lines 73–80)

The sense of the last three lines is to distance the regimen at hand from commodified medical knowledge, like the proprietary information purchased from a learned apothecary like 'maister antonye' or 'mayster hughe'. Instead, Lydgate's vernacular dietary makes health 'Of soule and Body' accessible to all who can read it. The generic flexibility that apparently helped to make Lydgate's *Dietary* so popular is also internal to the poem's meaning: its theme is the inextricability of *physic* and ethics, of body and soul, and of medicine and broader practices of self-governance.

Does it make sense to treat Lydgate's poem as a medical text? Perhaps no more than it does to treat Robert Thornton's Lincoln codex as a medical book. Both transmit vernacular medical knowledge, but neither maintains medicine as an autonomous, stable, or professional discourse. Lydgate's poem flourishes in the same borderlands spanned by the Lincoln manuscript and mapped by means of its generic divisions. In these borderlands, expertise in healing is marked by difficulty and even esoteric opacity (characteristic of 'master antonye' and 'master hughe' and evidenced by Thornton's own difficulties in copying the *Liber*), but that opacity simultaneously begins to dissolve in the very motions of medicine's vernacularization. Lydgate's regimen and Thornton's codex participate alike in this process of vernacularization. Both poem and manuscript realize some of the mercurial possibilities of Middle English medical writing during the period of its dissemination and help us today better to query the practices of medical reading in fifteenth-century England.

Afterword
Robert Thornton Country

Rosalind Field with Dav Smith

Robert Thornton, as is well known, lived at East Newton Hall in the parish of Stonegrave in the North Yorkshire wapentake of Ryedale. His identity as the copyist of the Thornton manuscripts was established in the middle of the last century, and much has been done by George Keiser, Michael Johnston and others to explore the networks, among local associates and clerics in particular, that provided Thornton with his materials for copying and indeed the intellectual stimulus for undertaking such a task.[1] There is still a need however to return to the matter of place, as Derek Brewer puts it, 'the significance of where he lived'.[2]

Place is a primary base of networks, formed as people go about their daily business, associate with their neighbours, travel familiar and established routes. This is all the more so when a place is closely associated with a family over several generations. So it is necessary to look again, and more closely, at the country in which Thornton lived his long and apparently uneventful life and in which his predecessors and descendants lived for several centuries.

The small parish of Stonegrave lies in the middle of Ryedale, north of York, south of the Whitby moors, west of Malton and east of the Vale of Mowbray. Thornton's home of East Newton Hall is in the west of the parish, where it borders the neighbouring parish of Oswaldkirk.

These days Ryedale is a prosperous rural area, featuring market towns, large farms, a concentration of heritage sites and handsome stone villages. Like many such areas, it has a strong sense of local identity and is distanced, even somewhat detached, from the political and social events of the metropolis. Perhaps because of this, awareness of Thornton's local world has shown a tendency to vagueness or geographic inexactitude. Carl Horstmann may be excused for

---

[1] G. R. Keiser, 'Lincoln Cathedral Library MS. 91: Life and Milieu of the Scribe', *Studies in Bibliography* 32 (1979), 158–79; G. R. Keiser, 'More Light on the Life and Milieu of Robert Thornton,' *Studies in Bibliography* 36 (1983), 111–19; and M. Johnston, *Romance and the Gentry in Late Medieval England* (Oxford, forthcoming 2014).

[2] D. S. Brewer, 'Introduction', in *The Thornton MS*, intro. Brewer and Owen, pp. vi–xi (p. xi).

placing Thornton 'near' Hampole as he had a European perspective and a need to associate Thornton with Rolle,[3] but there is less excuse for the more recent and misleading tendency to associate Thornton with Pickering.[4] Furthermore, even in the most sympathetic and detailed accounts of Thornton's milieu, there tends to be a note of surprise that an achievement such as Thornton's was possible, 'even in rural Yorkshire'.[5]

Medieval Ryedale

Medieval Ryedale would have been very different from its modern version in many ways. The medieval economics of power being land-based, an area such as Ryedale was far from a backwater. It was fertile, easily accessible with no natural boundaries other than rolling hills, a road system dating back to the Romans and within easy reach of York, for much of the medieval period the second city of England and at times the temporary capital.

For a relatively small area it figures largely in various medieval networks. Walter Espec of Helmsley, who founded Rievaulx Abbey and led the English army at the battle of the Standard in 1138, was also part of an early lay book-reading network. He borrowed a manuscript of Geoffrey of Monmouth's *Historia regum Britanniae* from Robert of Gloucester and lent it to the FitzGilbert family in Lincolnshire, whose chaplain, Geffrei Gaimar, used it as a source and model for his *Estoire des Engleis*.[6] Geoffrey's fiercest critic, William of Newburgh, took his name from the Ryedale priory. In the fourteenth century, Robert Mannyng was asked to write his chronicle by a certain 'Robert of Malton'.[7] Richard Rolle began his hermit career in his likely birthplace of Thornton le Dale outside Pickering.

Even before the dynastic wars of Thornton's lifetime, the population of Ryedale would have been well aware of events in the wider world. Four of the Magna Carta barons – Vesci, Mowbray, Percy and Ros – held lands in or near Ryedale, as did some of their most important allies. Helmsley was one of the

---

[3] *Yorkshire Writers: Richard Rolle of Hampole and His Followers*, ed. C. Horstmann, 2 vols. (London, 1895–6; repr. Cambridge, 1999).

[4] This goes back at least as far as the 1898 edition of the *Dictionary of National Biography* and is still found in T. Turville-Petre, *The Alliterative Revival* (Cambridge, 1977), p. 44.

[5] Keiser, 'Lincoln Cathedral Library MS. 91', p. 167.

[6] I. Short, 'Gaimar's Epilogue and Geoffrey of Monmouth's *Liber vetustissimus*', *Speculum* 69 (1994), 223–43.

[7] T. Summerfield, *The Matter of Kings' Lives: The Design of Past and Present in the Early Fourteenth-Century Verse Chronicles by Pierre de Langtoft and Robert Mannyng* (Atlanta, 1998), pp. 136–7.

few rebel strongholds to hold out against King John in the ensuing civil war.[8] A century later, after the battle of Bannockburn in 1314, northern England was left largely defenceless, and after their subsequent victory at the battle of Byland in 1322, the victorious Scots army came south to raid Rievaulx and Byland abbeys and several market towns, and Robert Bruce briefly set up his headquarters in Malton.[9] A Scots attack on Pickering Vale, from Helmsley to Pickering, was bought off for 200 marks.[10] Local magnates rebelled against first Richard II and then Henry IV in the rebellions of 1399 and 1402. Ralph Hastings of Slingsby had joined the Scrope rebellion in 1405, continued to support Owen Glendower, was executed in 1410 and his head was displayed in Helmsley. During Robert Thornton's lifetime, clashes between York and Lancaster, or more locally Neville and Percy, affected the whole area.[11] Thomas Roos was executed after the battle of Hexham in 1464 and his castle at Helmsley given to Richard of Gloucester. The Thorntons seem to have kept out of politics, although even that did not save Robert from being falsely implicated in the Percy attempt to kidnap the Earl of Salisbury outside Sheriff Hutton in 1453 and losing his post as tax collector as a result.[12]

As Figure 1 shows, Stonegrave parish was close to many of these events. Furthermore, it was on East Newton land that the 'regalis via' of Hambleton Street running west/east from the Vale of Mowbray to the Humber crossed over the road that ran south from Pickering and Helmsley.[13] Far from living in a backwater, Thornton was well placed to build the networks that provided his material. If we take the distance of 9 miles or 15 kilometres as representing a day's journey in medieval times,[14] some places important to Thornton's networks such as York (16 miles) and Mount Grace (18 miles) are at a greater distance than this, but he would have been within easy reach of many of the local centres of power and culture, both lay and ecclesiastical.

---

[8] J. C. Holt, *The Northerners* (Oxford, 1961), pp. 31–2: 'Indeed, if the movement [against King John] had any single geographic centre, it was in and around the North Yorkshire Moors. Here was concentrated the power of Vesci at Malton, Mowbray at Thirsk, Brus at Skelton and Danby, Stuteville at Rosedale, Percy around Whitby and Ros at Helmsley.'

[9] For discussion and illustrations of the economic effects of the Scots invasion see R. A. Butlin, *Historical Atlas of North Yorkshire* (Otley, 2003), pp. 87–8, fig. 6:13.

[10] J. Rushton, *The History of Ryedale* (Pickering, 2003), p. 113.

[11] A. J. Pollard, *North-Eastern England during the Wars of the Roses* (Oxford, 1990), ch. 10–12.

[12] Keiser, 'More Light', pp. 163–4.

[13] J. McDonnell and R. H. Hayes, 'Roads and Communications, I (Pre-Conquest and Mediaeval)', in *A History of Helmsley, Rievaulx and District*, ed. J. McDonnelly, Yorkshire Archaeological Society (York, 1963), pp. 60–70.

[14] See Butlin, *Historical Atlas*, p. 82.

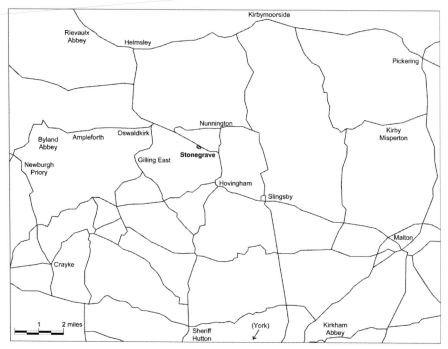

Figure 1. Map of Ryedale, North Yorkshire

Place and manuscript contents

It has always been the ecclesiastical and monastic network that offers researchers the clearest connections with the contents of the Thornton manuscripts. Stonegrave Minster itself is witness to the antiquity of ecclesiastical building in the area. Within an easy day's travel from Stonegrave were a number of major religious houses: the Cistercian abbeys of Byland and Rievaulx are easily accessible, and Byland was a major landowner in the area. To the south of Byland lies the village and castle of Crayke held by the bishops, and later, county, of Durham from the time of Athelstan to the mid nineteenth century. Crayke castle was visited by every king from John to Edward IV, and Bishop Robert Neville undertook a large rebuilding project as part of his efforts to support his family's ambitions in the region.[15]

To the east lay the Augustinian priory of Kirkham, founded, like Rievaulx, by Walter Espec, and the Gilbertine Priory of Malton, and to the west, the Augustinian priory of Newburgh. The Carthusian priory of Mount Grace was across the northern moors beyond Rievaulx. The importance of York as

[15] For Bishop Neville's political activities see Pollard, *North-Eastern England*, pp. 123, 251–2.

an ecclesiastical and cultural centre was paramount and movements between that centre and the outlying religious houses would provide further access to libraries containing the range of religious material collected by Thornton.

It is the romances and other secular material in the manuscripts that have always proved more difficult to place in terms of transmission and ownership. The exception is the *Liber de Diversis Medicinis*, which is evidently the result of a close local network, having been copied from a manuscript lent by the Pickering family of the neighbouring parish of Oswaldkirk and some of its recipes provided by the Oswaldkirk rector.[16] But there is no such clear evidence of transmission for the romances in Thornton's manuscripts. This is particularly the case with what might be seen as the narratives of the Nine Worthies, apparently originally aimed at courtly audiences.[17]

However, as many centres of secular power as of religious influence surround the parish of Stonegrave. The castle of the Roos family at Helmsley is within four or five miles as is that of the Hastings family at Slingsby. The de Etton castle at Gilling is even closer. It has been shown that some of these families did own numbers of books, even if information about secular texts is difficult to come by.

Perhaps the most suggestive is the power base of the Neville family at Sheriff Hutton in the Forest of Galtres, six miles to the south. Rosamund Allen has argued for a Neville origin for the *Awntyrs off Arthure* based on place names associated with Neville lands in Westmorland and, indeed, that a possible author for that poem can be identified in the clerical member of the family – Robert, later bishop of Durham.[18] She dates *Awntyrs* to 1424–5 and suggests Joan Neville as the likely patron.[19] Ralph Neville settled Sheriff Hutton on Joan, his second wife, and she held it as his widow from 1425 until her death in 1440.[20] As well as being an intriguing poem in its own right, with a complexity belied by its brevity, *Awntyrs* is a witness to the reception of earlier Arthurian poems – the alliterative *Morte Arthure* and *Sir Gawain and the Green Knight*.

---

[16] Keiser established that the exemplar was borrowed from the Pickerings and not from the rector of Oswaldkirk as was previously thought ('More Light', p.114).

[17] I am grateful to M. Johnston for the opportunity to read his forthcoming book, *Romance and the Gentry in Late Medieval England* which places Thornton's gentry romances in their political and cultural context.

[18] R. Allen, 'The *Awntyrs off Arthure*: Jests and Jousts', in *Romance Reading on the Book: Essays on Medieval Narrative Presented to Maldwyn Mills*, ed. J. Fellows, R. Field, G. Rogers and J. Weiss (Cardiff, 1996), pp. 129–42; and R. Allen, 'Place-Names in *The Awntyrs off Arthure*: Corruption, Conjecture, Coincidence', in *Arthurian Studies in Honour of P. J. C. Field*, ed. B. Wheeler (Cambridge, 2004), pp. 181–98.

[19] Allen, 'Place-Names', pp. 193–5.

[20] W. Page, ed., *Victoria History of the County of York, North Riding*, 5 vols. (London, 1907–74), II, 172–87.

There is no evidence that *Sir Gawain* ever crossed Thornton's path, but his copying of both *Morte Arthure* and *Awntyrs* in the early years of his scribal career indicates an interest in, and availability of, these northern poems in the area. That this could be due to transmission between Neville households is an intriguing possibility.[21] This is not to argue that Thornton was on social terms with families such as the Nevilles; indeed Johnston has shown that his circle of acquaintance was that of local gentry. However, his friends the Pickerings of Oswaldkirk were themselves retainers of the Nevilles.[22] But the households of the great lords were cultural hubs, employing literate men who would not be out of Thornton's social sphere and who would have provided an audience appreciative of the complex moral challenges these poems examine. Both the *Morte Arthure* and *Awntyrs* are opaque in their meaning, as is the case with many of the best alliterative poems. Their appeal to magnates such as the Nevilles may have been in their celebration of aristocratic mores and values – such as the detailed hunting scene with which *Awntyrs* opens, to appeal, as Allen implies, to Richard Neville, warden of the royal forests north of the Trent, but also, perhaps, to the audience of Galtres Forest. More seriously, the poems share an aristocratic ideology that is sceptical of royalty, in that the Round Table, and especially Gawain, are the champions, the conscience and finally the victims of royal power. And both poems have a wider appeal, one perhaps more suited to the clerical reader or to the serious-minded layman such as Thornton (or that other copyist and adaptor, Thomas Malory) in their demonstration that earthly glory is at the mercy of Fortune and justice may challenge power. Whatever the case, the response of modern day readers to both poems confirms the breadth of their appeal, and indeed that one of Thornton's greatest achievements was the preservation of the unique copy of the *Morte Arthure*.

Stonegrave Minster

At the present day the monasteries and priories are in ruins, as are most of the power bases of the Ryedale nobility, with the castles of Helmsley, Slingsby, Sheriff Hutton and Pickering in ruins, while others such as Newburgh, Crayke and Gilling were modernized into family estates. Thornton's home at East

---

[21] See Pollard, *North-Eastern England*, map 3 for the Neville estates across Westmorland and the North Riding.

[22] Rushton, *History of Ryedale*, p. 151. Pollard, *North-Eastern England*, p. 248, notes that in 1454 Sir James Pickering was one of those organizing and leading Neville gangs against Percy retainers.

Newton is now a largely seventeenth-century building, improved and partially demolished by a succession of occupants.[23]

It is in the parish churches that the material memorials can still be found, and it is in the parish church of Stonegrave that the Thorntons have left their mark. The Thornton family were benefactors of Stonegrave Minster (Church of the Holy Trinity) from the mid fourteenth century, following the decline of the earlier patrons, the de Stonegraves. There is still a discernible footpath from the door of the church to East Newton hall.

The parish church of Stonegrave Minster can claim to be the oldest minster in England,[24] the subject of a papal letter concerning a disputed appointment in 757. It still contains a fine Saxon wheel cross and other Anglo-Saxon pieces and was extensively rebuilt after the Conquest. Robert Thornton's father was responsible for a programme of rebuilding in the early fifteenth century.

In the north aisle are medieval tombs belonging to the two families of Stonegrave and Thornton. The earlier tomb, of the early fourteenth century, has the effigy of a man wearing a long surcoat and a coif. The legs are crossed and the feet rest on a lion. This is believed to be that of Roger de Stonegrave, who was held prisoner after the fall of Acre in 1291 until released thirty years later following an appeal from Edward II to the pope to negotiate his release. Fittingly, throughout the medieval period, there was a chapel in the north aisle dedicated to Saint Leonard, patron saint of prisoners.

The second tomb is that of Robert Thornton's parents, apparently commissioned during the lifetime of Robert Thornton the elder, who died in 1418. The tomb is re-set into the north wall beneath a reused medieval canopy (possibly part of an Easter Sepulchre) (see Figure 2). It shows the recumbent figures of Thornton and his wife, both wearing long gowns with their hands in prayer, her feet resting on a curiously porcine dog. The Thornton coat of arms, a chevron between three thorn trees, occurs on a shield on the base of the tomb and on another shield suspended from the man's left sleeve.

But there is no tomb for Robert Thornton, or indeed for any later members of the family. There is no doubt that the north aisle was the site of the Thornton family tombs, but they were demolished by the Victorian rebuilding of the 1860s, as Dav Smith describes below. It is left to the coats of arms on the tomb, the roof, and in a modern window to testify to the importance of the Thornton family across several generations.

---

[23]   N. Pevsner, *The Buildings of England: Yorkshire: The North Riding* (Harmondsworth, 1966), p. 151.

[24]   Minster here refers to the 'Old Minsters', missionary stations staffed by monks and serving a large area.

Figure 2. Effigies of Thornton's parents, Stonegrave Minster

Thornton's reputation

Robert Thornton's memory and reputation have fared little better than his tomb. Although his family were evidently instrumental in preserving his manuscripts,[25] they were less successful in preserving his memory and next to nothing is known of him in the locality. The Rev. Harold Pobjoy accumulated the fullest history of the Minster in the 1960s and his egregious remarks about Thornton are the only detailed memorial surviving to this day:

> This Robert Thornton was succeeded in 1418, by his son, another Robert, a studious fellow, who in the days before printing, made his own 'Library' by copying out from books he borrowed, whatever took his fancy. This collection, known as The Robert Thornton MSS is still preserved in Lincoln Cathedral Library. It contains some 70 selections, including
> A life of Alexander, translated from Latin

[25] See Brewer, 'Introduction', pp. viii–ix; and Thompson, *London Thornton MS*, pp. 5–7.

The Lamentations of a Sinner in Purgatory
A Poem, 'Morte Arthure', written in Chaucer's time
A Life of St Christopher, in couplets
The Miraculous Conversion of a Wicked Knight with several Romance, Prayers and Sermons and ending with a Collection of Medical Receipts, several of which he says he obtained from the Rector of Oswaldkirk. They mainly consist of common herb concoctions, but sometimes included more unusual ingredients.
For sore eyes: boiled slug juice is recommended
For toothache: among 16 remedies is 'laying to the tooth rubbed strawberry stalks, pepper or even the filth of a badger; the latter will break the tooth and so stop the pain'. Unfortunately these MSS have not yet been printed.[26]

Apart from this there is a short descriptive notice on the Thornton tomb, but the existence of the London manuscript is never noted, and the importance of Thornton established in scholarship from the 1830s to the present day did not come to the attention of the Rev. Pobjoy or any other historians of the church.

Somewhat ironically, while the Thornton tombs were being tidied away in 1863, Thornton scholarship was gathering apace. The Camden Society had published J. O. Halliwell's *Thornton Romances* in 1844. George Perry, Dean of Lincoln, published volumes of the religious material in 1866 and 1867 and an edition of the *Morte Arthure* in 1865, all with the Early English Text Society, and Horstmann's *Yorkshire Writers* appeared in 1895–6.[27] Although there was still some doubt as to the identification of the scribe of the manuscript, Robert Thornton of East Newton had been preferred by Halliwell, and he appeared in the *Dictionary of National Biography* of 1898 and the *Victoria History of the County of York* of 1914.[28]

By the time Pobjoy wrote his history of Stonegrave in 1965, Thornton had long been credited with both the Lincoln manuscript (which Pobjoy knew about) and the London manuscript (which apparently he didn't). All the major works, the romances, the mystical writings, *Wynnere and Wastoure, Parlement of the Thre Ages*, had been edited and a good proportion of them were in university syllabuses. William Matthews's ground-breaking *Tragedy of Arthur* was

[26] This was published in a local history magazine, *In Former Days*, no. 52 (1965).

[27] *The Thornton Romances*, ed. J. O. Halliwell, Camden Society 30 (London, 1844); *Morte Arthure*, ed. G. G. Perry, EETS OS 8 (London, 1865); *The English Prose Treatises of Richard Rolle de Hampole*, ed. G. G. Perry, EETS OS 20 (London, 1866); *Religious Pieces in Prose and Verse, from R. Thornton's MS*, ed. G. G. Perry, EETS OS 26 (1867); and *Yorkshire Writers*, ed. Horstmann.

[28] A. F. Pollard, 'Robert Thornton', *Dictionary of National Biography*, 1st edn, ed. S. Lee (London, 1885–1900), LVI, 303; *Victoria History of the County of York*, I, 561–6.

published in 1960 and established the *Morte Arthure* as a significant work.[29] The facsimile edition of the Lincoln manuscript would be published in 1975, and John Thompson's study of the London manuscript in 1987.[30] The increasing amount of interest and scholarship devoted to the two manuscripts and their contents does not need rehearsing for readers of this volume.

That none of this activity apparently registered in Thornton's own country is a measure of the knowledge gap between the world of modern scholarship and that of the educated and interested population at large. It is a fair assumption that if one of the rectors of Stonegrave had been a paid-up member of the Early English Text Society or one of the other nineteenth-century subscription societies – as many country clergy were – matters might have been different.[31] But the situation now is that while the material culture and history of church buildings often arouses local interest, the literary-historical culture that Thornton represents – although of course he is in many ways a one-off – fails to bridge the divide between one world and the other.

Nor does Thornton scholarship provide much for those interested in historical personalities. Something is known about the part he played on the local stage, as family man, landowner and (briefly) tax collector, but next to nothing is known of his personality, other than a piety indicated by some of his comments and choices in his manuscripts. It is perhaps permissible to infer that he would have had the personal qualities necessary to build a sizeable network of acquaintances who could be persuaded to provide him with the exemplars from which to copy his texts. But as a personality, he is eclipsed by his seventeenth-century descendant, Alice Thornton (1626–1707). Her lively autobiography survives in which she records her responses to the politically turbulent times, and to her own struggles with illness and the deaths of six of her nine children.[32] Throughout she voices a consistent and individual piety, and it was her ambition to restore the family chapel dedicated to Saint Peter at East Newton Hall that had been established by Robert Thornton's father in 1397–8.[33] Although the depredations of a hopelessly spendthrift husband made this impossible, in 1961, when the south aisle chapel was restored, it was dedicated to St Peter in order finally to fulfil her ambition.

This historical awareness at Stonegrave Minster also applies to her son-in-

---

[29] W. Matthews, *The Tragedy of Arthur: A Study of the Alliterative* Morte Arthure (Berkeley, 1960).

[30] *The Thornton MS*, intro. Brewer and Owen; and Thompson, *London Thornton MS*.

[31] See D. Matthews, *The Making of Middle English 1765–1910* (Minneapolis, 1999), p. 160.

[32] Her autobiography was first published in 1875. A. Thornton, *The Autobiography of Mrs. Alice Thornton, of East Newton, Co. York*, ed. C. Jackson, Surtees Society Publications 62 (Durham, 1875; repr. Cambridge, 2010).

[33] Keiser, 'More Light', p. 111.

law, Thomas Comber, who also wrote a memoir of his life and times.[34] He began his career as a curate at Stonegrave and as a lodger at East Newton Hall, where he married the fifteen-year-old daughter of the house, another Alice. He went on to a glittering ecclesiastical career, canon of York Minster, dean of Durham Cathedral, chaplain to William and Mary, and author of *A Companion to the Temple*, an influential defence of the Book of Common Prayer.[35] He was responsible for passing the Thornton manuscript to Lincoln Cathedral Library through his contacts with the dean, Daniel Brevint.[36] He returned to Stonegrave to die, aged 55, and is buried in the chancel. The church displays a contemporary portrait and a copy of his book.

So the absence of awareness of Robert Thornton is not due to a lack of local interest in history and in the personalities that have belonged to Stonegrave.[37] Indeed, it could be argued that he has been crowded out by the historical richness of the place. For while Stonegrave Minster is recognized and valued as a site of Christian worship for over 1200 years, and its history a source of local pride, Robert Thornton has been lost from the record.[38]

The Victorian rebuilding of Stonegrave Minster[39]

The 1860s was a decade of restoration and rebuilding for many of Ryedale's parish churches,[40] and Stonegrave Minster was not spared. Between 1861 and 1863 the York-based architect George Fowler Jones largely rebuilt the church, preserving only the tower and nave walls. The twelfth-century north aisle,[41] which had been appropriated from an early date as the burial place for the Thornton and Comber families, was entirely demolished and replaced with the

---

[34] T. Comber, *The Autobiographies and Letters of Thomas Comber*, ed. C. E. Whiting, Surtees Society Publications 156–7, 2 vols (Durham, 1946–7).

[35] T. Comber, *A companion to the temple, or, A help to devotion in the use of the common prayer* (London, 1672).

[36] G. R. Keiser, 'A Note on the Descent of the Thornton Manuscript', *Transactions of the Cambridge Bibliographical Society* 6 (1976), 346–8.

[37] See the local publication, *People of the Minster*. Post-medieval figures include a Victorian rector who studied 120 languages, and the influential twentieth-century poet and critic Herbert Read.

[38] At the time of writing, proposals are being developed to place a memorial to Thornton in the church to restore his memory in the locality of his life and works. For further information, see http://www.ampleforthbenefice.org/StonegraveMinster.html.

[39] This section is authored by Dav Smith.

[40] See D. Smith, 'Vandalism or Social Duty: The Victorian Rebuilding of the "Street Parish" Churches' (unpublished thesis, University of York, forthcoming).

[41] T. Bulmer, *Bulmer's History and Directory of North Yorkshire* (Preston, 1890), p. 1122.

Figure 3. Photograph by George Fowler Jones, *c.* 1862, showing Stonegrave Minster from the south-west and capturing the Victorian restoration in progress, with the medieval south aisle having been removed. The chancel, clerestory and north aisle were shortly to follow.

present aisle. Jones was a keen early photographer, and the recent discovery of several photographs taken *c.* 1862 during the restoration at Stonegrave sheds new light on the pre-Victorian church. The first, rather dramatic, photograph shows Stonegrave Minster from the south-west following the demolition of the medieval south aisle (see Figure 3). Elements of the fabric soon to be lost to the rebuilding can still be seen, including the south wall of the chancel, revealing that it was tall, windowless, and contained a simple twelfth-century priest's door. Also visible is the early fifteenth-century clerestory featuring fine perpendicular Gothic windows.[42] Looking through the south arcade into the church interior, it is possible to discern that the chancel arch had been replaced by a plain, rectangular opening. The second image reveals the interior of the nave and north aisle shortly before the aisle's demolition and rebuilding, but following the removal of the internal fixtures and fittings (see Figure 4). The eye is immediately drawn to the nave wall paintings, in particular the depiction

---

[42] This clerestory, of which the internal corbels survive, was constructed as part of the remodelling of the church by Robert Thornton's father.

Figure 4. Photograph by George Fowler Jones, *c.* 1862, showing Stonegrave Minster's nave and north aisle during the restoration. The north aisle was soon to be demolished and rebuilt.

of 'time and death' represented by a skeleton holding a spear and hourglass.[43] The two dark marks near its feet may relate to the fixing of a later singer's loft against the west wall (the horizontal parallel lines tracing the loft's outline are visible across the arch and legs). Several rectangular panels containing scriptural texts[44] are also visible, as is a highly decorative coat of arms.[45] Before their

[43] 'Time and death' murals survive at: Westborough, Lincolnshire; Yaxley, Huntingdonshire; Patricio, Powys; and Llangar, Denbighshire. Lost examples are recorded at: 'Wakefield Cathedral', http://freepages.rootsweb.ancestry.com/~wakefield/cathedral/cath17.html; and 'Kirkby Malham' in Yorkshire, http://www.kirkbymalham.info/LHfocus.html. Post-Reformation wall paintings have received very little academic attention to date. For further information see E. C. Rouse, 'Post-Reformation Mural Paintings in Parish Churches', *Lincolnshire Historian* 1 (1947), 8–14.

[44] See R. Whiting, *The Reformation of the English Parish Church* (Cambridge, 2010), pp. 131–3.

[45] The shield is divided in two vertically (party per pale) and depicts the Thornton arms on the left, and a rampant lion (colours unknown), possibly representing the Wandsford arms on the right. The motto below reads: 'Sapiens Dominabitur' (The wise man will rule).

Figure 5. Stonegrave Minster, Victorian north aisle, looking east and showing the Thornton double effigy. The eastern bay of the aisle was originally planned as the Comber tomb; today it serves as the vestry and is enclosed by a reused seventeenth-century timber screen.

Victorian whitewashing, these wall paintings were dated as contemporary with the chancel screen and wooden panelling (*c.* 1637).[46]

Together, these photographs contribute to our understanding of the north aisle prior to its Victorian rebuilding and thus aid in the search for Robert Thornton's tomb. Like its Victorian successor, the twelfth-century north aisle comprised four bays (three nave bays and a single chancel bay). The medieval chancel bay, which equates to the vestry in the present Victorian aisle, contained

---

[46] 'Associated Architectural Society Reports, Vol. VI (1861–2)', *Yorkshire Architectural Society 21st Annual Report* (1862), p. cxv.

a chapel dedicated to Saint Leonard.[47] The west wall of the north aisle was blank, while the north wall contained a simple Norman door leading to the churchyard[48] and three windows. The north door likely mirrored the present south doorway, corresponding to the western bay of the north arcade. Rev. Eastmead's description of 1824 records a single, wall-mounted memorial tablet – to Thomas Jackson, of Nunnington (d. 1702) – to the left [west] of the north door.[49] The north aisle fenestration comprised 'two lancets and a Perpendicular window, and an east window of three lights with ogee flowing tracery'.[50] The tracery of this fourteenth-century east window has been copied in its Victorian replacement, which is visible in Figure 5. The lancet windows may have been contemporary with the construction of the aisle, and corresponded to the central and eastern bays of the nave arcade. The fifteenth-century perpendicular Gothic window is partially visible in Figure 3, confirming that it was in the north wall of the Saint Leonard chapel.

Internally the north aisle contained no pews or stalls, and its floor was raised on brick burial vaults to near the height of the nave pews. Sadly, Figure 4 was taken after the north aisle interior had been stripped; however the remains of part of the brick vaults can be seen to the far right. This raised floor level was accessed by a set of steps, and Eastmead records that the two recumbent effigies were to the left upon ascending them, while to the right were tombs commemorating Thomas Denton (*c.* 1626–1709) and his son Robert Denton (1699–1747), both rectors of Stonegrave.[51] This description suggests the steps were located in the chancel, which would fit with the nave arcade being blocked by box stalls. The double effigy of Robert Thornton's parents was, as today, located within a recess in the north wall,[52] although it is unclear if it sat beneath the same, seemingly reused, canopy (see Figure 2).

Contemporary descriptions of the pre-Victorian church note that the north aisle had been appropriated for the burial of the Comber and Thornton families from an early date,[53] suggesting that there were identifiable funerary monuments associated with both families. At the time of Robert Thornton's burial, the eastern bay of the north aisle was still in use as a chapel, so he was almost certainly buried within the nave bays. Eastmead provided detailed

---

[47] 'Stonegrave Minster, Stonegrave, North Yorkshire', http://www.ampleforthbenefice.org/StonegraveHistory.html.

[48] 'Associated Architectural Society Reports', p. cxv.

[49] W. Eastmead, *Historia Rievallensis* (London, 1824), p. 194.

[50] 'Associated Architectural Society Reports', p. cxv.

[51] Eastmead, *Historia Rievallensis*, p. 191.

[52] 'Associated Architectural Society Reports', p. cxv.

[53] See, for example: Eastmead, *Historia Rievallensis*, p. 191; and T. Whellan, *History and Topography of The City of York: and The North Riding of Yorkshire*, 2 vols. (Beverley, 1859), II, 886.

descriptions of the church's notable funerary monuments in 1824, almost all of which survive in the present church.[54] That there are no descriptions of Robert Thornton's tomb suggests that it was either unremarkable or unidentifiable by the early nineteenth century. The funerary monuments retained in the Victorian church are in comparatively good condition; however, the north aisle had suffered several vicissitudes in the post-medieval period – during the seventeenth century the lead was stripped off the roof and some of its windows were blocked up.[55] If Robert Thornton's tomb survived, it and many other Thornton monuments were lost during the Victorian restoration. The 1861 Faculty for this work specifically mentioned the re-interment of any burials found in the raised tombs.[56] The Comber family defrayed the cost of rebuilding the north aisle,[57] and its eastern bay was intended as 'The Comber tomb'.[58] Therefore, although Robert Thornton's tomb is lost, it is likely that his remains were reburied beneath the present vestry.

[54] Eastmead, *Historia Rievallensis*, pp. 187–96. Very few of the retained funerary monuments were replaced in their original locations.

[55] Alice Thornton left money and materials in her will for the repair of the north aisle roof, and for the re-opening and glazing of the windows. See Thornton, *The Autobiography*, ed. Jackson, pp. 305, 333–4, 337.

[56] University of York Borthwick Institute for Archives, Fac. 1861/2.

[57] *The Falcon*, ed. T. J. Wilkinson, 2 vols. (Thirsk, Yorkshire, 1889–91), II, 263.

[58] Borthwick Institute for Archives, Fac. 1861/2. Note the architectural delineation of the eastern bay in Figure 5.

Bibliography

Published primary sources

The Alliterative Morte Arthure: *A Critical Edition*, ed. V. Krishna (New York, 1976).

Altenglische Legenden, ed. C. Horstmann (Paderborn, 1875).

Altenglische Legenden: Neue Folge, ed. C. Horstmann (Heilbronn, 1881).

Apocrypha of the New Testament, trans. A. Walker, in *The Ante-Nicene Fathers*, ed. A. Roberts and J. Donaldson, rev. C. Coxe, 10 vols. (New York, 1903), VIII, 368–598.

Auchinleck Manuscript, ed. D. Burnley and A. Wiggins (Edinburgh, 2003), http://www.auchinleck.nls.uk/editorial/project.html.

Augustine, *The City of God against the Pagans*, ed. and trans. R. W. Dyson (Cambridge, 1998).

The Awnytrs off Arthure, ed. H. Phillips (Lancaster, 1988).

The Awntyrs off Arthure at the Terne Wathelyn, ed. R. Hanna (Manchester, 1974).

The Awntyrs off Arthure at the Terne Wathelyne, ed. R. J. Gates (Philadelphia, 1969).

Bishop Percy's Folio Manuscript: Ballads and Romances, ed. J. W. Hales and F. J. Furnivall, 3 vols. (London, 1867–8). *Breton Lays in Middle English*, ed. T. C. Rumble (Detroit, 1965).

Carmina medii aevi posterioris latina, II/1–3: Lateinische Sprichwörter und Sentenzen des Mittelalters in alphabetischer Anordnung A-E, F-M, N-P , ed. H. Walther (Göttingen, 1963–5).

Cleanness, ed. J. J. Anderson (Manchester, 1977).

Codex Ashmole 61: A Compilation of Popular Middle English Verse, ed. G. Shuffelton (Kalamazoo MI, 2008).

Comber, T., *A companion to the temple, or, A help to devotion in the use of the common prayer* (London, 1672).

—— *The Autobiographies and Letters of Thomas Comber*, ed. C. E. Whiting, Surtees Society Publications 156–7, 2 vols. (Durham, 1946–7).

The Commonplace Book of Robert Raynes of Acle: An Edition of Tanner MS 407, ed. C. Louis (New York, 1980).

The Complete Harley 2253 Manuscript in Three Volumes, ed. and trans. S. Fein, with D. Raybin and J. Ziolkowski (Kalamazoo MI, forthcoming 2014)

'A Critical Edition of *The Privity of the Passion* and *The Lyrical Meditations*', ed. S. M. Day (unpublished Ph.D. thesis, University of York, 1991).

Cursor Mundi (The Cursur of the World): A Northumbrian Poem of the XIVth Century, ed. R. Morris, 7 vols., EETS 57, 59, 62, 66, 68, 99, 101 (London, 1874–93).

The Cyrurgie of Guy de Chauliac, ed. M. Ogden, EETS OS 265 (London, 1971).

The Death of King Arthur, trans. S. Armitage (New York, 2012).

Der mittelenglische Versroman über Richard Löwenherz, ed. K. Brunner, Wiener Beiträge zur englischen Philologie 42 (Vienna, 1913).

The Destruction of Troy, ed. H. Matsumoto, 3rd edn (Okayama-shi, 2011).

The Douay-Rheims Catholic Bible, www.drbo.org.

Early English Books Online, www.eebo.chadwyck.com.

The Early English Carols, ed. R. L. Greene, 2nd edn (Oxford, 1977).

Eleven Gawain Romances and Tales, ed. T. Hahn (Kalamazoo MI, 1995).

Les Enfaunces de Jesu Crist, ed. M. Boulton, ANTS 43 (London, 1985).

The English Charlemagne Romances, Part II. 'The Sege off Melayne' and 'The Romance of Duke Rowland and Sir Otuell of Spayne', ed. S. J. Herrtage, EETS ES 35 (London, 1880).

English Mystics of the Middle Ages, ed. B. Windeatt (Cambridge, 1994).

The English Prose Treatises of Richard Rolle de Hampole, ed. G. G. Perry, EETS OS 20, 2nd edn (London, 1921).

English Writings of Richard Rolle Hermit of Hampole, ed. H. E. Allen (Oxford, 1931).

The Erl of Tolous and the Emperes of Almayne, ed. G. Lüdtke, Sammlung englischer Denkmäler 3 (Berlin, 1881).

Evangelia Apocrypha, ed. Constantinus Tischendorf (Leipzig, 1853).

The Form of Perfect Living and Other Prose Treatises, by Richard Rolle of Hampole, A.D. 1300–1349, trans. G. E. Hodgson (London, 1910).

The Four Leaves of the Truelove, in *Moral Love Songs and Laments*, ed. S. G. Fein (Kalamazoo MI, 1998), pp. 161–254.

Four Middle English Romances: Sir Isumbras, Octavian, Sir Eglamour of Artois, Sir Tryamour, ed. H. Hudson (Kalamazoo MI, 1996).

A Good Short Debate between Winner and Waster, ed. I. Gollancz, Select Early English Poems 3 (London, 1920).

'The Gurney Series of Religious Lyrics', ed. R. H. Robbins, *PMLA* 54 (1939), 369–90.

'*Have Mercy of Me* (Psalm 51), An Unedited Alliterative Poem from the London Thornton Manuscript', ed. S. G. Fein, *Modern Philology* 86 (1989), 223–41.

Hilton, W., *The Scale of Perfection*, ed. T. H. Bestul (Kalamazoo MI, 2000).

Historical Poems of the XIVth and XVth Centuries, ed. R. H. Robbins (New York, 1959).

'Hs. Brit. Mus. Additional 31042', ed. K. Brunner, *Archiv* 132 (1914), 316–37.

Hymns to the Virgin & Christ, The Parliament of Devils, and Other Religious Poems, ed. F. J. Furnivall, EETS OS 24 (London, 1868).

The Idea of the Vernacular: An Anthology of Middle English Literary Theory, 1280–1520, ed. J. Wogan-Browne, N. Watson, A. Taylor and R. Evans (University Park PA, 1999).

The Infancy Gospels of James and Thomas, ed. and trans. R. F. Hock (Santa Rosa CA, 1995).

King Arthur's Death: The Middle English Stanzaic Morte Arthur *and Alliterative* Morte Arthure, ed. L. D. Benson, rev. E. E. Foster (Kalamazoo MI, 1994).

'Kleine Publicationen aus der Auchinleck-hs. III.', ed. E. Kölbing, *Englische Studien* 8 (1885) 115–19.

'Kleinere mittelenglische Texte', ed. M. Förster, *Anglia* 42 (1918), 145–224.

The Lay Folks' Cathechism, or the English and Latin Versions of Archbishop Thoresby's

Instruction for the People, ed. T. F. Simmons and H. E. Nolloth, EETS OS 118 (London, 1901).

The 'Liber de Diversis Medicinis' in the Thornton Manuscript (MS. Lincoln Cathedral A.5.2), ed. M. S. Ogden, EETS OS 207 (London, 1938).

Libri de nativitate Mariae: Pseudo-Matthaei evangelium, textus et commentarius, ed. Jan Gijsel, vol. 1 (Turnhout, 1997).

The Life of Richard Rolle Together with an Edition of His English Lyrics, ed. F. M. M. Comper (London, 1928).

'Literary Associations of an Anonymous Middle English Paraphrase of Vulgate Psalm L', ed. J. J. Thompson, *Medium Ævum* 55 (1988), 38–55.

'*Lyarde* and Goliard', ed. J. Reakes, *Neuphilologische Mitteilungen* 83 (1982), 34–41.

Lydgate, J., *The Minor Poems of John Lydgate I–II*, ed. H. N. MacCracken, 2 vols., EETS OS 107, 192 (London, 1911–34).

'Lydgatiana: III. The Three Kings of Cologne', ed. H. N. MacCracken, *Archiv* 192 (1912), 50–68.

'Lydgatiana: 14. O Flos Pulcherrime!', *Archiv* 131 (1913), 60–3.

Markham, G., *The English Housewife: containing the inward and outward virtues which ought to be in a complete woman …*, ed. M. R. Best (Montreal, 1986).

'"Mercy and Justice": The Additional MS 31042 Version', ed. J. Brazire, *Leeds Studies in English* n.s. 16 (1985), 259–71.

The Middle English Breton Lays, ed. A. Laskaya and E. Salisbury (Kalamazoo MI, 1995).

The Middle English Charters of Christ, ed. M. Spalding (Baltimore, 1914).

Middle English Debate Poetry: A Critical Anthology, ed. J. W. Conlee (East Lansing MI, 1991).

The Middle English Penitential Lyric, ed. F. A. Patterson (New York, 1966).

The Middle English Poem, Erthe upon Erthe, Printed from Twenty-Four Manuscripts, ed. H. M. R. Murray, EETS OS 141 (London, 1911).

Middle English Religious Prose, ed. N. F. Blake (London, 1972).

Middle English Romances, ed. S. H. A. Shepherd (New York, 1995).

Middle English Romances, ed. W. H. French and C. B. Hale, 2 vols. (New York, 1930).

The Middle English Stanzaic Versions of the Life of St. Anne, ed. R. E. Parker, EETS OS 174 (London, 1928).

'A Middle English Versified Prayer to the Trinity', ed. C. F. Bühler, *Modern Language Notes* 66 (1951), 312–14.

'A Minor Comic Poem in a Major Romance Manuscript: "Lyarde"', ed. M. Furrow, *Forum for Modern Language Studies* 32 (1996), 289–302.

The Minor Poems of the Vernon MS., Part I, ed. C. Horstmann, EETS OS 98 (London, 1892).

Morte Arthure, ed. E. Björkman (Heidelberg, 1915).

Morte Arthure, ed. J. Finlayson (London, 1967).

Morte Arthure: A Critical Edition, ed. Mary Hamel, Garland Medieval Texts 9 (New York, 1984).

Morte Arthure: An Alliterative Poem of the 14th Century, from the Lincoln MS, ed. M. M. Banks (London, 1900).

Morte Arthure, Edited from Robert Thornton's MS (ab. 1440 A.D.) in the Library of Lincoln Cathedral, ed. G. G. Perry, EETS OS 8 (London, 1865).

Morte Arthure, or The Death of Arthur, ed. E. Brock, EETS OS 8 (London, 1871).

Morte Arthure: The Alliterative Romance of the Death of King Arthur, ed. J. O. Halliwell (Brixton, 1847).

'Nachträge zu den Legenden: 1. Kindheit Jesu aus Ms. Addit. 31,042', ed. C. Horstmann, *Archiv* 74 (1885), 327–39.

The Northern Passion, ed. F. A. Foster, 2 vols., EETS OS 145, 147 (London, 1913–16).

Octavian, ed. F. McSparran, EETS OS 289 (London, 1986).

Octavian, ed. G. Sarrazin (Heilbronn, 1885).

Of Love and Chivalry: An Anthology of Middle English Romance, ed. J. Fellows (London, 1992).

The Old French Evangile de L'enfance, ed. M. Boulton (Toronto, 1984).

The Parlement of the Thre Ages, ed. M. Y. Offord, EETS OS 246 (London, 1959).

The Parlement of the Thre Ages, in *Alliterative Poetry of the Middle Ages: An Anthology*, ed. T. Turville-Petre (Washington DC, 1989), pp. 67–100.

The Parlement of the Three Ages: An Alliterative Poem on the Nine Worthies and the Heroes of Romances, ed. I. Gollancz, Select Early English Poems 2 (London, 1915).

Paston Letters and Papers of the Fifteenth Century, Vols. I–III, ed. N. Davis, R. Beadle and C. Richmond, 3 vols., EETS SS 20, 21, 22 (Oxford, 2004–5).

Peter Idley's Instructions to His Son, ed. C. D'Evelyn (Boston, 1935).

Piers Plowman: The A Version, ed. G. Kane, rev. edn (London, 1988).

Piers Plowman: The B Version, ed. G. Kane and E. T. Donaldson, 2nd edn (London, 1988).

A Pistel of Susan, in *Alliterative Poetry of the Middle Ages: An Anthology*, ed. T. Turville-Petre (Washington DC, 1989), pp. 120–39.

The Prick of Conscience (Stimulus Conscientiae), ed. R. Morris (Berlin, 1863).

Prik of Conscience, ed. J. H. Morey (Kalamazoo MI, 2012).

The Prose Alexander: A Critical Edition, ed. M. Neeson (Los Angeles, 1971).

The Prose Alexander of Robert Thornton: The Middle English Text with a Modern English Translation, ed. J. Chappell (New York, 1992).

The Prose Life of Alexander from the Thornton MS, ed. J. S. Westlake, EETS OS 143 (London, 1913).

Pseudo-Bonaventure, *Meditationes vitae Christi* (or *Our lorde god stronge and myghty, and myghty in battayle, he is kynge of glorye*), trans. Nicholas Love (London, 1507).

The Quatrefoil of Love, ed. I. Gollancz and M. M. Weale, EETS OS 195 (London, 1935).

Religious Pieces in Prose and Verse, ed. G. G. Perry, EETS OS 26 (New York, 1905).

Religious Lyrics of the XIVth Century, ed. C. Brown (Oxford, 1924).

Reliquiæ Antiquæ, ed. T. Wright and J. O. Halliwell, 2 vols. (London, 1841–3).

'A Revelation of Purgatory', trans. E. Spearing, in *Medieval Writings on Female Spirituality*, ed. E. Spearing (New York, 2002), pp. xlvii, 205–25.

A Revelation of Purgatory by an Unknown Fifteenth-Century Woman Visionary: Introduction, Critical Text, and Translation, ed. M. P. Harley (Lewiston NY, 1985).

Richard Morris's Prick of Conscience: *A Corrected and Amplified Reading Text*, ed. R. Hanna and S. Wood, EETS OS 342 (Oxford, 2013).

Richard Rolle and þe Holy Boke Gratia Dei: An Edition with Commentary, ed. M. L. Arntz, S.N.D. (Salzburg, 1981).

Richard Rolle: Prose and Verse, ed. S. J. Ogilvie-Thomson, EETS OS 293 (Oxford, 1988).

Richard Rolle: The English Writings, trans. R. S. Allen (Mahwah NJ, 1988).

Richard Rolle: Uncollected Prose and Verse, ed. R. Hanna, EETS OS 329 (Oxford, 2007).

Robert Mannyng of Brunne: The Chronicle, ed. I. Sullens, Medieval and Renaissance Texts and Studies 153 (Binghamton NY, 1996).

The Romance of Sir Degrevant, ed. L. F. Casson, EETS OS 221 (London, 1949).

The Romances and Prophecies of Thomas of Erceldoune, ed. J. A. H. Murray, EETS OS 61 (London, 1875).

Sammlung altenglischer Legenden, ed. C. Horstmann (Heilbronn, 1878).

Scottish Alliterative Poems in Riming Stanzas, ed. F. J. Amours, Scottish Text Society 27, 38 (1892; repr. London, 1966).

Secular Lyrics of the XIVth and XVth Centuries, ed. R. H. Robbins (Oxford, 1964).

Sentimental and Humorous Romances, ed. E. Kooper (Kalamazoo MI, 2006).

The Siege of Jerusalem, ed. E. Kölbing and M. Day, EETS OS 188 (London, 1932).

Siege of Jerusalem, ed. M. Livingston (Kalamazoo MI, 2004).

The Siege of Jerusalem, ed. R. Hanna and D. Lawton, EETS OS 320 (Oxford, 2003).

The Siege of Jerusalem Electronic Archive, ed. T. J. Stinson, www.siegeofjerusalem.org.

The Sinner's Lament, in *Moral Love Songs and Laments*, ed. S. G. Fein (Kalamazoo MI, 1998), pp. 361–94.

Sir Degrevant, ed. K. Luick, Wiener Beiträge zur englischen Philologie 47 (Vienna, 1917).

Sir Eglamour: A Middle English Romance, ed. A. S. Cook (New York, 1911).

Sir Eglamour. Eine englische Romanze des 14. Jahrhunderts, ed. G. Schleich, Palaestra 53 (Berlin, 1906).

Sir Eglamour of Artois, ed. F. E. Richardson, EETS OS 256 (London, 1965).

Sir Ferumbras, ed. S. J. Herrtage, EETS ES 34 (London, 1879).

Sir Gawain and the Green Knight, ed. J. R. R. Tolkien and E. V. Gordon, rev. N. Davis, 2nd edn (Oxford, 1967).

Sir Perceval of Gales, ed. J. Campion and F. Holthausen (Heidelberg, 1913).

Sir Perceval of Galles and Yvain and Gawain, ed. M. F. Braswell (Kalamazoo MI, 1995).

Six Middle English Romances, ed. M. Mills (London, 1973).

Smithers, G. V., 'Two Newly-Discovered Fragments from the Auchinleck MS', *Medium Ævum* 18 (1949), 1–11.

Some Minor Works of Richard Rolle with The Privity of the Passion by S. Bonaventure, trans. G. E. Hodgson (London, 1923).

A Source Book in Medieval Science, ed. E. Grant (Cambridge MA, 1974).

The Southern Version of Cursor Mundi: Volume II, ed. R. R. Fowler (Ottawa, 1990).

The Southern Version of Cursor Mundi: Volume III, ed. H. J. Stauffenberg (Ottawa, 1985).

'Spätme. Lehrgedichte', ed. K. Brunner, *Archiv* 164 (1933), 178–99.

Syr Gawayne: A Collation of Ancient Romance-Poems by Scottish and English Authors Relating to the Celebrated Knights of the Round Table, ed. F. Madden (London, 1839).

Syr Perecyvelle of Gales, ed. F. S. Ellis (Hammersmith, 1985).

Thesaurus hymnologicus sive hymnorum canticorum sequentiarum circa annum MD usitatarum collectio amplissima, ed. H. A. Daniel, 5 vols. (Leipzig, 1855).

'Thesaurus Pauperum: An Edition of B.M., M.S. Sloane 3489, a Fifteenth Century Medical Miscellany, with Introduction, Notes and Glossary', ed. P. A. Cant (unpublished Ph.D. dissertation, University of London, 1973).

Thomas of Erceldoune, Parts 1–2, ed. I. Nixon (Copenhagen, 1980–3).

Thornton, A., *The Autobiography of Mrs. Alice Thornton of East Newton, Co. York*, ed. C. Jackson, Surtees Society Publications 62 (Durham, 1875; repr. Cambridge, 2010).

The Thornton Manuscript (Lincoln Cathedral MS. 91), intro. D. S. Brewer and A. E. B. Owen (London, 1975).

The Thornton Romances, ed. J. O. Halliwell, Camden Society 30 (London, 1844).

Three Alliterative Saints' Hymns, ed. R. Kennedy, EETS OS 321 (Oxford, 2003).

Three Early English Metrical Romances, ed. J. Robson, Camden Society 19 (London, 1842).

The Three Kings of Cologne: An Early English Translation of the Historia Trium Regum, ed. C. Horstmann, EETS OS 85 (London, 1886).

Three Middle English Charlemagne Romances, ed. A. Lupack (Kalamazoo MI, 1990).

Three Receptaria from Medieval England: The Languages of Medicine in the Fourteenth Century, ed. T. Hunt and M. Benskin, Medium Ævum Monographs n.s. 21 (Oxford, 2001).

'Two Unpublished Middle English Carol-Fragments', ed. K. Hodder, *Archiv* 205 (1969), 378–83.

'Unpublished Verses in Lambeth Palace MS. 559', ed. S. J. Ogilvie-Thomson, *Review of English Studies* n.s. 25 (1974), 387–9.

Wace's Roman de Brut: A History of the British, ed. J. Weiss, 2nd edn (Exeter, 2002).

The Wars of Alexander, ed. H. N. Duggan and T. Turville-Petre, EETS SS 10 (Oxford, 1989).

The Works of Sir Thomas Malory, ed. E. Vinaver (Oxford, 1947, 2nd edn 1967).

Writings Ascribed to Richard Rolle Hermit of Hampole and Materials for His Biography, ed. H. E. Allen (New York, 1927).

Wynnere and Wastoure, ed. S. Trigg, EETS OS 297 (Oxford, 1990).

Wynnere and Wastoure, in *Alliterative Poetry of the Middle Ages: An Anthology*, ed. T. Turville-Petre (Washington DC, 1989), pp. 38–66.

Wynnere and Wastoure and The Parlement of the Thre Ages, ed. W. Ginsberg (Kalamazoo MI, 1992).

Yorkshire Writers: Richard Rolle and His Followers, ed. C. Horstmann, 2 vols. (London 1895–6; repr. Cambridge, 1999).

Secondary sources

Akbari, S. C., 'The Hunger for National Identity in *Richard Coer de Lion*', in *Reading Medieval Culture: Essays in Honor of Robert W. Hanning*, ed. R. Stein and S. Pierson Prior (Notre Dame, 2005), pp. 198–227.

——'Incorporation in the *Siege of Melayne*', in *Pulp Fiction of Medieval England: Essays in Popular Romance*, ed. N. McDonald (Manchester, 2004), pp. 22–44.

Allen, R., 'The Awntyrs off Arthure: Jests and Jousts', in *Romance Reading on the Book: Essays on Medieval Narrative Presented to Maldwyn Mills*, ed. J. Fellows, R. Field, G. Rogers and J. Weiss (Cardiff, 1996), pp. 129–42.

—— 'Place-Names in *The Awntyrs off Arthure*: Corruption, Conjecture, Coincidence', in *Arthurian Studies in Honour of P. J. C. Field* , ed. B. Wheeler (Cambridge, 2004), pp. 181–98.

Ambrisco, A., 'Cannibalism and Cultural Encounters in *Richard Coeur de Lion*', *Journal of Medieval and Early Modern Studies* 29 (1999), 499–528.

Ashley, K. M., 'The Guiler Beguiled: Christ and Satan as Theological Tricksters in Medieval Religious Literature', *Criticism* 24 (1982), 126–37.

'Associated Architectural Society Reports, Vol. VI (1861–2)', *Yorkshire Architectural Society 21st Annual Report* (1862).

Aston, M., *Lollards and Reformers: Images and Literacy in Late Medieval Religion* (London, 1984).

Aveling, H., *Northern Catholics: The Catholic Recusants of the North Riding of Yorkshire, 1558–1790* (London, 1966).

Bahr, A. W., 'Reading Codicological Form in John Gower's Trentham Manuscript', *Studies in the Age of Chaucer* 33 (2011), 219–62.

Beadle, R., 'Prolegomena to a Literary Geography of Later Medieval Norfolk', in *Regionalism in Late Medieval Manuscripts and Texts: Essay Celebrating the Publication of* A Linguistic Atlas of Late Mediaeval English, ed. F. Riddy (Cambridge, 1991), pp. 89–108.

Beck, T. R., *The Cutting Edge: The Early History of the Surgeons of London* (London, 1974).

Beckwith, S., *Christ's Body: Identity, Culture and Society in Late Medieval Writings* (London, 1993).

Bejczy, I., 'Jesus' Laughter and the Childhood Miracles: The *Vita Rhythmica*', *South African Journal of Medieval and Renaissance Studies* 4 (1994), 50–61.

Bell, K. K., and J. N. Couch, eds., *The Texts and Contexts of Oxford, Bodleian Library, MS Laud Misc. 108: The Shaping of English Vernacular Narrative*, Medieval and Renaissance Authors and Texts 6 (Leiden, 2011).

Bennett, H. S., *The Pastons and Their England: Studies in an Age of Transition*, 2nd edn (1922; repr. Cambridge, 1970).

Benskin, M., 'The "Fit-Technique" Explained', in *Regionalism in Late Medieval Manuscripts and Texts: Essay Celebrating the Publication of* A Linguistic Atlas of Late Mediaeval English, ed. F. Riddy (Cambridge, 1991), pp. 9–26.

Benson, L. D., 'The Alliterative *Morte Arthure* and Medieval Tragedy', *Tennessee Studies in Literature* 11 (1966), 75–87.

Bestul, T. H., *Satire and Allegory in* Wynnere and Wastoure (Lincoln NE, 1974).

—— *Texts of the Passion: Latin Devotional Literature and Medieval Society* (Philadelphia, 1996).

Birenbaum, M., 'Affective Vengeance in *Titus and Vespasian*', *Chaucer Review* 43 (2009), 330–44.

Blake, N. F., *Caxton and His World* (London, 1969).

Blanchfield, L. S., 'Rate Revisited: The Compilation of the Narrative Works in MS

Ashmole 61', in *Romance Reading on the Book: Essays on Medieval Narrative Presented to Maldwyn Mills*, ed. J. Fellows, R. Field, G. Rogers and J. Weiss (Cardiff, 1996), pp. 208–20.

—— 'The Romances in Ashmole 61: An Idiosyncratic Scribe', in *Romance in Medieval England*, ed. M. Mills, J. Fellows and C. Meale (Cambridge, 1991), pp. 65–87.

Boffey, J., 'The Charter of the Abbey of the Holy Ghost and Its Role in Manuscript Anthologies', *Yearbook of English Studies* 33 (2003), 120–30.

—— and A. S. G. Edwards, *A New Index of Middle English Verse* (London, 2005).

—— and J. J. Thompson, 'Anthologies and Miscellanies: Production and Choice of Texts', in *Book Production and Publishing in Britain, 1375–1475*, ed. J. Griffiths and D. Pearsall, Cambridge Studies in Publishing and Printing History (Cambridge, 1989), pp. 279–315.

Boro, J., 'Miscellaneity and History: Reading Sixteenth–Century Romance Manuscripts', in *Tudor Manuscripts 1485–1603*, ed. A. S. G. Edwards, English Manuscript Studies 1100–1700, vol. 15 (London, 2010), pp. 123–51.

Brewer, D. S., 'Introduction', in *The Thornton Manuscript (Lincoln Cathedral MS. 91)*, intro. D. S. Brewer and A. E. B. Owen (London, 1975), pp. vii–xi.

—— and A. E. B. Owen, 'Collation of the Manuscript', in *The Thornton Manuscript (Lincoln Cathedral MS. 91)*, intro. D. S. Brewer and A. E. B. Owen (London, 1975), p. xii.

Briquet, C.-M., *Les filigranes*, 4 vols. (Leipzig, 1923).

British Library Catalogue of Illuminated Manuscripts, www.bl.uk./catalogues/illuminatedmanuscripts.

Bühler, C., *The Fifteenth-Century Book: The Scribes, the Printers, the Decorators* (Philadelphia, 1960).

Bulmer, T., *Bulmer's History and Directory of North Yorkshire* (Preston, 1890).

Butlin, R. A., *Historical Atlas of North Yorkshire* (Otley, 2003).

Carlson, J. I., 'The Alliterative *Morte Arthure*: A Hyper-Critical Edition' (unpublished Ph.D. dissertation, University of Virginia, 2006).

—— 'Scribal Intentions in Medieval Romance: A Case Study of Robert Thornton', *Studies in Bibliography* 58 (2007–8), 49–71.

Carpenter, C., 'Religion', in *Gentry Culture in Late-Medieval England*, ed. R. Radulescu and A. Truelove (Manchester, 2005), pp. 134–50.

Cartlidge, D. R., and J. K. Elliott, *Art and the Christian Apocrypha* (London, 2001).

The Catholic Encyclopedia, http://www.newadvent.org.

Christianson, C. P., *Memorials of the Book Trade in Medieval London: The Archives of Old London Bridge* (Cambridge, 1987).

—— 'The Rise of London's Book Trade', in *The Cambridge History of the Book in Britain: Volume 3, 1400–1557*, ed. L. Hellinga and J. B. Trapp (Cambridge, 1999), pp. 128–47.

Citrome, J. J., *The Surgeon in Medieval English Literature* (New York, 2006).

Cohen, J., *Christ Killers: The Jews and the Passion from the Bible to the Big Screen* (Oxford, 2007).

—— *The Friars and the Jews: The Evolution of Medieval Anti-Judaism* (Ithaca NY, 1984).

Cook, T. D., with P. Whiteford and N. M. Kennedy, 'XXIV. Tales', in *A Manual of the*

Writings in Middle English, 1050–1500, ed. A. E. Hartung, vol. 9 (New Haven, 1993), pp. 3138–330, 3471–570.

Copeland, R., 'Lollard Writings', in *The Cambridge Companion to Medieval English Literature, 1100–1500*, ed. L. Scanlon (Cambridge, 2009), pp. 111–23.

Cordery, L., 'Cannibal Diplomacy: Otherness in the Middle English Text *Richard Coer de Lion*', in *Meeting the Foreign in the Middle Ages*, ed. Albrecht Classen (New York, 2002), pp. 153–71.

Corpus of Middle English Prose and Verse, http://quod.lib.umich.edu/c/cme/.

Coss, P., *The Foundations of Gentry Life: The Multons of Frampton and Their World* (Oxford, 2010).

Couch, J. N., 'Misbehaving God: The Case of the Christ Child in Ms Laud Misc. 108 "Infancy of Jesus Christ"', in *Mindful Spirits in Late Medieval Literature: Essays in Honor of Elizabeth Kirk*, ed. B. Wheeler (New York, 2006), pp. 31–43.

Crofts, T. H., 'The Occasion of the *Morte Arthure*: Textual History and Marginal Decoration in the Thornton MS', *Arthuriana* 20 (2010), 5–27.

Cullmann, O., 'Infancy Gospels', in *New Testament Apocrypha: 1. Gospels and Related Writings*, ed. W. Schneemelcher, trans. R. McL. Wilson, rev. edn (Louisville KY, 1991), pp. 414–69.

Dagenais, J., *The Ethics of Reading in Manuscript Culture: Glossing the 'Libro del buen amor'* (Princeton, 1994).

Dalrymple, R., *Language and Piety in Middle English Romance* (Cambridge, 2000).

Daly, O. J., 'This World and the Next: Social and Religious Ideologies in the Romances of the Thornton Manuscript' (unpublished Ph.D. dissertation, University of Oregon, 1977).

Davis, N. Z., *The Return of Martin Guerre* (Cambridge MA, 1983).

D'Evelyn, C., and F. A. Foster, 'V. Saints' Legends', in *A Manual of the Writings in Middle English, 1050–1500*, ed. J. B. Severs, vol. 2 (New Haven, 1970), pp. 410–57, 553–639.

Digital Publication of the 'Piccard' Collection of Watermarks, German Research Foundation, http://www.landesarchiv-bw.de/web/44577.

Donovan, M. J., C. W. Dunn, L. H. Hornstein, R. M. Lumiansky, H. Newstead and H. M. Smyser, 'I. Romances', in *A Manual of the Writings in Middle English, 1050–1500*, ed. J. B. Severs, vol. 1 (New Haven, 1967).

Dove, M., *The First English Bible: The Text and Context of the Wycliffite Versions* (Cambridge, 2007).

Doyle, A. I., 'Publication by Members of the Religious Orders', in *Book Production and Publishing in Britain, 1375–1475*, ed. J. Griffiths and D. Pearsall, Cambridge Studies in Publishing and Printing History (Cambridge, 1989), pp. 109–23.

—— 'Remarks on the Surviving Manuscripts of *Piers Plowman*', in *Medieval English Religious and Ethical Literature: Essays in Honour of G. H. Russell*, ed. G. Kratzmann and J. Simpson (Cambridge, 1986), pp. 35–48.

—— 'Review of *Robert Thornton and the London Thornton Manuscript*, by J. J. Thompson', *Review of English Studies* n.s. 41 (1990), 241–2.

—— and M. B. Parkes, 'The Production of Copies of the *Canterbury Tales* and the *Confessio Amantis* in the Early Fifteenth Century', in *Medieval Scribes, Manuscripts, and Libraries: Essays Presented to N. R. Ker*, ed. M. B. Parkes and A. G. Watson (London, 1978), pp. 163–210.

Duffy, E., *The Stripping of the Altars: Traditional Religion in England, 1400–1580* (New Haven, 1992).

Duggan, H. N., 'Alliterative Patterning as a Basis for Emendation in Middle English Alliterative Poetry', *Studies in the Age of Chaucer* 8 (1986), 73–105.

—— 'Extended A-Verses in Middle English Alliterative Poetry', *Parergon* 18 (2000), 53–76.

—— 'Final -e and the Rhythmic Structure of the B-Verse in Middle English Alliterative Poetry', *Modern Philology* 86 (1988), 119–45.

—— 'Scribal Self-Correction and Editorial Theory', *Neuphilologische Mitteilungen* 91 (1990), 215–27.

—— 'The Shape of the B-Verse in Middle English Alliterative Poetry', *Speculum* 61 (1986), 564–92.

Dzon, M., 'Boys Will Be Boys: The Physiology of Childhood and the Apocryphal Christ Child in the Later Middle Ages', *Viator* 42 (2011), 179–225.

—— 'Cecily Neville and the Apocryphal *Infantia Salvatoris* in the Middle Ages', *Mediaeval Studies* 71 (2009), 235–300.

—— 'The Image of the Wanton Christ-Child in the Apocryphal Infancy Legends of Late Medieval England' (unpublished Ph.D. dissertation, University of Toronto, 2004).

—— 'Joseph and the Amazing Christ-Child of Late-Medieval Legend', in *Childhood in the Middle Ages and the Renaissance: The Results of a Paradigm Shift in the History of Mentality*, ed. Albrecht Classen (Berlin, 2005), pp. 135–57.

—— and T. Kenney, 'Introduction: The Infancy of Scholarship on the Medieval Christ Child', in *The Christ Child in Medieval Culture: Alpha es et O!*, ed. M. Dzon and T. Kenney (Toronto, 2012), pp. xiii–xxii.

Eastmead, W., *Historia Rievallensis* (London, 1824).

Edwards, A. S. G., 'Lydgate Manuscripts: Some Directions for Future Research', in *Manuscripts and Readers in Fifteenth-Century England: The Literary Implications of Manuscript Study. Essays from the 1981 Conference at the University of York*, ed. D. Pearsall (Cambridge, 1983), pp. 15–26.

Elliott, J. K., 'Birth and Infancy Gospels', in *The Apocryphal New Testament: A Collection of Apocryphal Christian Literature in an English Translation Based on M. R. James*, ed. J. K. Elliott (Oxford, 1993), pp. 46–122.

Evans, M. J., *Rereading Middle English Romance: Manuscript Layout, Decoration, and the Rhetoric of Composite Structure* (Montreal and Kingston, 1995).

Fein, S., 'The Epistemology of Titles in Editing Whole-Manuscripts: The Lyric Sequence, in Particular', *Poetica* 71 (2009), 49–74.

—— 'The Literary Scribe: The Ludlow Scribe of Harley 2253 and Robert Thornton as Case Studies', in *Insular Books: Vernacular Miscellanies in Late Medieval Britain*, ed. M. Connolly and R. Radulescu, Proceedings of the British Academy (London, forthcoming 2015).

——, ed. *My Wyl and My Wrytyng: Essays on John the Blind Audelay* (Kalamazoo MI, 2009).

—— 'Quatrefoil and *Quatrefolia*: The Devotional Layout of an Alliterative Poem', *Journal of the Early Book Society* 2 (1999), 26–45.

——, ed., *Studies in the Harley Manuscript: The Scribes, Contents, and Social Contexts of British Library MS Harley 2253* (Kalamazoo MI, 2000).

Field, P. J. C., '"Above Rubies": Malory and *Morte Arthure* 2559–61', in *Malory: Texts and Sources*, ed. P. J. C. Field (Cambridge, 2001), pp. 196–8.

Field, R., 'Popular Romance: The Material and the Problems', in *A Companion to Medieval Popular Romance*, ed. R. L. Radulescu and C. J. Rushton (Cambridge, 2009), pp. 9–30.

Finlayson, J., 'The Concept of the Hero in *Morte Arthure*', in *Chaucer und seine Zeit: Symposium für Walter F. Schirmer*, ed. A. Esch (Tubingen, 1968), pp. 249–74.

—— 'The Context of the Crusading Romances in the London Thornton Manuscript', *Anglia* 130 (2012), 240–63.

—— 'Reading Romances in Their Manuscript: Lincoln Cathedral Manuscript 91 ("Thornton")', *Anglia* 123 (2005), 632–66.

Fredell, J., 'Decorated Initials in the Lincoln Thornton Manuscript', *Studies in Bibliography* 47 (1994), 78–88.

—— '"Go Litel Quayer": Lydgate's Pamphlet Poetry', *Journal of the Early Book Society* 9 (2006), 51–74.

—— 'The Pearl-Poet Manuscript in York', *Studies in the Age of Chaucer* 36 (forthcoming, 2014).

Frederiksen, P., *Augustine and the Jews: A Christian Defense of Jews and Judaism* (New York, 2008).

Friedman, J. B., *Northern English Books, Owners, and Makers in the Late Middle Ages* (Syracuse, 1995).

Frost, U., *Das Commonplace Book von John Colyns: Untersuchung und Teiledition der Handschrift Harley 2252 der British Library in London*, Europäische Hochschulschriften 14, vol. 186 (Frankfurt, 1988).

Getz, F. M., 'Charity, Translation, and the Language of Medical Learning in Medieval England', *Bulletin of the History of Medicine* 64 (1994), 1–17.

—— 'Medical Education in Later Medieval England', in *The History of Medical Education in Britain*, ed. V. Nutton and R. Porter (Amsterdam, 1995), pp. 76–93.

Gillespie, A., 'Poets, Printers, and Early English *Sammelbände*', *Huntington Library Quarterly* 67 (2004), 189–214.

Gillespie, V., 'Dial M for Mystic: Mystical Texts in the Library of Syon Abbey and the Spirituality of the Syon Brethren', in *The Medieval Mystical Tradition in England, Ireland and Wales*, ed. M. Glasscoe (Cambridge, 1999), pp. 241–68.

Ginzburg, C., *The Cheese and the Worms: The Cosmos of a Sixteenth-Century Miller*, trans. J. Tedeschi and A. Tedeschi (Baltimore, 1980).

—— 'Microhistory: Two or Three Things That I Know about It', trans. J. Tedeschi and A. C. Tedeschi, *Critical Inquiry* 20 (1993), 10–35.

Glasscoe, M., *English Medieval Mystics* (London, 1993).

Goldberg, P. J. P., 'Lay Book Ownership in Late Medieval York: The Evidence of Wills', *The Library* 6th ser. 16 (1994), 181–9.

Göller, K., 'Reality versus Romance: A Reassessment of the Alliterative *Morte Arthure*', in *The Alliterative* Morte Arthure: *A Reassessment of the Poem*, ed. K. Göller (Cambridge, 1981), pp. 15–28.

Gordon, E. V., and E. Vinaver, 'New Light on the Text of the Alliterative *Morte Arthure*', *Medium Ævum* 6 (1937), 81–98.

Gorny, D., 'Reading Robert Thornton's Library: Romance and Nationalism in Lincoln, Cathedral Library MS 91 and London, British Library MS Additional 31042' (unpublished Ph.D. dissertation, University of Ottawa, 2013).

Green, M., 'Salerno on the Thames: The Genesis of Anglo-Norman Medical Literature', in *Language and Culture in Medieval Britain: The French of England, c. 1100–c. 1500*, ed. J. Wogan-Browne, with C. Collette, M. Kowaleski, L. Mooney, A. Putter and D. Trotter (York, 2009).

Green, R. F., 'Friar William Appleton and the Date of Langland's B Text', *Yearbook of Langland Studies* 11 (1997), 87–96.

Greene, R. L., 'XIV. Carols', in *A Manual of the Writings in Middle English, 1050–1500*, ed. A. E. Hartung, vol. 6 (New Haven, 1980), pp. 1743–52, 1940–2018.

Grindley, C. J., 'Reading *Piers Plowman* C-Text Annotations: Notes toward the Classification of Printed and Written Marginalia in Texts from the British Isles 1300–1641', in *The Medieval Professional Reader at Work: Evidence from Manuscripts of Chaucer, Langland, Kempe, and Gower*, ed. K. Kerby-Fulton and M. Hilmo, English Literary Studies 85 (Victoria BC, 2001), pp. 73–141.

Grounds, A., 'Evolution of a Manuscript: The Pavement Hours', in *Design and Distribution of Late Medieval Manuscripts in England*, ed. L. R. Mooney and M. Connolly (York, 2008), pp. 118–38.

Guddat-Figge, G., *Catalogue of Manuscripts Containing Middle English Romances* (Munich, 1976).

Hall, T. N., 'The Miracle of the Lengthened Beam in Apocryphal and Hagiographical Tradition', in *Marvels, Monsters, and Miracles: Studies in the Medieval and Early Modern Imaginations*, ed. T. S. Jones and D. A. Sprunger (Kalamazoo MI, 2002), pp. 109–39.

Hamel, M., 'Arthurian Romance in Fifteenth-Century Lindsey: The Books of the Lords Welles', *Modern Language Quarterly* 51 (1990), 341–61.

—— 'The "Christening" of Sir Priamus in the Alliterative *Morte Arthure*', *Viator* 13 (1982), 295–307.

—— 'Scribal Self-Corrections in the Thornton *Morte Arthure*', *Studies in Bibliography* 36 (1983), 119–37.

—— 'The *Siege of Jerusalem* as a Crusading Poem', in *Journeys toward God: Pilgrimage and Crusade*, ed. Barbara N. Sargent-Baur (Kalamazoo MI, 1992), pp. 177–94.

Hanna, R., 'The Growth of Robert Thornton's Books', *Studies in Bibliography* 40 (1987), 51–61.

—— 'Humphrey Newton and Bodleian Library, MS Lat. Misc. C.66', *Medium Ævum* 69 (2000), 279–91.

—— 'The London Thornton Manuscript: A Corrected Collation', *Studies in Bibliography* 37 (1984), 122–30.

—— 'Miscellaneity and Vernacularity: Conditions of Literary Production in Late

Medieval England', in *The Whole Book: Cultural Perspectives on the Medieval Miscellany*, ed. S. G. Nicholas and S. Wenzel (Ann Arbor, 1996), pp. 37–51.

—— 'The Production of Cambridge University Library MS. Ff.1.6', *Studies in Bibliography* 40 (1987), 62–70.

—— *Pursuing History: Middle English Manuscripts and Their Texts* (Stanford CA, 1996).

—— 'Sir Thomas Berkeley and His Patronage', *Speculum* 64 (1989), 878–916.

—— and A. S. G. Edwards, 'Rotheley, the De Vere Circle, and the Ellesmere Chaucer', *Huntington Library Quarterly* 58 (1996), 11–35.

Hardman, P., 'Compiling the Nation: Fifteenth-Century Miscellany Manuscripts', in *Nation, Court and Culture: New Essays on Fifteenth-Century English Poetry*, ed. H. Cooney (Dublin, 2001), pp. 50–69.

—— 'Domestic Learning and Teaching: Investigating Evidence for the Role of "Household Miscellanies" in Late-Medieval England', in *Women and Writing c. 1340–1650*, ed. A. Lawrence-Mathers and P. Hardman (York, 2010), pp. 15–33.

—— Introduction to *The Heege Manuscript: A Facsimile of National Library of Scotland MS Advocates 19.3.1*, Leeds Texts and Monographs n.s. 16 (Leeds, 2000), pp. 1–57.

—— 'Reading the Spaces: Pictorial Intentions in the Thornton MSS, Lincoln Cathedral MS 91, and BL MS Add. 31042', *Medium Ævum* 63 (1994), 250–74.

—— 'The *Sege of Melayne*: A Fifteenth-Century Reading', in *Tradition and Transformation in Medieval Romance*, ed. R. Field (Cambridge, 1999), pp. 71–86.

—— 'The Unity of the Ireland Manuscript', *Reading Medieval Studies* 2 (1976), 45–62.

—— 'Windows into the Text: Unfilled Spaces in Some Fifteenth-Century Manuscripts', *Texts and Their Contexts: Papers from the Early Book Society*, ed. J. Scattergood and J. Boffey (Dublin 1997), pp. 44–70.

Harley, M. P., 'The Middle English Contents of a Fifteenth-Century Medical Book', *Mediaevalia* 8 (1982), 171–88.

Harris, K., 'John Gower's "Confessio amantis": The Virtues of Bad Texts', in *Manuscripts and Readers in Fifteenth-Century England: The Literary Implications of Manuscript Study. Essays from the 1981 Conference at the University of York*, ed. D. Pearsall (Cambridge, 1983), pp. 27–40.

—— 'The Origins and Make-up of Cambridge University Library MS Ff.1.6', *Transactions of the Cambridge Bibliographical Society* 8 (1983), 299–333.

—— 'Ownership and Readership: Studies in the Provenance of the Manuscripts of Gower's *Confessio amantis*' (unpublished D.Phil. thesis, University of York, 1993).

Harriss, G., *Shaping the Nation: England 1360–1461* (Oxford, 2005).

Hebron, M., *The Medieval Siege: Theme and Image in Middle English Romance* (Oxford, 1997).

Hellinga, L., *William Caxton and Early Printing in England* (London, 2010).

Heng, G., *Empire of Magic: Medieval Romance and the Politics of Cultural Fantasy* (New York, 2003).

Holt, J. C., *The Northerners* (Oxford, 1961).

Horobin, S., 'Adam Pinkhurst and the Copying of British Library, MS Additional 35287 of the B Version of *Piers Plowman*', *Yearbook of Langland Studies* 23 (2009), 61–83.

—— 'Adam Pinkhurst, Geoffrey Chaucer, and the Hengwrt Manuscript of the *Canterbury Tales*', *Chaucer Review* 44 (2010), 351–67.

—— '"In London and opeland": The Dialect and Circulation of the C Version of *Piers Plowman*', *Medium Ævum* 74 (2005), 248–69.

—— 'A Manuscript Found in Abbotsford House and the Lost Legendary of Osbern Bokenham', in *Regional Manuscripts 1200–1700*, ed. A. S. G. Edwards, English Manuscript Studies 1100–1700, vol. 14 (London, 2008), pp. 132–64.

—— 'Mapping the Words', in *The Production of Books in England 1350–1500*, ed. A. Gillespie and D. Wakelin (Cambridge, 2011), pp. 59–78.

—— 'The Scribe of Bodleian Library, MS Digby 102 and the Circulation of the C Text of *Piers Plowman*', *Yearbook of Langland Studies* 24 (2010), 89–112.

—— and A. Wiggins, 'Reconsidering Lincoln's Inn MS 150', *Medium Ævum* 77 (2008), 30–53.

Horrall, S. M., '"For the cummun at understand": *Cursor Mundi* and Its Background', in *De Cella in Saeculum: Religious and Secular Life and Devotion in Late Medieval England*, ed. M. G. Sargent (Cambridge, 1989), pp. 97–107.

—— 'The London Thornton Manuscript: A New Collation', *Manuscripta* 23 (1979), 99–103.

—— 'The Manuscripts of *Cursor Mundi*', *TEXT: Transactions of the Society for Textual Scholarship* 2 (1985), 69–82.

—— 'The Watermarks of the Thornton Manuscripts', *Notes and Queries* n.s. 27 (1980), 385–6.

Hourihane, C., *Pontius Pilate, Anti-Semitism, and the Passion in Medieval Art* (Princeton, 2009).

Hudson, A., 'Lollard Book Production', in *Book Production and Publishing in Britain, 1375–1475*, ed. J. Griffiths and D. Pearsall, Cambridge Studies in Publishing and Printing History (Cambridge, 1989), pp. 125–41.

Hughes, J., *Pastors and Visionaries: Religion and Secular Life in Late Medieval Yorkshire* (Woodbridge, 1988).

Hunt, T., *Popular Medicine in Thirteenth-Century England* (Cambridge, 1990).

Huws, D., 'MS Porkington 10 and Its Scribes', in *Romance Reading on the Book: Essays on Medieval Narrative Presented to Maldwyn Mills*, ed. J. Fellows, R. Field, G. Rogers and J. Weiss (Cardiff, 1996), pp. 188–207.

Jefferson, J. A., and A. Putter, 'Alliterative Patterning in the *Morte Arthure*', *Studies in Philology* 102 (2005), 415–33.

Johnson, L., 'The Alliterative *Morte Arthure*', in *The Arthur of the English*, ed. W. R. J. Barron (Cardiff, 2001), pp. 90–9.

Johnston, M., 'A New Document Relating to the Life of Robert Thornton', *The Library* 7th ser. 8 (2007), 304–13.

—— 'Robert Thornton and *The Siege of Jerusalem*', *Yearbook of Langland Studies* 23 (2009), 125–62.

—— *Romance and the Gentry in Late Medieval England* (Oxford, forthcoming 2014).

Jones, C., 'Discourse Communities and Medical Texts', in *Medical and Scientific Writing in Late Medieval English*, ed. I. Taavitsainen and P. Pahta (Cambridge, 2004), pp. 23–36

Jones, P. M., 'Four Middle English Translations of John of Arderne', in *Latin and Vernacular: Studies in Late-Medieval Texts and Manuscripts*, ed. A. J. Minnis (Cambridge, 1989), pp. 61–89.

—— 'Medicine and Science', in *The Cambridge History of the Book in Britain, Vol. 3: 1400–1557*, ed. L. Hellinga and J. B. Trapp (Cambridge, 1999), pp. 433–48.

Jordan, R., *Handbook of Middle English Grammar*, trans. E. J. Crook, *Janua Linguarum* Series Practica 218 (The Hague, 1974).

Jurath, H., S. H. Kuhn, *et al.*, *Middle English Dictionary* (Ann Arbor MI, 1954–2001), http://www.quod.lib.umich.edu/m/med.

Kane, G., 'The Text', in *A Companion to 'Piers Plowman'*, ed. J. A. Alford (Berkeley and Los Angeles, 1988), pp. 175–200.

Kato, T., *A Concordance to the Works of Sir Thomas Malory* (Tokyo, 1974).

Keiser, G. R., 'Lincoln Cathedral Library MS. 91: Life and Milieu of the Scribe', *Studies in Bibliography* 32 (1979), 158–79.

—— 'Medicines for Horses: The Continuity from Script to Print', *Veterinary History* n.s. 12 (2004), 125–48.

—— 'Medicines for Horses: The Continuity from Script to Print', *Yale University Library Gazette* 69 (1995), 111–28.

—— 'The Middle English *Planctus Mariae* and the Rhetoric of Pathos', in *The Popular Literature of Medieval England*, ed. T. J. Heffernan (Knoxville, 1985), pp. 167–93.

—— 'More Light on the Life and Milieu of Robert Thornton', *Studies in Bibliography* 36 (1983), 111–19.

—— 'MS. Rawlinson A.393: Another Findern Manuscript', *Transactions of the Cambridge Bibliographical Society* 7 (1980), 445–8.

—— 'The Nineteenth-Century Discovery of the Thornton Manuscript', *Papers of the Bibliographical Society of America* 77 (1983), 167–90.

—— '"Noght how lang man lifs; but how wele": The Laity and the Ladder of Perfection', in *De Cella in Saeculum: Religious and Secular Life and Devotion in Late Medieval England*, ed. M. G. Sargent (Cambridge, 1989), pp. 145–59.

—— 'A Note on the Descent of the Thornton Manuscript', *Transactions of the Cambridge Bibliographical Society* 6 (1976), 347–49.

—— 'Reconstructing Robert Thornton's Herbal', *Medium Ævum* 65 (1996), 35–53.

—— 'Review of *Robert Thornton and the London Thornton Manuscript*, by J. J. Thompson', *Envoi* 2 (1989), 155–60.

—— 'Robert Thornton's *Liber de Diversis Medicinis*: Text, Vocabulary, and Scribal Confusion', in *Rethinking Middle English: Linguistic and Literary Approaches*, ed. N. Ritt and H. Schnedel (Frankfurt, 2005), pp. 30–41.

—— 'Þe Holy Boke Gratia Dei', *Viator* 12 (1981), 289–317.

—— 'The Theme of Justice in the Alliterative *Morte Arthure*', *Annuale Mediaevale* 16 (1975), 94–109.

—— '"To Knawe God Almyghtyn": Robert Thornton's Devotional Book', in *Spätmittelalterliche geistliche Literatur in der Nationalsprache*, vol. 2, Analecta Cartusiana, ed. J. Hogg (Salzburg, 1984), pp. 103–29.

—— 'Two Medieval Plague Treatises and Their Afterlife in Early Modern England', *Journal of the History of Medicine* 58 (2003), 292–324.

—— 'XXV. Works of Science and Information', in *A Manual of the Writings in Middle English, 1050–1500*, ed. A. E. Hartung, vol. 10 (New Haven, 1998).

Kellogg, A. B., 'The Language of the Alliterative *Siege of Jerusalem*' (unpublished Ph.D. dissertation, University of Chicago, 1943).

Kennedy, B., 'Cambridge MS Dd.4.24: A Misogynous Scribal Revision of *The Wife of Bath's Prologue?' Chaucer Review* 30 (1996), 343–58.

—— 'Contradictory Responses to the Wife of Bath as Evidenced by Fifteenth-Century Manuscript Variants', *Canterbury Tales Project Occasional Papers* 2 (1997), 23–39.

Kennedy, R., 'The Evangelist in Robert Thornton's Devotional Book: Organizing Principles at the Level of the Quire', *Journal of the Early Book Society* 8 (2005), 71–95.

Ker, N. R., *Medieval Libraries of Great Britain: A List of Surviving Books*, Royal Historical Society Guides and Handbooks 3, 2nd edn (London, 1964).

Kerby-Fulton, K., and D. L. Despres, *Iconography and the Professional Reader: The Politics of Book Production in the Douce* Piers Plowman, Medieval Cultures 15 (Minneapolis, 1998).

'Kirkby Malham', http://www.kirkbymalham.info/LHfocus.html.

Kiser, L., 'Elde and His Teaching in *The Parlement of the Thre Ages', Philological Quarterly* 66 (1987), 303–14.

Kline, D. T., 'The Audience and Function of the Apocryphal *Infancy of Jesus Christ* in Oxford, Bodleian Library, MS Laud Misc. 108', in *The Texts and Contexts of Oxford, Bodleian Library, MS Laud Misc. 108: The Shaping of English Vernacular Narrative*, ed. K. K. Bell and J. N. Couch, Medieval and Renaissance Authors and Texts 6 (Leiden, 2011), pp. 137–55.

Kwakkel, E., 'Late Medieval Text Collections: A Codicological Typology Based on Single-Author Manuscripts', in *Author, Reader, Book: Medieval Authority in Theory and Practice*, ed. S. Partridge and E. Kwakkel (Toronto, 2012), pp. 56–79.

—— 'A New Type of Book for a New Type of Reader: The Emergence of Paper in Vernacular Book Production', *The Library* 7th ser. 4 (2003), 219–48.

Ladurie, E. L. R., *Montaillou: The Promised Land of Error*, trans. B. Bray (New York, 1978).

Lagorio, V. M., and M. G. Sargent, with R. Bradley, 'XXIII. English Mystical Writings', in *A Manual of the Writings in Middle English, 1050–1500*, ed. A. E. Hartung, vol. 9 (New Haven, 1993), pp. 3049–137, 3405–71.

Lawton, D., 'Gaytryge's Sermon, "Dictamen", and Middle English Alliterative Verse', *Modern Philology* 76 (1979), 329–43.

—— 'Titus Goes Hunting and Hawking: The Poetics of Recreation and Revenge in *The Siege of Jerusalem*', in *Individuality and Achievement in Middle English Poetry*, ed. O. S. Pickering (Woodbridge, 1997), pp. 105–18.

Leverett, E., 'Holy Bloodshed: Violence and Christian Piety in the Romances of the London Thornton Manuscript' (unpublished Ph.D. dissertation, The Ohio State University, 2006).

LeVert, L., '"Crucifye Hem, Crucifye Hem": The Subject and Affective Response in Middle English Passion Narratives', *Essays in Medieval Studies* 14 (1997), 73–90.

Levi, G., 'On Microhistory', in *New Perspectives on Historical Writing*, ed. P. Burke, 2nd edn (University Park PA, 2001), pp. 93–113.

Lewis, R. E., and A. McIntosh, *A Descriptive Guide to the Manuscripts of the* Pricke of Conscience, Medium Ævum Monographs n.s. 12 (Oxford, 1982).

——, N. F. Blake and A. S. G. Edwards, *Index of Printed Middle English Prose* (New York, 1985).

Liddy, C. D., 'William Frost, the City of York and Scrope's Rebellion of 1405', in *Richard Scrope: Archbishop, Rebel, Martyr*, ed. P. J. P. Goldberg (Donington, 2007), pp. 77–82.

Lohman, M. E., 'Thornton', freepages.genealogy.rootsweb.ancestry.com/~celticlady/thornton/England_Thorntons.pdf.

Louis, C., 'XXII. Proverbs, Precepts, and Monitory Pieces', in *A Manual of the Writings in Middle English, 1050–1500*, ed. A. E. Hartung, vol. 9 (New Haven, 1993), pp. 2957–3048, 3349–404.

Lucas, P. J., *From Author to Audience: John Capgrave and Medieval Publication* (Dublin, 1997).

Lyall, R. J., 'Materials: The Paper Revolution', in *Book Production and Publishing in Britain, 1375–1475*, ed. J. Griffiths and D. Pearsall, Cambridge Studies in Publishing and Printing History (Cambridge, 1989), pp. 11–29.

Machan, T. W., *Textual Criticism and Middle English Texts* (Charlottesville VA, 1994).

Manion, L., 'The Loss of the Holy Land and *Sir Isumbras*: Literary Contributions to Fourteenth-Century Crusade Discourse', *Speculum* 85 (2010), 65–90.

Mann, J., 'Malory: Knightly Combat in *Le Morte D'Arthur*', in *The New Pelican Guide to English Literature: 1. Medieval Literature. Part One: Chaucer and the Alliterative Tradition*, ed. B. Ford (Harmondsworth, 1982), pp. 331–9.

Marsh, D., '"I see by sizt of evidence": Information Gathering in Late Medieval Cheshire', in *Courts, Counties and the Capital in the Later Middle Ages*, ed. D. E. S. Dunn (New York, 1996), pp. 71–92.

Marshall, S. C., 'Manuscript Agency and the Findern Manuscript', *Neuphilologische Mitteilungen* 108 (2007), 339–49.

Matheson, L. M., '*Médecin sans frontières?* The European Dissemination of John of Burgundy's Plague Treatise', *American Notes and Queries* 18 (2005), 17–28.

Matthews, D., *The Making of Middle English 1765–1910* (Minneapolis, 1999).

Matthews, W., *The Tragedy of Arthur: A Study of the Alliterative* Morte Arthure (Berkeley, 1960).

McDonald, N., 'Eating People and the Alimentary Logic of *Richard Coeur de Lion*', in *Pulp Fictions of Medieval England: Essays in Popular Romance*, ed. N. McDonald (Manchester, 2004), pp. 124–50.

McDonnell, J., ed., *A History of Helmsley, Rievaulx, and District* (York, 1963).

—— and R. H. Hayes, 'Roads and Communications, I (Pre-Conquest and Mediaeval)', in *A History of Helmsley, Rievaulx and District*, ed. J. McDonnell, Yorkshire Archaeological Society (York, 1963), pp. 60–70.

McIntosh, A., 'A New Approach to Middle English Dialectology', *English Studies* 44 (1963), 1–11.

—— 'The Textual Transmission of the Alliterative *Morte Arthure*', in *English and Medieval Studies Presented to J. R. R. Tolkien on the Occasion of His Seventieth Birthday*, ed. N. Davis and C. L. Wrenn (London, 1962), pp. 231–40.

——, M. L. Samuels and M. Benskin, with M. Laing and K. Williamson, *A Linguistic Atlas of Late Mediaeval English*, 4 vols. (Aberdeen, 1986).

McNamer, S., *Affective Meditation and the Invention of Medieval Compassion* (Philadelphia, 2010).

Meale, C., 'The Compiler at Work: John Colyns and BL MS Harley 2252', in *Manuscripts and Readers in Fifteenth-Century England: The Literary Implications of Manuscript Study. Essays from the 1981 Conference at the University of York*, ed. D. Pearsall (Cambridge, 1983), pp. 82–103.

Mehl, D., *The Middle English Romances of the Thirteenth and Fourteenth Centuries* (London, 1968).

Mills, R., 'The Early *South English Legendary* and Difference: Race, Place, Language, and Belief', in *The Texts and Contexts of Oxford, Bodleian Library, MS Laud Misc. 108: The Shaping of English Vernacular Narrative*, ed. K. K. Bell and J. N. Couch, Medieval and Renaissance Authors and Texts 6 (Leiden, 2011), pp. 197–221.

Minnis, A. J., *Medieval Theory of Authorship*, 2nd edn (Philadelphia, 2010).

Moll, R., *Before Malory: Reading Arthur in Later Medieval England* (Toronto, 2003).

Mooney, L. R., 'Chaucer's Scribe', *Speculum* 81 (2006), 97–138.

—— 'A Holograph Copy of Thomas Hoccleve's *Regiment of Princes*', *Studies in the Age of Chaucer* 33 (2011), 263–96.

—— 'Locating Scribal Activity in Late Medieval London', in *Design and Distribution of Late Medieval Manuscripts in England*, ed. M. Connolly and L. R. Mooney (York, 2008), pp. 183–204.

—— 'Manuscript Evidence for the Use of Medieval Scientific and Utilitarian Texts', in *Interstices: Studies in Middle English and Anglo-Latin Texts in Honour of A. G. Rigg*, ed. R. F. Green and L. R. Mooney (Toronto, 2004), pp. 184–202.

—— and S. Horobin, 'A *Piers Plowman* Manuscript by the Hengwrt/Ellesmere Scribe and Its Implications for London Standard English', *Studies in the Age of Chaucer* 26 (2004), 65–112.

—— and L. M. Matheson, 'The Beryn Scribe and His Texts: Evidence for Multiple-Copy Production of Manuscripts in Fifteenth-Century England', *The Library* 7th ser. 4 (2003), 347–70.

——, D. W. Mosser, E. Solopova and D. H. Radcliffe, *The Digital Index of Middle English Verse*, www.dimev.net.

Moran, J. A. H., 'A "Common Profit" Library in Fifteenth-Century England and Other Books for Chaplains', *Manuscripta* 28 (1984), 17–25.

—— *The Growth of English Schooling, 1340–1548: Learning, Literacy, and Laicization in Pre-Reformation York Diocese* (Princeton, 1985).

Morey, J. H., *Book and Verse: A Guide to Middle English Biblical Literature* (Chicago, 2000).

Moriya, Y., 'Identical Alliteration in the *Alliterative Morte Arthure*', *English Language Notes* 38 (2000), 1–16.

Morrisroe, P., 'Imposition of Hands', in *The Catholic Encyclopedia*, vol. 7, www.newadvent.org.

Morrissey, J. W., '"Termes of Phisik": Reading between Literary and Medical Discourses in Geoffrey Chaucer's *Canterbury Tales* and John Lydgate's *Dietary*' (unpublished Ph.D. dissertation, McGill University, 2011).

Mueller, A., 'The Historiography of the Dragon: Heraldic Violence in the Alliterative *Morte Arthure*', *Studies in the Age of Chaucer* 32 (2010), 295–324.

Muir, E., 'Introduction: Observing Trifles', in *Microhistory and the Lost Peoples of Europe*, ed. E. Muir and G. Ruggiero, trans. E. Branch (Baltimore, 1991), pp. vii–xxviii.

Mustain, J. K., 'A Rural Medical Practitioner in Fifteenth-Century England', *Bulletin of the History of Medicine* 46 (1972), 469–76.

Narin van Court, E., 'The *Siege of Jerusalem* and Augustinian Historians: Writing About Jews in Fourteenth-Century England', *Chaucer Review* 29 (1995), 227–48.

—— 'The *Siege of Jerusalem* and Recuperative Readings', in *Pulp Fiction of Medieval England: Essays in Popular Romance*, ed. N. McDonald (Manchester, 2004), pp. 151–70.

Neddermeyer, U., *Von der Handschrift zum gedruckten Buch: Schriftlichkeit und Leseinteresse im Mittelalter und in der frühen Neuzeit: Quantitative und qualitative Aspekte*, 2 vols. (Wiesbaden, 1998).

Nolan, M., 'Lydgate's Worst Poem', in *Lydgate Matters: Poetry and Material Culture in the Fifteenth Century*, ed. L. H. Cooper and A. Denny-Brown (New York, 2008), pp. 71–87.

Oakden, J. P., *Alliterative Poetry in Middle English*, 2 vols. (Manchester, 1930–5).

O'Loughlin, J. L. N., 'The Middle English Alliterative *Morte Arthure*', *Medium Ævum* 4 (1935), 153–68.

Olson, L., 'Romancing the Book: Manuscripts for "Euerich Inglische"', in K. Kerby-Fulton, M. Hilmo and L. Olson, *Opening Up Middle English Manuscripts: Literary and Visual Approaches* (Ithaca NY, 2012), pp. 95–151.

Orlemanski, J., 'Jargon and the Matter of Medicine in Middle English', *Journal of Medieval and Early Modern Studies* 42 (2012), 395–420.

Orme, N., 'Education and Recreation', in *Gentry Culture in Late-Medieval England*, ed. R. Radulescu and A. Truelove (Manchester, 2005), pp. 63–83.

—— *From Childhood to Chivalry* (London, 1984).

Owen, A. E. B., 'Collation and Handwriting', in *The Thornton Manuscript (Lincoln Cathedral MS. 91)*, intro. D. S. Brewer and A. E. B. Owen (London, 1975), pp. xiii–xvi.

—— 'The Collation and Descent of the Thornton Manuscript', *Transactions of the Cambridge Bibliographical Society* 6 (1975), 218–25.

Page, W., ed., *Victoria History of the County of York, North Riding*, 5 vols. (London, 1907–74).

Parker, D. *The Commonplace Book in Tudor London: An Examination of BL MSS Egerton 1995, Harley 2252, Lansdowne 762, and Oxford Balliol College MS 354* (Lanham MD, 1998).

Parkes, M. B., *English Cursive Book Hands 1250–1500* (Oxford, 1969).

—— 'The Literacy of the Laity', in *Scribes, Scripts and Readers: Studies in the Communication, Dissemination and Presentation of Medieval Texts* (London, 1991), 275–97.

Patterson, L., *Negotiating the Past: The Historical Understanding of Medieval Literature* (Madison WI, 1987).

Pearsall, D., 'Editing Medieval Texts: Some Developments and Some Problems', in *Textual Criticism and Literary Interpretation*, ed. J. McGann (Chicago, 1985), pp. 92–106.

—— 'The Manuscripts and Illustrations of Gower's Works', in *A Companion to Gower*, ed. S. Echard (Cambridge, 2004), pp. 73–97.

——, ed., *Studies in the Vernon Manuscript* (Cambridge, 1990).

Pevsner, N., *The Buildings of England: Yorkshire: The North Riding* (Harmondsworth, 1966).

'Pickering Church', at Britain Express, www.britainexpress.com/attractions. htm?attraction=4600.

'Pickering Parish Church', www.pickeringchurch.com/wallpaintings.html.

Pinker, S., *The Better Angels of Our Nature: Why Violence Has Declined* (New York, 2011).

Pollard, A. J., *North-Eastern England during the Wars of the Roses* (Oxford, 1990).

Pollard, A. W., and G. R. Redgrave, *A Short-Title Catalogue of Books Printed in England, Scotland, and Ireland, and of English Books Printed Abroad, 1475–1640*, 2nd rev. edn, ed. W. A. Jackson, F. S. Ferguson and K. F. Pantzer (London, 1976–86).

Pouzet, J.-P., '"Space this werke to wirke": Quelques figures de la complémentarité dans les manuscrits de Robert Thornton', in *La Complémentarité: Mélanges offerts à Josseline Bidard et Arlette Sancery à l'occasion de leur depart en retraite*, ed. M.-F. Alamichel (Paris, 2005), pp. 27–42.

Purdie, R., *Anglicising Romance: Tail-Rhyme and Genre in Medieval English Literature* (Cambridge, 2008).

Putter, A., J. A. Jefferson and M. Stokes, *Studies in the Metre of Alliterative Verse*, Medium Ævum Monographs n.s. 5 (Oxford, 2007).

Rawcliffe, C., *The Hospitals of Medieval Norwich* (Norwich, 1995).

—— *Medicine for the Soul: The Life, Death and Resurrection of an English Medieval Hospital, St Giles's, Norwich, c. 1249–1550* (Stroud, 1999).

Raymo, R. R., 'XX. Works of Religious and Philosophical Instruction', in *A Manual of the Writings in Middle English, 1050–1500*, ed. A. E. Hartung, vol. 7 (New Haven, 1986), pp. 2255–381, 2467–582.

Renoir, A., and C. D. Benson, 'XVI. John Lydgate', in *A Manual of the Writings in Middle English, 1050–1500*, ed. A. E. Hartung, vol. 6 (New Haven, 1980), pp. 1809–922, 2071–176.

Rice, N. R., *Lay Piety and Religious Discipline in Middle English Literature* (Cambridge, 2008).

—— 'Spiritual Ambition and the Translation of the Cloister: The Abbey and Charter of the Holy Ghost', Viator 33 (2002), 222–60.

Richmond, C., 'Religion and the Fifteenth-Century Gentleman', in *The Church, Politics and Patronage in the Fifteenth-Century*, ed. B. Dobson (Gloucester, 1984), pp. 193–208.

Rickert, E., *Ancient English Christmas Carols* (New York, 1915).

Rigg, A. G., *A Glastonbury Miscellany of the Fifteenth Century: A Descriptive Index of Trinity College, Cambridge, MS O.9.38* (London, 1968).

Robbins, R. H., 'The Findern Anthology', *PMLA* 69 (1954), 610–42.

—— 'XIII. Poems Dealing with Contemporary Conditions', in *A Manual of the Writings in Middle English, 1050–1500*, ed. A. E. Hartung, vol. 5 (New Haven, 1975), pp. 1385–1538, 1631–1726.

Robinson, P. R., 'The "Booklet": A Self-Contained Unit in Composite Manuscripts', *Codicologica* 3 (1980), 46–69.

—— 'Booklets in Medieval Manuscripts: Further Considerations', *Studies in Bibliography* 39 (1986), 100–11.

—— 'A Study of Some Aspects of the Transmission of English Verse Texts in Late Mediaeval Manuscripts' (unpublished B.Litt. thesis, Oxford University, 1972).

Rouse, E. C., 'Post-Reformation Mural Paintings in Parish Churches', *Lincolnshire Historian* 1 (1947), 8–14.

Rushton, J. H., *The History of Ryedale* (Pickering, 2003).

—— 'Life in Ryedale in the 14th Century', 2 Parts, *Ryedale Historian* 8 (1976), 19–29, and 9 (1978), 29–51.

Sargent, M., 'The Transmission by the English Carthusians of Some Late Medieval Spiritual Writings', *Journal of Ecclesiastical History* 27 (1976), 225–40.

Saul, N., *English Church Monuments in the Middle Ages: History and Representation* (Oxford, 2009).

Scase, W., ed., *The Making of the Vernon Manuscript: The Production and Contexts of Oxford, Bodleian Library MS Eng. poet. a. 1*, Texts and Transitions 6 (Turnhout, 2013).

—— 'Reginald Pecock, John Carpenter and John Colop's "Common-Profit" Books: Aspects of Book Ownership and Circulation in Fifteenth-Century London', *Medium Ævum* 61 (1992), 261–74.

Schelp, H., *Exemplarische Romanzen im Mittelenglischen*, Palaestra 246 (Göttingen, 1967).

Schibanoff, S., 'The New Reader and Female Textuality in Two Early Commentaries on Chaucer', *Studies in the Age of Chaucer* 10 (1988), 71–108.

Schmidt, A. V. C., *The Clerkly Maker: Langland's Poetic Art* (Cambridge, 1987).

Scott, K. L., *Dated and Dateable English Manuscript Borders c. 1395–1499* (London, 2002).

—— 'A Late Fifteenth-Century Group of *Nova Statuta* Manuscripts', in *Manuscripts at Oxford: An Exhibition in Memory of Richard William Hunt (1908–1979), Keeper of Western Manuscripts at the Bodleian Library Oxford, 1945–1975, on Themes Selected and Described by Some of His Friends*, ed. A. C. de la Mare and B. C. Barker-Benfield (Oxford, 1980), pp. 102–5.

—— *Later Gothic Manuscripts: 1390–1490*, 2 vols. (London, 1996).

—— 'Newly Discovered Booklets from a Reconstructed Middle English Manuscript', in *Regional Manuscripts 1200–1700*, ed. A. S. G. Edwards, English Manuscript Studies 1100–1700, vol. 14 (London, 2008), pp. 112–29.

Severs, J. B., A. E. Hartung and P. G. Beidler, eds., *A Manual of the Writings in Middle English, 1050–1500*, ed. 11 vols. (New Haven, 1967–2005).

Sharpe, R., J. P. Carley, R. M. Thomson and A. G. Watson, *English Benedictine Libraries: The Shorter Catalogues*, Corpus of British Medieval Library Catalogues 4 (London, 1996).

Sheingorn, P., 'Joseph the Carpenter's Failure at Familial Discipline', in *Insights and Interpretations: Studies in Celebration of the Eighty-Fifth Anniversary of the Index of Christian Art*, ed. C. Hourihane (Princeton, 2002), pp. 156–67.

—— 'Reshapings of the Childhood Miracles of Jesus', in *The Christ Child in Medieval Culture: Alpha es et O!*, ed. M. Dzon and T. Kenney (Toronto, 2012), pp. 254–92.

Short, I., 'Gaimar's Epilogue and Geoffrey of Monmouth's *Liber vetustissimus*', *Speculum* 69 (1994), 223–43.

Skemer, D. C., *Binding Words: Textual Amulets in the Middle Ages* (University Park PA, 2006).

Smith, D., 'Vandalism or Social Duty: The Victorian Rebuilding of the "Street Parish" Churches' (unpublished D.Phil. thesis, University of York, forthcoming).

Smith, K. L., 'A Fifteenth-Century Vernacular Manuscript Reconstructed', *Bodleian Library Record* 7 (1966), 235–41.

Stern, K., 'The London "Thornton" Miscellany: A New Description of British Museum Additional Manuscript 31042', *Scriptorium* 30 (1976), 26–40.

—— 'The London "Thornton" Miscellany (II): A New Description of British Museum Additional Manuscript 31042', *Scriptorium* 30 (1976), 201–18.

Stevens, M., and D. H. Woodward, eds., *The Ellesmere Chaucer: Essays in Interpretation* (San Marino CA, 1995).

'Stonegrave Minster, Stonegrave, North Yorkshire', http://www.ampleforthbenefice.org/StonegraveHistory.html.

Strickland, D. H., 'The Jews, Leviticus, and the Unclean in Medieval English Bestiaries', in *Beyond the Yellow Badge: Anti-Judaism and Antisemitism in Medieval and Early Modern Visual Culture*, ed. M. Merback (Leiden, 2007), pp. 203–32.

Summerfield, T., *The Matter of Kings' Lives: The Design of Past and Present in the Early Fourteenth-Century Verse Chronicles by Pierre de Langtoft and Robert Mannyng* (Atlanta, 1998).

Sweetinburgh, S., *The Role of the Hospital in Medieval England: Gift-Giving and the Spiritual Economy* (Dublin, 2004).

Thompson, J. J., 'Another Look at the Religious Texts in Lincoln, Cathedral Library, MS 91', in *Late-Medieval Religious Texts and Their Transmission: Essays in Honour of A. I. Doyle*, ed. A. J. Minnis (Cambridge, 1994), pp. 169–87.

—— 'Collecting Middle English Romances and Some Related Book-Production Activities in the Later Middle Ages', in *Romance in Medieval England*, ed. M. Mills, J. Fellows and C. Meale (Cambridge, 1991), pp. 17–38.

—— 'The Compiler in Action: Robert Thornton and the "Thornton Romances" in Lincoln Cathedral MS 91', in *Manuscripts and Readers in Fifteenth-Century England: The Literary Implications of Manuscript Study. Essays from the 1981 Conference at the University of York*, ed. D. Pearsall (Cambridge, 1983), pp. 113–24.

—— *The Cursor Mundi: Poem, Texts and Contexts*, Medium Ævum Monographs n.s. 19 (Oxford, 1998).

—— *Robert Thornton and the London Thornton Manuscript: British Library MS Additional 31042*, Manuscript Studies 2 (Cambridge, 1987).

—— 'Textual Instability and the Late Medieval Reputation of Some Middle English

Religious Literature', *TEXT: Transactions of the Society for Textual Scholarship* 5 (1991), 175–94.

—— 'Textual *Lacunae* and the Importance of Manuscript Evidence: Robert Thornton's Copy of the *Liber de Diversis Medicinis*', *Transactions of the Cambridge Bibliographic Society* 8 (1982), 270–75.

—— 'Thomas Hoccleve and Manuscript Culture', in *Nation, Court and Culture: New Essays on Fifteenth-Century English Poetry*, ed. H. Cooney (Dublin, 2001), pp. 81–94.

Thomson, R. M., *Catalogue of the Manuscripts of Lincoln Cathedral Chapter Library* (Cambridge, 1989).

Thurston, H., 'Christian Names', in *The Catholic Encyclopedia*, vol. 7, www.newadvent.org.

Trapp, J. B., 'Literacy, Books and Readers', in *The Cambridge History of the Book in Britain: Volume 3, 1400–1557*, ed. L. Hellinga and J. B. Trapp (Cambridge, 1999), pp. 31–43.

Truelove, A., 'Literacy', in *Gentry Culture in Late-Medieval England*, ed. R. Radulescu and A. Truelove (Manchester, 2005), pp. 84–99.

Turville-Petre, T., 'The Ages of Man in *The Parlement of the Thre Ages*', *Medium Ævum* 46 (1977), 66–76.

—— *The Alliterative Revival* (Cambridge, 1977).

Tyerman, C., *England and the Crusades, 1095–1588* (Chicago, 1988).

Utley, F. L., 'VII. Dialogues, Debates, and Catechisms', in *A Manual of the Writings in MiddleEnglish, 1050–1500*, ed. A. E. Hartung, vol. 3 (New Haven, 1972), pp. 669–745, 829–902.

Vale, M. G. A., *Piety, Charity and Literacy Among the Yorkshire Gentry, 1370–1480*, Borthwick Papers 50 (York, 1976).

Vaughan, M. F., 'Consecutive Alliteration, Strophic Patterns, and the Composition of the Alliterative *Morte Arthure*', *Modern Philology* 77 (1979), 1–9.

Vitz, E. B., 'The Apocryphal and the Biblical, the Oral and the Written, in Medieval Legends of Christ's Childhood: The Old French *Evangile de L'enfance*', in *Saturna: Studies in Medieval Literature in Honour of Robert R. Raymo*, ed. N. M. Reale and R. E. Sternglantz (Donington, 2010), pp. 124–49.

Voigts, L. E., 'Multitudes of Middle English Medical Manuscripts, of the Englishing of Science and Medicine', in *Manuscript Sources of Medieval Medicine: A Book of Essays*, ed. M. R. Schleissner (New York, 1995), pp. 183–95.

—— 'Scientific and Medical Books', in *Book Production and Publishing in Britain, 1375–1475*, ed. J. Griffiths and D. Pearsall, Cambridge Studies in Publishing and Printing History (Cambridge, 1989), pp. 345–402.

—— and P. D. Kurtz, *Scientific and Medical Writings in Old and Middle English: An Electronic Reference*, CD–ROM (Ann Arbor, 2000).

—— and M. R. McVaugh, 'A Latin Technical Phlebotomy and Its Middle English Translation', *Transactions of the American Philosophical Society* 74 (1984), 1–69.

Voigts-Kurtz Search Program, University of Missouri-Kansas City, http://cctr1.umkc.edu/cgi–bin/search.

'Wakefield Cathedral', http://freepages.rootsweb.ancestry.com/~wakefield/cathedral/cath17.html.

Wakelin, D., 'Writing the Words', in *The Production of Books in England 1350–1500*, ed. A. Gillespie and D. Wakelin (Cambridge, 2011), pp. 34–58.

Watt, D., '"I this book shal make": Thomas Hoccleve's Self-Publication and Book Production', *Leeds Studies in English* n.s. 34 (2003), 133–60.

West, C., *Democracy Matters: Winning the Fight against Imperialism* (New York, 2004).

Whellan, T., *History and Topography of The City of York: and The North Riding of Yorkshire*, 2 vols. (Beverley, 1859).

Whitehead, C., 'Middle English Religious Lyrics', in *A Companion to the Middle English Lyric*, ed. T. G. Duncan (Cambridge, 2005), pp. 96–119.

Whiting, R., *The Reformation of the English Parish Church* (Cambridge, 2010).

Wiggins, A., 'A Makeover Story: The Caius Manuscript Copy of *Guy of Warwick*', *Studies in Philology* 104 (2007), 471–500.

Wilkinson, T. J., *The Falcon*, 2 vols. (Thirsk, Yorkshire, 1889–91).

Windeatt, B., 'The Scribes as Chaucer's Early Critics', *Studies in the Age of Chaucer* 1 (1979), 119–41.

Woolf, R., *The English Religious Lyric in the Middle Ages* (Oxford, 1968).

Yeager, S. M., *Jerusalem in Medieval Narrative* (Cambridge, 2008).

—— 'Jewish Identity in *The Siege of Jerusalem* and Homiletic Texts: Models of Penance and Victims of Vengeance for the Urban Apocalypse', *Medium Ævum* 80 (2011), 56–84.

Youngs, D., 'Cultural Networks', in *Gentry Culture in Late-Medieval England*, ed. R. Radulescu and A. Truelove (Manchester, 2005), pp. 119–33.

—— *Humphrey Newton (1466–1536): An Early Tudor Gentleman* (Woodbridge, 2008).

Index of Manuscripts Cited

Note: Boldface numbers indicate figures.

General Index

This index contains the topics, names of people and titles of works discussed in the text and footnotes. It does not include references to works or authors cited in the Bibliography and not discussed further. Boldface numbers indicate figures.

YORK MEDIEVAL PRESS: PUBLICATIONS

God's Words, Women's Voices: The Discernment of Spirits in the Writing of Late-Medieval Women Visionaries, Rosalyn Voaden (1999)

Pilgrimage Explored, ed. J. Stopford (1999)

Piety, Fraternity and Power: Religious Gilds in Late Medieval Yorkshire 1389–1547, David J. F. Crouch (2000)

Courts and Regions in Medieval Europe, ed. Sarah Rees Jones, Richard Marks and A. J. Minnis (2000)

Treasure in the Medieval West, ed. Elizabeth M. Tyler (2000)

Nunneries, Learning and Spirituality in Late Medieval English Society: The Dominican Priory of Dartford, Paul Lee (2000)

Prophecy and Public Affairs in Later Medieval England, Lesley A. Coote (2000)

The Problem of Labour in Fourteenth-Century England, ed. James Bothwell, P. J. P. Goldberg and W. M. Ormrod (2000)

New Directions in later Medieval Manuscript Studies: Essays from the 1998 Harvard Conference, ed. Derek Pearsall (2000)

Cistercians, Heresy and Crusade in Occitania, 1145–1229: Preaching in the Lord's Vineyard, Beverly Mayne Kienzle (2001)

Guilds and the Parish Community in Late Medieval East Anglia, c. 1470–1550, Ken Farnhill (2001)

The Age of Edward III, ed. J. S. Bothwell (2001)

Time in the Medieval World, ed. Chris Humphrey and W. M. Ormrod (2001)

The Cross Goes North: Processes of Conversion in Northern Europe, AD 300–1300, ed. Martin Carver (2002)

Henry IV: The Establishment of the Regime, 1399–1406, ed. Gwilym Dodd and Douglas Biggs (2003)

Youth in the Middle Ages, ed. P. J. P. Goldberg and Felicity Riddy (2004)

The Idea of the Castle in Medieval England, Abigail Wheatley (2004)

Rites of Passage: Cultures of Transition in the Fourteenth Century, ed. Nicola F. McDonald and W. M. Ormrod (2004)

Creating the Monastic Past in Medieval Flanders, Karine Ugé (2005)

St William of York, Christopher Norton (2006)

Medieval Obscenities, ed. Nicola F. McDonald (2006)

The Reign of Edward II: New Perspectives, ed. Gwilym Dodd and Anthony Musson (2006)

Old English Poetics: The Aesthetics of the Familiar in Anglo-Saxon England, Elizabeth M. Tyler (2006)

The Late Medieval Interlude: The Drama of Youth and Aristocratic Masculinity, Fiona S. Dunlop (2007)

The Late Medieval English College and its Context, ed. Clive Burgess and Martin Heale (2008)

The Reign of Henry IV: Rebellion and Survival, 1403–1413, ed. Gwilym Dodd and Douglas Biggs (2008)

Medieval Petitions: Grace and Grievance, ed. W. Mark Ormrod, Gwilym Dodd and Anthony Musson (2009)

St Edmund, King and Martyr: Changing Images of a Medieval Saint, ed. Anthony Bale (2009)

Language and Culture in Medieval Britain: The French of England c.1100–c.1500, ed. Jocelyn Wogan-Browne et al. (2009)

The Royal Pardon: Access to Mercy in Fourteenth-Century England, Helen Lacey (2009)

Texts and Traditions of Medieval Pastoral Care: Essays in Honour of Bella Millett, ed. Cate Gunn and Catherine Innes-Parker (2009)

The Anglo-Norman Language and its Contexts, ed. Richard Ingham (2010)

Parliament and Political Pamphleteering in Fourteenth-Century England, Clementine Oliver (2010)

The Saints' Lives of Jocelin of Furness: Hagiography, Patronage and Ecclesiastical Politics, Helen Birkett (2010)

The York Mystery Plays: Performance in the City, ed. Margaret Rogerson (2011)

Wills and Will-making in Anglo-Saxon England, Linda Tollerton (2011)

The Songs and Travels of a Tudor Minstrel: Richard Sheale of Tamworth, Andrew Taylor (2012)

Sin in Medieval and Early Modern Culture: The Tradition of the Seven Deadly Sins, ed. Richard G. Newhauser and Susan J. Ridyard (2012)

Socialising the Child in Late Medieval England, c. 1400–1600, Merridee L. Bailey (2012)

Barking Abbey and Medieval Literary Culture: Authorship and Authority in a Female Community, ed. Jennifer N. Brown and Donna Alfano Bussell (2012)

Christians and Jews in Angevin England: The York Massacre of 1190, Narratives and Contexts, ed. Sarah Rees Jones and Sethina Watson (2013)

Reimagining History in Anglo-Norman Prose Chronicles, John Spence (2013)

Henry V: New Interpretations, ed. Gwilym Dodd (2013)

Rethinking Chaucer's Legend of Good Women, Carolyn P. Collette (2014)

York Studies in Medieval Theology

I   *Medieval Theology and the Natural Body*, ed. Peter Biller and A. J. Minnis (1997)

II   *Handling Sin: Confession in the Middle Ages*, ed. Peter Biller and A. J. Minnis (1998)

III   *Religion and Medicine in the Middle Ages*, ed. Peter Biller and Joseph Ziegler (2001)

IV   *Texts and the Repression of Medieval Heresy*, ed. Caterina Bruschi and Peter Biller (2002)

York Manuscripts Conference

Manuscripts and Readers in Fifteenth-Century England: The Literary Implications of Manuscript Study, ed. Derek Pearsall (1983) [Proceedings of the 1981 York Manuscripts Conference]

Manuscripts and Texts: Editorial Problems in Later Middle English Literature, ed. Derek Pearsall (1987) [Proceedings of the 1985 York Manuscripts Conference]

Latin and Vernacular: Studies in Late-Medieval Texts and Manuscripts, ed. A. J. Minnis (1989) [Proceedings of the 1987 York Manuscripts Conference]

Regionalism in Late-Medieval Manuscripts and Texts: Essays celebrating the publication of 'A Linguistic Atlas of Late Mediaeval English', ed. Felicity Riddy (1991) [Proceedings of the 1989 York Manuscripts Conference]

Late-Medieval Religious Texts and their Transmission: Essays in Honour of A. I. Doyle, ed. A. J. Minnis (1994) [Proceedings of the 1991 York Manuscripts Conference]

Prestige, Authority and Power in Late Medieval Manuscripts and Texts, ed. Felicity Riddy (2000) [Proceedings of the 1994 York Manuscripts Conference]

Middle English Poetry: Texts and Traditions. Essays in Honour of Derek Pearsall, ed. A. J. Minnis (2001) [Proceedings of the 1996 York Manuscripts Conference]

Manuscript Culture in the British Isles

I   *Design and Distribution of Late Medieval Manuscripts in England*, ed. Margaret Connolly and Linne R. Mooney (2008)

II   *Women and Writing, c.1340–c.1650: The Domestication of Print Culture*, ed. Anne Lawrence-Mathers and Phillipa Hardman (2010)

III   *The Wollaton Medieval Manuscripts: Texts, Owners and Readers*, ed. Ralph Hanna and Thorlac Turville-Petre (2010)

IV   *Scribes and the City: London Guildhall Clerks and the Dissemination of Middle English Literature, 1375–1425*, Linne R. Mooney and Estelle Stubbs (2013)

Heresy and Inquisition in the Middle Ages

Heresy and Heretics in the Thirteenth Century: The Textual Representations, L. J. Sackville (2011)

Heresy, Crusade and Inquisition in Medieval Quercy, Claire Taylor (2011)